THE LAST BIWA SINGER

This page is intentionally left blank.

THE LAST BIWA SINGER

A Blind Musician in History, Imagination and Performance

HUGH DE FERRANTI

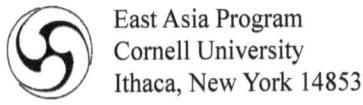

East Asia Program
Cornell University
Ithaca, New York 14853

The Cornell East Asia Series is published by the Cornell University East Asia Program (distinct from Cornell University Press). We publish books on a variety of scholarly topics relating to East Asia as a service to the academic community and the general public. Standing orders, which provide for automatic notification and invoicing of each title in the series upon publication, are accepted.

If after review by internal and external readers a manuscript is accepted for publication, it is published on the basis of camera-ready copy provided by the author who is responsible for any copyediting and manuscript formatting. Alternative arrangements should be made with approval of the Series. Address submission inquiries to CEAS Editorial Board, East Asia Program, Cornell University, Ithaca, New York 14853-7601.

Cover photos: Yamashika preparing to play biwa before the grave of Hori Kōjun. Photograph by Kimura Yoshio. Used by permission of Mrs. Kimura Yoshio.
Cover design, book layout and formatting: Lindsay Rowlands

Number 143 in the Cornell East Asia Series
Copyright ©2009 by Hugh de Ferranti. All rights reserved.
ISSN: 1050-2955
ISBN: 978-1-933947-13-6 hc
ISBN: 978-1-933947-43-3 pb
Library of Congress Control Number: 2009925879

24 23 22 21 20 19 18 17 16 15 14 13 12 11 10 09   9 8 7 6 5 4 3 2 1

CAUTION: Except for brief quotations in a review, no part of this book may be reproduced or utilized in any form without permission in writing from the author. Please address all inquiries to Hugh de Ferrranti in care of the East Asia Program, Cornell University, 140 Uris Hall, Ithaca, NY 14853-7601.

For Claudio Yoshiyuki Zani de Ferranti

Born as you were,
one hundred years after Yamashika —
weaving threads of song
to bind each day and night
without a word.

This page is intentionally left blank.

CONTENTS

List of Figures, Tables and Examples   x
Note on Conventions in the Text   xii

INTRODUCTION   1
The Setting: Kyushu and Kumamoto   6
The Biwa Music Traditions   9
Biwa and *Biwa Hōshi* in Modern-day Japan   13
The *Biwa Hiki*, Yamashika Yoshiyuki   14

1   IMAGES AND HISTORIES   19

Characteristics of the Blind Biwa Traditions   20
Biwa and Blindness   20
Biwa and Sanctity   28
Biwa and Gender   36
Biwa and Musical Narrative   40

The Social Status of Blind Musicians and Itinerant Performers   42
Images and Depictions of Biwa Hōshi   44

Biwa Hōshi and Mōsō: Entangled Musical, Literary and Religious Figures   48
The Established Accounts   48
A New Approach: Mōsō as Biwa Hōshi *Who Gained Buddhist Patronage*   51
Ancient and Medieval Period Biwa Hōshi   52
Heike *Recitation and the* Biwa Hōshi *Guild, the* Tōdō-za   55
Biwa Hōshi *and Zatō after the Waning of* Heike *Recitation's Popularity*   58
Mōsō *and* Mōsōbiwa *Traditions*   60
Mōsō *Groups' Dispute with the* Tōdō-za *and Its Consequences*   63

2   BIWA MUSIC OF THE HIGO REGION   69

Varieties of *Mōsōbiwa* in Kyushu   70
Terms That Identify the Biwa Traditions and the Musicians   71
Writings on Zatōbiwa, Higobiwa *and* Mōsōbiwa   74
Populist Accounts and Depictions   85

Performers' Consciousness of Tradition and Accounts of Origins	88
Tradition and "History"	88
Historical Evidence	93
Repertories of the Kyushu Biwa Traditions	108
Tales	109
Rites	125

3 IMAGINING, ENCOUNTERING AND DOCUMENTING YAMASHIKA — 143

Documentation of "The Last Biwa Hōshi"	144
Academic Documentation	145
Representations for the Broader Public	148
Yamashika and His Interlocutors	154
Scholars	155
The Kimuras	157
Foreigners	158
Kimura's *Kikigaki* Life History of Yamashika	163
Kimura Rirō and His Various Writings on Yamashika	164
The Text and Its Construction	166

4 TALES IN PERFORMANCE — 177

Performance Contexts and Procedures	177
Settings and Audiences	178
Kadobiki and Zashikibiwa	179
Other Contexts: Myōon Kō, Nabiraki and Yogomori	185
Concert Performances Since the 1960s	185
Formal Elements in Narrative Performance	187
Framing Tales	187
Sonic Elements of Performance	190
Tales in Performance: The Oral Compositional Process	202
Performance and Narrative Units: The Shōdan Model	202
Fixity and Variability: Yamashika's Dōjōji	205
Dōjōji (Performance of October 14, 1989)	208

5 THE LIFE OF THE ROAD: YAMASHIKA REMEMBERS ... 231

Becoming a *Biwa Hiki* ... 232
Yamashika's Choice of Vocation in Context ... 232
Apprenticeship ... 240

Participation in Local *Biwa Hiki* Groups and Acquisition of a Professional Name ... 252
Yamashika's Participation in the Tamagawa-ha ... 253
Acquisition of Professional Status and a Performer's Name ... 256

Making a Living as a *Biwa Hiki* ... 258
Acquisition of Skills and Repertory from Other Biwa Hiki ... 259
Kadozuke and Discrimination against Biwa Hiki ... 262
Discrimination and Its Persistence ... 265
Working Regions and Remuneration ... 270

6 BLIND BIWA SINGERS FORGOTTEN, REMEMBERED AND REHABILITATED ... 277

Effects of the Social Re-positioning of Biwa Hiki ... 279
Fragmentary Transmission of Yamashika's Repertory ... 280
Another "Last" Biwa Hōshi ... 282
Contemporary Biwa Hōshi *and Public Demand* ... 284

ACKNOWLEDGEMENTS ... 287

APPENDICES ... 290
Appendix 1
Map 1. Kyushu, showing prefectures and their approximate correlation with pre-Meiji provinces. ... 291
Map 2. Principal places in central Kyushu that are mentioned in the text. ... 292

Appendix 2
Transcription of the First shōdan of Dōjōji
(Yamashika Yoshiyuki; performance of October 14, 1989) ... 293

Bibliography ... 301
Audiography and Videography ... 312
Index ... 313

List of Figures, Tables and Examples

Figure 1.1
Eighteenth-century Chinese devotional image of
Sarasvati showing her names in Tibetan, Chinese, Mongolian
and Manchu. (Walter E. Clark, *Two Lamaistic Pantheons*, vol. 1,
288. Cambridge, MA: Harvard University Press 1937)   30

Figure 1.2
Fourteenth-century *Benzaiten-zu* (detail).
Collection of Hōjōin, Mt. Koya. (Tokyo: *Nihon e gakkan*,
Kodansha International Ltd. 1971)   31

Figure 1.3
Biwa hōshi depicted in the fourteenth-century scroll
painting *Boki ekotoba* (detail). Collection of Nishi Honganji.
(*Zoku Nihon emakimono taisei*, vol. 4.
Tokyo: Chūō Kōronsha 1985)   47

Figure 2.1
Yamashika preparing to play biwa before the grave of Hori Kyōjun.
Photograph by Kimura Yoshio. Used by permission of
Mrs. Kimura Aiko.   90

Figure 2.2
Yamashika preparing *gohei* for a *kamado-barai*.
Photograph by the author (April 1989).   134

Figure 2.3
Yamashika performing the *kamado-barai*. He is wearing a priest's *kesa*
garment because at the time he was temporarily a member of the
Gensei Hōryū *mōsō* sect. Photograph by the author (April 1989).   135

Figure 2.4.
Performance of a tale after a *kamado-barai* held in Yanagawa.
Photograph by the author (April 1989).   136

Figure 4.1
Yamashika performing while seated on a chair behind a banner
bearing his professional name, Tamagawa Kyōen (-shi).
Photograph by the author (November 1991).   182

Table 4.1
Profiles of Yamashika's primary *fushi* set.   196

Example 4.1
Tetrachordal formations in all Yamashika's *fushi* types.   201

Figure 4.2.
Depiction of Kiyohime in distress on the banks of the
Hidaka River. Chikanobu Toyohara, *The Boatman*, 1898.
Triptych from the Bamboo Knots (*Take no hitofushi*) series.
(http://commons.wikimedia.org/wiki/File: Chikanobu_The_Boatman.jpg)   207

Table 4.2
Shōdan articulation in *Dōjōji* (performance of October 14, 1989).   225

Table 4.3
Narrative events and *fushi* structure in four performances
of *Dōjōji*.   226

Figure 5.1
Yamashika outside his teacher's house in
Amakusa. Photograph by Kimura Rirō (used with permission).   241

Notes on Conventions in the Text

Japanese and Chinese names are rendered as family name first, personal name second, except for individuals whose professional lives have made them known in the English-speaking world, or whose work has been published in translation using the opposite name-order.

Pitches are designated using the Western system of letter-names (*a, b, c, d, e, f, g*), but without any implication of absolute or fixed pitch. From the lowest octave to the highest, pitches are represented as follows: an upper case letter with prime symbol (A'), upper case alone (A), lower case alone (a), and lower case with prime (a'). When staff-notation examples or transcriptions are referred to, the octave *A - a* corresponds to that from *A* below middle-*c* (that is, on the top line of the bass clef) to *a* above.

Titles of Japanese works, other than tales in the repertories of *biwa hiki* and other tales from oral tradition, are given in italics with only the initial letter and the first letter of proper nouns capitalised. In the titles of tales all words are capitalised (for example *Kikuchi Kuzure*).

The following abbreviations for reference volumes have been used in the book's text and footnotes:

    ODJ   = *Ongaku daijiten*
    NKBD = *Nihon koten bungaku daijiten*
    NMD   = *Nihon minzoku daijiten*
    NMJ   = *Nihon minzokugaku jiten*
    NODJ = *Nihon ongaku daijiten*

INTRODUCTION

Popular culture in late-twentieth-century Japan repeatedly fixed upon images that valorise older values and ways of life—"traditional Japan." This was specially so in representations of the country's peripheral rural areas of the far north and south, whose people were framed again and again by the nostalgic gaze of Tokyo-based journalists, film directors and television producers. Elderly musicians and practitioners of regional performing arts traditions who had made their living as performers since before the Second World War and Occupation were of strong interest to the creators of this romantic imagery for consumption in the metropolises of central Japan. Their songs, tales, dances and lives were interpreted in terms of ideas about folk culture, tradition, and regional and national identity that had been in circulation since Japanese modernity gained impetus in the 1920s, but also in accordance with values reflective of folk heritage preservation movements that emerged from North America and Britain in the post-war era. Inevitably, a group of blind men who played an ancient string instrument while singing tales or chanting invocations to local gods in remote parts of Kyushu became caught up in this evocation of a dreamlike past.

The Kyushu blind musicians were also the subject of my own work during most of the 1990s, but this book is centred on just one of them, Yamashika Yoshiyuki (1901–1996). He was a man almost unknown beyond the vicinity of his village in Kumamoto Prefecture, Kyushu, until his late sixties, when he began to acquire renown and eventual fame as "the last" of the *biwa hōshi*, blind *biwa* (lute)-playing bards who performed ritual placations for the angry ghosts of warriors killed in battle, and who first popularised the medieval *Tale of the Heike*, which became Japan's "national epic" in modern times (Bialock 2000). From at least the end of the Second World War until the 1980s, Yamashika lived a life of apparent, and at times actual, privation in the rural district where he was born. In many respects his life was one of hardship and considerable tragedy. The visible evidence for this aided some researchers and many photographers, journalists and artists in their portrayals of Yamashika as a living relic of the image of the *biwa hōshi* as it exists in the popular imagination—namely, a solitary blind man, dishevelled and pitiful, yet rich in his knowledge of rites and old lore. From the early 1970s there was much academic, media and public interest in Yamashika, manifested in a variety of publications, events and documentations: academic and commercial books and journals; recordings; performances in Tokyo; photographic exhibitions and a photo-essay on his lifestyle and character; television specials; and national honours and awards. In 1992 a full-length documentary film was produced, and photographs and articles about Yamashika appeared in the *Japan Times*, the *New York Times* and the *International Herald Tribune* (see de Ferranti 1992b; Sanger 1992). With the Japanese Education Ministry's 1993 approval of the film *Biwa hōshi Yamashika Yoshiyuki* for use in high schools, Yamashika's posthumous fame became assured, for he soon became known to many young people throughout Japan as "the last *biwa hōshi*."

I first heard of Yamashika Yoshiyuki while a student in Tokyo from 1985, but was not able to meet him until 1989, when I visited Kyushu shortly before returning to Australia. The meeting was a decisive one for me, and I resolved to undertake fieldwork research with any former blind biwa players whom I could locate. During 1991 and 1992 I worked with three such musicians, including Yamashika. The bulk of textual and musical analysis in my previous work documents the music of Ōkawa Susumu (1918–2000), for the reason that among the three his explanations of performance practice were the most lucid, and his melodic style most consistent (de Ferranti 1997, 2003). I have taken an altogether different approach in writing this book because I came to view Yamashika and his practice as significant for broader cultural and historical reasons—not solely as a key to oral compositional processes and performance techniques of the kind that occupied me in the early 1990s. While Ōkawa and another former *biwa hiki*,[1] Hashiguchi Keisuke

1. *Biwa hiki* was among the most common of vernacular terms for blind biwa players in central Kyushu (see further chapter 2).

(b. 1914), were fully trained musicians who had made a living from biwa before the Second World War, both had turned to other trades soon after the war. The media and field researchers remained largely unaware of them; they were never drawn to Ōkawa and Hashiguchi in the way they were to Yamashika, who almost invariably became the face of traditional biwa music in Kyushu whenever it was mentioned publicly or written about.

This work, and the form of documentation offered in this book, has been shaped to varying degrees and at various times by topics and theoretical concerns that arise from Japanese and English-language academic writing. They include the genre of biwa music (*biwagaku*) in the context of Japanese music history, with its concomitant forms of ritual and narrative, as addressed by scholars of Japanese religion, folklore and literature; Japanese society's treatment of the blind, and in particular the historical status of blind musicians; questions of musical style and oral compositional performance practice as addressed by music historians, folklorists and ethnomusicologists; the significance of individual musicians in the shaping and transmission of a musical tradition; and questions of representation and identity in the making and reception of ethnographic texts, which have occupied a central place in cultural studies and anthropology since the 1980s. Those concerns are not so much a unitary set whose elements intrinsically belong together, as a field of topics within which I have sought to interpret the musical activities of Yamashika and other blind biwa players.

These topics and concerns are addressed in various sections of my text, but it must be emphasised here, at the beginning, that synthesis and interpretation of materials of Japanese origin have been the central activities in the preparation of this book. The performance traditions of blind biwa players in south-western Japan have come to be regarded as important for themes at the interstices of the disciplines of literature, musicology and history as they are practised in Japan, and that importance is reflected in texts of many kinds produced by amateur and professional scholars since the late 1980s. In addition to the primary material of performances and interviews themselves, the principal representations of and tools for contemplating *biwa hiki* are three kinds of Japanese sources: those on biwa music and its history;

portrayals and accounts of Yamashika Yoshiyuki, including the 1994 partial life-history by Kimura Rirō, *Higo biwa hiki Yamashika Yoshiyuki yobanashi* (Fireside tales of a *biwa hiki* of Higo, Yamashika Yoshiyuki);[2] and extensive analytical writings on performance and professional practice among Kyushu *biwa hiki*—much of it data about Yamashika—including the seminal works produced in the 1990s by the researcher of oral and medieval literature, Hyōdō Hiromi. I give primary emphasis to these sources unapologetically, while giving due consideration to writings in European languages that touch upon biwa, music traditions of the blind, and ritual "begging" in Japan, as well as some of the pertinent theoretical issues I have referred to above.

An important common theme emerged from working with the latter two of these three kinds of Japanese sources: the appropriateness of characterising a performance tradition through examination of the practice of a prominent individual. While Kimura's book about Yamashika makes no claims to being a source for knowledge of the broader practice of biwa music among blind professionals in Kumamoto Prefecture or other regions of Kyushu, as one of only two monographs on the Higo-region biwa tradition it bears considerable weight as a resource. Scholarly sources on the *biwa hiki*, their tales, rites and music include texts that focus solely on Yamashika (Murayama 1986), or else position him as a central figure among surviving musicians (Ga 1972; Narita 1985a). Similarly, notwithstanding Hyōdō Hiromi's occasional suggestions that Yamashika's narrative practice was unorthodox, data about this individual has come to be treated as data about "the tradition" of Kyushu *biwa hiki* largely because a scholar of Hyōdō's stature devoted a long article and much of two subsequent articles on biwa narrative to discussion of Yamashika's training and performances (Hyōdō 1991, 1993, 1999).

In Euro-American scholarship since the mid-1990s there has been increased attention to the individual's embodiment of "culture" and "performance tradition," which are core concepts in the disciplines of anthropology and ethnomusicology (Danielson 1997; Reed-Danahay

2. Reasons for my choice of wording in the title translation are given in chapter 3. Note that I often quote the first-person speech by Yamashika that makes up the bulk of Kimura's text, but also draw upon passages in which Kimura presents his own authorial voice; the latter are identified as such, although both kinds of passage are referenced as Kimura 1994.

1997). The processes through which ideas of culture and tradition can be "created" by researchers, namely, intersubjective experience and authorial representation, have been broached in anthropological theory (Jackson 1998; Marcus 1999), but are touched upon little in musical ethnography (Kisliuk 1998). In recent ethnomusicology monographs, the relationship between researcher and researched is consistently problematised, but few include extensive documentation of those individual musicians whose knowledge of tradition underpins much of what is written (Bakan 1999; Keister 2004; Babiracki 2008), and even fewer provide first-person expositions of such knowledge and its acquisition (Walton 1996).

Two basic questions arise from a focus on individuals in documenting music traditions: Firstly, in what sense did a tradition exist that bound together the repertories and styles of disparate performers? Secondly, was the practice of the individual sufficiently similar to that of other musicians for it to be treated as representative? For the narrative and ritual music that Yamashika performed, the first question can only be answered by a combination of historical research and ethnographic documentation of ways in which *biwa hiki* spoke about their lineage and affiliations as musicians, while the second calls for examination of commentary by Yamashika and others, and ultimately comparative analysis of the range of archive performances by *biwa hiki* recorded since the 1960s. In this book I address the first question, and provide some suggestions toward answering the second, chiefly in light of my knowledge of the profiles and performance styles of Yamashika, Ōkawa and Hashiguchi.

For these reasons, I do not present Yamashika's practice as representative of the music of *biwa hiki* as it was in the twentieth century—much less how it "always" had been in earlier times. As chapter 2 shows, even the twentieth-century history of this music is hardly documented; there are not even partial repertory lists from before the 1960s, for example, and the sole pre-1950 aural record of performance has never been made available to researchers—if indeed it still exists. The primary diachronic element in this study is that of Yamashika's life and experiences, as accessed through my own recordings and memories of his words, and through the words of other researchers to whom he spoke over several decades.

My approach to Yamashika and the performance tradition he has come to represent acknowledges the complexity of an individual's identity, and the processes of its documentation and production through textual and other media. Consequently this book also documents the meanings created through interaction between Yamashika's own words and actions (including performative ones for audiences) and a variety of verbal and cultural texts about him in late-twentieth-century Japan. All of those texts, in turn, must be considered in relation to images of blind singers yielded by history, for Yamashika was a twentieth-century practitioner of a narrative tradition that bore significant points of similarity to ones practised by blind males in Japan during the best part of a millennium. Qualities of the *biwa hōshi* depicted in scroll paintings, folk tales, drama and other media since at least the fourteenth century took root in a particular form in popular imagination in the modern era, for reasons that I discuss in chapter 1. Remoteness, sanctity, fear, poverty and suffering are a set of core characteristics in commonly held images of the *biwa hōshi*. Some or all those characteristics are ever-present in portrayals of Yamashika, his life and music.

The Setting: Kyushu and Kumamoto

Historically, blind performers of biwa have been active in many regions of Japan, but it is only in south-western Honshu and Kyushu that *mōsō* (blind Buddhist priests who played biwa in various contexts) and *biwa hiki* remained active until the mid twentieth century. Of the two regions, by far the majority of musicians were in Kyushu, and *biwa hiki* were concentrated in the centrally positioned prefecture of Kumamoto (which approximates the former Higo Province), where at least eight were still capable of performing in the early 1970s.

Kyushu (see appendix 1, map 1, which shows the island with its modern prefectures and pre-modern provinces) is the southernmost of Japan's four principal islands, but is a place of great historical significance. The likelihood that the founders of the Imperial lineage came from Kyushu is reflected in the Sun Goddess Amaterasu Ō Mi-Kami's legendary descent to earth at a mountain in Miyazaki Prefecture. The proximity of the Korean peninsula to the west and the Ryūkyū archipelago to the south produced broad cultural contact from earliest times—possibly yielding the introduction of biwa-playing, according to one theory. The military and political power of Kyushu regimes, in particular that of Satsuma Province's Shimazu clan and the Satsuma samurai-class figures who dominated much political life in the period 1870 to 1899, was a decisive factor in the formation of the Meiji-era (1868–1912) state and its ideology.

Biwa has been played by blind males throughout Kyushu, but in the former provinces of Satsuma (Kagoshima and southern Miyazaki Prefecture), Higo (Kumamoto Prefecture and the Amakusa islands) and Chikuzen-Chikugo (Fukuoka and parts of Saga Prefecture) concentrations of players were sustained by limited support from religious institutions and widespread belief in the efficacy of agrarian rites performed with biwa. Buddhist institutions for association among "blind"[3] priests still exist and exercise authority over members in several regions of Kyushu, but in the former Higo region the Higobiwa Hozonkai, a governmental organisation established in the 1970s to preserve the regional tradition that some called *higobiwa*, has become effectively obsolete, and no local musicians have maintained competence in performance.[4]

The localities most important for the aspects of Yamashika Yoshiyuki's professional life presented in this book are all contained in a region approximately sixty kilometres square which straddles central and northern Kumamoto Prefecture and the southern reaches of Fukuoka Prefecture, where Yamashika spent his ninety-five years of life (see appendix 1, map 2): Nankan, Tamana, Yanagawa, Yamaga, Ōmuta, Amakusa, and the prefectural capital, Kumamoto. The first four are towns of diverse sizes in an area around what was once the Higo-Chikugo provincial border. Nankan is where Yamashika was born and lived, with the exception of two years in Amakusa in the

3. Very few member priests today are blind, and only one blind member plays biwa in rites for his *danka* (parishioners; see chapter 6).
4. The background to the term "*higobiwa*," as well as its potential inaccuracy, is explained in chapter 2. Katayama Kyokusei, a Kyoto-based musician who learned some pieces from Yamashika, occasionally performs "*higobiwa*," and has taught a small group of Kumamoto residents to play beginners' pieces (see chapter 6). Among *biwa hiki*, however, competence in performance meant far more than this rudimentary level of skill.

1920s and nearly twenty years spent in the coastal town of Yanagawa during the 1940s to 1960s. Nankan is written with characters meaning "southern gate"(南関), a reference to the fact that in the Edo period the barrier gate between Higo, domain of the Hosokawa clan daimyō (provincial ruler), and Chikugo, the southern half of the Kuroda clan's domain, was located nearby on the Buzen Kaidō Road. The old Nankan town had prospered as a point of accommodation for travellers waiting to pass through the gate, but declined with the advent of railways in the 1890s, when what became the Kagoshima Line was laid far away, along the coast.[5] Being adjacent to the old domain border (which was taken as the basis for the modern borders of Fukuoka and Kumamoto prefectures), the local culture and dialect of Nankan inhabitants drew strongly upon both Higo and Chikugo traditions. For most of the twentieth century Nankan was a farming village that produced rice, barley and vegetable produce for the markets of Ōmuta, Tamana and other towns whose economies derived from their positions as ports, transportation hubs, and attractive natural resources (the last applies to Yamaga, known for its hot springs since the Edo period).

The Ōhara area of Nankan (now known as Kobaru) in which Yamashika grew up and lived most of his life is today picturesque, as the population is small and the remaining farmhouses are large and in good repair, and because both the urban and suburban settings that frame most Japanese people's lives seem remote from the place.[6] Yet in the past living conditions for many there were far from comfortable. Poverty was not rare in rural Japan in the first half of the twentieth century. Unlike the Tōhoku region of northern Honshu where famine occured in the early 1930s, the milder climate of Kyushu meant that there was always some form of food available (the last famine in Kyushu was in Meiji 4, 1871). Yet for rural Nagasaki Prefecture and Kumamoto Prefecture's Amakusa islands (where Yamashika spent just over two years during his unfinished apprenticeship), poverty and lack of education have been cited as principal reasons for these regions'

---

5. This now runs from Fukuoka in the north to Kagoshima in the south, but was laid only as far as Yatsushiro, some thirty kilometres south-east of Kumamoto, by the end of the Meiji period.

6. This is in part because noise from the expressway that passes about three hundred metres to the south is barely perceptible, due to sound baffles.

inordinate representation among the numbers of Japanese prostitutes in brothels throughout the Japanese empire and adjacent regions in the first half of the twentieth century.[7]

Finally, the city of Kumamoto, some thirty-five kilometres from Nankan, had been the castle town of the rulers of Higo, the Hosokawa. Always subsidiary in size and importance to Fukuoka in the modern era, it is nonetheless one of three large cities in Kyushu and has been home to over 500,000 people since the mid-1970s. In the time I knew Yamashika he visited Kumamoto rarely—and most often for performances arranged by scholars and amateur folklorists who worked with him. Most of the officials and governmental bodies charged with documenting and preserving the regional blind biwa tradition were based in Kumamoto, and the Folklore Studies division of Kumamoto National University has been an important centre for research on biwa music in central Kyushu.

The Biwa Music Traditions

Apart from court ensemble music and modern instrumental compositions, the bulk of biwa repertory has been vocal music, either melodic recitation of poetic narrative or ritual recitation, accompanied by biwa. It is a major genre of traditional music practised in various regions, but especially prevalent on Kyushu. While modern styles of biwa music are played by professionals and amateurs of both sexes, prior to the Meiji period it seems that only males performed biwa narrative (see chapter 1), and the majority of styles were practised solely by blind professionals.

Biwa is not an indigenous Japanese instrument. The origins of the various forms of biwa that have developed in Japan are in the transmission of Continental Asian short-necked lutes and portions of their repertories to Japanese musicians, by at latest the eighth century. The principal historical traditions of biwa can be divided into four groups:

---

7. See the accounts of the experiences of some women from those areas in Yamazaki (1972; published in English as Yamazaki 1999).

Biwa in *gagaku*—The earliest documented transmission was of several forms of short-necked lute performed by both men and women for instrumental, dance and song forms within the music repertories of the court and major Buddhist ecclesiastical institutions, from as early as the eighth century. The court music repertory, generically referred to as *gagaku*, continues on a reduced scale today, and the four-stringed *gaku biwa* (or *gagaku biwa*) is considered to be a form of the instrument little changed since its introduction from the Asian continent.

Singers of tales with biwa: *zatō* and *biwa hōshi*—In sources from the tenth century on there are accounts of blind male musicians, most commonly called *zatō*, a general term for blind men of low status. Such blind musicians were also often referred to as *biwa hōshi*, a literary term for which the earliest documented usage is a poetic diary of the 980s. These blind musicians were not associated with court society and in most cases lacked any formal Buddhist affiliation. As itinerants whose shaven heads and apparel often gave them the appearance of priests, they could be referred to as *hōshi* (literally, "teacher of the Buddhist law," or one who has given up a home for the purpose of practising austerities). They are thought to have performed recitations of war tales as a ritual means of placating the souls of slain warriors; hence they are important figures in accounts of the creation of representative *gunki monogatari* (tales of war) during the twelfth to fourteenth centuries. The *biwa hōshi* are best known for their role in shaping the most representative work of medieval Japanese narrative literature, the *Heike monogatari* (*The Tale of the Heike*). Performers of *heike* recitation with biwa (*heikebiwa*) began as low-status itinerant musicians in the early thirteenth century. After developing their recitational art over centuries, they received Shogunal patronage, and established a formal guild, the *tōdō-za*. Low-status *zatō* who recited *heike* and other local repertories with either biwa or *shamisen* accompaniment existed in several regions of Japan, in varying relation to the administrative network of the centrally-administered *tōdō-za*. While the guild frequently made efforts to force all such musicians into membership, many continued to work outside its jurisdiction.[8] After the guild's

---

8. In addition to Kyushu, such performers are documented for northern Honshu—most famously in Bashō's account in *Oku no Hosomichi* of a blind biwa player's

dissolution in the 1870s, traces of its organisational practices remained among regional blind musicians, and among a small number of blind and sighted *heikebiwa* players who transmitted that tradition until the present day.

Biwa-playing Buddhist priests (*mōsō*) and other blind biwa players in Kyushu—The word *mōsō* appears in early Japanese sources, but only to refer to priests who are blind; its use to designate members of particular social groups whose members were blind and played biwa dates from much later, in the late seventeenth century, when blind males who performed certain sutras and ritual narratives with biwa sought patronage from powerful Buddhist sects. It is reasonable to interpret *mōsō* as a designation for *biwa hōshi* who gained affiliation from the late seventeenth century with regional and national institutions, both Buddhist and "Shintoist" in nature. In the case of Satsuma *mōsō*, the patronage of the powerful Shimazu daimyō was also secured. As a result of these affiliations, *mōsō* engaged in a greater range of ritual activity than other *biwa hōshi*. This position, which I present at length in chapter 1, was developed by Komoda (2004), and has largely displaced the understanding of *mōsō* and *mōsōbiwa* as ancient institutions and traditions, which was standard to musicological reference sources of the latter half of the twentieth century.

It is likely that legitimate status as "monks" or "priests" was rare for blind biwa players until the modern period, but in Kyushu and the westernmost reaches of Honshu (Yamaguchi and Hiroshima prefectures), both *zatō*—that is, low-status *biwa hōshi*—and *mōsō* were important as celebrants of rites central to local veneration of deities of fire and earth, known most simply as Kōjin and Jijin. Exorcism (*harai*) of these deities was performed in a range of rites carried out for householders, such as the *Jijin-barai* and *kamado-barai*, as well as in formal group rites within *mōsō* temples, such as the Jijin-kyō Hōraku of the Fukuoka-based Chikuzen *mōsō* sect and the Myōon Jūnigaku of the Kagoshima-based Satsuma sect.

In music scholarship, the term *mōsōbiwa* has had two usages, a broader and a narrower one. The former sense is as a collective term

---

performance of tales of the *oku jōruri* repertory (see Hirose 1997, 116), which continued in fragmentary form into the twentieth century as a *shamisen*-accompanied genre.

for the biwa performance traditions that have been practised by blind males in south-western Japan; as such, it remains in currency as the broadest and most common general term for the blind traditions of Kyushu. Hence it encompasses both the ritual and secular repertories of Yamashika and other *biwa hiki* of the former Higo Province—*zatō* who were bearers of what has been called the *higobiwa* tradition (see chapter 2)—and the biwa music of certified member priests of two *mōsō* organisations, the Gensei Hōryū and the Jōrakuin Hōryū. When used in its narrower sense, *mōsōbiwa* denotes the musical repertories of member priests of those two sects. As the head temples of these sects are in the former (pre-Meiji) provinces of Satsuma and Chikuzen, respectively, scholars have distinguished the repertories and ritual practices as the *Satsuma mōsōbiwa* and *Chikuzen mōsōbiwa* traditions.

Chikuzenbiwa and satsumabiwa—Early in the Edo period (1603–1867), a new form of biwa playing emerged from interaction between *mōsō* and the samurai class in the province of Satsuma. It subsequently became well known throughout Japan from the end of the nineteenth century, at the start of a period of popularity for "modern biwa" (*kindai biwa*) that lasted until the 1930s. Equally as popular as *satsumabiwa* (the term by which this music became known) was a style called *chikuzenbiwa*, which had its origin in the 1890s in the Chikuzen region of Kyushu, and drew upon elements of the music of *mōsō* in the region, as well as *shamisen* music and *satsumabiwa* instrumental techniques. By the 1920s both styles were played for leisure by tens of thousands of amateurs and several hundred professionals in all of the country's major centres. *Chikuzenbiwa* and *satsumabiwa* are the two styles of biwa narrative that have been most widely practised in Tokyo, Osaka and other cities since the late Meiji period. The histories of both styles up until the time of their popularisation among urban audiences in central Japan, between 1880 and 1920, are inseparable from the histories of biwa performance by blind males in the Chikuzen and Satsuma regions. Distinct four- and five-string instruments are played in each style; in the case of *chikuzenbiwa* the four-string *chikuzen biwa* instrument[9] was a little-altered form of a type of biwa played by Chikuzen-region *mōsō*.

---

9. In this text, forms of instrument will be denoted by separation of the word "*biwa*" from what precedes it, hence *mōsō biwa*, *heike biwa*, *satsuma biwa*, and so forth.

Biwa music performed today in the cities of Japan is almost invariably that of schools within these two styles.[10] In addition to the instrument played, what most distinguishes "modern biwa" music from the recitations of Kyushu *biwa hiki* (and from other traditional narrative genres such as *jōruri*) is the uniformity of vocal delivery style throughout a *satsumabiwa* or *chikuzenbiwa* piece; even when first-person speech phrases are recited, change in sonic quality of the voice occurs only briefly.

Biwa and *Biwa Hōshi* in Modern-day Japan

There are now only a limited number of contexts in which most people have contact with biwa, the instrument or its music. The word *mōsō* is unknown to most people, as is the fact that in the late twentieth century there were blind priests in rural Kyushu who played biwa in ritual contexts. The biwa's most common and immediate association is with the expression *biwa hōshi*, which in turn conjures up a set of images acquired principally from two sources: compulsory study of the *Tale of the Heike* for a few days during high school, and the one story about biwa that almost everyone knows—*Mimi Nashi Hōichi*, as rendered by the Irish-Greek essayist and documentor of Meiji-period Japan, Lafcadio Hearn, or as recast in film, manga, anime and other media. Through exposure to these sources most Japanese come to think of the biwa as a battered old string instrument played by a decrepit blind man who looks like a Buddhist priest and wanders about chanting old tales about war and ghosts.

Live performances of biwa narrative singing are on the whole rare, and almost all performers are practitioners of *chikuzenbiwa* and *satsumabiwa*.[11] These traditions were popular during the first decades of the twentieth century largely because they expressed the prevailing nationalist, militarist sentiments of late-Meiji imperialist ideology. The repertories of both *chikuzenbiwa* and *satsumabiwa* changed greatly in the post-war era as they came to be seen as refined classical pursuits,

---

10. There are also a small number of *heikebiwa* performers active in Nagoya, Tokyo and Sendai.

11. As biwa narrative singing continues in these two "modern biwa" traditions, the title of this book is not intended literally, but as a characterisation to be understood in light of the array of representations of Yamashika that I discuss.

and today they may be heard far more often than *heikebiwa*. There is no general awareness of this, however, nor of the fact that the instruments and music of modern biwa traditions are not those of *biwa hōshi* of times past.

Apart from at occasional performances, the biwa itself can often be seen in the benevolent arms of the goddess Benzaiten at her numerous shrines, and in images of the Seven Lucky Gods (*shichi fukujin*) in homes, shops and offices. Notwithstanding, for Japanese I have spoken with over the last fifteen years, it is not these everyday objects or images that come to mind when the biwa is mentioned, but rather the *biwa hōshi* and Hearn's story of the blind priest, "Earless" Hōichi. Most are not quite sure what the instrument sounds like, and few can recognise its tones without being prompted by accompanying visual references to ghosts and medieval warriors offered in films and television programs. In all cases there is an emphatic sense that the biwa cannot be a thing of contemporary Japanese life and experience, but is tied forever to the world of the *Tale of the Heike*; a gloomy world of martial valour and samurai ghosts. Outside the realms of scholarship and the few who are involved in learning and performing, then, biwa narrative music is no longer experienced even as a marginal genre "inscribed within the nostalgic register as vanishing" (Ivy 1995, 242). Notwithstanding, the biwa's association with the provision of solace for the dead and appeasement of the gods continues to be fixed in the public imagination.

The *Biwa Hiki*, Yamashika Yoshiyuki

Born in 1901, in the Ōhara district of Nankan in northern Kumamoto Prefecture, Yamashika lost sight in his left eye at the age of four. His right eye was also weak, and had virtually failed by the time he reached his twenties, although he retained some ability to make out shapes and light contrast until his eighties. In his teens he became fond of a *shamisen*-accompanied narrative style that had been extremely popular since the last decade of Meiji, *naniwa-bushi*, and dreamed of becoming a professional performer. His father, however, forbade this, and insisted that he train as a professional biwa player, as he felt that "even if the tales (*gei*) lose their audience, there'll always be ritual (*harai*) work for you" (Murayama 1986, 430–431).

Introduction

In 1923 Yamashika was apprenticed for five years to a biwa player named Ezaki Shotarō (performer's name Tamagawa Kyōsetsu) in Amakusa. The teacher, a skilled performer in Yamashika's opinion, had been a student of Tamagawa Kyōjun, a renowned *biwa hiki* of the Nankan area and the founder of the Tamagawa line (*ha*), who is said to have received his performer's name from the last of the Higo daimyō. He taught infrequently, however, and by his third year of apprenticeship Yamashika had learned only a handful of short pieces. When his father took sick in 1926, Yamashika returned to Nankan, where for a few years he proceeded to work the family's small plot (something he could do because he still had partial sight in one eye) while also doing *kadobiki*, biwa performance door-to-door for whatever payment the occupants would offer, and learning new tales and some ritual procedures from a number of other biwa players in the area. From time to time, too, he was associated with a group of blind performers in the Chikugo region, whose purpose was to assist in organising concerts and other events to generate members' income (Hyōdō 1991, 16). Yamashika took the performing name Tamagawa Kyōen and, despite the fact that his apprenticeship had been cut drastically short, declared his "professional" status with a ceremonial name-taking performance in 1927.[12] He also learned to perform some *naniwa-bushi* and *jōruri* recitations, both of which styles had enjoyed great popularity in northern Kyushu.

From the 1930s to the late 1960s, Yamashika supported himself and his family through formal biwa engagements, ritual activities and *kadobiki*, supplemented by produce grown in a field near his home in Nankan. The small family plot was especially important as a source of sustenance during the years of war against the United States of America and the Occupation years (1945–1951) that followed, when biwa engagements were rare. In 1973 Yamashika applied to the Gensei Hōryū *mosō* sect in Fukuoka to become certified as a Tendai priest, both in an effort to ensure a continuing income from ritual work, and to fulfil a long-held aspiration for professional recognition and legitimacy.[13] Also in 1973, the so-called *higobiwa* tradition was declared

---

12. There is some doubt as to the exact year of the ceremonial performance; see chapter 3.
13. This was Kimura Rirō's interpretation, expressed in conversation, but Yamashika himself later gave confirmation. To judge from Yamashika's statement to Murayama

to be an Intangible Cultural Asset by the national government's Office of Cultural Affairs. Following this, a number of prestigious awards were given to Yamashika by governmental and private cultural foundations, including the Imperial Fifth Order of the Sacred Treasure (*Zuihō-shō*) in 1980. Yamashika had married several times and had children, but from 1988 on he lived alone.[14] Although his career as an active performer had effectively ended by 1990, he continued to be asked to perform in occasional events instigated by researchers and aficionados of local culture. In the first week of July 1992 he performed in Tokyo for two nights, to well-above capacity houses at the Mokubatei, a small theatre in Asakusa. The concert was organised by the producers of the 1992 documentary, *Biwa hōshi Yamashika Yoshiyuki*, and footage of the event forms the denouement of the film (Aoike 1992). A few months after returning from Tokyo, he fell from steps and was hospitalised. Although he recovered, and was able to spend most of 1993 in his home, he maintained, in October of that year, that he was absolutely incapable of holding the biwa, and that "without the biwa, my voice just won't work."[15] His health failed again in 1995, so that he entered a nearby old people's home where he died on June 24, 1996.

*   *   *

In writing this work I have assumed that most readers will have little or no prior knowledge of biwa music, nor of Japanese scholarship on historical performance traditions. Even in musicological and literary research on Japan published in English, there has been no extensive writing about *biwa hōshi* since Susan Matisoff's 1978 book on Semimaru.[16] Accordingly, chapter 1 provides a general account of

in 1974 that he no longer received any requests to do *kamado-barai* rites, this strategy for generating work as a Gensei-sect *mōsō* was hardly successful (Murayama 1986, 439). It should be noted that Yamashika was not included in the Heisei 3 (1991) directory of member priests of the Gensei Hōryū, as he had not paid dues for some years (Yasuda 2001, 22–23).

14. According to Kimura Rirō, Yamashika's first wife, Ine, bore five children, of whom only Tetsuo lived beyond childhood (1994, 101). Tetsuo died in his twenties, and one son by another of Yamashika's four wives remained alive in 2007.

15. Telephone conversation of October 1993.

16. In German, Fritsch (1996) deals with the history and origin-stories of the *mōsō* blind priests and the *biwa hōshi*, as well as other blind musicians and ritualists. Matisoff's

available historical evidence on blind male performers of biwa, as well as past and modern-day images of *biwa hōshi*, while chapter 2 concerns blind biwa players in central Kyushu and presents an overview of the repertory of *"higobiwa,"* with most detail about Yamashika's known repertory, as the largest and best documented among the *biwa hiki* whom researchers contacted since the 1960s. In chapter 3, I examine closely the problems of such "contact," and representations of Kyushu biwa traditions and of Yamashika the individual musician that they have given rise to in scholarship, the mass media and populist writings. Chapter 4 deals with the changing contexts for performances by Yamashika and with the performance process itself in a rendition of the *Dōjōji* tale. Chapter 5 concerns how Yamashika came to train as a *biwa hiki*, and the circumstances and characteristics of his training and professional life from the 1920s through 1960s. The final chapter, "Blind Biwa Singers Forgotten, Remembered and Rehabilitated," concerns the interstices of history, representation and the individual in the social rehabilitation of *biwa hiki*, whom most locals had considered little better than beggars until the late 1960s, and the subsequent transmission of some of Yamashika's repertory to sighted musicians that this change enabled. Efforts since Yamashika's death to pass the mantle of "the last *biwa hōshi*" to a blind Tendai-sect priest in Miyazaki Prefecture are also examined, to suggest the enduring cultural meanings that the perceived persistence of this kind of premodern musician has in Japan.

The concerns of this book for social and individual history, as well as imaginings and interpretations of those histories, have necessitated inclusion of only a limited amount of analysis of the performance process and musical and textual elements of the narrative and song repertories.[17] Nonetheless familiarity with the music of *biwa hiki* (and Yamashika Yoshiyuki's performances in particular) will enrich the reading of all that follows. Despite Yamashika's fame among the research community and folklore enthusiasts since the 1970s, at the time of his death no recordings of representative repertory had been made commercially available. I sought to rectify that lack by working

---

book is now available again as a reprint (2006).
   17. I have presented extensive analyses of the oral compositional process elsewhere (see de Ferranti 1995, 1997 and 2003).

with Kimura Rirō and the Japan Traditional Cultures Foundation over several years to produce a compact disc anthology with extensive documentation in Japanese and English (Nihon Dentō Geinō Shinkō Zaidan 2007). As one of the three discs includes Hyōdō Hiromi's field recording of the performance of *Dōjōji* that is presented in full in chapter 4, I would urge readers to seek out the CD-set and familiarise themselves with how Yamashika's performances sounded during the 1970s and 1980s.[18] I have also deposited a number of field recordings of performances by Yamashika with the Pacific and Regional Archives for Digital Sources in Endangered Cultures (PARADISEC), some of which will be made publicly accessible.[19]

18. A fuller sense of performance can of course be gained from audiovisual resources, of which a selection is listed in the Audio-Videography. As this book was going to print, a wonderful audiovisual resource appeared in the form of a twenty-minute excerpt from a 1989 performance of *Shuntokumaru*, on the DVD included with Hyōdō Hiromi's book *Biwa hōshi* (2009, Tokyo: Iwanami Shinsho).

19. On the archive website, paradisec.org.au, search the catalogue for the set of field recordings whose persistent identifier is HDF1-YY.

1

IMAGES AND HISTORIES

Today all except one of the forms of biwa music described in the introduction continue, albeit among far smaller numbers of performers and audiences. The exception is the performance of songs and narratives by blind males of low social status commonly called *biwa hōshi*. Late in his life Yamashika Yoshiyuki became broadly identified as a twentieth-century *biwa hōshi*—and seemingly "the last *biwa hōshi*"—for the reason that his professional activities as a performer and his lifestyle accorded with the essential features of the historical *biwa hōshi* as represented in scholarship, and selectively imparted by education and the media. As an icon of the past and its remoteness, the term *biwa hōshi* has a marketing value that has been immediately apparent to writers on Yamashika, as well as to television and film producers who documented his lifestyle. The publisher of Kimura Rirō's 1994 book, moreover, opted to exploit that same value in the rhetorical phrase that serves as the book's sub-title, "He's been called the last *biwa hōshi*, but . . ." (*hito wa saigo no biwa hōshi to iu keredo*). The image of the medieval *biwa hōshi*—a combination of a blind priest and an entertainer—hovers in the background of almost every text on Yamashika; "the last *biwa hōshi*" expresses a view of Yamashika in terms of stereotypic images from national history.

While *biwa hōshi* have long been regarded as key historical figures for canonical genres of national literature and performing arts, the practice of biwa music in Higo remains a topic of interest primarily for local scholars and enthusiasts. If not for the framing concepts of the *biwa hōshi* and their significance for the development of canonical performed narrative (*katarimono*) genres, it is doubtful that knowledge of Yamashika would have extended beyond Kumamoto and Kyushu folklorists and historians. Kimura's book was put together at a time—the early 1990s—when Yamashika's national significance had been emphatically established by the activities of scholars and a film-maker, and the construction of his text implicitly argues for a local and personal significance that supercedes the claims of "outsiders" who appropriated Yamashika for their own intellectual and ideological agendas. While aware of my status as one of the latter group, in this chapter I aim to convey the density of historical and ethnographic layering that bears upon representations of Yamashika and other blind biwa players of the modern era.

Characteristics of the Blind Biwa Traditions

The treatment of blind biwa players in historical documents and representative literature reflects a set of characteristics that *biwa hōshi, mōsō* and *zatō* (or *biwa hiki* as they were often called in central Kyushu) have had in common: blindness, maleness, a degree of association with sacred and supernatural phenomena, and various degrees of engagement in performance of narratives for entertainment.

Biwa and Blindness

As in many societies, music and narrative performance have been common professions for the blind throughout much of Japanese recorded history.[1] Among musicians, blind professionals were of central importance for most major genres (the exceptions being court music and genres of theatre music) from the thirteenth to nineteenth centuries, and among blind musicians, biwa players figure in sources spanning nearly one thousand years. In folklore and literature, stories about biwa players other than those of the court music tradition are invariably about blind *biwa hōshi* and *zatō*. Apart from the modern biwa traditions, and *gaku biwa* as played in the *gagaku* ensemble, most professional biwa performers were blind throughout recorded history.[2]

---

1. For a brief but thorough overview of blind musicians in Japanese history, much of which concerns *biwa hōshi*, see Groemer (1999, 3–19). A more extensive treatment is given in German by Ingrid Fritsch (1996). The principal studies in Japanese are Nakayama (1934), Katō (1974), Nagai (2002) and several chapters in Hirose (1997).

2. Note that in the Tsugaru tradition of *heikebiwa* (*heikyoku*), non-blind professionals were not uncommon. Since the late twentieth century, moreover, a small number of

By no means, however, should it be assumed that all "blind" biwa players were completely lacking the sense of vision and knowledge of writing. The denotation of words for blind people, the most common of which were *mōjin*, *zatō* and *mekura* (a slang word now officially listed as a discriminatory expression), must be acknowledged at the start of any historical assessment of blind biwa performers. There is little doubt that many people called by these terms were in fact only impaired in their vision. It is also worth remembering that many blind people became so only gradually, or else suddenly as adults, due to illness or accident, so that they were able to learn to read and write. In reading sources on the blind biwa traditions of Kyushu, and talking with blind performers in the early 1990s, I have often been struck by the fact that representative figures (for example, Yamashika and the Kunisaki-peninsula *mōsō*, Takagi Seigen) had had sufficient sight in one eye for them to read and even write some characters into their early adulthood (Kimura 1994, 164–178; Nagai 2002, 362). What is more, Yamashika and other former *"higobiwa"* performers spoke on several occasions of professional players and teachers who were sighted and in some cases literate.[3] The records of the Jōjuin or Gensei Hōryū *mōsō* tradition, moreover, include evidence that even during the Edo period sighted men were often admitted, even if their numbers were small (Nagai 2002, 13, 126, 333). Statutes of the Gensei Hōryū from its establishment in 1907 contain no requirements for blindness, and by the 1930s sighted men had already become a majority in the sect's membership (Fukuoka-ken Kyōiku Iin Kai 1983).[4] Any study of blind biwa performance in Japan must take into consideration the potential role of sighted participants in the tradition, in particular in the production of written texts and their utilisation in transmission of repertory.

---

both male (for example, the established *satsumabiwa* player Suda Seishū) and female (for example, Hashimoto Toshie) non-blind performers of *heikebiwa* have been active.

3. For a discussion of the implications of this in the case of Ōkawa Susumu's performance tradition, see de Ferranti (2002).

4. In 2002 the Gensei Hōryū had no blind members, while in the Jōrakuin Hōryū there were four blind priests, of whom only one played biwa in the households of his *danka*. A few sighted priests of both *hōryū* did so; among them, the practice of Ōkawa Gyōshun, of Hiradojima near Nagasaki, has been partially documented by researchers (*Fugeki mōsō gakkai kaihō* 1991).

The earliest documentation of biwa playing outside the court traditions refers to blind male performers. What might have been the historical roots of this association, beyond the practical consideration of the instrument's portability for itinerant performance by people with visual impairment? Blindness and the playing of lutes for alms were linked in Indian Buddhist culture in the early centuries of the first millennium of the Christian era. One of the central episodes among the origin stories of blind biwa players recounted in documents of the *mōsō* sects and the *biwa hōshi* guild concerns Prince Kunala, son of King Asoka, who is said to have become an itinerant player of the *vina*, led around by his wife or (in some versions) five-year-old son, after having his eyes ripped out at his stepmother's request. In Sanskrit, the tale is to be found in a fourth-century text, the *Asokavadana* (translated as *The Legend of King Asoka*; Strong 1983). In South Asia, then, from at least the fourth century there were blind itinerants, described as priests or holy men, who played lutes and received alms. The Kunala story was also popular throughout the Northern Buddhist cultures, and exists in a seventh-century Chinese version.[5] Scattered accounts of blind holy men who play lutes suggest that the practice of such semi-ritualistic performance was transmitted to East Asia with Buddhism. For example, in the sixth volume of the Tang-period chronicle *Xu gaoseng zhuang* there is a record of a blind man named Zhenyu who "preached" (presumably in chant) while playing *pipa*[6] and won many followers after being invited to perform at the Imperial compound (Hyōdō 1985b, 102).[7] Before the 1949 revolution, blind beggars who recited tales and travelled with *pipa* accompanists were common in the Shanbei region near Inner Mongolia (Wu Ben 1992, 58). It is also

---

5. *Hsi Yu Chi* [Records of Western Countries; mentioned on page 69 of Matisoff 1978 (2006)]. See also the bibliographic notes on page 151 of Strong (1983).

6. *Pipa* is the etymological source of the word biwa, and is written with the same two characters (琵琶), although historically the word has referred to a variety of plucked, fretted lutes played in China. From the seventh until at least the fourteenth centuries, the Chinese and Japanese terms denoted instruments that were structurally identical or similar, namely, forms of the four-stringed, pear-shaped lute played with a large plectrum (*gagaku biwa*) that has continued to be played in the *kangen* ensemble of *gagaku*. Structural modification to the *pipa* since the fifteenth century has produced an instrument, performance style and repertory unlike those of any forms of biwa.

7. The original text can be read in *Gaoseng Zhuan* (Biographies of eminent monks) (Shanghai: Shanghai guji chubanshe, 1991).

documented that in the 1970s under Maoism, blind itinerant narrative singers called *shuoshude* who played the three-stringed lute, *sanxian*, in household ritual contexts were protected and used by the Communist Party as "a potent force for social reform" (Tsao 2002, 258).

The Kunala story appears in many Japanese sources, including the fourth scroll of the early-twelfth-century *Konjaku monogatari-shū*.[8] The origins of blind biwa traditions in Japan remain unclear (see below), but the story of the most exalted individual among the Indian blind lute players probably contributed to emergent images of the *biwa hōshi* as blind musicians of an ambiguous sacred status. In part, that ambiguity of identity derived from a standard interpretation of blindness (along with other disabilities and disfiguring diseases such as leprosy) as a karmic punishment, in terms of the fundamental Buddhist doctrine of reincarnation or transmigration of the soul after death. In Yamashika's own performance repertory, this interpretation finds expression in the blinding of various characters for their sins. For example, after she has arranged for her suitor to fall into a torrent and drown, Ono no Komachi suddenly became "unable to tell night from day, unable to see the sunlight, unable to carry out her daily duties, so lost her position and was driven from her house to live in a wretched hut below the Ausaka no Seki'"[9] (Kimura 1994, 222).

Another circumstance that lent ambiguity to the identity of *biwa hōshi* throughout their history is the early use of the expression "*hōshi*" (法師) as one term for poor itinerants who presented themselves with some of the visual markers of Buddhist priests, namely, shaven pates and modest robes.[10] As itinerant begging was of itself a Buddhist tradition for adherents or teachers (*shi*) of the Law (*hō*), it was also

8. Narita (1985a) includes a brief comparative study of versions of the Kunara Taishi story, in both *mōsō* sources and the *Konjaku monogatari-shū* (pages 147–160). Matisoff (1978 [2006]) includes a translation of the latter.

9. This is the same place where the legendary blind Imperial prince, Semimaru, is said to have lived as a beggar musician in many sources (see further "Images and Depictions of *Biwa Hōshi*," below).

10. The word *hōshi* was a component in terms for many kinds of itinerant and performing artists of the twelfth to sixteenth centuries. It later came to be used as a generic suffix for itinerant performers who held various degrees of affiliation with large shrine-temple complexes, as in *sarugaku hōshi* and *dengaku hōshi*. Although these people did not always bear visual resemblance to priests, the continued use of the term reflected the origin in or association of many performance traditions with Buddhist ritual.

open to exploitation by people who had no such ascetic leanings; an early-tenth-century writer's comment suggests that while many *hōshi*, itinerants in the guise of priests, surely were religious, many more were regarded as opportunists and shysters:

> In every province there are peasants who flee from taxation and conscripted labor; cutting off their own hair, without authority they wear priestly robes. With the passing years the numbers of people like this are gradually increasing; two-thirds of the common people have become bald-pates of this sort. All of them have wives and children at home, and eat flesh. In their appearance they resemble monks, but in their hearts they are like butchers. (From *Iken jūni kajō*, a 914 document in the *Gunsho ruiju*, vol. 27, 128. Adapted from the translation in Matisoff 1978 [2006], 18–19.)

Was it only Buddhist lore and continental tradition which yielded blind biwa players an aura of both sanctity and marginality? Indigenous beliefs about the blind that pre-date the dissemination of Buddhist learning during the sixth to the ninth centuries may also have been important for the circumstances in which blind performers adopted biwa and the visual appearance of itinerant priests. It is generally acknowledged that in Japanese ritual life blind men and women had been respected as shamanic celebrants who bore numinous power because of their separation from the world experienced by others (Hirose 1997, 122–125; Nagai 2002, 51). Individuals accorded shamanic status by a local community required no official qualifications, but need only have demonstrated the power to placate malevolent spirits deemed responsible for sickness and suffering. Historically a great many such figures have been blind. Healing ritual that involves possession in Japan has been largely the province of blind mediums, but many *harai* (exorcism) rites have also been entrusted to blind celebrants.

In both contexts the sounding of plucked or struck string instruments has been important. The *azusa yumi* (catalpa bow[11]) was a tool for summoning deities in pre-Buddhist ritual, and may have been struck by a blind shaman. It continued to be used by blind female mediums (*miko* and *itako*) and was a precursor of the struck

---

11. This translation is inaccurate, as Japanese cherry birch was used, not catalpa (Groemer 2008, 26).

bow still used by some mediums in northern Honshu. The importance of instruments and vocal intonations for enabling trance, possession, and communication with deities and spirits of the dead is suggested in some of the earliest Japanese written sources. For example, in Book II of the *Kojiki*, the first collection of Japanese mythology and oral history (compiled in 712), the sound of a plucked zither (*koto*) is said to have induced possession and the delivery of divine instructions to the fourth-century Empress Jingū. In the late-eighth-century anthology of poetry, the *Manyōshū*, poem 1129 in Book 7 implies that the *koto* is able to act as a conduit for spirits of the dead:

As I take up the koto	koto toreba
I first hear a cry escape it.	nageki sakidatsu
Can it be that	kedashiku mo
within this koto	koto no shitahi ni
my wife's spirit has hidden?	tsuma ya komoreru

Shamanistic ability is implied in one of the most established interpretations of the primary role of early *biwa hōshi*: ritual performance of battle tales as a means to allay the fury of slain warriors' ghosts (*tamashizume*). In ancient and medieval contexts "*chinkon-sai*" often denotes a kind of exorcism to placate the dead. In the late Heian and Kamakura periods, belief in the dangerous potential of ghosts of those who had died bearing grievances (*goryō shinkō*) had considerable bearing upon political life. Of particular concern were the ghosts of warriors killed in battle. Historical references to the involvement of blind professionals in divination (*uranai*) abound,[12] but in the case of blind biwa players in south-western Japan, there is evidence that *mōsō* carried out not only divination but also *chinkon-sai* for harmful aggrieved spirits until well into the Edo period. For example, a record of events in the area of Soeda-chō in Buzen tells of four *mōsō* being engaged in Bunsei 12 (1830) to subdue the anger of a recently deceased resident, which was said to have caused the death of many livestock and other misfortunes. The fact that the earliest account of performance of narratives (as distinct from sutras) by blind biwa players in Chikuzen lists a series of tales that relate the fall of a castle or the course of a grand battle, has also been interpreted as evidence for the central function of such arratives in placatory rituals of the region.[13]

12. See, for example, Katō (1974, 80).
13. Tales of this sort were called *kuzure* in several regions of Kyushu (see further

The Ikime Jinja in Miyazaki has long been renowned throughout Kyushu as a shrine for the blind and sufferers of eye diseases. In conversations I had with elderly blind musicians in the Kumamoto region during 1991, the shrine's healing properties were repeatedly mentioned. When I later went to visit Ikime Jinja, I was told about—though refused permission to see—a collection of biwa that had been played within and donated to the shrine by musicians who had sought improvements in their eye conditions through the powers of the enshrined deities. Chief among the benevolent deities of the institution is the spirit of Kagekiyo, a famous warrior of the Heike clan who were swept from power by the Genji clan in the late twelfth century. The extensive lore about Kagekiyo includes a chapter in the *Tale of the Heike*, a noh play by Zeami and a puppet-play by Chikamatsu, but in regional Kyushu the most commonly known tale recounts how Kagekiyo was blinded when held prisoner by the Genji, then became an itinerant biwa player who made his way to the Miyazaki region. In the vicinity of the Ikime Jinja there are a number of relics identified as belonging to Kagekiyo himself; chief among these is the biwa said to have been brought by him from the region of the capital, Kyoto, over 700 years ago. The shrine is today unrelated to either of the *mōsō* groups, but petitioners to the shrine have included many of the blind or partially blind males who made their living in Kyushu carrying out *harai* rituals and reciting both Buddhist and secular tales with biwa. On their pilgrimages, the blind musicians would perform biwa, and sometimes offer their instruments to the shrine, as part of healing rituals of which they were the intended beneficiaries. The culture of the *zatō* (as both *biwa hiki* and *mōsō* were often called in the vernacular) has long been inseparable from the cult of healing surrounding biwa performance and the spirit of Kagekiyo.

Blindness and biwa are associated in the legends of the origins and early histories of the two pre-modern Japanese social institutions whereby blind males associated for the purpose of maintaining and furthering their livelihoods: the *tōdō* or *tōdō-za*,[14] a guild of *Heike* per-

---

chapter 3; Nagai 2002, 49–52).

14. *Tōdō* means "the true way" or "our way," and was an expression used by the leading exponents in various medieval performing arts. For example, after the age of seventy Zeami used this term to refer to his *sarugaku* teachings (Iwahashi 1951, 179). "*Za*" is usually translated as a guild or professional organisation, but there were many

formers which expanded from its base among musicians of the Kyoto region to become a national institution governing professions practised by the blind in the early Edo period, and various regional groups of biwa-playing blind ritualists called *mōsō* from the late eighteenth century on. As the condition of blindness was basic to membership of those organisations (albeit not mandatory for groups in northern Kyushu by the mid Edo period; Nagai 2002), their traditional accounts of ancestry ennoble their lineage, tracing it back through various quasi-historical blind Imperial figures such as Semimaru, the supposed son of the Emperor Daigo (reigned 897–930), Prince Saneyasu, the actual fourth son of the ninth-century Emperor Nimmyō (reigned 833–850), to the Indian Prince Kunala, son of King Asoka.[15] In the Edo-period *mōsō* documents, Prince Kunala is said to have performed the very rites for the deities Jijin and Kōjin that *mōsō* sects have claimed as their professional domain, as well as secret pieces for the biwa (*myōon no hikyoku*). In many such accounts, the lineage of blind biwa players ultimately is traced to an entirely legendary figure, a blind disciple of the historical Buddha Shakyamuni, called Gankutsu Sonja.[16]

Blindness and the biwa, then, were inseparable in all contexts except courtly *gakubiwa* performance, for at least the first thousand years of the instrument's practice in Japan. During the Edo period, moreover, *Heike* reciters who controlled the *tōdō-za* guild came to regulate the lives of most of the country's blind people, by achieving Shogunal authority for expansion of their guild's jurisdiction to cover all blind professionals. The guild was given authority to exact membership from blind practitioners of the professions of music, massage and acupuncture throughout Japan.[17] The historical importance of the

---

kinds of *za* in both medieval and Edo-period Japan, and distinction must be made between the centrally based, nationwide structure of the *tōdō-za* as it was from the time of its consolidation of Shogunal support in the seventeenth century, and medieval-period locally based troupes (*za*) of *sarugaku hōshi* and *biwa hōshi*.

15. Saneyasu is venerated as the founder of the *tōdō-za* guild and called Prince Amayo in various guild documents and ritual texts. Matisoff (1978 [2006]) provides a detailed account of how these various legends coalesce in representations of Semimaru through pre-modern Japanese literary and performing arts history.

16. Some sources give the alternative name Gankatsu Chōja.

17. As a centrally organised institution for the blind, the *tōdō-za* has drawn a lot of scholarly attention, and has been thoroughly documented by social and music historians. See Nakayama (1934 and 1936), Katō (1974), and Komoda (2003a); in English, Fritsch (1991) and Groemer (2001a), and in German, Fritsch (1996).

link between blindness and the biwa can be keenly appreciated when one considers why it was that, from the late seventeenth through nineteenth centuries, professional players of three of Japan's principal string instruments—*biwa, koto,* and *kokyū*—were also blind: as biwa professionals were the first musicians to take up each of those instruments and apply them in the performance of contemporary popular styles, they created and long protected a monopoly on the instruments and their newly established repertory through granting professional certification only to blind students.

A general point that arises from the centrality of blindness in the pre-Meiji history of biwa music is that text sources for historical performance repertory, whether ritualistic or secular, are by definition highly ambiguous in nature. In the case of the *heikebiwa* tradition, contemplation of the apparent paradox presented by a blind performance tradition of a large-scale narrative that has been circulated in many different text versions has led to a seachange in *Heike monogatari* studies since the 1980s. For *mōsō* traditions some of the ritual texts chanted are extracts or entire renditions of sutras contained in the standard Japanese Buddhist canon and its Chinese and Sanskrit precursors (the Heart Sutra is the most conspicuous example of this), and for those texts it seems that readings from standard printed versions have been memorised and adhered to. For many more ritual items, however, there exist only partial written texts or no text sources at all. With regard to secular narrative texts other than those of the *Heike* tradition, very few written sources have been located, but the participation of sighted, literate individuals in transmission of repertory appears to have been significant for particular individuals and performance lineages. This is an issue I will return to in chapter 2.

Biwa and Sanctity

> Biwa is a special instrument in Japan because it was devised by Benzaiten at the time Amaterasu hid herself in the cave. (Kimura 1994, 59)

> The original job of *biwa hiki* was to worship the gods and Buddhas, but already by the time I was a young man, there were very few people who knew how to do that properly. (ibid., 94)

Yamashika's pithy statement about the sacred origins of biwa expresses the same need to provide a distinguished lineage for the profession of the biwa player as do the blind priests' and *Heike* performers' traditional accounts of origin and lineage. Yet his mythological grounds for biwa's "special" status also reflect the fact that in the region where Yamashika led his professional life—as throughout most of Kyushu—for centuries biwa had been inseparable from the performance of rites important to local belief. It was an instrument of numinous power, and its blind performers were called upon to mediate with "the gods and Buddhas" as well as to entertain in the context of both ritual festivities and secular celebrations.

Yamashika's words reflect not only the important role of *biwa hiki* in local ritual life of the not-yet-distant past, but also the position of biwa within a web of associations with various sacred beings in Buddhism and East Asian regional syncretic practices. Short-necked lutes are played by celestial musicians found in Buddhist iconography throughout much of East and South-East Asia (*tian shi* in Chinese, and in Japanese, *tenshi* or *tennyo*). They are also played by *di guo tian* in Chinese and Korean representations—figures that correspond to the Guardian King of the East Dhritarashtra (Dhrtarastra), who in Indian tradition was also leader of the celestial musicians (*gandharvas*) and played a lute—and by avatars of the *vina*-playing Hindu goddess of music, wisdom and eloquence, Sarasvati, in Tibetan and Chinese iconographic images and sculptures (see figure 1.1). The latter are all female deities that have their Japanese counterpart in Benzaiten, one of the Japanese "Seven Lucky Gods" (*shichi fukujin*), who holds a biwa in the most common of her two forms (Bakshi 1979).

In Japanese iconography there are two female lute-playing deities whose identities have fused in various contexts: Benzaiten and Myōon (Gaku) Ten. Both have existed in Continental Asian tradition, and their lineage can be traced directly from Sarasvati through various forms in the Himalaya region and China (Ludvik 2001). While Benzaiten—or rather, Biancaitian in Chinese—was the original name for Sarasvati in rituals associated with recitation of the *Sutra of Golden Light* (in Sanskrit *suvarnaprabhaasa*, and in Japanese *Konkōmyōsaishō-ō Kyō*)[18] from the

18. The Kenrō Jijin-bon, the eighth chapter of this sutra, addresses manifestations of Jijin and is recited in group rites of both the Chikuzen (Gensei Hōryū) and Satsuma (Jōrakuin Hōryū) *mōsō* sects in Kyushu.

sixth century (ibid., 200–208), subsequent transformation into two distinctly named East Asian goddesses whose names reflect different aspects of Sarasvati's powers—eloquence in the case of Benzaiten ("Accomplished Speech" deity), sound and music in the case of Myōon Ten ("Miraculous Sound" deity)—is evident in eighth-century Chinese sources (ibid., 280).

Figure 1.1. Eighteenth-century Chinese devotional image of Sarasvati with her names shown in Tibetan, Chinese, Mongolian and Manchu.

A bodhisattva also named "Miraculous Sound," Myōon Bosatsu, is the subject of the twenty-fourth chapter of the *Lotus Sutra* but is not unequivocally gendered in the text. Both Biancaitian (Benzaiten) and Miaoyin(le)tian (Myōon [Gaku] Ten) are venerated in the *Mahâvairocana Sūtra*[19] that is the basis for the Womb World Mandala

---

19. This Sanskrit text was first translated into Chinese in the early eighth

and are gendered as female. Thereafter in the majority of Japanese sculptures and iconographic sources (few, if any, survive in China), a female form is shown holding the *pipa* (see figure 1.2).

Figure 1.2. Fourteenth-century *Benzaiten-zu* (detail). Collection of the Hōjōin, Mt. Koya.

Musicians of Japanese court society who had studied biwa traditions in Tang China during the eighth and ninth centuries probably brought back with them a cult of veneration of the "Miraculous Sound" goddess. The importance of this bodhisattva for biwa players in the Japanese capital is evident in the naming of the principal *mōsō* temple of the Kyoto region, the Myōondera Jōrakuin, said to have been established in 808. Many of her attributes were interchangeable with those of Benzaiten, and from the late Heian period (794–1185)

---

century (Ludvik 2001, 279) and brought to Japan by Kūkai some decades later.

the goddess variously referred to as Myōon Ten (Tennyo) or Myōon Benzaiten was in effect a patron deity for musicians of the court traditions.[20] By the Muromachi period (1392–1573) her influence had spread to musicians beyond court culture, in particular to the *biwa hōshi*, and by the Edo period, under *tōdō-za* regulation, rites for her worship were maintained by all groups of blind professional musicians as well as *itako* mediums who induced "trance" while striking a bow. Those rites continued until the mid twentieth century in some regions (Fritsch 1991).

In a little-known article of 1966, Hirai Yoshinobu examines particular grounds for association between biwa and the traditions of blind ritualists (*mōsō*, but *biwa hōshi* are also referred to in Hirai's text). His starting point is a Yanagita Kunio essay of 1932 on lore about the blind and their roles in literary history. Yanagita explores the relations between blind males and *kami* of water—almost always manifest as giant snakes or dragons who first appear as a beautiful female—and especially the pacification of this *kami* by players of the flute, who in many stories are blind (Yanagita 1998, 528–554). Hirai goes on to examine several other regional stories about water *kami*, blindness and instrumental performance, including ones about the skills of biwa players in rain-making rites. He reaches a conclusion that supports Yanagita's contention that the elements of flute-playing, Benzaiten as a water *kami*, blind performers' worship of both Benzaiten and the earth *kami* Jijin, and Benzaiten's representation as a biwa-playing female can all be tied together in light of these legends (ibid., 550): ritual instrumental performance to placate forms of water *kami*, as well as performance on flutes to control snakes, were probably roles associated with the blind from before the time they took up biwa-playing as a profession.

Another contributing factor in the adoption of biwa by the blind may have been the attribution of numinous power to plucked string sounds, as I have already described. Beliefs and practices concerning ritual performance of string instruments that were already common

---

20. Few accounts of her worship have been identified in contemporary sources, but one is given in a passage in the thirteenth-century treatise on biwa traditions, *Bunkidan*, about the famous eleventh-century biwa player Minamoto no Tsunenobu's veneration of Myōon Tennyo. See Iwasa Miyoko (1989, page 51 [Kikutei-bon text] and pages 171–172 [Fushinomiya-bon]). I am grateful to Professor Steven Nelson for drawing this to my attention.

in Japan may well have contributed to the establishment of biwa as a ritual vehicle. One of the services of early *biwa hōshi* associated with shrine-temple complexes was *goryō chinkon* ritual performance. *Biwa hōshi*'s accounts of battle were an important means of allaying the wrath of warrior ghosts, for it was believed that the vengeful spirits could be appeased by narrative tellings of the circumstances of their deaths (Hyōdō 1985a, 33–34; Plutschow 1990). The fact that early *biwa hōshi* performed war tales as a form of exorcism reflects a confluence of the historical links between oral narrative and indigenous *chinkon* rites on the one hand and between the *biwa* and Buddhist ritual on the other.

The sanctity of biwa performed by blind ritualists is expressed in lore about the many places whose name contains the characters or sounds "biwa." The most well known of these is of course Japan's largest lake, Lake Biwa, near Kyoto. Most lore about the lake's association with various *kami* refer to the important Benzaiten shrine on Chikubushima, an island in its northern reaches. For instance, in the *Heike monogatari* when the great biwa player Taira no Tsunemasa performs on the island before the Benzaiten shrine, the deity appears to express its delight in the form of a white dragon. Yet throughout much of Japan there are "biwa valleys," "biwa hills," "biwa ponds," "biwa bridges" and the like. Such places are especially numerous in Kyushu, and associated with many of them are stories about blind ritualists and performers who may have buried instruments or offered them to the waters at the place.[21]

The legacy of the biwa's numinous power is also inherent in a body of lore about the sacred nature of both instruments and repertory, found in texts from the late Heian period on. These stories concern *gakubiwa* and music of the court milieu brought from Tang China, whose ritual efficacy continued to be acknowledged centuries later. The best known are the accounts of the instruments named *Seizan* given in the *Heike monogatari* and references in multiple texts to *Ryūsen*, *Takuboku* and *Yōshinsō*, three secret pieces that Fujiwara Sadatoshi is said to have learned from a Tang master in the 830s. Each of these

---

21. A list of some of these places is given in the entry for "*biwa no chimei*" in *Nihon minzokugaku jiten*: 1060–1061. See also Yanagita 1998 (vol. 5, 213) for a discussion of the many places along rivers and ponds where *zatō* are said to have fought snake demons.

pieces is characterised as having been played by bodhisattvas or other Buddhist deities and attributed power to "open the mind to the realm of gods and Buddhas" (Matisoff 1978 [2006], 77).

In the late twentieth century, *mōsō* (and to a lesser extent *biwa hiki*) maintained lore about the sanctity and "cosmology" of the biwa itself. As has been documented by Murayama (1978, 1986) and Kawano (2001, 120–123), the sacred nature of the biwa as a ritual tool is described not only in ritual texts called *shakumon* but also in oral lore passed to *mōsō* by their teachers and older fellows. According to that lore, each part of the instrument is an embodiment of a Buddhist deity or of one of the five elements and cardinal directions fundamental to Daoist and Yin-Yang (*ommyō-dō*) cosmology. The cosmological associations accorded to the instrument by the *mōsō* were mostly lost in the development of secular performance traditions among sighted players, but certain of them live on in the names used for frets on the four- and five-stringed *chikuzen biwa*: wood, fire, earth, metal and water, in ascending order. For Yamashika and other *biwa hiki*, such lore was manifested in comments and stories about the origin of the characters for biwa ("in the characters for biwa there are lots of kings lined up next to one another"[22]) as well as aspects of the instrument's design. For example, the symbolism of the instrument's principal parts is recounted as follows in Yamashika's version of the *watamashi* ritual, learned from a local biwa player named Sakamoto Saichi:

> *biwa ni wa Amaterasu Ō Mi-kami no kurai o tori*
> Biwa has the status of the great goddess Amaterasu,
> *sono shōkō ni biwa no hidari ni matsuwaru Gattenshi,*
> and the proof of this is: the venerated Moon deity, at the left on
>   the [face of the] biwa,
> *migi ni iwau Nittenshi*
> and the celebrated Sun deity, at the right —
> *futatsu no jitsugetsu o manabase tamau*
> in the form of the sun and the moon.
> *itsutsu no tsubo wa nijūgo no Kanzeon no itoku o arawashi*
> The five frets that are the virtues of the twenty-five Kanzeon
>   bodhisattvas,

---

22. Kimura 1994, 118. Here the use of the character for king (王), doubled side by side at the top of both BI and WA, is taken as an indication of a noble heritage and ritual power.

itomaki wa tenjin no kurai o tori
the tuning pegs that have the status of celestial beings,
fukuju wa Ama no Iwato no katachi o manabase tamau
and the tail-piece in the form of the Cave of Heaven.
haraita wa chikyū no katachi o tori
The soundboard is in the form of the Earth,
yosuji no ito wa toshi ni shisetsu no fujō o harai
and the four strings that exorcise impurity in all four seasons...

(From text transcription given in Kimura 1994, 183–184. Punctuation and line divisions follow those given by Kimura.)

The origin account of the Satsuma *mōsō* sect (the Jōrakuin Hōryū) varies in different documents of the sect, but in all cases describes how initial transmission of the Jijin sutra from Shakyamuni to his blind disciple was followed by transmission of secret *"myōon"* biwa music, either by or to the goddess Benzaiten herself together with her divine children.[23] In the *Jijin mōsō kongen*,[24] for example, the origin in Japan of both biwa-playing and recitation of the Jijin Darani-kyō (sutra in honour of Jijin, deity of the earth) and the rites of Do-Kōjin by blind males is given as follows:

> The priest Gankutsu Sonja, a disciple of Shakyamuni, received the Jijin Darani-kyō and the Do-Kōjin rites, and Myōon Benzaiten received the Myōon music for biwa. At that time in central India the son of King Asoka, Prince Kunala, suddenly went blind and became a disciple of Gankutsu Sonja. Thereafter the disciples of Kunala included Shichioni Taishi and Akō Taishi of Tang China, who transmitted the rites to their motherland. Then in the reign of Emperor Kimmei, the son of the Jingi Daisei Daijin [a high-ranking government official], Yūkyō Reishi, went blind and was sent to the Udo Cave in Hyūga Province. At that time a blind priest from China came and taught him the rites. Reishi thereafter was called Daijinbō and built a temple, where he taught the rites to *mōsō* from six regions of Kyushu. (As summarised by Murata 1994, 148–149.)

---

23. Individually named deities who were Sarasvati's children exist in Hindu legend. On Benzaiten and her *dōshi* children, see Fukushima (1987, 71), and Bakshi (1979, 121–122).

24. This is a document of unknown date held by the Jōrakuin Hōryū. Murata describes it as unique in relating the origin of blind biwa-playing priests throughout Kyushu, rather than only those of the Satsuma region (1994, 148).

What is significant in this legend of origin is the sanctity it accords to the biwa itself and the legitimacy accorded to the *mōsō* tradition through association with historical rulers and high officials. While there is no question of its historical inaccuracy—for example, the historical Buddha's disciples lived nearly two hundred years before King Asoka's time—the legend may reflect the general path of transmission of a Buddhist rite long associated in Japan with blind lute players.

There is little in the recent practice of institutional Buddhism in China and Korea which links lutes with groups of blind ritualists, but important commonalities exist in terms of texts for the *Jijin Darani-kyō* sutra that is central to rites of the *mōsō* sects. I have not had access to data on Chinese blind ritualists' practices, but it seems likely that the association of this text with blind supplicants of the earth spirit was common throughout East Asian Buddhism, as it has been an important text in the repertory of Korean blind ritualists and was performed as one of seven indispensable sutras of rites for protection of agrarian households, carried out soon after the New Year.[25]

Biwa and Gender

Images of women of Heian-period court society playing biwa abound, and in the twentieth century some of the most celebrated biwa players of the *chikuzenbiwa* and *satsumabiwa* styles were female.[26] Yet with the exception of avocational performance by women in the court music tradition, for the thousand years between those most ancient and modern contexts for biwa performance, biwa was a male profession. Defined by both blindness and maleness, the two social institutions of the *mōsō* and the *tōdō-za*, whereby biwa players were sustained as priests or *biwa hōshi*, admitted no female members.

---

25. Nagai 2002, 25, 260, 336. It is also worth noting here that in Korean shamanistic rites of divination and exorcism, carried out by female *mudang*, the drummer-reciter whose sounds are essential for the *mudang*'s entry into trance is called a *popsa*, written with the characters for "*hōshi*" in historical sources (see Takamatsu Keikichi, "Poppusa [Hōshi]," in *Kadai Shigaku*, n. 45, 1997, 33–58).

26. Among them are Suitō Kinjō and her student Tsuruta Kinshi (*nishikibiwa* and the *Tsuruta-ryū*), Yamazaki Kyokusui (*Chikuzenbiwa Tachibana-kai*), and Uehara Mari (who trained as a *Chikuzenbiwa Asahi-kai* player, but since the 1980s has performed *Heike monogatari* episodes in a style that draws upon her experience as a Takarazuka actor and singer).

To date there has been no substantial research on the question of whether there were blind females who played biwa prior to the introduction of the three-stringed lute, *shamisen*, in the sixteenth century. There are, however, a few clues to be followed:

1. In Tang China it had been common for women to play *pipa*, and for later periods there are documentary accounts of blind performers of both sexes.[27]

2. It was common for women of court society from the Heian through Muromachi periods to learn biwa from their childhood days; one of the best known among such skilled players was Nijō, author of the *Towazugatari*.[28]

3. In the same early-fourteenth-century text there is an account of biwa being played by a sighted female entertainer (Nijō, trans. Brazell 1973, 182). There are also suggestions in late-Heian poetry that low-status female itinerants (of a group then referred to as *kugutsu-me*) may have performed biwa at that time (Nakayama 1934, 53; Law 1997, 96).

4. There is a single reference to two female blind performers, Aiju and Kikuju, in the diary of Gosukōin, *Kanmon Gyoki*, for the seventeenth day of the eighth month, 1418. What the women performed is described as "*ku*"—a term that usually denoted episodes of the *Heike* corpus—but there is no indication whether a biwa was played.

---

27. See for example the early-nineteenth-century book *Qing Jia Lu*, in which several references to blind female *pipa* players who performed both narratives and songs in earlier eras are cited (Gu lu 1999, 134–135). Iwahashi also refers to accounts of a Ming dynasty regional tradition, *taozhen* (陶真), in which male and female blind *pipa* players recited "historical and contemporary tales" (1951, 171).

28. Nijō wrote that she "mastered all the usual court pieces" and at age ten performed in a palace rehearsal for celebrations of Emperor Go-Saga's fiftieth birthday (Nijō, trans. Brazell 1973, 96). References to women performers include them among successors to important solo biwa traditions, in particular within the Saionji clan. In the mid thirteenth century, moreover, Gyōbukyō no Tsubone, granddaughter of the renowned author of treatises on biwa, Fujiwara no Takamichi, taught the instrument to several members of the Imperial family (Terauchi 1996, 147–149).

5. As there were no female members of the *tōdō-za*, women performers of biwa (as distinct from *shamisen* or *koto*-playing *goze*) are not mentioned in Tōdō documents. During the Edo period, when blind *heikebiwa* professionals taught narrative recitation to sighted amateur enthusiasts in the metropolises of Edo, Kyoto and Osaka, a few women were taught to recite— and perhaps also to play biwa. The most well documented among them is Fujii Masako, wife of the painter Fujii Setsudō (Tateyama 1911, 566). It appears that their involvement with *heikebiwa* was purely recreational and that they were highly exceptional figures.

Itinerant women performers of various kinds were common in the medieval period, and most images and descriptions depict them playing the *tsuzumi* drum. In the Edo period blind professional female singers called *goze* accompanied themselves on the *shamisen* or *koto*, the latter instrument being played by relatively affluent blind women who taught it to the wives of samurai and merchants. Only *shamisen* and its wooden imitation, *gottan*, were played for *kadozuke*, performance for alms from house to house.[29] *Goze* were not uncommon in Kyushu, and are mentioned in late-eighteenth-century documents concerning the *tōdō-za* guild. While they held annual ceremonies (Myōon Kō) similar to those of the guild's ceremonies, they were not bona fide members. *Shamisen* performance continued to be a viable profession for blind women in rural Kyushu until the mid twentieth century; the last of Yamashika's wives (Misao) had been trained as a professional *shamisen* player and singer, as had the wife of Ōkawa Susumu, a former *biwa hiki* whom I interviewed several times between 1991 and 1995.[30]

During ten years of research on blind musicians in Kyushu, I did not once hear of nor find reliable references to blind female biwa players. After fieldwork in the early 1970s, Murayama described at length the

29. On *goze*, see Groemer (2001a and 2008), Fritsch (1991) and Harich-Schneider (1959) in English, and Fritsch (1996) in German. There are many sources in Japanese, including Groemer's recent synoptic historical study (2007). On *gottan*, see Kikkawa (1984, 394).
30. A photograph of such a blind *shamisen* professional and her guide—women who may have been members of a Kyushu *goze* troupe—taken in the Sue Mura region of southern Kumamoto Prefecture in the 1930s by John Embree or his wife, Ella, may be seen in Wiswell and Smith 1982 (unnumbered plate) and in de Ferranti (2000, 36).

impression made upon him by the powerful voice of a female ritualist on Tsushima who carried on the work of her *mōsō* husband after his death, but he is ambiguous on the question of whether she played biwa; he states only that she had little or no skill on the instrument, so it is feasible that she struck its strings percussively while chanting ritual texts, as have *mōsō* in some other regions (1978, 8–10). The possibility exists that there were women *biwa hiki*, but documentary evidence for them has yet to be found. The closest thing to such a reference is the program of a concert entitled "Dai ikkai higobiwa ensōkai" on July 9, 1922, at which ten people performed. Among the ten were both men with elements in their names that mark them as professional—and most probably blind—*biwa hiki* (such as Miyazaki Maki no Ichi[31]) as well as a woman named Sakanishi Sukiko (Yasuda 2001, 75). Yet there is no way of knowing whether she was a blind performer, and the fact that Shimada Dangetsu's activities at that time (see chapter 2) had encouraged a small number of sighted amateurs to learn the local biwa tradition makes it probable that she was one of them. As yet there is little published research on the *goze* groups in Kyushu and western Japan,[32] by comparison with the many books on *goze* of northern Japan, and evidence for female biwa players may yet emerge among documents pertaining to Kyushu *goze*. In view of the restriction of *goze* to *shamisen* performance elsewhere in Japan, however, it seems likely that any blind female biwa players would have been maverick figures rather than members of either *goze* or *zatō* professional organisations.

There is a gender puzzle at the core of the blind traditions of biwa performance: while the patron deity of music venerated by both *biwa hōshi* and *mōsō*, Benzaiten-Myōon Bōsatsu (the Bodhisattva Miraculous Sound), is depicted as a female who plays biwa, blind females were not admitted to membership of the professional organisations of either group. The puzzle is further compounded by the fact that *goze* guild members also participated in annual group ceremonies for the goddess. A solution to this puzzle may yet come from historians who

---

31. The word "ichi," most often written with the character for capital or city (都) or that for market (市) was common in the names of blind professionals throughout the Edo period. The origins of such names may lie in the affiliation of *Heike* performers with the Muromachi period ICHIkata school. The name of the fictitious blind swordsman Zatō Ichi, played by Katsu Shintaro in twenty-five films made from 1962 through the mid-1970s (and more recently by "Beat" Takeshi), draws upon this convention.

32. The most extensive account is given by Groemer (2007, 67–91).

direct their attention to gender-related passages in the documents of all three blind institutions—*goze, mōsō* and the *tōdō-za*. For the time being, only speculation may be offered as to why blind women did not earn their living with biwa: What seems most plausible is that exclusion of blind women musicians from biwa-playing served the economic function of yielding a greater amount of professional work for *biwa hiki* and *mōsō*.[33]

By the late twentieth century that economic imperative had long ceased to operate. In a 1991 interview, the late Kunisaki-region *mōsō*, Takagi Seigen, made the following observation: "So you see, I can't just give up hope for this biwa music. There are nuns, and *mōsōbiwa* performed by nuns would be something great, wouldn't it? They've got such good voices, after all" (Nagai 2002, 368). The comment was made in the context of a discussion about the many possible vocations and opportunities for blind people in modern-day Japan so that no blind youths wanted to become *mōsō*. Notwithstanding their exclusion in the past, then, Takagi was willing to acknowledge the potential beauty of performance of *mōsōbiwa* repertory by females and the possibility that females might carry on the tradition in the absence of males.

Biwa and Musical Narrative

The expression "musical narrative" is an awkward one, for it implies a division between storytelling and musical performance that poorly renders the experience of performers and audiences in most of the genres to which the term is applied, among which are Celtic and Continental European ballad singing, West African and South Asian epic singing, Malay and Sundanese *pantun*, and Korean *pansori*. Such musical narrative is first and foremost a performing art, which in many cases involves oral composition (as in Yamashika's biwa repertory). Musical and textual elements can be analytically extracted as distinct entities but are generated in performance as a unity, through the mechanism of what I describe in chapter 4 as text-music systems. When oral compositional technique is no longer transmitted, the narrative in performance becomes a musical rendition of a fixed literate (although not always written) entity.

33. The converse was not true. Even after blind female performers turned from the drum to *shamisen* and *koto* as their preferred instruments, *zatō* who performed *shamisen* competed with *goze* singers for custom in some regions.

There is no established explanation of how narrative performance with lute accompaniment first came to be practised in Japan. The Tang *pipa* brought to Japan as part of the court and ritual music that came to be called *gagaku* had no documented tradition of use in oral narrative. It remains subject to debate whether the earliest biwa narrative arose through innovative use of the *gagaku biwa* (or a smaller version of the instrument), development of a tradition of tales on Buddhist themes by ritualists later known as *mōsō*, or imitation of Continental Asian narrative performance with lute accompaniment, such as various precursors of Chinese *tanci*. Records of a performance genre called *tanci* date back only to the late Yuan dynasty, that is, the mid fourteenth century, long after the time of the first records of oral narrative recitation with biwa in Japan. Influences from Ming dynasty Chinese practices are unlikely but cannot be ruled out, for there is the following reference to Chinese narrative performance traditions in the *Jikaishū* of the fifteenth-century Rinzai-sect Zen priest Ikkyū (1394–1481): "In China blind players of *pipa* perform historical recitations (史) at the gates of houses" (Iwahashi 1951, 171).

Biwa hōshi who recite tales are first referred to in the mid-eleventh-century *Shin sarugaku-ki*, but in sources from the twelfth to fourteenth century they figure as the primary oral disseminators of *gunki monogatari*, including not only the *Heike monogatari* but also the *Hōgen monogatari*, *Heiji monogatari*, *Soga monogatari*, and *Taiheiki*. Each of these narratives tells a version of historical events of great importance in medieval Japan, and their texts were themselves treated as historical sources for many centuries (Hyōdō 2000; Bialock 2000).

The importance ascribed to *biwa hōshi* in the creation of medieval narrative literature (*chūsei katarimono bungei*) has led scholars to write about them from historical, literary, iconographic, folkloric and other perspectives. Music and performing arts historians also position them at the start of a lineage that leads down to the modern period, through the central stream of performed narrative genres called *katarimono*. This is a broad category of performance traditions that includes genres in which a tale is presented through an act of narrating (*katari*), which in some cases also involves dramatic enactment by one or more performers. Among *katarimono* are the *ningyō jōruri* or *bunraku* puppet theatre, much of the stylised recitation of the music of *kabuki* theatre, the semi-theatrical recitation tradition of *kōwaka-mai*, the medieval *sekkyō-bushi* narratives (for which a reconstructed nineteenth-century performance tradition exists), and the various biwa narrative traditions. What enables construction of such a historical lineage for *katarimono* is the fact that *biwa hōshi* or *zatō* were the first performers to popularise *shamisen* on a broad scale, from the early seventeenth century, at a time when many of them were moving away from the *Heike* stories and developing the earliest forms of *jōruri* narratives that would become the basis for Edo-period theatre music. The so-called *ko-jōruri* tales ("old" or "early" *jōruri*) were commonly performed with either biwa or a fan that could be used for both gesticulation and percussive effect, and in turn with *shamisen*. It is the role of blind biwa players in this, the established version of the historical transition from medieval to Edo-period narrative, which shaped the perceptions of the first scholars of music history and performing arts who wrote about Kyushu *biwa hiki* in the 1960s; hence they often characterised the regional performance tradition as "*jōruri* with biwa."

Shamisen had supplanted biwa as the standard instrument for musical narrative performance in central Japan by the late seventeenth century, and thereafter biwa-playing was confined to *Heike* (*heikebiwa* or *heikyoku*) until the Meiji era and the popularisation of *satsumabiwa* and *chikuzenbiwa*. Yet those "modern" biwa traditions came into existence in the late nineteenth century only because in western Japan, and Kyushu in particular, biwa had continued as a vehicle for musical storytelling by blind males throughout the Edo period.

The Social Status of Blind Musicians and Itinerant Performers

I have described a generalised stigma historically associated with blindness in Japanese society, in part as the result of a Buddhist interpretation of the condition as a form of karmic punishment. Yet marginalisation and discriminatory treatment of blind musicians has occurred for more complex reasons, which need to be addressed in terms of specific historical and regional practices. Throughout history, music and performance have figured prominently among professions of the blind, but those whose families lacked the resources to care for them beyond childhood did work of many kinds. There is most documentation of the blind, their professions and their treatment for the Edo period, although for bureaucratic purposes they were not treated as a distinct category of people except in the matter of responsibility for heading a household (*teishu*), which they were required to yield to their sons and brothers, and through membership of the *tōdō-za* guild, whereby blind males in particular professions were afforded privileges. The blind were registered and subject to restrictions on activity in accordance with their societal rank: Commoner townsmen (*chōnin*) and warrior-rank blind were therefore allowed to engage in the professions available to all of similar rank, within the constraints of their visual impairment, while blind members of agrarian households were expected to do what labour they could to contribute toward payment of the land taxes (Katō 1974, 31–33). Notwithstanding, among all blind people the most common professions were music, massage, acupuncture and moxa therapy. Ritual work, such as that particular to the *mōsō* and *zatō* of Kyushu, and to the *itako* female mediums of Tōhoku, was common in some regions.

Two broad categories of itinerant performers are recognised in Japanese scholarship: those whose performances have been presented in public outdoor spaces (*daidō geinin*) and those who perform in front of houses in expectation of being invited to perform inside or otherwise receiving payment from householders (*kadozuke geinin*). A great variety of performers of both kinds existed from earliest documented times until the mid twentieth century.[34] While the most affluent of blind musicians were able to make a living during the Edo period as teachers and performers based at their homes, for most—both male *zatō* and female *goze*—*kadozuke* was important for their survival. The latter has been generally regarded as a form of begging (*monomorai*) but is also widely recognised as having important ritual associations that shape its reception. In the historical practice of agrarian seasonal rites and celebrations, door-to-door performances of drama, song and dance, such as *senju manzai, ebisu mawashi, daikoku-mai* and many forms of lion dance, were carried out by professional performers attached to shrines and temples. From the medieval period, such groups of performers were accorded low status and many were associated with *sanjo* districts for the discriminated classes (*senmin*; Wakita 1978).

34. See entry for *kadozuke* in *Nihon minzoku daijiten*, 375. Documentation of the variety of arts still being practised in the late 1960s was undertaken by Ozawa Shōichi in the book and LP series *Nihon no hōrōgei* (Ozawa 1982 [1974]).

In social and cultural theory, such *kadozuke* performances for the new year, harvest and other agrarian festivals have been constructed as a practice derived from a fundamental mode of folk ritual in Japan, in which *kami* in the form of other-wordly creatures or strange individuals visit homes during community festivals to rid them of impurity, then receive gifts from individual householders. Orikuchi Shinobu's seminal ethnographic writings on ritual life developed the theory of *marebito*—mysterious, often fearful but seasonally valued visitors— which has come to be used as a pivotal concept in much socio-cultural analysis of Japanese ritual and performance, and helps to account for the willingness of householders in many regions of Japan to give food and money to itinerant performers who could appear in a steady stream during festival periods.[35] *Kadozuke* was also shaped by Buddhist cultural traditions, in particular that of giving alms (*kisha*) to itinerant figures as an act that brought merit (*hodokoshi*).

These historical circumstances for the reception of blind and *kadozuke* performers had ramifications for the lives and perceived identities of *biwa hiki* in regional Kyushu even in the latter half of the twentieth century, which I will return to in a discussion of Yamashika's experiences of discrimination in chapter 5.

Images and Depictions of *Biwa Hōshi*

Throughout their long history, *biwa hōshi* have often been portrayed in iconographic and literary sources. There exist portraits and accounts of *biwa hōshi* who were wealthy and powerful—mostly Edo-period *tōdō-za* leaders with their sumptuous lifestyle and political intrigues—but it is portrayals of low-status *biwa hōshi*, almost invariably referred to simply as *zatō*, which have most shaped the images of *biwa hōshi* that prevail today. Three key elements of those images can be summarised as follows: *biwa hōshi* are solitary and pitiable; they are mysterious, frightening and potentially dangerous; and they are ridiculous figures to be made fun of, at times with unbridled cruelty. These elements are consistently present in pictorial and narrative depictions of *biwa hōshi*, although it is rare for all three to figure in a single source, perhaps

---

35. In English, see the survey of *kadozuke-gei* in Raz (1983, 36–41) and the extensive discussion of ritual *kadozuke* and Orikuchi's theories in Law (1997, 49–88).

because the second and third elements are seemingly contradictory.³⁶

The elements of solitude and pathos are most prominent in the corpus of stories and portrayals of Semimaru, the quasi-historical beggar musician who appears as the author of poems in stories of oral tradition, plays and other writings of the tenth through eighteenth centuries, principally as a blind biwa player. As Matisoff showed in her monograph on the legendary figure, new literary portrayals of Semimaru appeared in accordance with the norms of each historical period. Accordingly, in the early eighteenth century Chikamatsu could portray him as a man about whom "many women have felt envious of his attention to others" (trans. Matisoff 1978 [2006], 232), but after going blind and being abandoned at Mount Ausaka, "holding his lute and leaning on his bamboo staff, he breaks down, collapses" (ibid., 239), he becomes again the pitiful individual portrayed in Zeami's noh play, *Semimaru*—and Chikamatsu proceeds to quote directly from Zeami's text to enforce this image.

Similar sentiments underpin some *minwa* folk tales about *biwa hōshi*. Among them are tales such as "*Bosama no yome tori*" (A *bosama* takes a wife):³⁷ A biwa-playing blind performer (called *bosama* in the Tōhoku region) wins as bride the beautiful daughter of a farmer, but tells her it is better to die than spend her life with him, then jumps into a river and drowns, having mistakenly thought that she tried to drown herself when he heard the sound of her bundle of wedding-gifts falling into the water. The woman weeps uncontrollably with pity and sadness for the fate of the *bosama*.

In folklore, *biwa hōshi*'s association with ghosts through *chinkon* ritual performance, as well as their own occult power after wrongful death, are frequently the material for mysterious and frightening tales. By far the best-known example of the former kind is *Mimi Nashi Hōichi* (Earless Hōichi), the folktale re-written in 1903 from oral sources by Lafcadio Hearn.³⁸ Hearn wrote his story in English about a young *biwa*

36. Other recurrent elements in iconographic sources include dogs that bark at the blind man and the presence of a young guide (Ishii 1996, 1997a, 1997b). See figure 1.3.

37. The term *bosama* referred most commonly to blind male *shamisen* players from the mid Edo period but biwa-playing *bosama* are also recorded. A version of this folktale is given in Yanagita (1998, vol. 2, 30–31).

38. Hearn's rendering of the tale was first published in the *Atlantic Monthly* magazine in 1903, then included in the collection entitled *Kwaidan*, published in Boston in 1904.

hōshi who suffers at the hands of the very ghosts for whose solace he performs episodes from the *Heike*, but a Japanese translation of his text appeared by at least 1926.³⁹ The tale has remained so popular that in the 1990s it was almost invariably the first association brought to mind for Japanese whom I told of my interest in blind biwa players. As one of the most accomplished and eerie renderings of a *biwa hōshi* in film, the *Mimi Nashi Hōichi* segment of Kobayashi Masaki's *Kwaidan* (1964) has strongly reinforced the association of *biwa hōshi* with fearsome ghosts that most people bear from reading or hearing the tale as Hearn told it. "Zatō Sakura" is an example of the second kind of folk tale, about the vengeful ghosts of *biwa hōshi*; in it the curse of a *biwa hōshi* beheaded after being tricked brings death and illness to many.⁴⁰

Biwa hōshi are treated with ridicule in the category of *kyōgen* plays called *zatōmono*, as well as many of the folktales about blind people collected by Yanagita. In *kyōgen*, the most common pattern is for one or more blind *zatō* to be deliberately tricked so that they become lost, walk in the wrong direction, suffer losses or engage in arguments on the basis of misunderstandings provoked by sighted people solely for their own amusement (Golay 1973). Two well-known plays of this kind are *Tsukimi zatō* (The moon-viewing *zatō*) and *Saru zatō* (A monkey and a *zatō*). In the former, a *zatō* enjoys the annual moon-viewing celebrations in the fields outside the capital (despite the fact that he cannot see the moon) when he meets another Kyoto resident with whom he can talk, sing and drink. Yet after they part, the sighted man grabs hold of the *zatō* and turns him around and around so that he loses his sense of direction. The play ends as the disoriented blind man is attacked by dogs. *Saru zatō* also starts with the enjoyment of annual celebrations, in this case by a *zatō* and his pretty wife having a blossom-viewing party. A man who entertains with monkeys sees them and tries to steal the blind man's wife; he succeeds in taking her away after substituting a monkey for her at the end of a rope that the *zatō* has tied to her after his first attempt to seduce her.

39. The *Honyaku bungaku mokuroku* gives Taisho 15 as the date for the first published translation (National Diet Library 1959, 438), but the *Koizumi yakumo jiten* mentions publication of a nine-volume set of English texts with parallel Japanese translation in 1921 (2000, 728). The contents of the volumes is not specified, but it seems likely to have included the popular tale.

40. Collected by Yanagita Kunio and presented in a 1932 essay on the role of the blind in creating folk literary arts (*minkan bungei*) (Yanagita 1998, 541–542).

A similar sense of *biwa hōshi* as bizarre, somewhat frightening figures who can nevertheless be taunted is conveyed in many medieval picture scrolls. There are scrolls in which people look out from their houses at the biwa players and appear to be laughing or jeering at them. Images of children chasing or running in fright from *biwa hōshi* who are doing *kadozuke* and of dogs barking at them, are also so common as to form a visual trope in many kinds of *emaki* (see figure 1.3).

Figure 1.3. *Biwa hōshi* depicted in the fourteenth-century scroll painting *Boki ekotoba* (detail). Collection of Nishi Honganji.

Biwa Hōshi and Mōsō: Entangled Musical, Literary and Religious Figures

The Established Accounts

Until the post-war era most music scholars paid attention to the biwa music of the blind only when writing about the *Heike* or *heikyoku* tradition (for example, Kanetsune 1913, 6, 49). Among musicologists, only Tanabe penned a few paragraphs on *mōsōbiwa* (1941, 321–322), but he wrote of it merely as a historical source for both the instruments and music of biwa genres of the modern era. In writings on Japanese music of the first three decades of the twentieth century, the fact that even after the heyday of *Heike* there were blind professionals who performed biwa music that was not *Heike* narrative is apparent in just two contexts: discussion of the origins of the *jōruri* narrative traditions (including fleeting references to the *okuni* or *oku jōruri* narrative of northern Honshu, in which *shamisen* did not displace biwa until the mid Edo period), and of *satsumabiwa*, in which local *biwa hōshi* or *mōsō* of the southern province are said to have been asked to fashion music for a new instrument by a sixteenth-century Shimazu lord (Iba 1928, 444; Iba 1934, 154; Tanabe 1941). It was only social and performing arts historians, chiefly Nakayama Tarō and Iwahashi Koyata, who wrote about the copious evidence for performances of many kinds by *biwa hōshi*, and about the long dispute between *tōdō-za* biwa players and *mōsō*. This was perhaps because music scholars of the time usually sought to give expositions of traditions that were still played, and none of them knew that even as they wrote there were hundreds of blind professionals in Kyushu and western Honshu playing biwa as part of their livelihood.

Until the late 1990s most writers of reference-book accounts of biwa, in particular musicological texts, attributed substance (directly or implicitly) to the *mōsō* sects' claims of pre-Nara-period origin and explained early accounts of performances of songs and narrative by blind biwa players (*biwa hōshi*) as music that had emerged from earlier *mōsō* ritual practices (see for example, Kikkawa 1965 and 1986, 60). This account was buttressed by explanations of the origin and development of a distinct instrument-type called the *mōsō biwa*, first proposed by

Tanabe Hisao (Tanabe 1947b, 83–84; 1964).[41] A second account by other writers, by contrast, hypothesised a trickle-down process in which biwa was first played by the elite, both purely instrumentally and to accompany vocal performance, in court and high-ecclesiastical contexts, then in time by low-status musicians who had heard the instrument at the temple compounds where they gathered, then started to recite popular sutras and eventually secular tales with a modified form of the *gagaku biwa*. For example, in the 1930s Nakayama Tarō interpreted evidence for the use of biwa in rites of esoteric Buddhism performed by high-placed priests and nobles as an important route by which the instrument reached the hands of blind men living in temple compounds (1934, 65–69).

Much of the writing about relations between secular biwa narrative performance by Kyushu *biwa hiki* and ritual performance by *mōsō* that underpinned the established explanation until the late 1990s was characterised by a belief that the documented twentieth-century repertory of Kyushu *mōsō* was a reliable guide to ancient *mōsō* practice. As a means to account for the ritual functions of early *Heike* performance, the music historian Hirano Kenji suggested that the *Heike* narrative corpus could be related to an originary form of ritual narrative in a similar way to battle tales called *kuzure* that were recited until the early twentieth century by *mōsō* in Kyushu:

> If we can think of the *kuzure* tales as having developed from the *mōsōbiwa* narratives on Buddhist themes—the *shakumon* and *wasan*..., then it can even be thought that the so-called *heikebiwa* and *Jōrurihime Monogatari* tales were generated from such narratives. (Hirano 1975, 36)

The last writer in English to deal with these questions at length was Susan Matisoff, in her 1978 study of the Semimaru legend. After surveying most of the Japanese materials available at the time, she made a strong statement in favour of the first of the two positions adopted by Japanese writers:

> No Japanese scholar has unearthed any concrete evidence concerning the origins of *biwa hōshi* that would prove a history radically different

---

41. To make this assertion Tanabe extrapolated from Kishibe Shigeo's writings on the dual lineage of four- and five-string forms of Tang-dynasty *pipa* (Kishibe 1936, 1944).

from the general picture shown by the Tokugawa *mōsō* documents. If the *biwa hōshi* are accepted as the descendents of the *mōsō*, we are dealing with one continuous tradition of low-class blind men, loosely connected with the Tendai sect, whose art as sutra chanters, storytellers and oral poets spread gradually from Kyūshū throughout Japan. (1978 [2006], 34)

Yet some thirty years later, a plausible means for dissemination of the *mōsō* tradition from Kyushu still cannot be described, and there is little evidence for affiliation of blind biwa players with any temples in central Japan other than the late-thirteenth-century accounts of musicians in records of the Ichijōin of the Kōfukuji temple complex. Even in the case of the Ichijōin *zatō* (who are not called *mōsō* in historical sources), documents describe individuals' recitations of the Jijin-kyō sutra and various secular entertainments, not formal ritual activity (Iwahashi 1951, 193–194).

The performing arts historian Iwahashi Koyata stood outside these two streams of explanation, for he did not concern himself with the question of a route by which biwa came to the hands of blind men. He adopted an approach to the historical relations of *biwa hōshi* and *mōsō* that was not reflected in writings on music for nearly fifty years after his *Nihon geinōshi: chūsei kabu no kenkyū* (1951):

Performers of *heikebiwa* became strictly *tōdō-za* musicians, and chanters of the Jijinkyō became strictly *mōsō*, so the blind men who performed songs and tales with biwa in Satsuma and Chikuzen were the ones who really preserved the original form of *biwa hōshi*. . . . It can be concluded that originally there had been no clear distinction between *mōsō* and *tōdō-za* biwa players. It follows that the *mōsō* themselves were originally *biwa hōshi* entertainers. (1951, 191–192)

Notwithstanding an implied strict separation of the two groups' repertories that does not accord with documented recitation of the Jijinkyō by some *tōdō-za* musicians, and of *kuzure* tales by many *mōsō*, Iwahashi's statement about pre-modern-era blind biwa players in Kyushu preserving the "original form of *biwa hōshi*" is itself prescient of later writers' approaches to musicians such as Yamashika Yoshiyuki. Iwahashi's inversion of the standard chronology for *mōsō* and *biwa hōshi* was not proposed again in music history scholarship until the work of Komoda Haruko, more than four decades later.

A New Approach: *Mōsō* as *Biwa Hōshi* Who Gained Buddhist Patronage

While a few writers—notably Araki Hiroyuki—have continued to argue for the plausibility of the *mōsō* sects' legends of transmission of the Jijin-kyō rites directly from Korea or China to eastern Kyushu, research since the early 1990s has yielded a new understanding of the relations between *biwa hōshi* and *mōsō* that has displaced the long-accepted accounts outlined above. Firstly, there has been a reassessment of the significance of the Jijin rites as a marker of blind biwa players' identity. The earliest verifiable account of performance of the Jijin-kyō sutra was in fact by an early-fifteenth-century biwa player described as a performer of the *Heike* (Hirose 1997, 146).[42] Edo-period *zatō* below the *tōdō-za* rank of *shūbun* were given permission to recite the Jijin-kyō, but could not rise above that rank without forgoing performance of the sutra. Nagai Akiko has shown that, because of such activity, some of those low-rank *zatō* were even included, along with *mōsō*, in lists of the blind who came under the protection of the Kyoto temple, the Shōren-in, from the late eighteenth century (2002, 31–32). Several groups of biwa players who had been conventionally described as Yamato and Kumano "*mōsō*" in fact seem to have been performers of historical and legendary narratives—*biwa hōshi*—who nonetheless performed Jijin rites and loosely served major religious complexes such as the Ichijōin of Kōfukuji and shrines in the Yoshino and Kumano regions of the mountainous Kii peninsula (Nakayama 1936, 30–31; Hirose 1997, 160–175).

During the same period, the folklorist Yasuda Muneo and the musicologist Komoda Haruko have constructed new accounts of the emergence of *mōsō* as social institutions and the development of the "*mōsō biwa*" instrument, respectively. According to their accounts, groups of biwa players identified as *mōsō* became established with varying degrees of affiliation with Buddhist institutions only in the

---

42. The account, in the *Kanmon Gyoki*, is an entry for the 5th day of the 8th month 1423.

late seventeenth and eighteenth centuries, after the *tōdō-za* guild won the Shogunate's support in 1674 (Empō 2) for a ban on professional performance of string instruments by non-guild members, except for the use of biwa in Jijin rites, and for mandatory changes to the structure of instruments played for the latter purpose (Komoda 2003a, 314–329; Yasuda 2004a, 4–6). The conventional understanding of historical relations between *biwa hōshi* and *mōsō* is thereby turned on its head in a way that had been anticipated by Iwahashi in the 1950s.

Taken together, Komoda's writings on biwa history and Yasuda's on Higo-region biwa players accord continuity with earlier *biwa hōshi* practices to the many regional blind traditions typified by dual roles of entertainer and ritualist; to the twentieth-century practices of *biwa hiki* of the former Higo region; and even to the eighteenth-century repertory of biwa narrative in Satsuma Province which became the "classic" stratum of modern *satsumabiwa*. The performances of *biwa hōshi* included *Heike* and *jōruri* tales and other corpuses of narrative, on the one hand, and rites adapted to local custom such as recitation of the Jijin-kyō, on the other. In this way, all of the biwa traditions of Kyushu (regardless of the status of *satsumabiwa* and *chikuzenbiwa* as music practised nationwide in the modern era) can be understood as distinct elements within the legacy of the *biwa hōshi*.

Ancient and Medieval Period *Biwa Hōshi*

Among the earliest references to *biwa hōshi* are those in a poem by Taira Kanemori, of the 980s (Matisoff 1978 [2006], 26), and in Fujiwara no Akihira's *Shin sarugaku-ki*, of between 1058 and 1065. The latter is the earliest account of the recitation of tales by a *biwa hōshi*, and depicts a kind of performance quite unlike that of most early depictions—a *biwa hōshi* who appears as a presenter of *monogatari*, or miscellaneous historical and fictitious narratives, as one of a stream of performers whom Akihira anticipates he and his family will watch during an evening's entertainment.

A point that has hardly been raised in considerations of the origins of biwa's use to accompany songs and musical storytelling by *hōshi* is evidence for seemingly boisterous performance of biwa (although apparently not yet musical narrative) as early as the eighth century, in depictions of two kinds of biwa as instruments of the *sangaku* performances illustrated on a hunting bow in the Shōsōin collection (these illustrations are called *dankyū shitsuga*). It is difficult to gain an idea of the extent of public (as opposed to courtly) representation in the audiences for *sangaku*, but the Chinese performance tradition represented may have inspired vernacular imitation by other entertainers. If so, the predecessors of *biwa hōshi* who appear singing songs and tales with biwa in tenth- and eleventh-century sources could well have included just such popular performers, in addition to priests from Kyushu or performers associated with court society. Such a lineage seems especially apt for the lively sort of *biwa hōshi* described in the introduction to *Shin sarugaku-ki*.

In the centuries prior to the pre-eminence of the *Heike* narratives of the Gempei war of the 1180s, just what did *biwa hōshi* perform, and what may have been the basis for their role in late Heian society? A number of Japanese scholars from the fields of literature and folklore have considered these questions, principally for the light that they shed upon the significance of *biwa hōshi*'s role in the creation and dissemination of the *Heike monogatari*. To summarise their conclusions, during the eleventh and twelfth centuries *biwa hōshi* probably had the following characteristics and societal functions:

1. Like oral storytellers in many cultures, *biwa hōshi* conveyed knowledge of major events to people unable to read. Recited accounts of battles and political disputes such as those that comprise the *Hōgen monogatari* and the *Heiji monogatari* were probably performed in remote regions well after the events took place, so that they did not constitute "news" so much as chronicles that helped listeners make sense of those events. The titles and contents of specific tales recited by *biwa hōshi* are not recorded in any pre-twelfth-century source. Knowledge of blind biwa players' involvement in production of the episodes that make up the *Hōgen monogatari* and the *Heiji monogatari* is based upon later accounts such as the *Futsū shōdōshū* of 1297 (NKBD 1998, 1135).[43]

43. Reference to the performance of a fictitious narrative by a blind biwa player, said to have occurred about fifty years after the performances recorded in the *Shin sarugaku-ki*, is found in the *engi* documents of Kyūnōji temple, which claim that in the Eikyū era (1113–1118) a priest-scholar authored a fictional battle tale called the

2. From the late Heian period many kinds of low status performer-beggars called *hōshi* were loosely associated with temples and shrines, including *biwa hōshi, sarugaku hōshi, dengaku hōshi, and etoki hōshi* (Nakayama 1934, 78–79). Perhaps in return for permission to live in the shrine precincts or vicinity, they developed, recited and performed versions of *engi* narratives, that is, tales of gods and Buddhas involved in the origins and establishment of major temples and shrines. In this way they helped to confirm and spread knowledge of the power of those institutions, although they participated little or not at all in formal institutional rites.
3. Performance of battle tales as a form of *chinkon* rite was probably an important function of early *biwa hōshi*. This entailed a combination of ritual function and secular narrative repertory that points to the very heart of the problem of drawing a distinction between *biwa hōshi* and *mōsō* prior to the Edo period: If *biwa hōshi* of the late Heian period often functioned as ritualists when performing accounts of battle and had various kinds of association with temples or shrines, then consistent grounds for their distinction from *mōsō* ritual professionals are hard to maintain.
4. It seems the provision of sheer entertainment, through singing *imayō* and other popular song forms, was integral to the ways early *biwa hōshi* earned a living (Iwahashi 1951, 179). Even after the *Heike* narratives became their signature repertory in the fourteenth century, the majority of *biwa hōshi* probably continued to perform a range of genres, including humorous stories and emphatically "low-brow" entertainment as part of their stock-in-trade, as the research of Ishii Masami has shown

---

"Mumyō hosshō gassen monogatari" and taught it to a blind singer (Iwahashi 1926, 157–176). The narrative itself has not been transmitted, either among biwa players or as a historical battle tale (*gunki monogatari*), and although the extant text for it is of late medieval origin, this claim reflects the fact that the singing of battle tales by blind males was commonplace long before the development of the *Heike* tale corpus by *biwa hōshi*. See further Nakayama (1934, 84–89). Susan Matisoff has pointed out that the explanation of the tale's origin—a priest-scholar devises the tale then teaches it to a *biwa hōshi*—follows the same pattern as Yoshida Kenko's explanation of the origin of the *Heike* (personal communication). This may reflect the fact that loose association between blind biwa players and some temples already existed as well as the *biwa hōshi's* need to attribute tales to a respectable source.

(1986, 1988). High-ranking members of the *tōdō-za* may have been able to sustain themselves by performing nothing but the *Heike* for centuries, but even they eventually had to adopt *koto* and *shamisen* as the principal instruments of Edo-period urban music culture. In fact it was low-status *biwa hōshi* who were able to maintain popular audiences for their recitational art, through their participation during the sixteenth century in development of the new narrative repertory of *jōruri*, and their eventual adoption of *shamisen* rather than biwa as its accompaniment instrument.[44]

Heike Recitation and the *Biwa Hōshi* Guild, the *Tōdō-za*

A century after the *Shin sarugaku-ki* account, extraordinary political events and war provided *biwa hōshi* with the body of stories that would sustain them, and enable in time the establishment of a professional guild that lasted until the start of the modern era. The key role of *biwa hōshi* in the making of the textual repository of those stories, the *Heike monogatari* (*The Tale of the Heike*), has been acknowledged since the mid fourteenth century when Yoshida Kenkō wrote as follows in *Tsurezuregusa* (Essays in Idleness):

> Archbishop Jien [an Enryakuji Abbot] made a point of summoning and looking after anyone, even a servant, who could boast of an accomplishment; thus, he granted this Shinano Novice an allowance. Yukinaga composed the *Tale of the Heike* and taught it to a blind man, Shōbutsu, so that the man might narrate it.
> ... When it came to warriors and the martial arts, Shōbutsu, who was an easterner, put questions to warriors and had Yukinaga write what he learned. People say that our present-day *biwa hōshi* imitate Shōbutsu's natural voice. (*Tsurezuregusa*, sec. 226, cited in McCullough 1988, 7)

The authorial model of this account, wherein an original text was created by one man, a former courtier, through consultation with a

---

44. It is worth emphasising that the same pressing need to satisfy diverse audiences in many contexts led Yamashika Yoshiyuki and other young *biwa hiki* of his generation to adapt stories and techniques from *naniwa-bushi*, the most popular narrative art of the day, as well as to maintain a stock of humorous and erotic stories, and even gag routines (*kyokubiki*) such as the *hachinin-gei* (see chapter 2).

biwa hōshi and others, prevailed until the modern era, when it became the basis for a grand critical enterprise of establishing just which among the extant texts for the *Tale of the Heike* was closest to the original text. While a few scholars still argue for the validity of that endeavour, it is now generally accepted that the work itself was not a stable entity for which an authoritative text existed until the production of the Kakuichi text in 1371, nearly two centuries after the events described by the narrative. The oral performance activity of *biwa hōshi* during those two centuries is seen as being significant for the development and definition of the tale corpus, and at least equal in importance to literary compositional activity by chroniclers, diarists and poets whose texts are reflected in the Kakuichi text.[45]

With the emergence of widely acclaimed and politically astute *biwa hōshi* such as Kakuichi (?-1371),[46] a learned blind man who became the most innovative and influential *biwa* performer of his time and gained access to many powerful figures, came the opportunity to ensure the social status of accomplished *Heike* performers and the continuation of their profession through a professional guild (*za*). The guild called the *tōdō-za* may have existed as a loose organisation of diverse schools of performance (the so-called six schools *Tōdō roppa*) prior to Kakuichi,[47] but it was most likely he who brought greater unity to the *za* and instituted a hierarchy which at first comprised four ranks: *kengyō, bettō, kōtō* and *zatō*.[48] As *Heike* flourished during the fourteenth and fifteenth centuries, the guild organisation became far more complex through

45. Even with the production of the Kakuichi text, other texts continued to be important for particular groups of performers, among which the Yasaka-ryū was most important. While the Kakuichi text has been the most widely read and has constituted the basis for most scholarship since the mid Edo period, moreover, it may not have constituted a model for professional performers until even more recently. On the significance of the Kakuichi and Yasaka texts for the history of the *Heike* as a performed and read body of narrative, see various articles in Hyōdō (2000) and, in English, Butler (1966) and Bialock (2000).
46. Although he is often referred to as Akashi no Kakuichi, his relations with the region of Akashi (near modern-day Kobe) remain subject to debate.
47. Hirano Kenji's entry on "Kakuichi kengyō" in NODJ 1989, 616.
48. The first two terms were already in use to denote high ranks within the Buddhist clergy, while *kōtō* was one of many categories of rank-and-file clergy (*Bukkyō daijiten*; Kyoto: Hōsōkan, 1987, 886–887). *Zatō* was the common-use term for *biwa hōshi*, and by the mid Edo period denoted blind performers in general, in particular those of low status. It is unclear whether the word predates its use as a rank term by the *tōdō-za*.

subdivision of each of these four ranks; by the sixteenth century (if not earlier), a total of 72 ranks and sub-ranks existed. This guild continued until its abolition in 1871 and became in that time a major societal institution which exercised considerable control over the professions of the blind throughout Japan, including most professional performers of biwa, *koto, shamisen* and *kokyū* throughout much of the Edo period. The disparity in power and wealth between those in the upper ranks and the majority of guild members became extreme. At the same time, the guild succeeded on many occasions in protecting the livelihood of its members from competition; the infamous legislative victory over the *mōsō* in 1674 (see below) is a case in point, along with regional edicts against non-blind performers of certain repertories.[49]

The skills of *biwa hōshi* stood in ambiguous relation to practices of narrative performance for religious proselytisation, perhaps until the Edo-period transformation of *Heike* into the antiquarian musical pursuit of *heikyoku* on the one hand and ceremonial performance for the Shogunate on the other. Throughout the medieval period, the performances of priests and a range of proselytising entertainers, male and female alike, were important media for the dissemination of new forms of Buddhist doctrine and practice. Street performers depicted in iconographic sources include diverse storytellers, singers and reciters, including *etoki hōshi, bikuni, sekkyō-shi,* and *biwa hōshi*. As already noted, early *biwa hōshi* seem to have been loosely associated with certain temples and shrines, and one of their repertories was *engi* narratives, that is, tales of gods and Buddhas involved in the origins and establishment of major temples and shrine complexes. It is clear that many segments of the *Heike* in its multiple versions comprise or include *engi* stories, renderings of old Buddhist tales and "parables," as well as sermons on morality and theology. In terms of musical style, aspects of the *kōshiki* genre of Buddhist ritual chant, and performative, often musical, sermonising called *shōdō,* are acknowledged as among the principal musical sources for *Heike* performance practice (Nelson 2001).

In the late sixteenth century, when Portuguese Jesuit priests were active proselytising to daimyō and commoners alike in Kyushu, a *biwa hōshi* from the Hizen region who was given the Christian name

---

49. In English, see Groemer (1999, 16).

Lorenzo (*Rorenso* in Japanese records) became the most renowned of their Japanese converts (Iseki 1982, 157–166).[50] Portuguese records show that he and some other *biwa hōshi* who became Christians put their great skills in recitational sermonising to use for the Jesuit cause.[51]

Biwa Hōshi and *Zatō* After the Waning of *Heike* Recitation's Popularity

The *Tale of the Heike*, as the fountainhead of the overarching literary and musical genre of *katarimono* and the primary performative account of events of epochal significance in Japanese history, has been a seemingly limitless resource for repertory in narrative and dramatic performance traditions, including *kōwaka-mai*, noh theatre, puppet drama and kabuki. Yet the performance of *Heike* episodes with biwa was itself an art whose popularity inevitably waned, although it lasted at least three centuries. Thereafter, while biwa players in the upper ranks of the professional guild enjoyed a secure, even a luxurious livelihood as performers and teachers of what came to be called *heikyoku* ("Heike music") into and throughout the Edo period (Komoda 1999), many low-status *biwa hōshi* diversified their activities by developing a new body of narrative that came to be called *jōruri*, and by adopting the new, more portable and melodically versatile lute, *shamisen*, as well as its bowed version, *kokyū*. In this way, blind musicians from the late sixteenth century on comprised not only professional biwa players—ranging from the *kengyō* of Kyoto, Edo, and some regional towns, to itinerant *biwa hōshi* or *zatō* —but also performers of many sorts of songs and narratives on *shamisen*, *kokyū*, and the portable zither, *tategoto*. These were collectively referred to as *zatō* arts (*zatō-gei*).

By the late seventeenth century *Heike* had become a tradition associated for the most part with the upper strata of Japanese society and practised under direct patronage of the Shogunate and associated high-ranking *samurai*. Dissemination of printed editions meant that even among this elite audience, moreover, knowledge of the narrative came to be primarily gained from reading, not from listening to and

---

50. See further Yūki (2005).
51. While no documentation of their Christian-based narrative texts exists, there are several references to the efficacy of renditions of tales from the Scriptures by *biwa hōshi* (Ruiz-de-Medina 2001, 178–180).

viewing performances. At the same time numerous text-scores (*fuhon*), with comprehensive performance notations, were produced for use in teaching sighted amateurs, most of them *samurai* and priests. The text of the most widely disseminated, the *Heike mabushi*, closely follows the wording of the Kakuichi text, although its episodes are grouped differently. By the end of the Edo period, *Heike mabushi* had become the authoritative text-score of almost all *heikyoku* practitioners.

By that time the wealth of the *tōdō-za*'s leaders, and their access to the ear of the Shogun, had become legendary. With the start of the new constitutional government in the Meiji period, efforts to break the old Shogunal bureaucratic networks led to forcible dissolution of the *tōdō-za* (along with the *mōsō* sects, as a second Edo-period institution for blind professionals) in 1871. This action led to an immediate reduction in numbers of active *heikyoku* musicians in both the cities and the regional centres as many professionals put aside biwa in favour of *koto* and *shamisen* or else adopted occupations other than music. By the 1960s, blind professional performers were reduced to just three men—all more active as *koto, shamisen* and *kokyū* players than as *heikyoku* performers— who maintained just eight episodes (or items) of the *Heike mabushi* text-score's hundred and ninety-nine. At the end of the century there was only one active blind professional, Imai Tsutomu (b. 1958). A number of non-blind performers, including the first female professional performers of *heikyoku*, have sought to continue the Tsugaru tradition of performing all episodes in the *Heike mabushi* as a concert musical art.

Just as the *heikyoku* tradition steadily diminished throughout the twentieth century, so too did the numbers of blind *zatō* performers of songs and narrative with *shamisen, tategoto* and other instruments in regional areas.[52] Together with the *biwa hiki* of Kyushu, the most resilient of *zatō* arts were the *shamisen*-accompanied *oku-jōruri* and certain song and narrative traditions among professionals called *bosama* in the northern Tōhoku region.[53] Performers of both traditions lived until the last two decades of the century.

52. The same can be said of *goze*, whose numbers in the Hokuriku region were comparable to those of *higobiwa* players during the 1960s, but likewise diminished to the point that no blind tradition-bearer remained active at the close of the century. "The last *goze*" of Niigata, Kobayashi Haru, died on April 25, 2005, at age 105.
53. See Groemer (1999, 35–42) for an account of the importance of blind *bosama* for the development of *shamisen* music in Tōhoku, in particular what came to be called *Tsugaru-jamisen*.

Mōso and *Mōsōbiwa* Traditions

In the modern era *mōsō* have firmly distinguished themselves from *zatō* by forming organisations (*hōryū*) under the aegis of the Tendai sect and engaging in strictly liturgical activity and performance. Their legal status since the early twentieth century has been that of Buddhist priests, and their social identity that of ritual specialists. This distinction had been foreshadowed during the two centuries between the 1674 legislation that granted a monopoly on entertainment with biwa to *tōdō-za* guild members and the temporary prohibition of all *mōsō* groups from 1871. Nevertheless during that long period of continued vigilance and efforts by *mōsō* groups to maintain autonomy from *tōdō-za*-controlled *biwa hōshi*, the majority of *mōsō*—who were especially numerous in Kyushu and south-western Honshū—performed rituals, didactic Buddhist narratives, and other songs and tales for sheer entertainment. Conversely, many *tōdō-za* members in Kyushu, including *zatō* in the Amakusa islands and in Higo Province, performed songs and tales as well as rites with biwa; it is only the organisations and institutional practices of the groups of *zatō* and blind priests, and their respective relations with the national entities of the *tōdō-za* and various religious institutions, that were distinct, while the performance activities of all but high-ranking *tōdō-za biwa hōshi* and *mōsō* were fundamentally similar (Yasuda 2001; Nagai 2002, 39). Going further back, prior to the late-seventeenth-century legislative partition by the Shogunate, moreover, it seems there were no consistently applicable grounds for distinction between biwa players who were professional performers of "secular" narrative and those who were ritualists.

There are nonetheless important historical precursors of the concept and practice of *mōsō*. Historically the word appears in early Japanese sources to refer only to priests who are blind—for example, the Nara-period founder of the Tōshōdaiji temple, Chien-chen or Ganjin, a Chinese priest who was blind when he arrived in Japan in 754. On the whole, the term *mōsō* is rare in surviving Edo-period documents, as it seems to have been used in preference to *zatō* or *biwa hōshi* primarily for the purpose of drawing distinction between *tōdō-za* guild and non-guild member performers of biwa and other string instruments.[54] The

---

54. As Nakayama Tarō observed in the 1930s, however, documents created and preserved by the victorious side are generally far more numerous than those of the

use of "*mōsō*" to designate particular groups affiliated with temples in the Tōhoku, Kii peninsula, Nara, western Honshū and various Kyushu regions, whose members were blind and played biwa, appears to date only from the mid-to-late seventeenth century, when the *tōdō-za* became most persistent in its efforts to wield exclusive jurisdiction over secular performance by the blind throughout Japan. "*Mōsō*" became entrenched as an important categorical term and concept in Japanese music and religious history largely because of its use in *tōdō-za* documents and because of the distinct identity since 1907 of the two Kyushu *hōryū* organisations, with their numerous documents of origin and lineage (almost all of them of Edo-period provenance).

Among groups that modern scholars have called *mōsō*, because of their affiliation with religious institutions, early references include a 1420 document of the Mount Kōra shrine in the Chikugo region of northern Kyushu. At a time when performance of *Heike* narrative was very popular in the capital region and *biwa hōshi* who made a living from *Heike* repertory alone were common, biwa players in the distant Chikugo Province established affiliation with a powerful regional shrine and thereby achieved support from a major institution in times of need (Nagai 2002, 67). In both these sources and early-Edo-period documents, the blind performers are identified as forming *za*, that is, guilds or troupes, with rank titles similar to those of the earliest form of the *tōdō-za*. In central Japan, such *za* in locales from Nara to Ise existed under the authority of the Ichijō-in temple, with which ritualists and entertainers of several kinds were associated; these were the blind musician-ritualists who came to be identified in twentieth-century scholarship as the "Yamato *mōsō*."[55] Other *za* that held a fair amount of autonomy from the Yamato *mōsō* umbrella organisation were those based in localities in the Kumano and Yoshino regions of the Kii peninsula (Hirose 1997, 155–180).[56] The blind performers

---

defeated side in a historical dispute, so almost all primary sources that predate the *mōsō*'s patronage by major Tendai institutions are in fact documents created by the *tōdō-za*.

55. Katō notes that a group he calls a "*Jijin mōsō no za*'" were already in dispute with the "*Heike-za*" (that is, the *tōdō-za*) in 1394, only a few decades after the formation of the latter as a guild of *biwa hōshi* in the capital region (1974, 257).

56. Hirose's own choice of "*mōsō*" is both deliberate and idiosyncratic: he prefers it as a term for *all* blind biwa players, whom he regards as most significant, in socio-historical terms, as ritualists, not bearers of oral narrative traditions (1997, 153).

are referred to only as *mōmoku zatō* or *Jijin(kyō) zatō* in seventeenth-century documents of the Ichijō-in which show that they engaged in several genres of entertainment, including *matsubayashi* and *Heike* recitation, in addition to rites for Jijin (Iwahashi 1951; Nishioka 1989). A document of 1641, moreover, claims that some of these musicians performed *Heike* narratives, while others played *shamisen* rather than biwa (Katō 1974, 89–90). Accordingly, it is only specification of the Jijinkyō as their characteristic ritual activity that distinguished the activities of these biwa players from *tōdō-za* musicians in the eyes of the document's authors.

If *mōsō* as a social institution only came into being from the late seventeenth century, what can be said of *mōsōbiwa* as a musical tradition? There is no longer any doubt that recitation of the Jijinkyō with biwa accompaniment has not been restricted to blind males certified as Buddhist priests, notwithstanding its centrality in the identity of *mōsō* since the 1670s. As I will describe in chapter 2, many of the rites and sacred repertory items performed by Gensei Hōryū and Jōrakuin Hōryū sect *mōsō* have also been performed by *zatō* or *biwa hiki*. As performance repertory, what are unique to the modernday *mōsō* sects are the music of *kaidan hōyō*, annual and occasional group ceremonies conducted within sect temples, and the narratives called *shakumon* and *wasan*—legends and tales on Buddhist themes—that were performed by Kunisaki- and Hyūga-region *mōsō*, and continue to be performed in 2007 by the Nobeoka priest, Nagata Hōjun.

The lack, until the early twentieth century, of centralised administration and contact between regionally defined *mōsō* groups has meant that ritual and musical practice among *mōsō* has been variable on both broad and localised geographical scales. Not only is it clear that blind priests in geographically disparate regions around Kyushu, such as the Kunisaki peninsula, the Amakusa islands and Miyazaki Prefecture, performed sutras and played biwa in quite different ways, but *mōsō* working in relatively close proximity also performed melodically-unrelated versions of sutras and ritual narratives whose titles and texts are similar.[57] There is little evidence

---

57. This observation can only be based upon evidence in recordings made since the 1960s, such as those compiled by Matsuoka Minoru for the Kunisaki peninsula and held in the Usa Minzoku Rekishi Shiryokan Museum, Oita Prefecture. For one region, however, this tendency is offset by claims that an *ippon-biki* (either "one-

for mechanisms, such as authoritative versions of ritual texts, records of ritual procedures or periods of residence of high-ranking *mōsō* from larger temples at remote ones, whereby uniformity of practice could have been imposed through combinations of textual and oral means. Moreover, as blind people, travel between such disparate regions would have been difficult and infrequent for *mōsō*, so opportunities for direct transmission of common repertory would have been rare. For aural evidence of this circumstance in recent practice, one has only to listen to various recordings of performances of identically titled ritual pieces by *mōsō* from Fukuoka (the former Chikuzen region), Oita (Kunisaki), Miyazaki (Hyūga) and Kagoshima (Satsuma), made during the 1960s to 1980s;[58] vocal delivery and melodic styles, biwa accompaniment, and, to a lesser extent, text are all different, at times strikingly so.

Mōsō Groups' Dispute with the *Tōdō-za* and Its Consequences

Shogunal edicts of 1674 stripped the Yamato *mōsō* and other regional non-*tōdō-za* musicians of ranks, titles and *kesa* priests' robes. Unlike in Kyushu, where *mōsō* sought and eventually found institutional protection from severe curtailment of their professional activities by the edicts, in Yamato such musicians were absorbed into the *tōdō-za* or forced to give up biwa as a profession.[59] What was the nature and background to this bitter dispute?

In an era of centralised bureaucratic control such as that established by the Tokugawa Shogunate, it became inevitable that the *tōdō-za* would encroach upon and force *mōsō* to achieve political legitimacy through the patronage of major religious institutions in the urban centres of power. Why was it important, from the mid seventeenth century, for the *Heike* performers' guild to strike out against *mōsō* who engaged in performing songs and narratives in addition to their ritual chants? The answer seems straightforward: they were facing a decline of audience and employment as biwa professionals and therefore had to protect themselves more stringently against competition—

---

string" or "one-finger") style of biwa playing was transmitted from *mōsō* in Yamaguchi Prefecture (Matsuoka 1987, 2).

58. See recordings listed in the Audiography and Videography.

59. Katō, however, presents some evidence that suggests the continued existence of *Jijin mōsō* affiliated with the Kōfukuji temple complex (1974, 90).

in particular perceived competition from biwa players who were unaffiliated with their guild. If one considers broad developments in the history of Japanese music, the seventeenth century is a time when the newly introduced *shamisen* rapidly achieved popularity in urban centres, largely through the performance of a new genre of narrative music that came to be called *jōruri* (Tokita 1999, 32–35). While *Heike* remained strong as a performing art supported by the Shogunate and some of the ruling warrior class, the populace's taste turned rapidly to the new *jōruri* tales recited by biwa-players turned *shamisen*-players. When combined with puppetry in a new medium this led to one of the most important developments in Japanese musical theatre, *ningyō jōruri* (later also called *bunraku*). By the mid seventeenth century many blind musicians who would formerly have been biwa players and reciters of *Heike* had taken up the new instrument or else developed biwa narrative repertory in the new style. The popularity of blind *zatō* who presented "*jōruri*" in northern Kyushu is apparent, for example, from the many such performances noted in the *Katō masafusa nikki*, a diary of daily life from 1675 to 1689 in Minagi village, in what is now Fukuoka Prefecture (Nagai 1997, 90–94).

Under such conditions, the continuing activities in western Japan of non-*tōdō-za* member biwa players as both entertainers and ritualists were intolerable to the *tōdō-za* leadership. For blind performers in all regions of Kyushu and western Honshu other than Satsuma,[60] the year Empō 2 (1674) is of critical significance, for in that year the Kyoto-based guild succeeded in a campaign that it had begun in the 1640s to have the rights and privileges of all non-*tōdō* biwa performers severely curtailed by an edict of the Tokugawa Shogunate. The "*Heike (no) zatō*," as the *tōdō-za* musicians were usually referred to in Kyushu, were thereafter granted exclusive rights to perform secular narratives with the *biwa*. The only use of the instrument permitted to blind persons not affiliated with the *tōdō-za* was as accompaniment of recitation of the *Jijin-kyō* and some other *harai* or exorcism rites.[61]

60. In the Satsuma region, the participation of both *mōsō* and sighted samurai-class males in biwa performance had enabled the continuation of a centuries-old local tradition until the 1870s, when performances in Tokyo stimulated the founding of a new style that soon found nation-wide appeal, and in turn inspired the creation of *chikuzenbiwa*.
61. See Yasuda (1991, 8–9). For extracts from documents related to the Shogunate's edicts of Empō 2, see Nakayama Tarō (1934, 360–365).

A particular example of the manifestation of this edict in a Kyushu domain can be found in the *Furejō-hikae*, a collection of documents pertaining to laws and edicts of the Higo domain during the Edo period. There are several entries in the *Furejō-hikae* that illustrate the attempt to strictly control the activities of the *mōsō*, referred to as "*jijinkyō mōmoku*" or "*bussetsu zatō*," and to grant privileges to the "*Heike zatō*." These include directives to take from *mōsō* any certificates or licences they may hold, to ensure that they do not call themselves *kengyō*,[62] wear coloured cassocks or other robes which might enable them to pass for *tōdō-za* musicians, and further to impose imprisonment on any persons who carried out "*jōruri, tsukushigoto, shamisen, kōkyū* and other such '*zatō*' performances" (entry for twelfth month of the year, Empō 2).

The edict also stipulated that physical changes be made to the biwa to distinguish it from the instrument played by *Heike zatō*: namely, that the frets should be fixed firmly to the neck, unlike the moveable frets of the *heike biwa*, and that the strings should be of hemp (*asa*).[63] Komoda has interpreted the objective of these stipulations as an attempt to ensure that non-*tōdō-za* biwa players would no longer be able to play currently popular songs and narratives of *shamisen* music, which *tōdō-za*-member musicians were appropriating as their own (Komoda 2003b, 2004). She argues, moreover, that the response of *mōsō* was to change both biwa and its performance techniques in yet other ways— heightening the frets and reducing the body size, most importantly. In so doing they gave birth to the instrument-type that has been known as the "*mōsō biwa*" since Tanabe Hisao first used the term in the 1940s. Tanabe's explanation for the fact that performance technique in the Kyushu biwa traditions involves depressing the strings between high frets (unlike the *gagaku biwa* and *heike biwa* with their low frets) had involved an elaborate theory of this instrument-type's transmission and evolution from the Indian *vina*, by a different route to the Persian-derived Tang lute that became the *gagaku biwa* and in turn the *heike biwa* (Tanabe 1947b, 1964). By contrast, Komoda's explanation, which has now displaced Tanabe's, presents the various forms of *mōsō biwa*—

---

62. *Kengyō* denoted the highest of the four principal ranks within the *tōdō-za* guild.

63. "Mōmoku no biwa wa asa no ito koma wo uchitsuke ni tsukamatsuri sōrō koto" (Atsumi et al. 1984, 31)

including so-called *higo biwa* (see chapter 2)—as developments from the form of *heike biwa* played by Muromachi-period *biwa hōshi*, under the circumstances I have described.

The Shogunal edicts were enforced inconsistently in most of the regions where they were issued, and numerous others had to be issued in subsequent years as the *tōdō-za* complained about the extent of violations. Yet the Shogunate's unequivocal support for the *tōdō-za* presented a crisis for all non-*tōdō* blind performers, and over the course of a century following the 1674 edicts, various of the groups of *mōsō* in Kyushu responded through a series of appeals for protection to major religious institutions in the land. Multiple and in some cases older bases of affiliation were maintained by many of these disparate *za* groups (Nagai 2002, 331–333). For example, in Chikuzen and Chikugo provinces, distinct groups attached to the Dazai-fu Tenmangu, the Mount Kōra Taisha shrine complexes, and various religious complexes in the coastal Yanagawa domain, received patronage from another powerful Tendai-sect institution, the Kan'eiji complex, which was responsible for burial rites of the Tokugawa Shoguns, in the Ueno district of Edo (ibid., 84).[64] In Satsuma, too, the Nansen-in temple that was the regional Tendai headquarters was a branch temple of the Kan'eiji, and by the 1780s Satsuma *mōsō* were able to claim affiliation with both the Kan'eiji and the Tōshōgu, a clan shrine established for worship of the first Tokugawa Shogun, Ieyasu (Murata 1994, 41–47).

Oppression of the *mōsō* by Shogunal edict continued for over a century until, in Temmei 3 (1783), all *mōsō* unaffiliated with other institutions of patronage were afforded protection by the powerful Shōren-in of the Tendai complex on Mount Hiei in Kyoto. In all cases, however, this patronage came to an end in 1871 when the Meiji government outlawed existing bodies of association among blind professionals. Only the establishment in 1907 of the two *hōryū* sects of Kyushu *mōsō* consolidated affiliation within the contemporary framework of Tendai Buddhism.

---

64. Nagai describes various appeals made by Chikuzen- and Chikugo-region *mōsō* to large Buddhist institutions, not all of which were part of the Tendai sect (2002, 77–89). Had appeals for Shingon or Zen sect patronage succeeded, the official histories of the *mōsō* groups would doubtless not have highlighted the importance of putative performances of the Jijin sutra at the founding of the Enryakuji.

* * *

The circumstances, strands of evidence and interpretations described above support the following summary observations about the historical nature of *biwa hōshi*:

1. There were biwa hōshi active in central and south-western Japan from at least the tenth century, and their distinction from groups called mōsō based in the latter region is of much later provenance—at earliest the late seventeenth century.

2. Performance of narrative in secular contexts as entertainment was the principal activity of blind biwa players in most of Japan, although the Jijin-kyō sutra was a ritual piece strongly associated with them.

3. Performance of a larger repertory of ritual pieces and formal participation in ceremonial life at temples or shrine complexes appears to have been an exceptional status.

4. The political legitimacy afforded to the tōdō-za guild of biwa hōshi in central Japan, due to the historical significance of the Heike narrative, caused a dispute with biwa players in south-western Japan that led to the institutionalisation of mōsō groups. These groups then provided a framework for the development of narrative repertories and instrumental resources from which the kindai biwa traditions of satsumabiwa and chikuzenbiwa were constructed, while in Higo Province the majority of blind biwa players remained outside the mōsō institutions.

The biwa traditions of blind performers that continued in Kyushu until the late twentieth century cannot be understood apart from the historical contexts of the *biwa hōshi* and extant evidence for the practices of blind ritualists. The ways in which Yamashika Yoshiyuki has been portrayed and interpreted, in particular by scholars and the media, are conditioned by images and knowledge of historical *biwa hōshi*. This chapter has described the principal elements of a historical canvas before which Yamashika has been identified as a twentieth-century *biwa hōshi* and in relation to which various blind biwa traditions of Kyushu have been documented and represented. The next will provide an account of available historical evidence about biwa and its repertories in the former Higo Province and adjacent regions where Yamashika made his living as a professional performer.

2

BIWA MUSIC OF THE HIGO REGION

Biwa *hōshi* continue to be painted in broad, stereotypic strokes as figures in Japanese history. The ongoing provision of new research data about the diverse activities and situations of *biwa hōshi* in different periods and regions has little or no effect on popular imagery of them. Such images and lore about *biwa hōshi* inevitably influence representation of all the biwa traditions, in ways that I will examine in portrayals of Yamashika Yoshiyuki in chapter 3. While the blind biwa traditions of Kyushu—and the fact that they continued in several regions until the late twentieth century—are now little known beyond academic research contexts, in Kumamoto Prefecture Yamashika and other blind biwa players have figured in a variety of media in the construction of local cultural histories and identities.

Notwithstanding the term *higobiwa*'s contrivance at the end of the Meiji era as a means for distinguishing local tradition from the *chikuzenbiwa* and *satsumabiwa* styles that were gaining spectacular popularity throughout Japan, *biwa hiki* in and around Kumamoto Prefecture have given their own accounts of the origins of their music and their identity as performers and ritualists. What follows is, first, a brief account of the regional diversity of blind biwa traditions in Kyushu, the nature of Higo-region practices in relation to other traditions, and the perspectives from which *higobiwa* musicians have been written about. This leads to exposition and commentary on the grounding of historical accounts given by both tradition-bearers and researchers. The second half of the chapter describes the repertory of songs, tales and rites that has been identified since research on Higo-region *biwa hiki* began some fifty years ago.

Varieties of *Mōsōbiwa* in Kyushu

Higobiwa has been one of several terms for musical traditions of blind biwa players in regional Kyushu. Until the 1990s, *higobiwa* was defined in most reference sources as a primarily secular performance tradition that had evolved to become independent of the ritual biwa performance practices of *mōsō*, who in the twentieth century typically had responsibility for a *danka* (parish) and a temple residence, and who in small numbers continued to play biwa in several regions of the island (see for example NODJ 1989, 442). This model for Kyushu biwa music mirrored the prevailing view, in 1960s to 1980s music research, of pre-Edo-period *biwa hōshi* as musicians whose primary vocation was entertainment and *mōsō* as solely ritualists whose primary rite was the Jijinkyō. Like that view, it was a simplification of a much more complex reality in which the identities of these groups were hard to distinguish. More recent research has shown that historical biwa performance by *mōsō* and non- *mōsō* cannot be so neatly separated, in part because certified blind priests and non-priests alike performed many of the same rituals for rural householders.

It is now usual for *higobiwa* to be described as a regionally distinctive form of *mōsōbiwa* (used here in its broadest sense to denote biwa performance by blind males in Kyushu and environs), characterised by the continuation of both ritual and non-ritual performances until the late twentieth century, and by the fact that very few of its practitioners were certified priests.[1] Even the Kumamoto folklorist, Yasuda Muneo, whose work has focussed on the history and practice of *higobiwa*, sees it as a practice that became distinctive only as a result of the gradual expulsion of *mōsō* from Higo under pressure of the *tōdō-za*: "Originally *higobiwa* was a tradition maintained by the *mōsō* of Higo Province, so that it was part of the *mōsōbiwa* tradition found in all regions of Kyushu" (2001, 3).

Yasuda's comment refers to circumstances in the pre-modern province of Higo, but it is not applicable to twentieth-century Kyushu, when *mōsō* were officially disallowed from performing secular songs and tales (though a minority continued to do so). Late in life Yamashika

---

1. Narita 1985a was the first text to position biwa music of Higo in this way, as it includes sections on *"Higo no zatō"* and *"Higo no biwa hōshi kikigaki"* as sections within a chapter entitled *"Mōsō no sekai".*

Yoshiyuki himself temporarily became a member of the Fukuoka-based Gensei Hōryū, but his membership lapsed as he did not participate in group rites and stopped paying dues, and in no way did it alter the nature of his professional activities. He had trained and began work as a *biwa hiki* nearly five decades before seeking membership, moreover, so despite the fact that his musical and ritual practice has sometimes been categorised as an aspect of *mōsōbiwa*, Yamashika cannot be considered a *mōsō*.

Terms That Identify the Biwa Traditions and the Musicians

The plethora of terms for what Japanese scholars have posited as among the oldest of Japan's oral narrative repertories reflects the fact that thorough research on both the history and recent practice of the biwa music of Kyushu and environs has been broached only since the mid-1980s. This, in turn, stems from the fact that, despite the historical importance ascribed to *mōsō* in scholarly literature, in the latter half of the twentieth century the music of *mōsō* and other blind professionals in regional Kyushu was certainly among the country's most peripheral traditions, in terms of the accessibility of performances and primary source documents. Terms used in publications of the last thirty years to describe aspects of *mōsōbiwa* practice in various regions of Kyushu include *katarimonobiwa, monogataribiwa, Jijinbiwa, Kōjinbiwa, kuzurebiwa, higobiwa* and *zatōbiwa*.[2] Some of these terms reflect vernacular usage in particular regions of Kyushu, while others are terms devised and used only by scholars. *Katarimonobiwa* (performed narrative biwa) and *monogataribiwa* (tale biwa) refer to the practice of performing secular narratives but imply that those who do so are as a group distinct from those who carry out recitations in a ritual context, which is not always the case. The terms *Jijinbiwa* and *Kōjinbiwa* include the names of the deities addressed in ritual recitations but have been used to refer to broader practices which include secular narrative

---

2. See Ga (1972), Hirano and Tanabe (1975), Kikkawa (1965 and 1986), Higobiwa Hozonkai (1991), Hyōdō (1991 and 1993), and NODJ (1989), among others. Some of this research has also examined twentieth-century *mōsō* of the Fukuoka-based Gensei Hōryū sect who were active in rural parts of Honshū's westernmost prefectures, but in most instances *mōsōbiwa* and the terms that follow are used to refer to Kyushu practices.

repertory. *Kuzurebiwa* uses a term for one category of secular narrative, the *kuzure*, to refer to the whole spectrum of narrative repertory. *Higobiwa* parallels the names of the two traditions of modern biwa recitation practised throughout Japan, *satsumabiwa* and *chikuzenbiwa*, in specifying the pre-Meiji province with which a tradition was associated, but unlike the latter it has yet to be shown that this term had meaning for professional performers, as opposed to literate aficionados of biwa narrative in the region that had been Higo. All of these terms refer to an actual or perceived regional form or particular practice within the broader set of practices identified as *mōsōbiwa*.

Hyōdō Hiromi has challenged interpretations of the performance tradition of which Yamashika was the best-known and most-documented representative as merely an aspect of *mōsōbiwa*. As part of a broad program of research on oral narrative and its historical agency in Japanese culture, Hyōdō has argued for a view of narrative performance that bypasses the categories imposed by past authorities so as to more accurately reflect the majority of listener-audience's perceptions of performers' identities and repertory meanings. On the strength of a decade of field work with Yamashika and other *biwa hiki*, from the early 1990s he proposed that *higobiwa* be regarded as a similarly regional manifestation of *"zatōbiwa"* (1991, 1993), a term that he devised to link biwa performance in south-western Japan to the history of professional blind performers elsewhere.[3] In an article published in 1991, Hyōdō proposed the expression *"Kyūshū no zatōbiwa"* as a comprehensive term for both the sacred and secular traditions of biwa music of pre-Meiji origin in Kyushu.[4] Hyōdō's proposed terminology both effectively situates the recent Kyushu practices in relation to the historical ones of the *biwa hōshi* of central Japan and expresses the dual functions of the Kyushu musicians in sacred and secular spheres of performance. He maintained that with reference to

---

3. It is possible that Hyōdō adopted the term from the expression *"zatō no biwa,"* used by Orikuchi in one of the earliest ethnographic reports on the activities of regional *mōsō* (Orikuchi 1954, 438ff). The origins of *"zatō"* itself are obscure, but the word certainly predates its use, from the mid fourteenth century, as the lowest of the four principal ranks within the *tōdō-za* hierarchy.

4. This article was re-printed with some modifications in 1992, in the *chūsei* (medieval age) volume of the anthology series *Nihon bungaku-shi o omu* (Yuseido Editorial Board 1992), then further revised for inclusion in the book *Heike monogatari no rekishi to geinō* (Hyōdō 2000).

regions other than Satsuma,[5] expressions such as "*Jijin mōsō*" were Edo-period constructions devised by the *tōdō-za* for the purpose of making unequivocal distinction between *mōsō*, as blind men who carried out rites of local belief, and *zatō* or *biwa hōshi*, who were musicians affiliated with the guild of blind *heike* professionals. As such, Hyōdō maintained that when referring to blind biwa players who were not guild members, *tōdō-za* documents deliberately avoid "*zatō*," despite its use to mean blind performers in common parlance throughout Japan. In the case of Kyushu biwa players, "*zatō*" appears to have been used in daily speech regardless of affiliation with the *tōdō-za* or the *mōsō* sects,[6] with prefixes added when necessary to form distinctions, such as *Jijinkyō zatō, bussetsu zatō, kamabarai zatō*, and *Heike (no) zatō* (see Hirano 1989, 441).

In written sources (as distinct from the regionally diverse spoken vocabulary of Kyushu), terms for the bearers of the blind biwa traditions have reflected writers' views of relations between these musicians and the national institutions or performance traditions of central Japan. "*Biwa hōshi*" has been common, because of the prominence of imagery about such figures, as discussed in chapter 1, and because of Tanabe Hisao's interpretation of *higobiwa* as a remnant of *ko-jōruri* once performed by *biwa hōshi*. Following Hyōdō's argument that *biwa hōshi* was a literary term applied to high-ranking musicians of the *tōdō-za*, while in common parlance blind biwa players of all kinds had been referred to as *zatō* for centuries, the latter term became common in sources of the 1990s. So too did the Kumamoto-region vernacular word *biwa hiki*, introduced by Ga Machiko in 1972 and used consistently in writings by Kimura Rirō. I adopt the term *biwa hiki* in this text because it was the one most commonly used by Yamashika. Finally, in recent writings on the Miyazaki-region Jōrakuin Hōryū priest, Nagata Hōjun (Kawano 2001; Kawano, Kojima, Komoda and Nakayama 2005), the neologism "*biwa mōsō*" is used to denote *all* blind players, regardless of their level of involvement in institutional Buddhism. As Yamashika is listed among late-twentieth-century *biwa*

---

5. Satsuma province is treated as an exception because Hyōdō accepted the Satsuma *mōsō* sect's account of its own history under patronage of the Shimazu daimyō.

6. See Hyōdō (1991, 14 and 44). In his writings on pre-Edo-period practice of *Heike* recitation, moreover, Hyōdō has mostly referred to the bearers of the performance tradition as *Heike zatō* (Hyōdō 2000).

mōsō, this usage is questionable—even inaccurate—for it elides the secular narrative repertory that set Kumamoto-region practice apart for much of the twentieth century.

What is starkly apparent from the fragmentary research on blind biwa players in various regions of Kyushu conducted over the last thirty years is that there was great regional variation in both ritual practices and secular narrative repertories. Given this variety (which has yet to be rigorously documented), the degree of uniqueness of the music of blind biwa players in the region of the former Higo Province probably was no greater than that in other politically and geographically distinct regions such as the Kunisaki peninsula or Satsuma. That much is certainly true of repertory and performance style; as for durability, however, Yasuda's historical research has shown that it is because of circumstances in Higo during the Edo and Meiji periods that Kumamoto Prefecture and its environs yielded numerous blind biwa players who maintained into the twentieth century a repertory that had been abandoned by the biwa-playing *mōsō* of other regions.

Writings on *Zatōbiwa*, *Higobiwa* and *Mōsōbiwa*

Yamashika Yoshiyuki was the recipient of awards, as well as recognition by the Japanese government's Office of Cultural Affairs (*bunkachō*), as a bearer of the *higobiwa* tradition, which was itself designated an Intangible Cultural Asset (*mukei bunkazai*) in 1973. Yet there remains much that is ambiguous about the history and nature of the musical practices to which the term has been applied. Although the great majority of performers of secular biwa narratives who remained active after the Second World War were residents of Kumamoto Prefecture—roughly the region that had been the pre-Meiji province (*kuni*) of Higo—the claim that the practice of *biwa* players in Higo was substantially different from that in other regions remains open to question.[7] Arguments for the distinctiveness of such a tradition are of two kinds, one of which concerns historical evidence for the musicians' institutional affiliations from the late eighteenth through early twentieth centuries, which resulted in Higo-region musicians'

---

7. Among the texts that question that claim are Hirano (1975), Uda (1992), Hyōdō (1991) and Kimura (1997).

retention of a large secular narrative repertory, and the other the consciousness of tradition among *biwa hiki* interviewed since the 1960s.[8] Those arguments arise from evidence presented in a range of research writings on the biwa traditions of Kyushu and the music of the Higo region in particular.

Scholarly sources on the biwa traditions of Kyushu are few in comparison to the scope of writings on the major traditions of Japanese music. Until the late 1980s these were among the most marginal of historical music traditions, in terms of the quantity of published research and documentation available. Thereafter, research markedly increased due to a convergence of the interests of scholars in the fields of literary and social history, folklore and performance studies. Since 1994, eleven books devoted in part or whole to these traditions have appeared.[9]

Early Studies

Until the 1950s, most published writings on the Kyushu blind traditions were little more than references in passing in synoptic histories or surveys of Japanese music (for example, Kanetsune 1913; Iba 1928). Brief histories of the Kyushu groups appeared in three 1920s articles on *biwa hōshi* and Yamato *mōsō* (Iwahashi 1922a-b, 1923), and in Nakayama's 1934 *History of the Blind* and its 1936 supplement. Folklorists' accounts of a *watamashi* ceremony performance by a *higobiwa* player of Tamana, a town west of Kumamoto, and of Fukuoka-region *mōsō* performances appeared in the mid-1930s (Noda 1935; Hirai 1936, in Fukuoka-ken Kyōiku Iin Kai 1983). In September 1936 a performance of *Kumagaya* by the literate amateur player Nagamatsu Daietsu (1873–1953), of Tamana, was relayed from Kyushu by the national broadcaster.[10]

---

8. Some writers have also argued that a unique type of instrument, a large "*sasa biwa*," was played in central Kyushu. I address the issue below. See, for example, NODJ (1989, 442).

9. Murata 1994; Araki and Nishioka 1997; Hirose 1997; Araki and Fukuda 2000; Fukuda and Yamashita 2003; Nagai 2002; Yasuda 2001; Kawano 2001; Kumamoto Shimin Kaikan 2004; Kawano, Kojima, Komoda and Nakayama 2005; Nomura 2007.

10. Nagamatsu subsequently recorded for himself (rather than for commercial release) a set of twenty-eight SP records of various *gedai* in 1935 and 1936, at the Dai Nihon Katei Ongaku Kai, in Fukuoka. The discs are thought to be in the possession of Nagamatsu's family, but have not been heard by researchers since Tanabe's visit to

Fieldwork with *biwa hiki* and scholarly interest in the remnant traditions dates from the mid-1950s, when Kimura Yūshō started producing text transcriptions and impressionistic sketches of biwa singers in northern Kumamoto Prefecture—in particular Yamashika—for local newspapers, and for folklore and historical journals (Higobiwa Hozonkai 1991, 130). Kimura was a radio-play scriptwriter and compiler of Kumamoto regional folklore who had studied in the 1930s with the theorist and historian of folklore and performing arts, Orikuchi Shinobu. A number of manuscripts written by Kimura before his sudden illness and death in 1965, later edited and printed in issues of the newsletter of the Higobiwa Preservation Society, *Higobiwa dayori*, include a 1963 outline of the history and repertory of *higobiwa* ("Higobiwa gaisetsu"; An outline of *higobiwa*), with profiles of twelve *biwa hiki* who were still able to perform.[11] This same article begins with a veiled criticism of the leading musicologist Tanabe Hisao's view of *higobiwa* as something valuable only because it embodies "the remnant form of an old [medieval musical] tradition" (Higobiwa Hozonkai 1991, 6) and rather stresses the need for research on "reception of biwa narrative by people of old-time village society" and the ways in which that society had "nurtured biwa."

Tanabe Hisao's Work

Kimura Yūshō was instrumental in bringing Tanabe Hisao to Kumamoto Prefecture in July 1963 to assess the local biwa tradition and to speak at a concert of four performers held under the auspices of a local newspaper firm. Tanabe's attention had been directed to Kumamoto-region performers by the renowned Tokyo-based *chikuzenbiwa* player, Hirata Kyokushū, who visited Kumamoto in March 1963 and brought back a tape of several performers heard in Kimura Yūshō's company. After listening to the tape with the music historian Kikkawa Eishi, Tanabe arranged for the 79-year-old Nishimoto Tsuneki to come to Tokyo in June, assisted by Kimura Yūshō, where

---

Kumamoto in July 1963. In 1991 I was told by Nagamatsu's son that they still existed.

11. In 1991 a selection of writings from the newsletter were published, together with some new articles, in book form (Higobiwa Hozonkai 1991), and this contains reprints of Kimura's writings which originally appeared in the *Higobiwa dayori* newsletter. His essay and transcription of the *Kikuchi Kuzure*, which appeared originally in the journal *Nihon dangi* between October 1963 and March 1964, is given as an appendix in Kimura Rirō's 1994 text.

he gave a small concert[12] and recorded part of a tale for the anthology *Nihon biwagaku taikei* (Kimura 1963b; Tanabe 1963a, 1963b ii, 18–19).[13] In the accompanying notes, and in several writings during the 1960s and 1970s (Tanabe 1963a, 1963b, 1964; Kokuritsu Gekijō 1976), Tanabe described the tradition as a kind of *"jōruri* with *biwa,"* and perhaps a remnant of the earliest *jōrūri* styles (*ko-jōrūri*).[14] This is a claim he first put in his report to the Education Ministry's Cultural Affairs Division on the so-called *higobiwa* tradition:

> *Higobiwa* is a different form of music to *satsumabiwa* and *chikuzenbiwa*. Whereas these are styles in which the words of a song/poem (*kashi*) are sung, *higobiwa* is a *katarimono* style of music, like *ko-jōruri* . . . In other words, it is *jōruri* that uses biwa. (1963a, 1)[15]

In a series of articles about his four days in the Kumamoto region for the August through December issues of the popular monthly magazine *Hōgaku on tomo* (1963b i–v), Tanabe substantiates the claim that *higobiwa* preserves *ko-jōruri* by referring (albeit without citing any sources) to the conventional story of the tradition's origin—in short,

---

12. This was the first among several occasional Tokyo concerts of Kyushu biwa music during the 1960s and 1970s. The most important among them were held at the National Theatre and yielded program booklets that include short but important research essays. One entitled "Kōjinbiwa" was part of the Medieval Performing Arts series in 1970 (Kokuritsu Gekijō 1970), then in 1976 Yamashika Yoshiyuki and Tanaka Tōgo appeared as representative *higobiwa* musicians in a concert showcasing the various Kyushu traditions, with commentary essays by both Tokyo- and Kyushu-based researchers (Kokoritsu Gekijō 1976; personal program copy).

13. In his 1964 book on instruments, *Nihon no Gakki*, Tanabe wrote of Nishimoto: "Today the 80-year-old Nishimoto Tsuneki is the sole person alive who has perfectly learned all of the piece, 'Tamayohime Ichi Dai Ki'; a few others can play it imperfectly, in fragments, and the tradition as a whole is about to vanish" (88–89).

14. Strictly speaking, the early puppet theatre repertory called *ko-jōruri* (early *jōruri*) had been performed by *shamisen* players with puppets from about 1600 until the 1680s, but *zatō* of various kinds, including biwa players, are recorded as having sung *jōruri* narratives from as early as the fifteenth century. The generic term for these narratives derives from the *Jōrurihime monogatari*, thought to be the earliest of them. See Dunn (1966, 14–20).

15. Tanabe's handwritten report to the Bunkachō was submitted in September 1963 (Tanabe 1963a). Although it is not publicly available, nor is there any longer a file containing Tanabe's report on *higobiwa* at the Bunkachō archive (personal communication from a Bunkachō official, December 2002), I was given a copy by an individual in Kumamoto. The report was an important stimulus to the Prefectural government's subsequent interest in the tradition.

that in the late seventeenth century blind biwa players in Higo had been taught *jōruri* of Kyoto tradition by an esteemed *tōdō-za* musician of the *kengyō* rank.

Following the then-accepted historical model's sharp historical distinction between *biwa hōshi* and *mōsō*, Tanabe took the position that the ritual work done by many *biwa hiki* in the region was properly the work of *mōsō* and not a part of the "original *higobiwa* tradition." Comic recitations, too, he characterised as aberrant activity that led to a decline in the public status of biwa performers (although he gave no evidence for the public's having held more respect for them in the past):

> Today almost all the bearers of the true tradition have died, and only a very few elderly blind men remain. Morover these persons have found it hard to make a living from *higobiwa* in its original form, and have managed only by doing comic recitations and ritual music. For this reason *higobiwa* has come to be despised by the public. (1963c, 3)

Tanabe also claimed that the instrument played by a minority of the surviving Kumamoto-region *biwa hiki* in the early 1960s was a marker of *higobiwa*'s identity as a tradition. Indeed, he regarded it as so distinctive that he dubbed it the *"higo biwa"*:

> The *higo biwa* is somewhat different in form to the *satsuma biwa* and *chikuzen biwa* instruments in that its body is narrower and longer, and its frets are fixed by insertion into the surface of the neck (unlike *chikuzen biwa* frets . . . , which are simply pasted onto the surface). Its most characteristic feature is that a long cord of beads that form a *juzu* [string of prayer beads] is attached to the back of the body and the neck, so that the instrument can be suspended from the neck when walking the streets, and the *juzu* can be removed for use when reciting sutras during the *kamado-barai* and other rites. This instrument is rarely seen any more. (1963b iii, 20)

Over forty years later, there is no agreement among Japanese scholars as to whether or not the *"higo biwa"* existed as a unique instrument type. This is because at least until the early twentieth century, the forms of biwa played by blind professionals in Kyushu—whether *tōdō*, non-*tōdō* or *mōsō* sect members—were highly variable, even within single regions such as Chikuzen, Chikugo, Higo or Satsuma. The principal characteristics described by Tanabe—shape, manner of fixing the frets to the neck, and the use of a string of beads as a shoulder strap—are not confined solely to instruments that were used in the Higo region, and the same can be said of other features that he did not draw attention to, such as the use of *takezawari*, a piece of bamboo inserted between the strings and tailpiece (*fukuju*).[16] What is suggested from commentary by Yamashika, however, is that the situation in 1963 documented by both Tanabe and Kimura Yūshō (Higobiwa Hozonkai 1991, 19), wherein very few players owned an instrument of the sort Tanabe described while the majority played instruments similar to the standard four-string *chikuzen biwa* (an instrument Yamashika referred to as the *marume* or "roundish" biwa), may well have already been so by the 1920s.[17]

Writings by Local Historians and Folklorists

However rigid Tanabe's view of the biwa tradition of Kumamoto and environs may have been, it was largely due to his writings and lobbying that *higobiwa* was declared an Intangible Cultural Asset (*mukei bunkazai*) in 1973. The Higobiwa Preservation Society (*Higobiwa Hozonkai*) was subsequently established under the auspices of the Cultural Affairs Division of the Kumamoto Prefectural Government. The Society's newsletter *Higobiwa dayori* appeared irregularly until 1988 and included articles on the repertory, history and current state of the tradition, as well as text and source manuscript transcriptions.

Articles by local researchers and enthusiasts have also appeared in journals published in Kyushu, and in some cases have included data not presented in the Preservation Society's publications (Haraguchi 1973; Yonemura 1973; Tamagawa 1990). Writings by Kimura Rirō have appeared chiefly in local media including the *Higobiwa dayori* (reproduced in Higobiwa Hozonkai 1991). In a short essay published in 1981 (whose title can be translated as "Research on biwa, rather than '*higobiwa*'") Kimura stressed that the historical veracity of the

---

16. This is reflected in notes written by Kimura Yūshō as early as 1951: "The form of the instrument played is common to *mōsō* and *higobiwa*. This is a further point that suggests the common origin of *higobiwa* and *mōsōbiwa*" (Higobiwa Hozonkai 1991, 44). See also Murayama's claim (1986, 456) to have seen many features of the "*Higo biwa*" in instruments found in Fukuoka and Nagasaki prefectures.

17. Yamashika recalled that *marume biwa* were widely used in the 1920s when he began to learn, but also that at that time they had been relatively recently adopted by *biwa hiki* in Amakusa and northern Kumamoto Prefecture, so that people would still comment that such biwa were "unusual" (Kimura 1994, 83).

expression *higobiwa* had yet to be established. Despite the fact that in the late 1970s "from Yamaguchi Prefecture [in south-west Honshū] to [all regions of] Kyushu there are still living biwa players who carry on biwa performance traditions of medieval narrative," he maintained that "one doesn't hear terms such as *chikugobiwa* and *hizenbiwa*" (Higobiwa Hozonkai 1991, 61). Kimura also related how Yamashika had told him "he'd first heard the term *higobiwa* used to describe his own biwa repertory in 1951," from Kimura's own father (62).

Kimura's book on Yamashika, which I examine in detail in chapter 3, was published in 1994 by a Tokyo firm for national distribution, but is critical of national scholars' agendas.[18] It includes little about the status of *higobiwa* as a historical tradition, apart from the following sentence at the end of Kimura's first commentary section:

> The term *higobiwa*, which even today is used as if its meaning were fixed, may have been a very general way of referring to *biwa hiki* who had travelled from Higo Province, among those who received them in adjacent provinces. (1994, 35)

Just after the book's publication he was invited to contribute to an anthology on literature of oral tradition that has become a widely known scholarly resource, a volume edited by Hyōdō Hiromi in the *History of Japanese Literature* Iwanami Kōza series (1997). Kimura's article, "*Zatōbiwa no katari*" (Zatōbiwa narrative), shows the influence of Hyōdō's ideas and editorial work—for example, in its insistence that "*higobiwa*'s lineage is from *zatōbiwa*, not *mōsōbiwa*" (72–73)—but also explores further the problem of *higobiwa* as a historical construction. Kimura concludes that "it appears that *higobiwa* undoubtedly did exist" (71) in the late Meiji era, but most *biwa hiki* probably did not use the term. He goes on to level a critique against claims that Higo-region biwa players were *mōsō* who engaged mostly in narrative performance.

Scholarship Since Tanabe

After Tanabe's writings of the mid-1960s interest in the biwa traditions of Kyushu increased among scholars in institutions beyond Kyushu.

---

18. Kimura's book displays the writer's substantial knowledge of scholarship on the subject of *higobiwa*, and at times gives abbreviated references while avoiding footnotes and other academic trappings that publishers perceive as discouraging to general readers.

Resultant publications can be grouped into those based on fieldwork with surviving *biwa hiki* and *mōsō*, studies of historical issues and text sources, and several bodies of work that combine both approaches.

Apart from Kimura Yūshō's, the first extensive fieldwork among *biwa hiki* was carried out by Ga Machiko for her graduation thesis in folklore studies at Ritsumeikan University in Kyoto. Her published research report includes profiles of eight biwa players in Kumamoto Prefecture, as well as a scheme for the division of their repertories according to narrative content (Ga 1972). The folklorist Murayama Dōsen's long essay of 1978, "*Biwa: wasurerareta oto no sekai*" (Biwa: A world of forgotten sounds), documents biwa as it was still played in the mid-1970s in several regions of Kyushu. Murayama went on to publish an article on Yamashika's life and the performance practices of four surviving players (Murayama 1986). From the late 1970s, articles appeared regularly on *mōsō* traditions by folklorists Araki Hiroyuki and Nishioka Yōko and the literary historian Narita Mamoru (who brought together both fieldwork data and literary analysis of *biwa hiki* tales and *mōsō shakumon* texts in a book on what he called "the Kyushu *mōsō* tradition" in 1985). In 1981–1982 a field documentation project on Kyushu blind biwa traditions was funded by the Toyota Foundation and carried out by a research team of literature, folklore and music specialists, including the project's director, Fujii Sadakazu, Murayama Dōsen and a youthful Hyōdō Hiromi.[19]

My own writings on the Kyushu biwa traditions are based largely on ten months of fieldwork during 1991 and 1992, and several shorter visits to the Kumamoto region. In addition to a 1997 doctoral thesis, these writings have appeared in diverse academic journals, anthologies and reference books. The doctoral text addresses analytical procedures in oral narrative performance studies and theories of the *Heike monogatari*'s development in oral performance by blind musicians. It examines the nature of the text-music relationship in different performances of single repertory items. Elements from diverse frameworks for analysis of oral narrative, including "text-centred" oral compositional studies, on the one hand, and "music-centred" *senritsukei* theory, on the other, are applied in a detailed analysis of two 1975 performances of the first *dan* of *Shiga Dan Shichi* by Ōkawa

---

19. Afterwards a report was lodged with the Toyota Foundation, but it has remained unpublished (Fujii et al. 1983).

Susumu. Yamashika's practice is considered for its points of sharp contrast with Ōkawa's, and the differences are interpreted in terms of the two performers' lineage, training and professional experiences. The causes and nature of differences in the men's performance practice are then related to Hyōdō's hypotheses on the significance of written texts in the development of *Heike* narrative performance among *biwa hōshi*. Among my published articles, one develops a model for text-music relations for a single *fushi* type (1995; see further chapter 5) while others deal with the role of humour in performance (1996a) and Yamashika's representation to academia and the general public at the end of his life (1994). An article in Japanese (2002) and a related paper in English (2003) present fieldwork data from discussions with Ōkawa during 1992 and 1997, which sheds further light on the performances analysed in the thesis. Apart from my own work, since Matisoff's study of 1978 (reprinted as Matisoff 2006) the only scholarly text in English that contains more than a passing reference to the blind biwa traditions of Kyushu is a 2003 article by Tokita that compares versions of the Atsumori tale in three biwa traditions.

Among studies with a historical focus, one of the earliest was a 1972 attempt to categorise the sacred and secular repertories of blind biwa players in an article accompanying source documents on *mōsōbiwa* in the *Anthology of Historical Documents of the Life of the Japanese Populace* (*Nihon shomin seikatsu shiryō shūsei*, volume 17; Gorai 1972). In a commentary essay with the 1975 record anthology *Biwa: sono ongaku no keifū*, the leading music historian Hirano Kenji argued on grounds of repertory content and musical style for the unity of all pre-Meiji styles of biwa narrative in Kyushu. In that essay he referred at length to Yamashika, who by then was already seen as the last active professional *higobiwa* singer. While Hirano focussed his account on the secular repertory, he revised Tanabe's position on the nature of *higobiwa*; he emphasised the importance of the *biwa hōshi*'s involvement in religious practice through rites of local belief such as the *kamadobarai* for the fire deity Sanbō Kōjin, and *watamashi*, a blessing ceremony for newly constructed houses, in which it was usual to engage the services of a biwa singer. He also linked the secular and sacred aspects of the *higobiwa* repertory by framing the following hypothesis:

> We can imagine that *heikyoku* and also the recitation of the *Jōrurihime Monogatari* were at first "*danmono*" or "*kuzure*" of the

kind still practised in Kyushu. If that is so, then the modern biwa styles, *heikyoku* itself and the *shamisen katarimono* traditions all have *mōsōbiwa* as their point of origin. It goes without saying that much deeper research into the history and practice of *mōsōbiwa* is needed... The old local tales of battle can be thought of as having originated in a similar manner to stories in the *Tale of the Heike*, namely, as accounts of battle which the blind priests performed in ritual incantations to placate the dead warriors' souls. (Hirano and Tanabe 1975, 36–37)

While arguing for the importance of the ritual practices of regional musicians, then, Hirano also reinforced Tanabe's identification of *higobiwa* as a research topic of great consequence for the study of oral narrative traditions that have been positioned centrally within the historical canon in accounts of Japanese music of the twelfth to sixteenth centuries.

In 1993 a 600-page volume of historical documents pertaining to Fukuoka-region *mōsō* and *zatō* appeared (Nishi Nihon Bunka Kyōkai 1993). Much of the work of its compilation was done by the historian of religion and performing arts, Nagai Akiko, who went on to publish an important monograph comparing the historical circumstances of Japanese and Korean *mōsō* (Nagai 2002). Also in 1993, essays on the historical functions and organisation of *mōsō* in various regions of Kyushu, which had previously been published in diverse journals, appeared in anthologised form (Nakano 1993). Araki and Nishioka's 1997 book presents the contents of primary documents from *mōsō* temples in several regions, while Murata Hiroshi's of 1994 is an anthology that brings together his writings on the Satsuma-region *mōsō* traditions over a thirty-year period.

Yasuda Muneo presented the first reliable data on the existence of *mōsō* and their association with temples in the Higo region prior to the *tōdō-za*'s campaign (Yasuda 1991, 1993). Subsequently the results of Yasuda's research on Edo- and Meiji-period documentary sources were included in his 2001 book *Higo no biwa-shi: kinsei kara kindai e no hensen* (The biwa players of Higo: transformation [of a tradition] in the pre-modern and modern eras). The book's concern with Edo-period evidence for *mōsō* and *tōdō-za* activities in Higo Province links it to work being done by others on the history of *mōsō* as a social institution.

During the 1990s the work of Hyōdō Hiromi shaped scholarly perceptions of the central Kyushu *biwa* traditions and their significance for studies of *heikebiwa* and other medieval narrative traditions. Hyōdō's extensive fieldwork on what he came to call "*zatōbiwa*" was part of a broader endeavour that occupied him throughout much of the 1980s and 1990s to develop theoretical tools for analysis of the role of oral compositional procedures in the formulation of texts of the literary genre of medieval narrative (*chūsei katarimono bungei*).[20] In 1992, Hyōdō told me that he saw his work with the Kyushu *biwa hiki* as perhaps the last opportunity to study the making of texts in performance in a narrative tradition transmitted for the most part without writing from the Edo period until the present and one which includes versions of many tales now thought of as part of the canon of national literature.[21] To that end, Hyōdō recorded and examined only secular repertory items, and in particular the lengthy narratives called *danmono*. His use of the term *zatōbiwa* in part reflects his wish to separate consideration of the narrative art of *biwa hiki* from their local significance as ritual celebrants; from the first, he acknowledged that his objectives were

> to overcome the "local" concerns of . . . viewing [this practice] as a regional performing art, and to raise questions from a comprehensive persective on oral narrative traditions. This sort of study can be thought to provide a certain number of suggestions for gauging the actual distance of the practice of narrative recitation in medieval times from that of what has been called *heikyoku* in more recent times. (1991, 14)

Hyōdō's series of articles, "*Zatō(-mōsō) biwa no katarimono denshō nitsuite no kenkyū*" (the *zatō-mōsō biwa* tradition of secular oral narrative; 1991,

---

20. While the historical importance of oral tradition has long been recognised in writings on Japanese literature and performing arts, the concept of oral composition, as developed by European and American researchers in the 1920s through 1950s, was not applied to Japanese *katarimono* until the 1970s. At that time, Satō Teruo (Satō 1973), Yamamoto Kichizō (Yamamoto 1976, 1977) and others began to examine both literate and non-literate forms of narrative in terms derived in part from those of Parry and Lord. Satō's 1973 book concludes with an examination of sections of the *Heike* in which formulas are prevalent, and considers their "oral" and "literate" qualities, relative to formulas used in the *Song of Roland*. Yamamoto's work examines non-literate narrative forms usually classified as folk performing arts (*minzoku geinō*), such as *sekkyō-bushi*, goze narrative songs and *kowaka-mai*.

21. Personal communication, February 1992.

1993 and 1999), is based on fieldwork with Yamashika and other *biwa hiki*. In his comprehensive introductory essay in the Oral Literature volume of the 1997 *Iwanami History of Japanese Literature* series, Hyōdō sketches two extreme conditions of performative textuality in Japanese oral narrative. On the one hand there is the oral performance style of Yamashika, in which a set of music-textual pattern types (*fushi*) named by the musician are aurally identifiable but are flexible and variable to the extent that they often seem to disintegrate and disappear for a time. At the other extreme is the very clearly recognisable patterning system of *heikyoku* as it has been performed since at least the eighteenth century. In the debate on the historical practice of the *Heike* tale-complex's performance by blind musicians, and the performance tradition's significance for the multiple extant manuscript forms of the text, Hyōdō's inferences from the recent practice of Yamashika and other *biwa hiki* are regarded as a seminal body of work.[22]

Populist Accounts and Depictions

There is a brief but important anecdote about the significance of biwa singing for the local populace in a 1956 essay anthology of writings by the nationally renowned essayist and founder of the field of women's studies in Japan, Takamure Itsue (1894–1964):

> One of the old *higobiwa* tales ... concerns Waifu Tajima no Kami Chikanaga. Whenever a *biwa hōshi* would appear and start to sing this tale, one of my grandmothers would run and shut herself away. The reason was that this tale makes out Tajima no Kami to have been a villain who betrayed the main branch of his clan. Now Waifu, like Takamure and other old words, apparently was the name of one of the aboriginal peoples of Higo.... This is what my mother heard from my grandmother about the matter: In order to secure stability within the province, the great conquerors of the *kinsei* [Edo] period made use of *higobiwa*; by spreading the story of Tajima no Kami as a traitor throughout Higo Province, they were able to ensure that all the descendents of the Wai clan would remain under their control. (Takamure 1971 [1956], 203–204)

While this anecdote could be of interest outside Kumamoto Prefecture

---

22. Hyōdō's ideas are presented and examined at length in de Ferranti (1997, chapters 2, 5 and 6).

only to specialist historians and folklorists, it suggests an important aspect of the historical socio-political roles of *biwa hiki* and the tales in their *danmono* repertory, as regional oral histories to which the majority of the population had frequent exposure.

A widely known anthology of recordings, the spoken commentary from which was also published as a series of books on Japan's "itinerant performing arts" (*hōrōgei*), appeared from the early 1970s under the authorship of the actor Ozawa Shōichi. Ozawa had travelled throughout Japan during the 1960s to record and photograph performers of historical traditions. The first of his books (Ozawa 1982, originally published 1974) contains an extensive account of the Kunisaki-peninsula *mōsō* tradition, including an interview with the priest Takagi Seigen (1931–1999), then in his forties, as well as several pages about *higobiwa*. Ozawa obtained a copy of Tanabe's 1963 report from the Kumamoto office of the national broadcaster, NHK, then went to visit several of the performers listed therein. He provides photographs of an unidentified, apparently very old player in the town of Hinagu, southern Kumamoto Prefecture, and of Yamashika, who is described only as an "old *biwa hōshi* who can recite for over two hours without showing signs of tiredness" (79–81).

Documentation of the blind biwa traditions in the mass media and film should be divided into those written or created by local media and those by Tokyo-based media (in particular the national broadcaster, NHK). On the whole it can be said that most media documentaries have been populist in their orientation to a general audience, and their domination by themes of nostalgia for a past, simpler lifestyle of communal spiritual and aesthetic experience. The locus for that sentiment is more generalised in the products of national media and their regional divisions, while locally produced ones are able to frame nostalgia in terms of more specific knowledge and experiences assumed to be commonly held by a regionally defined reading and viewing public. It is for the establishment of common interpretive ground for readers and audiences not familiar with regional culture that the image of the *biwa hōshi* has been mobilised; for example, in a 1971 episode of the NHK television documentary series, *Shin Nihon kikō* (A travel diary of the new Japan), Kunisaki-peninsula *mōsō* such as Takagi Seigen are identified as *biwa hōshi*. The many differences in practice between late-twentieth-century Kyushu figures and historical accounts of the activities of *biwa hōshi* are of less consequence than the communicative value of the generalised image of a *biwa hōshi* and its rough fit with the activities and appearance of biwa players filmed in Kunisaki and parts of Kumamoto Prefecture.

The 1983 film *Satsuma mōsōbiwa* by the Tokyo director, Suwa Atsushi, also makes some use of the term *biwa hōshi*, but its aims are in contrast to those of the television documentary and film discussed above. In giving a detailed documentation of the activities of the blind Jōrakuin Hōryū priest Fukijima Junkai (1916–1995), Suwa's focus of attention is on the Satsuma priest's status as a *Jijin mōsō*, a priest of the earth deity Jijin, and throughout his film the director uses imagery and commentary to argue that Fukijima and the Satsuma *mōsō* sect are intrinsic to the traditional sacred belief systems of rural Kagoshima. As such, this film is closer in approach to the majority of documents produced by local writers and film-makers in Kyushu.[23]

Programs on *higobiwa* made by Kyushu broadcasting services in the 1970s through 1990s generally take the approach of explaining how the performance tradition is related to local history and aspects of ritual and community life in remote parts of the prefecture (RKK Kumamoto 1975, 1986; NHK Fukuoka 1993, 1994). In such programs, the theories of Tokyo scholars about the significance of this music as a "remnant" of historical *jōruri* are usually quoted in terms that imply that the national significance of the tradition should be a point of pride for Kumamoto people.

Finally, a series of writings and recordings of *mōsōbiwa* with populist commentary has been produced by Kawano Kusumi since the mid-1990s. Kawano was a senior producer at NHK in Tokyo when he encountered the Nobeoka (Miyazaki Prefecture) *mōsō* Nagata Hōjun

---

23. At the same time it deliberately obscures one important aspect of Satsuma *mōsōbiwa* practice in an effort to distance itself from the secular *satsumabiwa* tradition that has been practised all over Japan since the early twentieth century: Posters made to advertise the film all show Fukijima bearing a slender *sasa biwa* (a small biwa with a narrow body that resembles the shape of a leaf of *sasa* bamboo) with six frets rather than the standard five. This is at odds with the fact that since at least the 1970s biwa players within the Jōrakuin Hōryū sect have, with the exception of the Hyūga-region *mōsō* Nagata Hōjun, performed on the standard *satsuma biwa* instrument. When giving a 2002 conference paper, Komoda Haruko claimed to have been told by a member of Fukijima's family that at the time the film's publicity photographs were taken, the additional sixth fret had been deliberately attached to the old instrument shown (unpublished paper delivered at the annual conference of the *Fugeki Mōsō Gakkai*, in Kyoto, May 2002).

in the mid-1980s. He made a series of radio programs about Nagata, then privately produced CDs of his and Takagi Seigen's ritual music (Kawano 1997; Kawano and Takagi 1997). In 2001 Kawano published a book compiled from notes written over 15 years of interaction with Nagata. Published by NHK, it is clearly directed at a general readership that equates with the audience for NHK Television's many documentaries on traditional arts and lifeways. At the same time, as an extensive text that includes entire chapters on history and forms of the biwa, it displays Kawano's erudition and concern for historical sources.[24] In 2005, Kawano and a team of collaborators produced a box set of DVDs and CDs of Nagata's ritual repertory (Kawano, Kojima, Komoda and Nakayama 2005). The set presents Nagata as the last practising "*biwa mōsō*" and if anything adopts a more populist tone than Kawano's earlier book—the accompanying booklet can be enjoyed as much for its full-page colour images of the priest laughing with his parish householders and walking beside rice fields and cherry blossoms as for the data and interpretations offered in short essays by the established musicologists Komoda Haruko and Kojima Tomiko.

Performers' Consciousness of Tradition and Accounts of Origins

Tradition and "History"

> I wonder what *higobiwa* really is. Perhaps someone made it up. *Naniwabushi* was started by Tenchūken Ungetsu, but who started *higobiwa*? I'm often asked who was the founder. What I think is—putting aside the story about the Hosokawa lords for the moment—that there was really only Hori Kyōjun. (Kimura 1994, 114)

This brief comment was made by Yamashika in the course of a discussion with Kimura about his experiences of being interviewed by the musicologist Tanabe Hisao in the summer of 1963 and performing for audiences in Tokyo in the 1970s. It expresses his awareness that

---

24. There is less concern for the voluminous research on Kyushu biwa traditions that appeared during the fifteen years of Kawano's work with Nagata, for almost none of it is mentioned.

Tanabe and others who came to the music as "cultural outsiders," from a local perspective, were generally concerned to know the origins and history of this music so that it could be identified in terms of canonical traditions of biwa and *shamisen* narrative performance.

Yet in the late twentieth century, blind biwa players' consciousness of affiliation with a tradition or community of performative practice was either regionally based, lineage-based or institutionally based (in the case of priests within the *mōsō* sects). Regional identity is reflected in the following account by Yamashika of a fellow *biwa hiki* who had appropriated Tamagawa lineage without any legitimate grounds:

> By the way, the fellow I travelled with, Kumaichi, was from Fukuoka Prefecture. He was born in Sanwa, in Yamato county, but grew up in Ōmuta. The style of *biwa* he played was neither Gensei-hōryū nor *higobiwa*. You might call it a kind of "*chikugobiwa*." He gave himself the name Tamagawa without ever having had anything to do with a Tamagawa teacher. (Kimura 1994, 130)

A similar sense that biwa styles and repertories were regionally distinct is expressed in the text of a book about Kyushu customs and traditions written in the early 1920s, the time of Yamashika's apprenticeship as a biwa hiki:

> While there's biwa performance in both the Higo and Nagasaki regions—*higobiwa* and *nagasakibiwa*—in which you'll sometimes hear obscene tales, the Kōjin priests of Chikuzen do kuzure performances. (Takeda 1925, quoted in Fukuoka-ken Kyōiku Iin Kai 1983, 8)

Lineage-based identity was important for groups of *biwa hiki* who comprised a *ha* (style or school) named after a prominent performer from whom they or their teachers learned. When Yamashika referred to his own teacher in Amakusa as a "Tamagawa" player, he meant that he had been a member of the Tamagawa-*ha* founded by Hori Kyōjun (1835–1909).[25] Hori was already a skilled *biwa hiki* before the Meiji Restoration and is said to have been granted the venerable name of Tamagawa for his style, as well as permission to use a unique "*jōruri-bushi*" pattern, by a Hosokawa daimyō for whom he performed at Kumamoto Castle. Yamashika's telling of this story to me included

---

25. The date of Hori's death is given as 1909 in Yasuda (2001, 39), while 1910 is given in Higobiwa Hozonkai (1991, 27).

the claim that Hori's skills impressed the Hosokawa lord so much that thereafter the music of Hori and his pupils was widely known as "*tono-sama biwa*" (the lord's biwa; interview of November 9, 1991). While there is no evidence for the truth of this claim, in memory of Hori's renown as a biwa player and his skill as a teacher, a stone monument in the form of a two-metre tall biwa was erected at his grave by a group of his former students. As an old man, Yamashika made efforts to visit the grave and offer prayers to Hori every few years.

Figure 2.1. Yamashika preparing to play biwa before the grave of Hori Kyōjun. Photograph by Kimura Yoshio. Used by permission of Mrs. Kimura Aiko.

Yamashika saw Hori as unequivocally the central figure in the past of his own performance style and repertory: "What I think is—putting aside the story about the Hosokawa lords for the moment—there was really only Hori Kyōjun." What is strongly suggested by these words is that his perception of history and tradition was grounded in personal experience, so that the *higobiwa* that scholars spoke of was for him a reference to the Tamagawa-*ha* style and repertory he had learned—however incompletely—from two men who had both been students of the renowned Hori Kyōjun. He acknowledges that some biwa singers tell a "story" about their repertory having origin in contact with a highly ranked Kyoto *heike* musician who had been engaged by the Hosokawa lords of Higo, but he discounts it; instead he affirms the priority of his personal lineage as a performer.

By contrast, Yamashika's comments on the "history" of biwa (as distinct from his own practice) were often in the register of legend, and even myth: "Biwa is a special instrument in Japan because it was devised by Benzaiten at the time Amaterasu hid herself in the cave." Only this short statement is included in Kimura's 1994 text (118), but in discussion Yamashika would often recount the tale of the biwa's beginnings at length. Yasuda sums up the tale as follows:

> The biwa was brought to Japan from India at the request of the goddess Benzaiten when the sun goddess Amaterasu hid herself in a cave in shame at the behaviour of her brother Susanō. Benzaiten succeeded in luring Amaterasu back into the world by playing the biwa in ensemble with other instruments. Subsequently, in Hyūga, she taught a farmer named Jiro to play the biwa. He in turn taught others, and eventually the music was disseminated throughout Kyushu. In Higo the first person to learn the biwa was Hori Kyōjun of Katakimura, near Tamana. He performed for the Hosokawa daimyō and was granted the name Tamagawa Ōmi no Ichi. "Tama" was from the placename Tamana, and "-gawa" from the placename "Kikuchigawa." (Yasuda 1991, 3)

This tale is recited in part in performances of the *watamashi* rite for blessing new houses and buildings and in a section of the piece *Miyako Gassen Chikushi Kudari* where the heroine Tamayohime talks about the crescent moon and sun markings on the biwa. Hyūga is named as the site of the biwa's first transmission to a human performer; the importance of the Hyūga region in the lore of Kyushu blind biwa players found representation in Yamashika's own set of stories about the origin of his instrument.[26]

In some tellings and performances, Yamashika would introduce another mythical action that accounts for the nature of the biwa played by Tamagawa-*ha* professionals, namely, that a sacred mirror was smashed by Amaterasu's outrageous brother, Susanō, and its fragments fell upon the biwa, forming the symbols of the sun and moon that are almost always inscribed upon instruments of Tamagawa tradition *biwa hiki*. In essence, what Yamashika's account of the origins of biwa music does is to tie the instrument, its practitioners and their tutelary deity, Benzaiten, into the corpus of mythology concerning the central deity of the Shinto pantheon, Amaterasu. The prestige of the Imperial house is accessed by this and by the setting of the account in Hyūga, the site of Amaterasu's appearance and the birthplace of the legendary first Emperor of the Imperial line, Jimmu. The standard form of the episode of Amaterasu's loss and recovery accords with Yamashika's version in that her brother's misbehaviour outrages her so much that she goes into seclusion, a calamity for the world that leads all of the deities to gather outside. It is from this point that Yamashika's version diverges. The standard account describes the dancing of Ama-no-Uzume, whose erotic behaviour causes the gods to laugh, arousing Amaterasu's curiosity to the extent that she can be lured out by her own reflection in a mirror forged by one of the gods. Yamashika not only appropriates the sacred mirror for the purpose of accounting for symbols of the sun and moon on Tamagawa-*ha* biwa, but also sustitutes Benzaiten for Ama-no-Uzume as the performer, and the sound of the biwa for the mirror's reflection as a means to arouse the sun goddess' curiosity.

Musicians' accounts of the origins of their traditions serve both to position their practices in relation to other contemporaneous practices and to strengthen the legitimacy of current practice through appeal to historical figures and institutions generally acknowledged as authoritative. As sources, they usually offer a mixture of historical

---

26. While to the best of my knowledge Yamashika never recounted either the Kunara (Kunala) Taishi story or the version of the Jijin-kyō and biwa music's transmission from Continental Asia that tells of the visit of a Korean or Chinese blind priest to the abode of "Yūkyō Reishi" in Hyūga, as given in *mōsō* documents, Yamashika spoke of Hyūga as the place where a human being first learned biwa from the goddess Benzaiten.

facts and legendary accounts that reveal cultural values and articulate political dynamics.[27] Historical fact and legend are not manifested as two distinct sets of elements, however, but are embedded within one another in such a way that cultural priorities are revealed in the kinds of events and circumstances privileged by musicians' accounts, and by the relative functions of historical and non-historical materials in the musicians' constructions of their identity as a group or tradition. By its incorporation of the legend of Amaterasu's seclusion in a cave, which figures in the earliest collections of Japanese mythology, and moreover by linking these stories to one about the beginnings of his particular school of performance, this alternative account offered by Yamashika claims great antiquity for both the biwa itself and the Tamagawa-*ha*, despite the fact that Hori Kyōjun is known to have lived from 1835 to 1909.[28] It also constitutes an overt appeal to political legitimacy by association with the Imperial House, which, in the mythology promulgated by Japanese governments between the 1870s and 1940s, was believed to be directly descended from the goddess Amaterasu. In this regard, and in its ahistoricity, it is similar to legendary accounts of origin among many groups of traditional performing artists.

Historical Evidence

The first historical reference to a blind biwa player in Kyushu is that of a poem of 1097 by Minamoto no Shunrai about biwa music heard at Ashiya, near the modern city of Kita Kyūshū. The sounds of the instrument move Shunrai to tears—perhaps because they brought to mind his late father, an accomplished performer of *gagaku biwa* in the Katsura style—but neither the poem nor its explanatory note tells us that the biwa player also sang or recited. It is only the use of the literary expression "*biwa hōshi*" that suggests the musician was a blind man (Nagai 2002, 29; see also Matisoff 1978, 26).

As suggested in chapter 1, the bulk of pre-twentieth-century sources that include references to the blind biwa traditions of Kyushu

---

27. In German, see Fritsch (1991) on the nature and significance of this mixture in the origin stories of *mōsō*, *goze* and *sekkyo-shi* groups. For a discussion in English of the Kyushu *mōsō* sect accounts and their reliability, see Matisoff (1978, 32–35).

28. He may therefore have performed for the last Hosokawa daimyō, but can hardly have been the first person in Higo to have learned the biwa.

are documents produced by *mōsō* groups or records of governance that pertain to the ongoing dispute between the *tōdō-za* and other biwa players. For some regions of Kyushu a limited number of documents produced by sighted *mōsō* or scribes employed at *mōsō* temples exist;[29] among them are temple legends and histories, chronicles of ceremonies and rites, records of orthodox procedure, and *danka* membership lists. Historical accounts of blind performers referred to variously as either *mōsō*, *zatō* or *biwa hōshi* are also given in diaries and essays. With regard to Kagoshima and the Satsuma region, the best-known early accounts were written by travellers from central Japan in the late eighteenth century. These Edo-period accounts foreshadow the general tendency in modern-day representations to identify regional blind biwa players in terms of images of *biwa hōshi*; prominent *biwa hōshi* of the day, *kengyō*-rank *heikebiwa* musicians of Kyoto and Edo renowned for their recitation of *heike* and their wealth and favour with the Shogunate, were foremost in the minds of the eighteenth-century travellers. An excerpt from an entry headed "*Biwa no myōju*" (The master of biwa) in the *Seiyūki*, a 1795 chronicle of a journey from Kyoto to southern Kyushu, is typical in this regard (although atypical in its critical tone):

> The biwa in Miyako is just for introducing the pitches of the voice. When singing (*utau ni*) the *Heike monogatari*. . . . It [is music that] has not survived among the general public. . . . When I hear this contemporary biwa music [of Satsuma and Ōsumi], I feel for the first time the power of the instrument to impress the water deity (Suijin), as it is said the Tajima no Kami once did when playing the biwa. Perhaps the old music of Kyoto has survived only here. (Shimazu 1997, 149–150)

For the Chikuzen region, the diary entitled *Katō masafusa nikki* gives accounts of daily life, including many kinds of performances, in the village of Minagi-mura for the early 1680s through 1690s (the Empō and Genroku eras). The diary entries describe *mōsō* and their rites as part of a panoply of local performance and ritual life (Nagai 1997, 90–94).

---

29. Some of these documents are examined in Araki and Nishioka (1997), Nakano (1993), Murata (1994), Nagai (2002) and Narita (1985a), and in European languages in Matisoff (1978) and Fritsch (1994).

Edo-period documentation of biwa playing in Higo Province is chiefly contained in records of organs of the Hosokawa daimyō administration (Kumamoto Han 1966; Hosokawa Han Seishi Kenkyūkai 1985).[30] Events in the Tenmei era (1781–1789) related to the struggle between the *tōdō-za* and biwa players who were not guild members are also recorded in the *Shimaya nikki*, a source that covers nearly two hundred years of local Kumamoto history, from the late seventeenth century.

Pre-Meiji Evidence
Origins—The standard account of the origins of *higobiwa* that has been circulated by scholars and some musicians runs as follows: In the third month of the second year of Empō (1674), a renowned *heikyoku* reciter of the Hatanoha[31] named Iwafune Kengyō (Funahashi Kengyō in some accounts) came to Higo from Kyoto at the request of the daimyō, Lord Hosokawa. He performed *heikebiwa*, then at the daimyō's request composed several tales on local historical and legendary themes including the *Kikuchi Kuzure* and *Miyako Gassen Chikushi Kudari* (also known by the titles *Botan Chōja* and *Tamayohime Ichidaiki*) and taught them to blind biwa players within the Higo domain. It is further claimed that Iwafune Kengyō brought most Higo-Province biwa players into the *tōdō-za* guild, so that local authority and the rank of *kengyō* were passed to his student Kosaka Naminoichi. Kosaka Kengyō is said to have taught in turn the masters Dairyū and Etsuzan. Dairyū's student Daiki was acclaimed for his skill in the Kan'ei era by the daimyō Hosokawa Mitsunao, and defined the bases of the style thereafter. Two students of Daiki are said to have founded performance schools of opposing characteristics: the restrained, elegant Shunki-*ha* and the flamboyant Taietsu-*ha*. Both styles were practised as a pastime among samurai-class residents of the Kumamoto castle town and are said to have been transmitted to professional performer-teachers active until the 1920s (Yasuda 2001, 42; 2004a, 3–4). Primary evidence is lacking for this account of origin and for the putative Edo-period lines of transmission and early divisions into *ha*. In post-war writings these accounts of Edo-period schools of performance based in Kumamoto

---

30. Additional, unpublished documents are held in the central library of Kumamoto National University.
31. Some sources give "Haruno-*ha*," apparently in error.

were given in publications by the local historian Hirakawa Atsushi, but with references to only a single source, an otherwise unknown text of 1925 (Hirakawa 1991a [original 1978], 25–26).[32] The same schools of performance are, however, mentioned in 1920s concert performance programs produced by a *Kai* (study group) headed by the *chikuzenbiwa* performer and supporter of *higobiwa*'s renewal, Shimada Dangetsu, so it is possible that he had read the text cited by Hirakawa.

An important point to be made about the standard account of the origins of the *higobiwa* tradition is that it suggests that biwa-playing *zatō* were already common in Higo Province in the late seventeenth century—so common, in fact, that some of them could confidently take on acquisition of Kyōto-style *jōruri* and *heikebiwa* performance skills as a supplement to their narrative repertory. About the nature of that repertory very little can be said except that it probably comprised both local historical tales such as the *Kikuchi Kuzure* and the *Tamayohime Ichidai Ki* and others from a body of oral literature and folklore disseminated through much of Japan by the Muromachi period (1392–1568). The above-mentioned *Masafusa* diary for the period 1675–1689, and indeed the wording of the 1674 Shogunal edict itself, show that *jōruri* recitations were already a staple in the repertory of some regional Kyushu *zatō*.[33]

Yasuda has also documented a number of little-known alternative accounts of origin, none of which has been located in pre-twentieth-century sources on biwa (2001, 41–42). What is common to all of these is the claim of Imperial or noble lineage for local biwa traditions.

Activities of the *tōdō-za*, *mōsō* and *zatō* in Higo Province—References to "*Jijin mōsō*" in Higo-domain documents from the late seventeenth century make no mention of their being affiliated with either local

---

32. Although the title of this document is given as "*Higobiwa chikuzenbiwa satsumabiwa genshoryū no hitobito*" (Performers of the current schools of Higo, Chikuzen and Satsumabiwa) on page 26 of Hirakawa's article, I have come across no other references to it. Yasuda (1991, 14, fn28) asserts that Hirakawa had not divulged his source for this account.

33. In this sense, Tanabe Hisao's claim that *higobiwa* of the 1960s preserved the fundaments of early-period *jōruri* was based on a perception of historical continuity, even if it lacked substantiation through comparison of modernday *biwa hiki*'s vocal and instrumental performance practice, as well as narrative style and text forms, with what was known of the characteristics of historical *ko-jōruri*.

temples or with powerful sects based elsewhere.[34] Without patronage to protect them from a rigorously enforced law that punished non-*tōdō-za* biwa players for performing the secular songs and narratives that provided much of their income, a great many players "converted" to membership of the *tōdō-za*. Yasuda discusses a Temmei 3 (1783) document of the Kyoto temple Shōren'in that responds to a successful petition for protection by blind ritualists of disparate regions who called themselves *mōsō* but notes that there were *no* such *mōsō* listed as resident in Higo Province (Yasuda 2001, 61). It is not clear to what extent the Shōren'in thereafter was able to exert Tendai-sect authority to protect blind ritualists in Higo, as it did from the 1780s elsewhere in Kyushu (ibid., 62). To judge from the fact that the word *mōsō* effectively vanished from documentary records of both the Higo *han* (administration) and the Amakusa islands (a region under direct rule of the Shogunate since the conclusion of the Amakusa-Shimabara rebellion in 1638) for the remainder of the Edo period. However, such protection was probably minimal. Yasuda goes on to conclude that it is the absence from Higo of *mōsō* temples of the kind that existed in other provinces and the lack of any framework for *mōsō* patronage during the latter half of the Edo period that explain the continued presence of specialists in biwa narrative performance well into the twentieth century (ibid., 69).

The *tōdō-za* established administrative offices in Higo Province by at latest the mid-1690s (ibid., 43), but there is no doubt that many blind musicians who engaged in both secular and ritual performance in fact were not registered as guild members. As in other regions of Japan remote from the guild's headquarters in Edo and Kyoto, in Higo the *tōdō-za* had repeatedly to urge authorities to identify and punish such musicians—but without lasting effect (Yasuda 2001, 66–67). Just how much control was exercised over members' performance activities is unclear. What seems to have been of paramount importance to the guild was membership and the income that flowed upward from it in the form of dues rather than implementation of a policy of separating narrative recitation from ritual performance; having become *tōdō-za* members,

---

34. Yasuda examines in detail the *Jijinkyō doku mōmoku meifu chō*, a survey of "punishable and non-punishable" blind professionals submitted to Edo by the Higo authorities a year after promulgation of the 1674 regulations against non-*tōdō-za* blind musicians (2001, 45–57).

biwa professionals were allowed to continue their activities as before:

> It is appropriate to say that the influence [of the *tōdō-za*] did not lead them to perform solely *heikyoku* and oral narratives; documents show that it allowed them to carry out ritual activities, too, as needed.... We can also say that, at least during the Edo period, it was impossible to clearly distinguish between [*tōdō-za zatō*] and [*mōsō*]. (Yasuda 1991, 12)

A new framework of local association became important for *biwa hiki* who were "*tōdō-za zatō*": small, regionally based groups of *za* members, called Myōon Kō (or Myō-on Kai). Myōon Kō is also the name of these groups' most important ceremony, conducted annually in honour of Myōon-Benzaiten. The Myōon Kō ceremony itself was shaped in imitation of the *tō-e* rite conducted by the highest ranks of the *tōdō-za* in Kyoto, and may have been introduced to Kyushu musicians by *heikyoku* professionals or other *tōdō-za* guild members.[35] At least three Myōon Kō groups still existed in the Amakusa islands in the early twentieth century. Each had a membership of over fifty professional performing artists, including *goze*, *biwa hiki* and others (Ga 1972, 37-38). Two documents associated with the last group that met, in 1943, were among the possessions of Morita Takashi, a musician from Amakusa who was the group's youngest member.[36]

To summarise the results of research on pre-Meiji biwa music in the Higo region: With regard to the standard account of origins, Yasuda and other writers have reached the conclusion that, as Iwafune Kengyō was a senior figure in the *tōdō-za* during the Empō era, he would not have travelled from central Japan to perform for the Higo daimyō and teach non-guild musicians, even if such a request had been made. The citing of him as a founder of sorts who

---

35. For an introductory discussion in English of the significance of the Myōon Kō ceremony for members of the *tōdō-za*, see Fritsch (1991, 148-9). For more detail, in German, see Fritsch (1996).

36. These documents are: the *Tōdō ryakki*, a manuscript bequeathed by one Kurokawa *kengyō* in 1798 which contains lore that pertains to the *tōdō-za* and accounts of the guild's origins; and a scroll painting of the patron deity Myō-on (Benzai)Ten (Higobiwa Hozonkai 1991, 254-257). On the Amakusa Myō-on Kai groups, see Ga (1972), Yasuda (1991), Uda (1991, 80-82), and Higobiwa Hozonkai (1991, 254-257). There is also documentary evidence in the form of a *Myō-on Kai junkai kichō* (Register of meetings of the Myō-on Kai) for a large Myō-on Kai which existed in the Tamana region until the turn of the century; see Higobiwa Hozonkai (1991, 258-261).

appeared in Empō 2 (1674) is regarded as an expression of the *tōdō-za*'s increased political significance for musicians in the Higo region from that year, when regional blind musicians' activities were circumscribed by a Shogunal edict that favoured the rights of guild members (Yasuda 2001, 42–43; see also Narita 1985a, 58–59). It has also been pointed out that the chronology of the events described is nonsensical, for the Kan'ei era was 1624–1630, and the daimyō Hosokawa Mitsunao died in 1649, long before the Empō era when a *tōdō-za* musician from the capital supposedly first taught Higo musicians (Satō 1982). No primary-source evidence for the purported history of *higobiwa* transmission and the two *ha* styles practised as a pastime among the samurai class in Kumamoto during the eighteenth and nineteenth centuries has yet been found. Other accounts of origin are similarly unsubstantiated by documentary evidence. The lack of any power base in Higo for non-*tōdō-za* blind ritualists, who in other provinces organised associations and gained patronage as *mōsō*, is seen as a key circumstance behind the survival of the local practice of biwa narrative that twentieth-century scholars called *higobiwa*.

The Modern Era: Meiji- and Taisho-Era Evidence

What is known about the activites of biwa players in and around Kumamoto Prefecture during the Meiji and Taisho periods (ca. 1870–1920) is significant for understanding the subsequent training and early professional experiences of the musicians whose recordings and oral accounts constitute the principal extant primary sources on *higobiwa*. Relevant documentary sources from Meiji and Taisho include newspaper references to biwa, articles by professionals who had learned to read and write before going blind, and a number of printed materials concerning the activities of groups of literate, amateur practitioners.[37] From the last decade of the Meiji era (ca. 1900s) the ever-growing popularity in Japanese cities of *satsumabiwa*, and in turn *chikuzenbiwa*, gave rise to a good deal of writing on those styles that makes passing mention of the historical *mōsōbiwa* traditions, as practices that contributed to the development of the biwa's newly gained popularity. Biwa-playing in the former Higo region was also the subject of occasional local

37. See also the chronological listing of references from Kyushu and Kumamoto newspaper articles for the years Meiji 13 to Taisho 15 (1880–1926), given in Yasuda (2001), and at greater length in Kumamoto Shimin Kaikan (2004).

newspaper articles, and the term "*higobiwa*" appears for the first time.[38] From the 1920s there are programs for the concerts organised by Shimada Dangetsu. Shimada gathered biwa professionals from across the prefecture for a "First Higobiwa Concert" at the Kumamoto-shi Kōkaidō on July 9, 1922. The concert program lists ten performers, two of whom are identified in a *Kyushu nichi nichi shinbun* article as elderly representatives of the two schools of performance established since the mid Edo period, the Shunki-*ha* and the Taietsu-*ha* (Kumamoto Shimin Kaikan 2004, 458).

Clearly, many characteristics of training, professional activities and performance style, as documented for *biwa hiki* still living in the 1970s through 1990s, were shaped by conditions during the Meiji and Taisho eras. They may be summarised under four headings: the relative importance of ritual activity and entertainment for the musicians' livelihoods; responses to the success of other forms of popular narrative entertainments, including *gundan, naniwa-bushi, gidayū, chikuzenbiwa* and *satsumabiwa*; attempts to renew and revise the tradition; and sighted, literate performers' participation in the tradition. I will deal with each of these in turn.

Most Edo-period references to biwa players in the region who were not *tōdō-za zatō* identify them as being "blind persons who chant the Jijin sutra" (*jijinkyō mōmoku*). Interviews with persons old enough to recall perceptions of *biwa hiki* in rural areas during the Taisho (1912–1926) and early Shōwa eras (to 1940) suggest, however, that while their services as celebrants of the *kamado-barai, watamashi* and other ceremonies continued to be important for some, the most immediate perception of them at the time was as *geinin* (entertainers) who appeared most commonly on festival days (Yasuda 1991, 12).

Yasuda suggests that this marked change began when the Meiji government banned the *tōdō-za* in 1871 and ordered a temporary prohibition of ritual activities of the blind (1991, 12). As yet little evidence has been found for the effects of these events on *biwa hiki* in the Higo region, but it is likely that they were inhibited for some years from doing *harai* and other rituals with biwa. Even *kadozuke*

---

38. The first use of the word to denote traditional biwa narrative of the Higo region is in a March 23, 1901 (Meiji 34) Kumamoto newspaper article entitled "Improving Higobiwa" (*Kairyō higobiwa*) that describes the ideas for making local biwa music more popular (Yasuda 2001, 1 and 121).

and *zashikibiwa* activities may have been constrained by the fact that from Meiji 7 (1874) performers had to register with the prefectural authorities (Kumamoto Shimin Kaikan 2004, 476) if they were to legally operate as professionals.

The decline in the *biwa hiki*'s opportunities for ritual work came during a period when a number of other forms of oral narrative were becoming established as both popular entertainments and amateur pastimes throughout Japan. *Gundan* (recitation of military tales) surged in popularity from the time of the Sino-Japanese War (1894–1895). A Kumamoto man who performed under the name Bitō Itchō became one of the most successful *gundan* performers nationwide for some fifteen years thereafter. By the years of the Russo-Japanese war (1904–1905), some *higobiwa* professionals sought to adapt elements of Bitō's performance style and texts he composed (Yasuda 2001, 99–100). In the same period the numbers of professional and amateur performers of *chikuzenbiwa* and *satsumabiwa* in the metropolises of central Japan grew tremendously, and representative narratives in these repertories came to be heard in the regional cities. This was equally true of the various styles of dramatic storytelling and narrative singing which came to be called *naniwa-bushi* and in turn *rōkyoku*.[39] A far older narrative practice, *gidayū-bushi*—the recitation of excerpts from *ningyō jōruri* (*bunraku*) puppet plays in the style of the chanter Takemoto Gidayū—also enjoyed a resurgence of popularity and amateur practice from the 1880s through 1930s (Gerstle 1999).

The widespread success of the urbane *satsumabiwa* and *chikuzenbiwa* styles, *naniwa-bushi*, *gidayū* recitation and related styles of *gundan*, had important consequences for practices of biwa singing even in remote parts of central Kyushu and Amakusa: One was that as performers based in central Japan began to make "concert tours" of northern and central Kyushu, some *biwa hiki* attempted their own public performances in this manner, albeit on a smaller scale. The former *biwa hiki* Ōkawa Susumu (performance name Miyagawa Kikujun; 1918–2000) told me of how he would sometimes

---

39. After its emergence from a number of earlier narrative styles around the turn of the century, *naniwa-bushi* soon became the most popular form of oral narrative throughout the country, and continued as such until perhaps the 1970s. For evidence of its great popularity in the late-1950s, see William Malm's references to it (Malm 1959). The term *rōkyoku* came into use in print from 1917 (Kikkawa 1984, 1058).

arrange to perform in the *zashiki* room of a large house, then spend the afternoon advertising his "concert" by walking about the village or town. Concerts of this kind might also be held collaboratively by two or more singers, each of whom presented a few scenes from a single tale. As for concerts in urban venues such as theatres and *yose*, it seems that performers of biwa other than the Satsuma and Chikuzen traditions rarely appeared.[40]

A second consequence of the general popularity of *naniwa-bushi* and *gidayū* was that as the four-stringed form of the *chikuzen biwa* came to be produced cheaply for a growing market from the 1900s, some *biwa hiki* began to use these instruments. While instruments of similar structure may have been previously used by players in central Kyushu, their production in large numbers for amateur enthusiasts of *chikuzenbiwa* recitation made them less expensive than the longer, narrower form of biwa that some *biwa hiki* continued to play (that is, the instrument described as the "*higo biwa*" by Tanabe) but with the same tuning and fret systems.

Perhaps the most significant effect of the success of new forms of musical narrative was to stimulate a series of calls for a renewal of the local tradition. From Meiji 34 (1901), writings in Kumamoto regional newspapers refer to or are ascribed to two blind biwa players (both of whom had been highly literate men before going blind) who felt that the local biwa tradition should be revised so as to make it more respectable, elegant and on a par with *satsumabiwa* and *chikuzenbiwa* in literary themes and aesthetic. The first of these reformers, Noguchi Kinryū, argued that *higobiwa* (as he called it, probably for the first time; see above) had lost interest for most audiences and must be renewed through production of new texts on themes that would capture the interest of enthusiasts of contemporary styles of biwa narrative. He composed and performed several such texts. The other reformer, whose professional name was Takano Shizu no Ichi, contributed several articles arguing for not only new, fixed-text repertory based on popular military tales (*gunsho*) but also revision of performance style in such a way as to enhance what most distinguished local biwa

---

40. In the music and entertainment sections of Kumamoto newspapers of the Meiji period the only references to such performances are the concerts organised by the reformers Noguchi and Takano, to showcase their new compositions and performance styles. Yasuda Muneo, personal communication, July 2002.

tradition from *satsumabiwa* and *chikuzenbiwa*. In that regard, according to Takano, *higobiwa*'s similarity to the *shamisen*-accompanied musical narrative tradition, *jōruri*, was most important (Yasuda 2001, 87–94).[41] Takano organised a concert in September 1907 at the Shikijima-za, a small theatre in Kumamoto, to present several new compositions on classical themes.[42]

From the second decade of the century a number of sighted, literate persons in the Kumamoto region became interested in local biwa traditions to the extent that some took up performance and composition of new texts on an amateur basis. A few of these persons also became skilled enough to teach biwa as a source of supplementary income. There appear to have been at least two approaches taken. The first was that of Shimada Dangetsu, the heir to a Kumamoto high-ranking samurai family, who learned *chikuzenbiwa* while at university in Tokyo between 1905 and 1910, then formed a study group back in Kumamoto for researching and renovating local biwa traditions. Shimada also composed new texts for biwa recitation, such as the *Shinsaku Sano Genzaemon* which he performed in a concert he organised in April 1925 (Yasuda 2001, 95).[43] A second approach was in effect to participate in the local music culture as a professional performer and teacher. A number of these literate singers met with great success, so that they became revered performers and leaders of their own *ha*. Among these musicians was Tajima Rintarō of the Aso region, a man for whom a monument was erected by his many students after his death.[44] Miyagawa Kyōgaku the First was another sighted biwa player of renown, who performed and taught in southern Kumamoto Prefecture and is said to have been selected along with

41. In concrete terms, he wrote of the way in which the instrumental and vocal elements were integrated as one, rather than separate as they are in other biwa styles (Yasuda 2001, 92).

42. These writings were identified only in the latter half of the 1990s through the research of Yasuda Muneo. Yasuda reached the conclusion that the aspirations of Noguchi and Takano were not realised: "The movement to renew *higobiwa* ended with the Meiji period, and had no influence on biwa players thereafter" (2001, 96).

43. Yasuda seems not to regard Shimada Dangetsu's efforts as a comparable "movement" of renewal to that of Noguchi and Takano, perhaps because it was initiated and maintained by Shimada, who was a sighted *chikuzenbiwa* player, rather than a professional *biwa hiki*.

44. For descriptions of this monument, and of that erected to Yamashika's teacher's teacher, Hori Kyōjun, see Higobiwa Hozonkai (1991, 27).

other Kyushu performers to tour the Japanese colonies of Korea and Taiwan during the 1930s.[45] Nagamatsu Daietsu, the Tamana musician whose performance first alerted Tanabe Hisao to Kumamoto-region biwa when broadcast on national radio in 1935, wrote down the texts of several existing items of repertory, and composed a new, multiple-*dan* narrative about Toyotomi Hideyoshi.

It is questionable whether the practices of these sighted performers had significant impact upon the blind tradition. Two modes of influence can be posited (but neither of them can be confirmed retrospectively): Performances by sighted persons such as Tajima Rintarō were based upon written, fixed versions of narratives and may have been emulated in various ways by blind singers who heard them; secondly, sighted performers who were also active as teachers may have exerted direct influence over the forms in which their blind students acquired narratives of their core repertory.[46] The actual extent of difference between the performance styles of literate, sighted singers and those of the blind, non-literate *biwa hiki* cannot begin to be gauged until such time as the recordings made by Nagamatsu Daietsu in the 1930s are made available for research purposes.[47]

Shōwa Era and Recent Practice (ca. 1925–1990s)

Acquiring knowledge of the conditions of professional practice for Kumamoto-region *biwa hiki* of the early-to-mid twentieth century entails seeking out something that was little known, little thought about by anyone but scholars and a few individuals interested in folkways,

45. Ōkawa Susumu, interview of December 4, 1991.
46. From my discussions with Ōkawa Susumu, I heard of one example of the latter mode of influence, in the figure of Miyagawa Kyōgaku the First. While the legacy of Miyagawa's approaches to composition and performance is inherent in Ōkawa's recorded performances and knowledge of narrative texts, neither recordings nor accounts of him performing exist as data for verification of this. (See further de Ferranti 2003.) References to sighted *biwa hiki* are scattered throughout writings on *higobiwa*; for example, Tamagawa Taikyō, whom Ga claims taught Yamashika two *gedai* (Ga 1972, 29; see also Higobiwa Hozonkai 1991, 158), and Morita Takashi, whom she says could see well enough to read and learn *gedai* from books (Ga 1972, 37–38).
47. Tanabe recommended in his report to the Office of Cultural Affairs (Bunkachō; Tanabe 1963a) as well as in one of a series of articles on *higobiwa* in the monthly magazine *Hōgaku no tomo* (Tanabe 1963b ii, 20) that the discs be re-recorded for safekeeping "as national archive material" as soon as possible. No documentation of such copies exists (email communication from Saito Hirotsugu, a Bunkachō official, December 17, 2002).

and hardly visible in primary source documents. Substantial amounts of data on Yamashika and on one other individual, Hashiguchi Keisuke, and a lesser amount of data on Ōkawa Susumu, have been documented since the mid-1970s by scholars whose work I have described. The experiences and repertories of a much larger number of men who were still well enough to perform and discuss their performance traditions in the 1960s are known only in the most fragmentary of forms.[48]

From the range of data available, however, this much can be said:

1. Perhaps because of the decline in demand for *biwa hiki*'s ritual services, the extent of knowledge of ritual repertory has varied greatly. Some of the men still playing biwa in the 1960s knew no ritual pieces at all, while others considered themselves to be primarily celebrants of rites (Ga 1972).
2. Forms of professional association with roots in the Edo period that continued in some regions brought *biwa hiki* together with other blind performers. Myōon Kō groups are known to have operated in several areas (for example, the three groups in Amakusa, discussed above), and included performers who made a living as *biwa hiki, goze, sekkyō-shi* and *jōruri-gatari*, all of whom in effect competed for the same audience in their capacity as storytellers, if not as ritualists.[49] Accounts by Hashiguchi Keisuke and Yamashika suggest that the annual gathering for the Myōon Kō ceremony served as an opportunity for senior performers to enforce a professional behavioural code on the group's members, and to regulate relative income by conferring on matters such as numbers of students who would receive professional names.[50] There is also evidence of new forms of professional association, unrelated to the Myōon Kō with its ceremonial obligations. According to Hyōdō (1991, 16), Yamashika described a group he was involved in

---

48. This will remain the situation at least until the research documents of the late Hirakawa Atsushi and others who interviewed musicians in the 1960s are made available.

49. Ōkawa Susumu described to me a group he belonged to in the 1930s in the Izumi area of northern Kagoshima. He said that all these professions were represented in his Myō-on Kai group (interview of June 22, 1992).

50. For descriptions of some aspects of the Amakusa-region Myōon Kō ritual and associated celebratory performances, as well as the group's organisation and regulations, see Ga (1972, 38), Yasuda (1991, 6–7) and Uda (1992, 28). For consideration of the socio-economic functions of the groups and their significance for repertory transmission, see Hyōdō (1993, 56–60).

in the Ōmuta area during the late 1920s, which included thirteen *biwa hiki*, six *goze*, several *gidayū* and "*saimon*" (which he interprets as meaning *naniwa-bushi* in this context) performers, as well as singers who played *yōkin* (Japanese cimbalon or dulcimer). In the 1950s Yamashika continued to be a member of a locally based blind performers' organisation, the Miyama Chiku Mōjin Yūgei Kumiai, which may have been a continuation of the pre-war group.[51]

3. At the time that Tanabe and others directed academic and bureaucratic attention to Higo-region biwa music in the mid-1960s, opportunities for performance had already become rare. Thereafter both performance settings and the social status of *biwa hiki* changed dramatically, as *biwa hiki* were presented by scholars and public officials as bearers of an important folk performance tradition (*minzoku geinō*). Of the few musicians still able to perform Yamashika was the one most often engaged for concert-style performances organised by bureaucrats and researchers.

4. Numbers of performers steadily decreased, with the most drastic falls probably occurring between 1941 and 1945 when entertainment unrelated to the war effort was officially discouraged, and in the immediate post-war period when for a time historical narrative was widely felt to be tainted by the ideology of those who led Japan to war and defeat. There were 345 registered professionals in 1907 (Yasuda 2001, 100). In 1963, Kimura Yūshō documented 12 men in Kumamoto Prefecture who were still capable of performance. In 1978 a total of 16 living former practitioners were listed by Hirakawa, but few among them could still play (Higobiwa Hozonkai 1991, 32). Three of those 16 remained alive in 1992, of whom 2 were capable of performance (de Ferranti 1997). Provision of welfare and education to the blind in rural areas, moreover, has meant that no blind people have learned *higobiwa* in the post-war era, and in 2007 only the *chikuzenbiwa* player Katayama Kyokusei is able to perform a small number of pieces he learned during the last years of Yamashika's life.[52]

---

51. Miyama is written "three mountains" and takes a character from the names of each county from which the group's members came: MIike-gun (三池郡) and SANkan-gun (山間郡). According to Yamashika, the group ceased to operate in 1960 (Kimura 1994, 165, 179–182). It seems likely that this, rather than a Myō-on Kai group, was the organisation Ga refers to in her 1972 article as having "continued until about 10 years ago" (31).

52. Katayama has taught at least one of those to others in Kumamoto; see further chapter 6.

* * *

Like many music traditions in Japan, *higobiwa* was a Meiji-era invention that scholars took to be a far older unitary practice. It was only toward the end of Meiji, in the first decade of the twentieth century, that the musical and ritual practices of blind musicians in the former Higo Province were thrown into relief against the practices of other blind biwa players in Kyushu (most of whom had become *mōsō* sect members and given up secular narrative repertory) and the newly popular *chikuzenbiwa* and *satsumabiwa* styles. The efforts in the first three decades of the twentieth century of Noguchi, Takano, Shimada and others to renew repertory and revise the performance style of the tradition they dubbed *higobiwa* did not yield it popularity comparable to that of the new biwa styles, let alone to the contemporary popular recitation styles of *gundan* or *naniwa-bushi*. Despite calls for renewal and revision, and the participation of some sighted practitioners in *higobiwa*, by 1922 in the city of Kumamoto the word "biwa" was generally assumed to refer to *chikuzenbiwa*.[53] Biwa narrative of local origin remained on the whole marginal and irrelevant for the contemporary musical marketplace, as an oral practice of blind males which was increasingly confined to rural parts. Although narratives on modern themes entered the repertory, it could be said that biwa music in the Higo region remained a "pre-modern" performance tradition: The great majority of its practitioners were not entertainers who sought to compete in the urban marketplace with professionals of other styles for the favour of large audiences and recording opportunities but blindmen of regional towns and villages who made a living from a combination of door-to-door performance, engagement to play in individual homes and ritual work. For Yamashika—who claimed not even to have heard the term *higobiwa* until the post-war era—and most likely for other *biwa hiki* who made their living in locales distant from the site of experiments with renewal in Kumamoto, tradition was conceptualised in terms of local experience and teaching lineage, and it remained so even after Tanabe and other authoritative researchers and bureaucrats declared them to be *higobiwa* performers.

53. "When you say 'biwa' in Kumamoto today, you mean *chikuzenbiwa*." Quoted from June 22, 1922 edition of *Kyūshū nichi nichi shinbun* (Kumamoto Shimin Kaikan 2004, 458).

Repertories of the Kyushu Biwa Traditions

We now turn to the substance of the musical and narrative practice of Kyushu biwa singers—their repertory of tales and ritual recitations. The historical importance of the *biwa hiki*'s and *mōsō*'s past roles in religious and ceremonial life in rural areas cannot be overlooked; arguably, it was the centrality of the *kamado-barai, Jijin-barai, watamashi* and other rites in local folk practice which ensured that in Kyushu and nearby parts of Honshu biwa continued to be used to accompany oral narrative beyond the eighteenth century, by which time elsewhere in Japan it had been displaced by the *shamisen* in all contexts except *heikyoku* performance. In other words, the dual role of biwa players as ritual celebrants and entertainers was probably crucial for the survival of the secular narrative tradition into the modern era. I have discussed evidence that by the early and middle decades of the twentieth century *biwa hiki* were treated primarily as entertainers. Notwithstanding, there were *biwa hiki* who regarded themselves as ritualists first and foremost, and Yamashika's concern for acquiring and perfecting ritual skills throughout his career suggests that for people who continued to believe in the efficacy of rites directed to the deities Jijin and Kōjin, the most important qualification of celebrants continued to be blindness and skills in biwa performance—not certification as a Buddhist priest.

Division of *biwa hiki*'s repertory into secular and sacred is somewhat artificial, for in certain contexts performance of secular narrative constituted the completion or even the central action of a ceremony or ritual event. For example, in a rite called *yogomori* (or *o-komori*), the *biwa hiki* performed tales over the course of an entire night for local community members gathered within a small shrine as a rite of protection during a period when the deity was considered to be absent.[54] In annual gatherings of the Myōon Kō, song and narrative performance by members constituted a supplement to the elaborate ceremony in honour of the deity Myōon–Benzaiten. *Kadozuke* performance of short secular items itself had ritual undertones, as I discuss in chapter 5. All such performances should be considered from the broader perspective of the place of *geinō* (performing arts) in Japanese ritual and ceremony: In both Buddhist and Shinto rites, and in rites of folk belief that developed as syncretic practices prior to the modern era,

---

54. See "*yogomori matsuri*" entry, *Shintō daijiten* 1977 (1937), 399.

music and dance that has no conspicuously sacred content is presented as an offering before images or symbols of *kami*. At the same time, the texts and rites for various manifestations of Jijin and Kōjin, which had been practised by both *mōsō* and *zatō* (as well as *yamabushi* and other ritualists of "folk religion") in most regions of Kyushu, comprised a distinct repertory and set of skills which professionals like Yamashika needed in order to maximise their opportunities for earning income.

Tales

In the modern era blind biwa players in and around the former Higo Province stood apart from those of other regions because of their maintenance until the late twentieth century of a large repertory of tales performed as entertainment. While secular narratives and songs are known to have been performed by blind biwa players in other parts of Kyushu (Gorai 1972, 117; Hyōdō 1991, 14), by the time of the consolidation of *chikuzenbiwa* and *satsumabiwa* as practices requiring literacy on the part of both amateur and professional performers, performances of the older body of tales with biwa had become rare in all regions other than Kumamoto Prefecture and nearby areas. Performance for entertainment had been a characteristic activity of *mōsō* (so much so that the *tōdō-za* had moved to outlaw it) until the early twentieth century.[55] *Shakumon* (tales about Buddhist deities) continued in ritual settings as the only remaining legitimate narrative form in the modern *mōsō* repertory.

The similarities between Kyushu blind biwa players and typical images of the *biwa hōshi* have given rise to a conceptual shortcoming in writings on the Kyushu traditions: Categories and terminology of literary and performing arts history developed to describe the narrative repertories of medieval and pre-modern *biwa hōshi* have been repeatedly applied to the secular repertories and performance

---

55. Without doubt some *mōsō* did continue to perform *kuzure*, *hauta* and other non-ritual pieces, but such activity was continually discouraged after the formation of the two *hōryū* in 1907. Morita Shōjō (1901–2000), a Gensei Hōryū priest of Amagi in Fukuoka Prefecture, was the last *mōsō* who knew such pieces. As a sighted, literate man, he was able to learn them from his blind father and document them in text-score notations. See Hyōdō (1999) for analysis of the notation and *fushi* system used in Morita's text-scores.

activities of twentieth-century *biwa hiki*. In my own discussions with three Higo-region musicians, I came to understand that they had little or no knowledge of many terms used by researchers to position their repertory of tales and songs in relation to canonical formations and to analytically describe the structure and compositional mechanisms of their performances. In what follows I will describe the terms in which scholarship has categorised the *biwa hiki*'s secular repertory and the same repertory as it has been characterised by Yamashika and other *biwa hiki*.

Research on the narrative repertory of Kyushu *biwa hiki* has been conducted in terms of the overarching historical genre of literary and performing arts, *katarimono*. This scholarly term has been used most broadly to denote narrative presented through one or more performative media—as verbal, music, dramatic or kinaesthetic performance. A narrower and, for the purpose of research on biwa, more practical use of the term has denoted orally performed narratives and their performance traditions, regardless of whether written versions of the repertories existed contemporaneously with their performance traditions. This model of *katarimono* encompasses genres of oral narrative from the ancient legends and "histories" of the Imperial house, thought to have been performed by professional reciters called *kataribe*, to the *naniwa-bushi* tales that were still hugely popular in mid-twentieth-century Japan.

The model is one that affords critical importance to the *biwa hōshi*, as the first professional performers of tales for whom both the use of a musical instrument and musical recitation techniques can be verified from documentary evidence (see Fukuda 1981, 108). The performative, clearly audience-orientated nature of *biwa hōshi*'s tales—in particular the *Heike* narrative corpus which underpinned representative musical and dramatic repertories from the fourteenth through nineteenth centuries—and the fact that those tales eventually came to be circulated in text versions enables the *biwa hōshi* to be positioned at the fountainhead of what comprises the central material of *katarimono* history, a body of narratives that became known throughout Japan chiefly through performative media but in time were also disseminated in iconographic and textual forms during the Muromachi and early Edo periods:

Most of the literary arts that emerged during the middle ages belong to the category of audience-orientated repertory literature. These arts were not canonical but repertory arts . . . aimed not at a practitioner-elite but at wide and disparate audiences of whom little or no demands were made, they had a great impact on Japanese society as a whole. It was this category that altered the course of Japan's literary history, and out of which was born Japan's first national literature. (Ruch 1977, 285-286)

This formulation by Ruch was dependent on historical genre concepts developed by Yanagita Kunio, Orikuchi Shinobu and other twentieth-century Japanese scholars who worked in and across the fields of literary and performing arts history. The medieval performers who disseminated this body of narratives to "wide and disparate audiences" were *biwa hōshi, goze, Kumano bikuni, sekkyō-shi* and *etoki*—among the principal figures whom Orikuchi had focussed upon as performers of narrative as a means of proselytising (*shōdō bungei*) (see "*Shōdō bungei josetsu*" in Orikuchi 1995).

Ruch stresses that the repertories borne by these artists were not canonical arts or literatures, but it was their popularisation through performance that eventually ensured they would become part of a literary and theatrical vernacular canon by the modern era. In accounts of music history, conversely, the centrality of canonical *katarimono* such as *Heike, gidayū-bushi* and various styles of *jōruri* played in kabuki and puppet theatre performance meant that in the 1960s, for leading music historians such as Tanabe Hisao, the primary perceived importance of *higobiwa* was as a remnant of "*jōruri* with biwa," suggestive of early forms in the performance lineage of the narrative music of the classical theatre.

As *katarimono*, and a form of oral narrative that continued to be practised in the second half of the twentieth century, the tales of Kyushu blind biwa players have also been viewed through lenses wrought from a body of theory about oral tradition and composition which was generated mid-century.[56] Here again, the most influential writings were those of Yanagita and Orikuchi, in the latter case produced largely in isolation from the major contemporary developments in Western oral

---

56. As will become apparent, not all secular items in the repertory are lengthy narratives—there are also shorter song forms, to which theories of oral composition are less applicable.

compositional research, namely the work of Parry and Lord (Lord 2000 [1960]). Whereas those two Western scholars approached questions of composition-in-performance under the influence of the structural analytical orientation of classical philology and some oral literature studies, the Japanese scholars approached *katarimono* and their performance with methods and concerns typical of literary history and indigenous folklore studies. Yanagita presented oral tradition as a realm of experience iconic of essential cultural identity and little touched by Japan's experiences of modernisation and Westernisation.[57] Both Yanagita and Orikuchi considered the relations between national mythology, regional folktales and written literature in terms of the dissemination and transformation of common materials by oral means. In works written during the mid-1930s Yanagita depicted oral and written literature as complementary sources for knowledge of cultural history and mythology. Without giving it extensive treatment, he also referred in passing to the practical mechanisms of oral transmission and the writing down of blind performers' texts (Yanagita 1946, 1947). Orikuchi further developed a theory of "oral tradition studies" (*kōtō denshōgaku*) based upon analysis of historical documents as records of oral traditions, and orally gathered data on contemporary folklore.[58] Their approaches to oral traditions of verbal art have served as frames of reference for later researchers; for example, Hyōdō Hiromi's analysis of *zatōbiwa* repertory as a resource for building a theory of both early *Heike* (*katari*) performance and the *Heike* textual tradition's formation within the framework of Muromachi-period politics was informed by—and in significant respects reacted against—Yanagita's and Orikuchi's concepts of *katarimono* (Hyōdō 1985a, 32–35; 2000, 283–292).

Among the *biwa hiki*'s narratives are versions of tales that were well known throughout Japan until the mid twentieth century because

57. Ivy (1995, chapter 3) discusses Yanagita's literary transformations of ethnographic data into the *Tōnō monogatari*. This aspect of Yanagita's treatment of folk culture, moreover, is an important instance of what Harootunian has discussed as an innately modernist response to a "loss of cultural reference" in the early twentieth century: "The appeal to native culture was, in fact, the very sign of capitalist modernity and its modernist ideological program rather than resistance to it" (Harootunian 2000, 49).
58. Demonstrations of this theory in application to the earliest records of Japanese history and mythology are contained in Orikuchi (1924, 1926) and many later works, including a study of folk culture on the island of Ikijima, near western Kyushu, which contains an account of *jijin mōsō* (Orikuchi 1954, 438ff).

they had been mainstays of the repertory of many narrative and stage arts since the medieval period as well as staple reading materials in school curricula until the Second World War. Among such tales of "national literature," as identified by Ruch, are episodes from the late-twelfth-century Genpei wars, such as *Ichi no Tani*, stories about figures in those wars such as Kagekiyo and Atsumori, folk legends such as *Dōjōji*, *Oeyama* and *Sumidagawa*, and *sekkyō* tales such as *Ishidōmaru*, *Shuntokumaru*, and *Oguri Hangan*. All these tales differ in various respects from the versions in which they exist in other performance traditions; indeed, it is the manifestation of multiple *oral* versions of tales that are well known as literary artefacts which incited prominent literature scholars' interest in Kyushu biwa players in the 1980s. The secular reportories have also included chronicles of Kyushu history,[59] relatively short items called *hauta* (short songs), and comic pieces known as *charimono*, *kerenmono* or *kokkeimono*.

The principal categories of repertory recognised by Higo-region *biwa hiki* interviewed during the 1970s and 1980s, or with whom I spoke in the early 1990s, include *hauta*, *charimono* and *gedai*.

Songs: *Hauta*

Most of the *biwa hiki* active in the 1970s and each of the three men still alive in the early 1990s knew a small number of single-section pieces that they referred to by a term common to several historical genres of music, *hauta*. Its contextual meaning is a "short" song, and such pieces are distinguished from the longer *danmono* by their use of only two pattern types (*fushi*) in performance, their relatively short duration of between ten and twenty minutes and by having a fixed text form. Texts for all of the documented *hauta* are in the 7 + 5 mora metre (with some single-mora deviations) that is a standard "line" (*ku*) unit for much Japanese poetry and song of the late Heian through Edo periods. For example, the opening lines of Yamashika's *Ikka Hiraite* as transcribed by Hyōdō in 1991 (180) are as follows:

---

59. Among such chronicles are accounts of both documented historical events, such as the battles described in *Kikuchi Kuzure* and ones that may be fictitious or legendary, such as the *Tamayohime Ichidaiki*.

ikka hiraite	*shihō no haru*	7 + 6
A flower blooms	Spring in all directions	
mina chiyo nare ya	*chiyo nare ya*	7 + 5
auspicious for all	how auspicious!	
kadomatsu iwaute	*futabashira*	8 + 5
A pine branch at the gate, celebrate	(between) the two pillars	
jitto hikishime	*mi-shimenawa*	7 + 5
pulled taut	the sacred rope.	

Comparison of multiple performances shows that the texts of *hauta* themselves had a far higher degree of fixity than texts of the *danmono* repertory. As such, the *hauta* have served a dual function: They were the first vocal items taught to apprentice *biwa hiki*, who would learn them by strictly imitating the teacher; and they were often used in door-to-door alms work (*kadozuke*, or *kadobiki* in the performers' terminology) as short items whose performance entailed only two kinds of musical pattern (see further chapter 5), the basic recitational form of *kotoba* or *katari* and the florid but aurally attractive *nagashi* pattern.[60] There were, moreover, a number of *hauta* sung only for special occasions such as the New Year celebrations.[61]

Charimono (*Kokkeimono* or *Kerenmono*) and *Kyokubiki*

The terms *charimono*, *kokkeimono* and *kerenmono* are variously used to denote a small number of comic narratives not considered to be *hauta*.[62] "*Chari*" is a common term in stage and narrative performance arts of Edo-period provenance and is probably derived from the verb *charu*, in a Kansai dialect, which means to fool around or to make jokes. "*Kokkei*" means humorous and "*keren*" means a gag or a trick. Yamashika and other former *biwa hiki* told me that they would sometimes present such pieces between longer recitations, when they

---

60. Hyōdō notes, moreover, that according to Yamashika they could often be shortened to just their opening and closing *nagashi* passages, if it seemed unlikely that longer performance would yield increased payment from a particular householder (1991, 180).

61. The text of a New Year's song (*shōgatsu no hauta*) sung by Yamashika is given in Kimura (1994, 223).

62. See de Ferranti (1996a) for a detailed treatment of *charimono*.

sensed that an audience was unresponsive and needed to be put at ease. Examples of *charimono* in Yamashika's repertory include *Tai no Mukoiri*, a story about a wedding between the son of a *tai* (sea bream) and the daughter of a *fugu* (blowfish), and the *Sakemochi Gassen*, in which armies of various types of *mochi* and *sake* from all over Japan do battle in a kitchen.

A related practice is *chari o ireru* (literally, "putting in *chari*"), which refers to the seasoning of *gedai* through the introduction of *chari*, generally in the form of short humorous interludes that highlighted nonsense, punning and ribaldry. The performance of such interludes was conditioned primarily by the musician's perception of the audience and its members' sense of propriety. Insufficient attentiveness to the make-up and mood of the audience might lead to a musician being scolded and abused for electing to throw in a *chari* scene: Yamashika spoke of audience members who would shout "Cut that stuff out!" (*so gyan wa yamero!*) when he had begun to recite in *chari* style. Use of *chari*, then, was optional for most tales, and contingent upon the performer's judgement of its potential success in the particular circumstances of a performance.

Closely related to *chari* was *kyokubiki*, which was a comical practice for entertaining with gags, rather than a category of songs or tales:

> After that you start the entertainment for the feast—you should do some *chari* and maybe some *kyokubiki*. The people who come to the *watamashi* have usually come to enjoy this part. Often one of them would call out "Hurry up and start the *chari!*" The *biwa hiki* is generally pretty relieved at this point, as the main part of his job's been done without hitch, so now he can have some *sake*. If the mood takes him he might grab a broom and play it like a biwa... There's the *osase gozen* and the *rokunin-gei* (which some people call the *hachinin-gei*) for these occasions, too. It was a lot of fun for both the audience and the *biwa hiki*. You just did what came to mind, and what felt right for the mood of the gathering. (Kimura 1994, 93–94)

Here the *kyokubiki* gags include the *hachinin-gei*, literally, the "eight-person performance," in which a *biwa hiki* would simultaneously perform on several instruments, by tying drums, bells and rattles to his biwa, then display his ability to play the instrument behind his back and head, as well as pluck the strings with razor blades and raw eggs, without cracking the shell. This is a form of gag documented for blind performers all over Japan and is sometimes also called the *rokunin-gei* or *shichinin-gei* (six- or seven-person performance).[63]

Gedai, Danmono, Kuzure and Their Classification

Biwa hiki usually refer to the longer narratives which comprise the bulk of their repertory as *gedai*, a widely used term for a play or "piece" in *kabuki* and other Edo-period stage arts.[64] While there are a small number of *gedai* tales made up of only a single section (for example, *Dōjōji* and *Ono no Komachi*), the majority of *gedai* comprise several discrete sections, referred to variously as *dan* or *seki*,[65] each of which lasts from thirty to ninety minutes in performance. The longest tales of the repertory have eight or more such sections, so their full performance takes many hours. Each section presents a major episode in the tale, and short breaks are taken before going on to a successive *dan* or another tale. The expression *danmono*, while rarely used by performers, has been used by some writers to distinguish the longer narratives from *hauta*. *Danmono* is a repertory term common to several genres of traditional music, including *jōruri* musical narrative, but would appear to have been introduced to *biwa hiki* by researchers during the last forty years.[66]

Another term often used in secondary sources on both *higobiwa* and past practice in other regions of Kyushu is *kuzure*. The word derives from the verb *kuzureru*, "to fall down," and may be translated as "collapse." It is not recorded as a performance term in any musical

---

63. See Groemer (1999, 38–39) for graphic descriptions of a variety of *hachinin-gei* performed by blind *bosama* in Tōhoku in the early twentieth century. In Japanese see Narita (1985b).

64. Ōkawa Susumu and Hashiguchi Keisuke both used this term in my presence. Ōkawa, it should be noted, seemed comfortable using the words *gedai* and *danmono* interchangeably.

65. While perhaps an older expression—in terms of its localised usage in the Higo region—in comparison to *dan*, "*seki*" is the same one used by many *naniwa-bushi* reciters to refer to a similar concept of structural division and may also have been adopted relatively recently through *biwa* singers' well-documented familiarity with *naniwa-bushi* of the 1920s and 1930s. See Ga (1972, 29) and Murayama (1986, 430), on Yamashika's skill in *naniwa-bushi* singing. Hashiguchi and Ōkawa also told me of their love for the style, and Hashiguchi sang part of a *naniwa-bushi* tale for me.

66. Of the three men I worked with, only Ōkawa Susumu would regularly use the term *danmono*. The first use of the term by a scholar that I am aware of is that of Tanabe Hisao, in his report to the Bunkachō about the *higobiwa* tradition (Tanabe 1963a).

traditions other than biwa recitation.⁶⁷ *"Kuzure"* has been used with four designations: for some of the longer *gedai* or *danmono* narratives sung by *biwa hiki* in the Higo region; for the practice of performing secular narratives and songs, regardless of their length, by *mōsō*;⁶⁸ and, in *satsumabiwa*, both in the title of some of the earliest documented repertory items (battle tales such as the *Akahoshi Kuzure* and the *Kino Kuzure*⁶⁹) and for the vigorous, flamboyant vocal and instrumental patterns performed when scenes of conflict and battle are recounted.

The historian Nagai Akiko presented evidence for the Chikuzen and Chikugo regions that early-Edo-period *mōsō* commanded a repertory of *kuzure* tales of battle whose original function may have been to allay the ghosts of warriors, as is thought to have been the case for tales in the *heike* narrative corpus (2002, 52, 62). In contrast to its widespread historical usage in northern Kyushu, *kuzure* seems to have had a more limited application in Higo. Two of the singers with whom I worked used this term only in reference to a tale considered to be the oldest of the *higobiwa* repertory, the *Kikuchi Kuzure*. The third singer, Ōkawa Susumu, said that he had never heard the term.⁷⁰ It is possible, nevertheless, that *kuzure* was formerly more widely used by some *biwa hiki* in Higo as, in the dialect of at least one locale, the Aso region of central Higo, the common expression for a professional biwa player was *"kuzure katari"* (Higobiwa Hozonkai 1991, 7).⁷¹

67. *Kuzushi*, the term for an unrelated popular song form of the late Edo period, is generally written with the same character (崩).
68. This is reflected in the term *kuzurebiwa*, used by some writers to refer to performance of tales by Kyushu *mōsō*, in particular those of the northern regions. Kimura Yūshō wrote in the early 1960s that *"Kuzure* are not unique to *higobiwa*, but are found all over Kyushu, which suggests one could even call the practice as a whole 'kuzurebiwa'"* (original undated manuscript, quoted in Kimura 1994, 160).
69. The *Kino Kuzure* is also listed by Shimazu as an early *satsumabiwa* repertory item found in Edo-period sources (2000, 33).
70. Interview of November 25, 1991. In Hyōdō's account of Yamashika's repertory (1991, 183), the *Kikuchi Kuzure* is listed as the only one of forty-five repertory items in which the word *kuzure* occurs. Only Kimura Yūshō writes of the word's use in the title of another tale, *Yanagawa Kuzure*, as an alternative name for the piece *Yanagawa Sōdō* (Higobiwa Hozonkai 1991, 16–17).
71. See Gorai (1972), pages 129, 158 and 173, respectively, wherein the selections from Morita Shōjō's *danmono* texts are headed *"Kuzure (biwa sekkyō = danmono),"* and two sets of *hauta* texts are also headed *"Kuzure."*

Yamashika Yoshiyuki, Ōkawa Susumu and Hashiguchi Keisuke classified *gedai* variously, according to the social status of the narrative's main protagonists or to the tale's overall emotional register. The most extensive categorisation was that described to me by Ōkawa:

i. *heikemono*: tales about the Gempei Wars between the Heike and the Genji clans

ii. *bushimono*: tales about famous *bushi*, that is, warriors or *samurai*

iii. *kassenmono*: tales favoured for their scenes of fighting or battle

iv. *sanjakumono* or *tōzokumono*: tales about criminals of the Edo-period underworld

v. *Bukkyō-biwa* tales: literally "Buddhism biwa," that is, tales with a specifically didactic intent ("something like *sekkyō* with the biwa," as Ōkawa put it)

vi. *zokumono*: tales about the lives of commoners, either farmers or townspeople of the merchant or artisan classes

vii. *ureimono*: tales favoured for scenes of personal tragedy and suffering

viii. *charimono/kerenmono/kokkeimono*: tales primarily enjoyed for their humorous scenes

In Ōkawa's usage there was clearly a hierarchical relationship among categories, such that narratives concerning persons of high social standing, including *heikemono*, *bushimono* and, to a lesser extent, *kassenmono* pieces, were considered to have the greatest degree of formality. As the most highly valued repertory items they were transmitted by his teachers with the stipulation that their words and musical patterning (*fushizuke*) not be altered in any way, in other words, that they *not* be subject to oral compositional elaboration.[72]

Yamashika Yoshiyuki and Hashiguchi Keisuke tended to use classificatory terms less specifically and knew of only four of Ōkawa's

---

72. According to Ōkawa, this was because the most formal tales of the repertory had been written down in authoritative versions (as a *daihon*) by a literate figure in his lineage, Miyagawa Kyōgaku the First. For all other tales, textual and musical variance arising from oral composition were allowable (see further de Ferranti 2003). As Yamashika's apprenticeship was curtailed after two years, it is not known whether his teacher would have followed a similar practice.

categories: *kassenmono, ureimono, Bukkyō-biwa* and *charimono*. Like Ōkawa, Yamashika spoke of a hierarchy of repertory categories that reflected Edo-period criteria of social status, with tales about samurai-class figures ranked highest. For Yamashika, the distinction between tales about samurai and ones about townsmen and merchants or farmers had clear performative implications, such that what he called the *jōruri* style of performance was only permissible in tales of samurai and feudal lords.[73]

Two *gedai* are recognised by performers as the oldest pieces in the *higobiwa* repertory and form a special group of sorts, although they are not placed in a separate category: *Kikuchi Kuzure* (also called *Kikuchi Gassen*, and *Shimabara Gunki*[74]) and *Miyako Gassen Chikushi Kudari* (also called *Tamayohime Chikushi Kudari*, and *Botan Chōja*). The *Kikuchi Kuzure* relates the events in the 1570s that led to a battle between the Shimazu of Satsuma, allied with the Waifu of Kikuchi, and the warlord Ryūzōji Takanobu of Hizen, in which the latter was defeated and killed. *Miyako Gassen Chikushi Kudari* is a tale about the origins of the name Tamana (a major town and shire north of Kumamoto) in the trials and salvation of Princess Tamayo, a *mōshigo* (a child considered to have been received through a deity's benevolence) of the Kiyomizu Kannon in Kyoto.

The repertory of *biwa hiki* was clearly affected by changes in rural lifestyle and tastes. By the late 1920s, the widespread use of wind-up record players, and in turn radio, meant that new styles of narrative popularised by star performers in Tokyo and Osaka became well known even in rural districts.[75] Yamashika, Ōkawa and Hashiguchi had been fond of *naniwa-bushi* in their youth, and had learnt a number of popular tales of that genre so that they might present them in adapted form. While none of these three musicians grouped such repertory in a clear-cut category, Yamashika would sometimes speak of *shimpa-mono* to refer to narratives that dealt with events since the start of Meiji; these included pieces likely to have been based on *shimpageki* dramas (which

73. Interview of May 22, 1990.
74. It is referred to by this title in Noda (1935, 27). Note that the early satsumabiwa *danmono* that recounts much the same tale, the *Akahoshi Kuzure*, is also called the *Shimabara Gassen*.
75. For example, see Groemer (1999, 43–44, 241–243) on the tremendous popularity of *naniwa-bushi* in Tōhoku and its influence on various regional performing arts. On *naniwa-bushi* in the Chikugo region where Yamashika did much of his work with biwa, see Sakata (1992).

became known in regional Kyushu through performances in the vibrant theatre districts of large towns, among them nearby Ōmuta) and on new compositions by sighted, literate practitioners of *higobiwa* such as the early twentieth-century individuals described above.

Narrative Language and Style

Standardisation of performative and literary language was of tremendous importance for the dissemination of narrative repertory in performance traditions of disparate regions. Although *biwa hiki* practised for the most part in areas of rural Kyushu renowned for their idiosyncratic dialects, the language used in all narrative texts, with the exception of some *charimono*, is that of standard Japanese. Colloquial speech forms of standard Japanese are also used occasionally but, as in most forms of popular Japanese narrative, there is little of the vocabulary and grammatical forms of dialect that constituted the everyday language of both the *biwa hiki* and his audience.[76] As Hyōdō has noted, this is a feature common to *katarimono* in many regions of Japan, and reflects the fact that

> both the performance and reception of *katarimono* are a kind of activity outside daily life, and this is related to the fact that the performers, too—as *hijōmin* ["non-common" people]—lead an existence which is out of step with that of ordinary people in the local society. (Hyōdō 1991, 26)

In *danmono*, narrative style is unlike that of *heikyoku*, in that narratives are structured in sequential episodes (*dan*), each of which can be over an hour in duration, while *heikyoku* repertory items are performed as single "pieces";[77] the late Heian- and Kamakura-period language

---

[76]. The importance of maintaining standard speech-forms in performance was made clear to me by Ōkawa Susumu, who expressed his annoyance while listening to the second of his 1975 performances of *Shiga Dan Shichi*, when he heard that he had made the "mistake" of using the dialect form, "*gamadasu*," for the verb "*hataraku*" (to work).

[77]. It is likely that before the Edo period, *Heike* narrative performance was less rigid in structure, such that the bounds of individual items were less well defined and sequential performance in a manner similar to the *dan* of a *higobiwa* item was possible; this is one of Hyōdō's conclusions in a series of three articles that attempts to infer aspects of medieval practice of *Heike* from the late-twentieth-century practice of *biwa hiki* (1991, 1993, 1999). See also de Ferranti (1997 and 2003).

forms retained in *heikyoku* do not occur, and terms for the *fushi* (music and performance patterns, some of which carry requirements for particular content and language registers) segments that shape the tales as aural events are not held in common. Nor is it like the styles of biwa-accompanied narrative that have been performed widely by literate musicians since Meiji, *satsumabiwa* and *chikuzenbiwa*. Since at least the early twentieth century, repertory items in those styles have been referred to as *biwa uta* (songs), for they are less than thirty minutes long in performance, largely adhere to the poetic metre of 7 + 5 syllable lines (*ku*) in the way that *hauta* of *higobiwa* do, and tend to focus upon vivid depiction of a number of isolated events in the tale. Narratives in the oldest stratum of *satsumabiwa* repertory, some of which may date from the seventeenth century, tend to be longer, divided into two or more *dan*, and provide more detail and narrative continuity; in this regard they are closer in narrative style to the *danmono* and *kuzure* of the blind traditions, and their designation as *kuzure* in some sources testifies to their historical proximity to *danmono* narratives performed by the blind in other regions of Kyushu.[78]

Narrative Articulation

How did the local detail of the text of a narrative form units meaningful for performers and listeners? Common terms for formal units rendered in translation as lines of poetry or phrases of poetic prose—units formed from conventional metric schemes of groups of moras—were not used by *biwa hiki*, and there was no functional equivalent for it in their parlance. In the absence of any written or memorised text form, and of any small-scale units for text segmentation proffered by *biwa hiki*, semantic, metrical and performative criteria must be taken into account in the identification of the smallest units of narrative discourse. I will address the first two of these criteria here and describe performance-based articulation in chapter 4.

Semantic articulation—The boundaries of semantic units are unambiguous throughout most of a performance. The text is made up of sentences and clauses whose unity is readily apparent and is lacking in poetic devices that create the ambiguity so common in Japanese

---

78. See Shimazu (2000, 15, 33) for information on early-nineteenth-century *satsumabiwa* sources that include several *kuzure*.

written poetry, such as enjambement and the use of pivot-words. This can be said despite the fact that many sentences are distributed over two or more performatively articulated units (hereafter called phrases), separated by pauses and strokes on the biwa.

Metrical articulation—Poetic or prosodic "metre" established through segmentation based on units of 7 or 5 moras is a common formal principle in Japanese (other than Ryūkyū or Okinawan) performed narrative and most poetry of pre-twentieth-century origin. Biwa narratives include two kinds of text, those in which no regular metrical groupings are apparent and those in which text-units of 7 or 5 moras predominate. In the latter case, passages in consecutive 7 + 5 phrases sometimes occur, but chains of freely mixed units of 7 or 5 are more common. Mora regulation is an important factor whenever it occurs because it usually underlines semantic formations. Its significance for listeners and performers alike, therefore, is as a poetic form for the organisation of narrative content on a small-scale level (the level equivalent to the "line" or *ku* in most written forms of poetry). It operates as a regulatory principle regardless of whether performative segmentation reinforces metrical segmentation; in other words, it operates sometimes in support of, and at other times in conflict with, performed phrases.

Metrically non-regulated text can be either declaimed in a manner close to speech or recited, but metrically organised text is either recited or sung (these modes of vocal delivery are defined in chapter 4). In metrical text segments, standard seven- or five-mora units are often slightly deviated from, but the majority of deviations involve shortening or lengthening of units by a single mora, as is evident in the following extract from Ōkawa Susumu's *Shiga Dan Shichi*:

fusoku nakereba ninin no onko	7 + 7
They lack nothing, and soon there are two children,	
ane no Osato ni imoto no Onobu	7 + 7
first Osato, then her sister Onobu.	
ane ga torite jūroku sai	6 + 6
The elder girl is now just 16	

Deviation by a single mora is also evident in the first two text-units of a passage that Yamashika sang as a *nagashi* pattern (see chapter 4) in a 1975 performance of the first *dan* of *Kikuchi Kuzure*:

4 moras	Isogeba	Hurrying
8	Kikuchi no Nobu-ko to	Lord (Taka)nobu of Kikuchi
5	kagiri nashi	against all odds
7	hi kazu mikka ni	three days
5	ataru hi wa	on that day
7	Kikuchi Wai-fu ni	in the Wai district of Kikuchi
5	tsuki ni keru	he arrived

In the following fragment from a performance of *Dōjōji*, the text metre is less regular but nonetheless is dominated by units of 7 or 8 moras:[79]

kaette mairanu	mō wa sankei mo	8 + 8
he's not returned,	though his pilgrimage	
sunde iru hazu		7
ought to be finished		
yūbe atari ni	kaeru ka to omoeba	7 + 9
by last night	he should have come back	
ikkanai ka na	kage mo katachi mo miezu	7 + 10
this is no good,	but there's no shadow, no trace of him	

Textual Formulaity

In both Yamashika's and Ōkawa's oral compositional practices, formulaic text occurs as "formulas" and "formulaic expressions," as oral-formulaic theory defines these terms (Lord 2000 [1960]). Formulas are text phrases that are the same in all occurrences, while formulaic expressions constitute a common initial sequence of words followed by alternative words or sequences of words suited to the content of a particular tale and scene. Most formulaic material of both sorts occurs as syllabically regulated text. For example, the following phrases sung by Ōkawa in both *Shiga Dan Shichi* and *Azekakehime* are all framed as single- or double-line combinations of 7- and 5-mora units:

---

79. This fragment is from the performance by Yamashika presented in chapter 4 (recorded by Hyōdō and included on *Nihon Dentō Geinō Shinkō Zaidan* 2007), but in this case with text units set out to show the underlying metre rather than to reflect performative articulation of phrases.

nō ika ni [*imoto no Onobu/Sayoteru yo*]	5 + 7/ 5 + 5
watto bakari ni [*nakidedashi/nakifuseru*]	7 + 5
aware to iu mo nakanaka ni *mōsu bakari zo nakari keru*	7 + 5, x 2

Syllabic regulation in 7- and 5-mora units is characteristic of formulaic text even within named performance segments (*fushi*) that are non-regulated overall.

Formulaic materials are usually performed as the same type of *fushi* in different repertory items; therefore formulas involve fixity of both verbal and musical expression. For example, the two single-line and one double-line formulas of Ōkawa given above always occur in segments performed as the *fushi* that he called *katari urei, fushi urei* and *otoshi*, respectively.

Even from the relatively small sample of transcribed tales available, a comparison of texts by Yamashika, Ōkawa and Hashiguchi yields some formulaic material that may have been part of a common "stock" available to *biwa hiki* in central Kyushu. In the following examples of material common to two or more singers, distinction is made between formulas, formulaic expressions and short fixed passages:

Formulas

    i. *nukeba tamajiru kōri no yaiba*   drawing his blade, which glints like ice
    ii. *kiryō sugata mo yo ni sugure*   his appearance was beyond compare

Formulaic expressions

    i. *Ato ni nokorishi* [*Kiyohime/Atsumori-ko/shūto haha-oya/tsuma ya ko wa*]
[Kiyohime/Atsumori/the mother-in-law/ wife and children] remained.

This expression is sung either immediately after or before a *nagashi* pattern by both Yamashika and Ōkawa, in description of characters who remain behind after others have left the scene.

    ii. *Koko ni aware wa/aware wa koko ni* [*Kiyohime/ Yotarō-dono*]
    At this, pity poor [Kiyohime/Yotarō].

This single line is used as a summary expression of the suffering that a character has just begun to experience and in Yamashika's practice is performed as the *ō-okuri* pattern.

Fixed passage
mizu wa hōen no ki ni shitagau	As water is shaped by its vessel
hito wa zen aku no tomo ni yoru	people are shaped by the moral worth of their friends—
toka ya kōre wa kojin no tatoe nari	so say the proverbs of the ancients.

This is a fixed formulaic passage for the short introductory text called *kingen* (see further chapter 4).

The heterogeneous nature of the singers' training and professional experiences may well account for the small amount of materials common to their stocks; a larger sample of texts from singers who were trained in or active in the same area might yield more such material.

Rites

Yamashika was unequivocal about his belief that blind biwa players had been ritualists first and foremost in the past:

> The original job of *biwa hiki* was to worship the gods and Buddhas, but already by the time I was a young man, there were very few people who knew how to do that properly. And of course I knew almost nothing about it because I didn't complete my training. Even so, my Amakusa teacher did almost no sacred work as a *biwa hiki*. . . . In my teacher's house there wasn't a Benzaiten, nor any of the gods that have to do with biwa. He did hardly any *kamigoto* [ritual work]. (Kimura 1994, 94)

Yet Yamashika did not learn the Kōjin exorcism rite until well after he left his apprenticeship and was first engaged to perform it in 1942, some twenty years after he started to acquire skills as a *biwa hiki* (Kimura 1994, 96). That fact, and his comments on the place of ritual work in his and his teachers' activities, corroborates the view that while in many parts of rural Kyushu biwa playing continued to be associated with the ritual work of *mōsō* until well into the twentieth century, in the former Higo region, for most people . . . the religious aspect of biwa playing seems not to have been recognised as all that important. In other words, in Kumamoto Prefecture, [the biwa players'] sacred activities were much depleted by Shōwa 10 [1935], and their performances for entertainment were more prominent in people's consciousness. (Yasuda 1991, 12)

By no means, however, should it be thought that *kamigoto* (the most common of the *biwa hiki*'s words for ritual work) was discontinued in the Higo and Amakusa regions. A variety of ceremonies, including the above-mentioned *harai*, exorcism or blessing rites for the hearth (*kamado-barai*), earth (*Jijin-barai*), wells (*Suijin-barai*) and for new houses and buildings (*watamashi*), as well as rainmaking ceremonies (*amagoi*), continued to be carried out by some *biwa hiki* as an integral part of their livelihoods until the 1960s. One *biwa hiki* of the Yamaga region, Tanaka Tōgo (1906–1989), thought of himself primarily as a ritualist and considered his performances of historical tales, too, to be solemn occasions for ethical and religious edification.[80] By contrast, Ōkawa Susumu, of northern Kagoshima Prefecture, referred to ritual practice as "*Jijinbiwa*," something distinct from what he saw as his own principal professional activity, peformance of *zashikibiwa*. Notwithstanding, having learned several ritual texts in the 1930s, Ōkawa occasionally engaged in *harai* activity even after the Second World War, when his work as a masseur and acupuncturist prevented him from doing *zashikibiwa* performances.

In Yamashika's case, secular narrative performance had from the first been the primary activity of his professional life—as it had also been for his teacher in Amakusa—but he soon found out that *biwa hiki* could be called upon to conduct a variety of rites. His sense of the importance of that task, as he explained it to Kimura, began with an experience of being taunted by an old woman for not knowing a particular section of the *watamashi* rite (1994, 90). As someone striving to achieve self-sufficiency as a *biwa hiki* at a time when diversification of leisure activities meant that demand for his services was relatively low even in remote rural districts, he did all he could to acquire proficiency in *kamigoto* performance so that more work would be offered to him.

---

80. Personal communication, Yasuda Muneo, 1992. See also Hyōdō (1993, 16).

Fundamental to the persistence of these rites in rural Kyushu is the fact that none of them had origin in or were earmarked by Buddhist institutions as solely Buddhist rituals; as such, all of the ritual activities of *biwa hiki*, and all except the formal group rituals (*hōraku hōyō*) of *mōsō*, are better understood as manifestations of folk religion, in other words as part of the typical practice of people throughout Japanese history, as distinct from those of institutional Buddhism and Shinto. A movement for separation of Buddhist and indigenous religious practices (*shinbutsu bunri*) gathered great momentum by the Meiji era, so that the Department of Rites (*jingikan*) issued laws that distanced rites related to the ideology of Imperial sanctity from the "foreign" cosmology of Buddhism and Buddhist clergy in the second year of the new government, 1869.[81] Prior to Meiji, the religious lives of most Japanese, and certainly the great majority of inhabitants of rural areas, were a mosaic of indigenous, Buddhist, Daoist, Yin-Yang cosmology and other beliefs and practices accumulated over many centuries, which scholars have collectively termed Japanese folk religion (*minzoku shūkyō* or *minkan shinkō*):

> Religious practices the Japanese have developed and maintained in response to daily needs—practices generally called "folk religion"— occupy them even more than the institutional religions . . . *Minzoku shukyō* is essentially indigenous "primitive" religion onto which elements from Shinto, Buddhism, Taoism, yin-yang dualism, Confucianism and other religions have been grafted. (Miyake 2001, 161)

In Kyushu, rites for such "daily needs" were performed by a variety of figures, including blind biwa players: *mōsō* and *zatō*. None of these were rigidly defined as either Shintoist or Buddhist ritualists until well into the modern era. Probably the most common among them were the *yamabushi* or *shugenja*, adherents of the complex of ascetic practices generically called Shugendō. Like *mōsō* and *zatō*, they provided impor-

---

81. In most regions, this campaign provoked attacks, and the wholesale destruction of temples associated with certain groups; Kagoshima, in the former Satsuma domain, was one of the regions in which razing of temples was widespread. Tamamuro Fumio has written of the mid-to-late nineteenth century that "One is tempted to say that those faiths central to the masses during the Edo period were eradicated . . ." and estimates that "two out of every three temples that existed during the [early] Edo period were burned to the ground as a result of the suppression of Buddhism" (1997, 504–505).

tant services for rural communities in many regions, and in their rites Buddhist, Daoist, *onmyōdō* or *on'yōdō* (*in-yō* or *yin-yang* cosmology and its attendant rites) and indigenous elements were inextricably embedded. *Yamabushi* had important roles to play in *matsuri* (festivals) for *kami* at local small shrines, but in northern Kyushu they sometimes competed with biwa players for the custom of local householders, as Kōjin rites were among those most frequently performed (ibid., 64; see also Nagai 2002, 89).[82]

With respect to the Edo period, the social historian Katō Yasuaki claimed that, as ritualists, *mōsō* in northern Kyushu had centred their activities on rites for their essentially agrarian constitutency and freely blended elements of all the traditions that contributed to the beliefs of the rural masses. They staked out a professional territory different to that of regular Buddhist priests, whose typical functions in the Edo period were the conduct of funerals and formal *hōe* (ceremonies within temples; 1974, 90). From a post-Meiji perspective, the ritual activities of both the Chikuzen- and Satsuma-region *mōsō* and of *zatō* such as Yamashika are profoundly hybrid in nature. They are rites and beliefs shaped prior to the ideologically driven schism imposed by government in the late nineteenth century, and their contents reflect a diverse array of sources. The inseparability of such elements in the ritual life of rural Kyushu and the activities of blind biwa players is demonstrated by Yamashika's explanation for why *mōsō* were called "biwa priests" (*biwa bōzu*):

> Most people don't believe in *kami* anymore. But they're really there. A *biwa bōzu* [*mōsō*] can tell you about that. Why do we call them "*biwa bōzu*"? Because Kōjin-san likes the biwa. (Kimura 1994, 98)

Here Kōjin, the deity of the oven and a *kami* of Japanese origin rather than one adopted from the pantheon of East Asian Buddhism, is cited as the basis for the *mōsō*'s qualification as Buddhist clergy.

---

82. The functions of *mōsō*, *biwa hiki* and some *yamabushi* were so similar that, in the late 1700s, comments of the following sort were made about sighted *mōsō* who had inherited a *danka* through their family: "Those *mōsō* who can see seem to be much the same as *yamabushi* (*mōsō no me no mie sōro mono ni shika, yamabushi no tagui naru goza sōro yoshi*)" (Nagai 2002, 126).

Jijin, Kōjin, Suijin and Their Manifestations

In the ritual culture of south-western Japan, Jijin and Kōjin have been *kami* of great importance to agrarian life. Both are manifest in multiple and regionally various contexts, one of which is as *yashikigami*, an array of deities whose favour is needed for the well-being of a family, household or small community, its lands and its homes. Both *kami* have existed in broader contexts as deities in both institutional and folk ritual contexts beyond the south-west regions of the archipelago (Takami 2006, 5–12), and the texts and ritual paraphernalia of blind biwa players' rites for these *kami* reflect their syncretic background.

As an Asian Continental and Buddhist deity, Jijin's pedigree goes back beyond the earliest sutras to Hindu texts such as the *Rig-veda*, in which she bears the name *drdhaprthivi*, goddess of the Earth and the mother of Indra. The deity's formal Buddhist titles are Jiten (a translation of the Chinese *ditiān*) and Kenrō Jishin/Jijin. As such she is venerated in the Kenrō Jijin-bon of the eighth chapter of the *Konkōmyōsaishō-ō Kyō* (the *Suvarnaprabhaasa* or "Sutra of Golden Light"), a sutra esteemed in early Japanese Buddhism as one of three whose recitation provided protection for the realm.[83] It is as Kenrō Jishin, *kami* of all the earth and its waters, that Jijin is venerated in both formal group rites of the *mōsō* sects, and the *shakumon* tales transmitted in similar forms by Satsuma, Hyūga and Chikuzen region *mōsō*.

The vernacular names by which Jijin is called vary, so that Jishin and Jichin are both common. Each of these pronunciations is represented with a different set of Sino-Japanese characters when written, the literal meanings of which are "earth deity" (地神), "earth heart (or soul)" (地心), and "earth's calm/ease" (地鎮). In central Kyushu, the name "Jikonjin" was often used:

> In a great house, in the middle of the rice paddies, in the mountains, and in the fields too, there is the god of the earth, Jikonjin. People believe that they own the land, but that's not so. If you build a house without regard to Jikonjin's presence, the luck of the house will turn bad . . . Jikonjin is invited to the celebrations. On that day a *nawabari* is hung and all is finished. Originally it all had to be done by a *kengyō-san*, and these days it's done by a *kannushi*, if it's done at all. But people used to come here to ask me to do it, too. (Kimura 1994, 95)

---

83. In *mōsō* practice, this sutra is recited as the central segment of the Jōjuin sect's annual ceremony in honour of the founder, Gensei, and in shortened form as a portion of the Jijinsai or earth-breaking rite.

The historian of Satsuma region *mōsō*, Murata Hiroshi, wrote that

> in Satsuma Jijin is called "Jigansaa," and he is worshipped at a place at the base of a tree at one corner of the house—usually the northwest corner. He is a *kami* who often directs his anger at people. It's believed that if human waste is thrown on that place by mistake,[84] the genitals of the person who threw it will soon start to hurt! (Murata 1974, 5)

A similar strength of belief in the deity of the ground on which a house is built is reflected in the advice that Yamashika gave to a household stricken by illness:

> [He told them] "This is happening because you've made your dwelling by beating and packing down the earth that belongs to the Jikonjin of this land . . ." (Kimura 1994, 96)

Kōjin, venerated as the *kami* of fire, in particular the stove, oven, hearth or kiln (*kamado*), has been worshipped in Japan since at least the earliest period of Buddhist history and has a place in Shugendō and esoteric rituals of the Tendai and Nichiren sects.[85] As such, the deity has been associated with major Buddhist sites, such as the complex and site of pilgrimage now called Kiyose Kōjin, near Takarazuka, since the early Heian period. Major performance traditions of *Kōjin kagura* have been important for local ritual practice in central and western Honshu, where Kōjin is commonly regarded as a *yashikigami*. Called simply *kamado-gami* (or *kamado no kami*) in daily usage, Kōjin appears to be a thoroughly syncretic entity; despite the formal title of Sanbō Daikōjin (protector of the three Buddhist Treasures, the Sanbō), there is no evidence for veneration of such a Buddhist deity outside Japan, and Kōjin is not significantly similar to deities of fire, the oven or kitchen as they exist in Continental Asian religious practice. Scholars have distinguished Kōjin's manifestations as *kami* of fire and the oven (*uchi Kōjin*) from those as *kami* of the house and village properties (*soto Kōjin*), and it is the former type that is by far most prevalent in Kyushu and south-western Japan (Fukuoka-ken Kyōiku Iin Kai 1983, 94). As I have shown, Kōjin's identity is intermixed with that of Jijin in regions

---

84. "Night soil" of this kind was often used as fertiliser.
85. A description of the fire deity is recorded in the *Zoku Nihongi*, of the 3rd year of Tempyō (731). Both the *Kōjin-kyō* and *Jijin-kyō* are contained in the *Shugen-Seiten* collection of Shugendō liturgy.

of Kyushu where *mōsō* were active in rites for both deities.[86]

As two of the most important *kami* in Kyushu regional belief, both Jijin and Kōjin are most often worshipped through *saimon* (prayers to and in many cases about an individual *kami*) and *gikyō* (folk sutras), in terms that acknowledge the *kami*'s antiquity and awe-inspiring powers, but give them an immediacy and intimacy for those who petition their favour. This was so regardless of whether the celebrant was a *mōsō*, *biwa hiki* or *yamabushi*. Most of the texts and symbolic paraphernalia of these rites include elements of the Buddhist canon (for example, the Heart Sutra is chanted in almost all of the ceremonies) along with folk texts whose contents suggest the influence of Taoist and Yin-Yang (*onmyōdō*) divination ritual practices in Kyushu. Such elements in Kyushu folk rites are often attributed to the influence of *yamabushi* in medieval rural Japan, and in turn of *onmyōdō* practitioners upon *yamabushi*.[87]

Jijin and Kōjin are closely related to another *kami* of fundamental importance for agrarian life, Suijin, the deity of water. A deity of rain, rivers and ponds (and thereby often related to Benzaiten and various snake and dragon deities), Suijin is in some manifestations classed as a *yashikigami* because of the importance of wells for each rural household. The inseparability in folk religious practice of Suijin and Jijin, in particular, is evident in the fact that *mōsō* in all parts of Kyushu—and *biwa hiki* with ritual skills—were required to carry out Suijin rites (*suijin matsuri*) and *amagoe* rain-making rites in addition to the *Jijin-* and *Kōjin-barai*.[88]

---

86. See Nagai's description of the blurring of Kōjin and Jijin's identities in the Chikuzen region (2002, 43–44).

87. See Lancashire (2002, 47–48). Despite its brevity, this is probably the most important source in English on evidence for the influence of both practices and belief systems in *kagura* performance.

88. A cosmological basis for this is expressed in the text for the second half of a *shakumon* ritual narrative known variously as "Nehan" and "Shaka no dan" in the traditions of both Jōrakuin- and Jōjuin-sect *mōsō*; Suijin, as *kami* of the sea and rivers (together with other *kami* of trees, rocks and roads) is said to be but a manifestation of Kenrō Jijin, who must be venerated appropriately if Shakyamuni's remains are to be buried or scattered in any of these places (Narita 1985a, 136–141; Murata 1974, 7–8).

Harai Rites for Kōjin and Jijin

Kimura Yūshō used to joke that "Kōjin-san calms down when he hears the sound of the biwa. It makes him easy to fool." (Kimura 1994, 98)

Harai rituals are an attempt to placate a deity or spirit who has both negative, harmful aspects and positive, beneficial ones. When the malevolent aspect of a spirit is manifested, the exorcism rite may involve the invocation of the spirit through or from the body of an afflicted individual. In this kind of rite mediums are usually required to invoke the spirit. In doing so, they may become possessed by it and in turn placate it or drive it away. The more common kind of exorcism is not of this kind, but is a preventative ritual that takes place seasonally or annually and involves appeasement of a spirit or deity's potential malevolence through the offering of ceremonial objects, the intoning of texts and the sounding of instruments. This is done in the understanding that if the spirit has been satisfied with the ritual's performance, those on whose behalf it has been carried out will be safe from the spirit's potential displeasure and harmful powers for a certain period of time.

The two *harai* that have been the core public rituals of the blind biwa traditions, in the sense that they were the rites for which *biwa hiki* and *mōsō* alike were most often engaged by individual householders, are the *Jijin-barai*, for the earth deity, and the *Kōjin-barai*, also called *kamado-barai*, for the fire or oven deity. On the whole, an important point of distinction in regional practice is that the *Kōjin-barai* was most common in northern Kyūshū and Higo (and for this reason the *mōsō* tradition in Chikuzen-Chikugo sources is often called *Kōjinbiwa*, both locally and in several scholarly publications),[89] while the *Jijin-barai* was prevalent in the Satsuma and Hyūga regions. Yamashika explained to Kimura Rirō that "the *watamashi*, *Kōjin-barai* and *Jijin-barai* were all similar, as rituals in praise of the household gods. They all involved placating the gods, and cleansing impurity" (1994, 94). This was achieved by a combination of acts: material and symbolic offerings to the deity, recitation of sacred texts with and without biwa,

---

89. See, for example, Kokuritsu Gekijō (1970) and the *"Kōjinbiwa"* segment, by Murata Hiroshi, of the *Nihon ongaku sōsho*, volume 5 (Kokuritsu Gekijō 1990, 183–187).

and performance of at least one *dan* of a tale at a community gathering on the same land where the formal rite had taken place.

Yamashika's *Kōjin-barai* (or *Kamado-barai*)

In published sources on *biwa hiki* practice there are no detailed accounts of the *kamado-* or *Kōjin-barai*. The following is based on a brief account by Ga (1972, 30–31), a *kamado-barai* performed by Yamashika that I observed in April 1989 at a house in the town of Yanagawa (Fukuoka Prefecture),[90] and documentation of a similar event in Tamana (Kumamoto Prefecture) in March 1982 (Fujii et al. 1983).

In pre-war houses of the region the *kamado* oven is set in a separate, earthen-floored space (*kamaya*) below the level of the rest of the house, but the *harai* always begins with an act carried out inside the house, the cutting and assemblage of the *gohei*—"wands" of diverse decorative and symbolic shapes cut from *washi* paper and attached to short bamboo rods that are placed in and around the ritual space. In 1989 I watched as Yamashika meticulously folded, cut the white paper with scissors and fixed the shapes to the rods, then laid out three distinct *gohei* for the assembled ethnographers to view and photograph.[91]

---

90. Yamashika had lived in Yanagawa for twenty years from 1947 on and during that period had done *harai* for both the owner of the house and others in the surrounding community of fishers. The event in 1989 was one that took place at the request and under sponsorship of media producers and researchers rather than residents.

91. Yamashika knew how to make many more *gohei* for various purposes: "There are actually thirty-three ways of cutting those *gohei*, but I couldn't do them all. There's even one cut in the form of a house—that's one of the ones I simply couldn't learn. I suppose it's because I'm blind. The ones I knew were: first of all, the *shintai gohei*, used for the main entrance to the house. That one has five steps to it. Then the *sode gohei* and the *kōjin gohei*, both of which have two variations, and there are the *gohei* that you attach to the tip of a pole and wave around. You know—the kind used by a *kannushi*. The one we used most for ceremonies was done in three pieces with three folds. For the *jibiraki* of a house, it'd be five folds and five pieces—but there were also ones used that were seven-folds and seven-pieces. The most difficult one was called the *ōgesa*, with thirteen folds and thirteen pieces! That was thick, so you couldn't really do the details well. For someone blind, like me, the cutting would start out well, but after a while the layers of paper would get all mixed up. The *suijin gohei* has a lot of excess decoration around the *shintate* rod. Apart from those, there were the *gohei* with the round heads, the *hotoke no gohei* and the one for offering to Jizo-san and other Buddhas. I really only knew the easy ones well." (Kimura 1994, 92)

Figure 2.2. Yamashika preparing *gohei* for a *kamado-barai*. Photograph by the author (April 1989).

The *gohei* are placed upright on a temporary altar in front of or atop the *kamado*, and according to Yamashika each has the following significance:

- Sanbō Kōjin *gohei*: placed in the centre as a symbol of Kōjin, the oven's *shintai*.
- Sode *gohei*: placed beside the Sanbō Kōjin *gohei* as a form of "conductor" between the three *gohei*.
- Shintate *gohei*: a symbol of the celebrant, it is carried into the ritual space by him and placed closest to him during the rite.

Offerings that symbolise the *sanbō* (three treasures) are placed on the altar; these can be of rice, salt, fish, fresh vegetable or sake. The *biwa hiki* sits before the *kamado* and altar to tune his instrument[92] but then puts it aside until it is first played from midway through the third of the following segments of vocal recitation:

92. Two tunings were used in ritual performance by Higo-region *biwa hiki*: the standard *hon-chōshi* (do-fa-do'-do') and another called *roku-chōshi* (do-fa-so-so, a tuning also called *ō-san-sagari* by Ōkawa Susumu; de Ferranti 1997, 147) for recitation of specific sutra texts. In Yamashika's case the latter tuning was used only for the Heart Sutra. No explanation for this alternative tuning has been given by either *biwa hiki* or researchers.

1. Clap. *Shingan-shi* prayer of supplication. (Note that Ga Machiko gives the alternative name *misogi-barai* for this; 1972, 30.)
2. *Rokkon-barai* concerns the cleansing of six forms of impurity.
3. *Hannya Shingyō* is the Heart Sutra, chanted three times in succession with the biwa in *roku-chōshi* tuning.
4. *Kōjin-barai* (proper) concerns the status of Sanbō Dai-Kōjin in myth, and his powers. (Note that Ga describes a more elaborate version of this segment, divided into the "*iwato-biraki*" and the "*yashiki no ji-gatame*," and states that the former is omitted in a shorter version of the rite; ibid., 31).
5. *Hi-wari getsu-wari.* Here Yamashika would change his performance style to single reciting-tones over fragmentary melodic phrases in the biwa as he envoked a deity for each of the thirty days of the lunar calendar's month. (Ga gives the alternative name *sanjū hotoke* for this segment.)
6. *Shingan-shi* again.

Figure 2.3. Yamashika performing the *kamado-barai*. He is wearing a priest's *kesa* garment because at the time he was temporarily a member of the Gensei Hōryū *mōsō* sect. Photograph by the author (April 1989).

The segments of ritual recitation take between thirty and forty minutes to perform. After a break (which was of only eight minutes at the 1982 rite, but in April 1989 was long enough to enable the assembled extended family, neighbours, eight ethnographers and Yamashika himself to gather around a large set of tables and start eating and drinking) the performance of a tale begins. On both occasions a single *dan* of about one hour's duration was performed, preceded by a ten-to-fifteen minute introductory talk.

Figure 2.4. Performance of a tale after a *kamado-barai* held in Yanagawa. Photograph by the author (April 1989).

Watamashi

Rites for the completion of a new house or the removal of possessions into a new house have been conducted in diverse ways in many regions of Japan. The title of these rites is a word that once meant moving one's house (NMD 2000, 833). Nevertheless some *biwa hiki* have given an explanation that suits their own role as celebrants of this rite in central Kyushu; namely, that *watamashi* should be written with the second character in bi-WA followed by TAMASHI (meaning the spirit), for the reason that by playing biwa and chanting, "the *biwa hiki* puts the spirit into a new house" (Kimura 1994, 93, 158). This explanation accords with the fact that at least until the mid twentieth century, there were parts of the Higo and Chikugo regions where the *watamashi* had to be carried out within a year of a dwelling's completion, and for that purpose *yamabushi*, *kannushi* or other ritualists could not be engaged; the rite had to be celebrated by a blind, biwa-playing *zatō* (Noda 1935, 25).[93]

Not having witnessed a *watamashi*, I rely on accounts and partial text transcriptions by Kimura Yūshō (reproduced in Higobiwa Hozonkai 1991, 16, 39–45, and 79–80; in Kimura 1994, 157–159) and by Ga (1972, 30; revised in Nomura 2007) as well as accounts by Yamashika himself, as documented in Kimura 1994.[94]

The physical setting for a *watamashi* was similar to that for the *Kōjin-barai*, but the offerings for the altar were specified in more detail:

> To carry out the ceremony, you must first make a *shintai*, with one *chō* and three *gō* of white rice, salt, a fish with the head and tail on, and fresh vegetables—those are the *sanbō* offerings. On top of all that you set up the *gohei*. (Kimura 1994, 93)

Two contrasting descriptions of the order of materials in the rite are given, perhaps because a shortened version existed; for that reason, two items are shown in parentheses after item 1. Descriptions of items 2, 3 and 5 are by Yamashika, as told to Kimura Rirō:

1. Clap before altar; *harai no kotoba* (an introductory prayer).

    (*Rokkon-barai*: as recited in the *Kōjin-barai*)

    (*Kan no maki*, also called *kangyo* or prayer of requests; Higobiwa Hozonkai 1991, 42; Kimura 1994, 159)

2. *Hannya shingyō*: the Heart Sutra is chanted (usually three times, as in the *Kōjin-barai*), and the biwa in *roku-chōshi* tuning is played, often starting from midway through the first rendition of the sutra.

3. *Watamashi* proper: a *honji suijaku no saimon* (a legendary tale of the origin of a sacred place or entity, in this case the biwa). It is

---

93. Noda wrote of the Tamana area. In other parts this was probably not the case, for sixteen years later Kimura Yūshō wrote that *watamashi* as a rite for new houses could be carried out by Buddhist priests or *kannushi*, but the internal segment called *watamashi* was only included when the celebrant was a blind biwa player (Higobiwa Hozonkai 1991, 43).

94. A new text transcription of parts 3 through 6 of the *watamashi* outlined below is given in Kimura and de Ferranti (2007) with a recording of Yamashika's *watamashi*.

told how the goddess Benzaiten brought the instrument to Japan to help lure the Sun Goddess, Amaterasu, from a cave.[95] The numinous symbolism of the biwa's frets and strings, and the sun and moon inscribed on the face of instruments used by Yamashika and other Tamagawa-lineage players, are also explained. In turn, the symbolism of parts of the *koto* is briefly described, and a final appeal is made to the benevolence of the Imperial house.

4. *Jibiraki*: The four seasons and their respective blessings and the bounty of nature's resources (most of all, water) are described.
5. *Hashira-date*: The names of numerous deities who protect the newly erected house from each of the cardinal directions and inhabit each of its pillars are then invoked.
6. *Hi-wari getsu-wari* or *sanjū hotoke*, as recited in the *Kōjin-barai*.

Items 3, 4 and 5 are unique to this rite, and the item for which the rite as a whole is named is densest in content; here it bears one of the core tales of the origin of biwa known to *biwa hiki* in Kyushu.

Like the *Kōjin-barai*, the *watamashi* was followed by a performance of one or more tales. As often as not, Yamashika said, the audience gathered wanted most of all to enjoy some of the *biwa hiki*'s repertory of *chari* while drinking (see *charimono*, above). This atmosphere of casual celebration is confirmed by a comment recorded by Ga Machiko (1972, 30) to the effect that for entertainment after the ritual part of *watamashi*, a *shamisen* could be played instead of *biwa*, and performances of folksongs known to all present were not uncommon.

Other Occasional *Kamigoto* Performances

The *harai* and *watamashi* were rites carried out for the benefit of a household or family associated with a given residence and plot of land. As such they were the *kamigoto* that *biwa hiki* were most commonly requested to perform, but from Yamashika's account it is clear that in the mid twentieth century occasional requests for a range of ritual services for both individuals and communities, comparable to those provided by *shugenja* prior to the Meiji period, were still being made of

---

95. This tale is of course a variant of the legend of the origin of Japanese performing arts in an erotic dance that restores light to the world by arousing Amaterasu's curiosity.

biwa hiki. Ga Machiko provides a listing of many kinds of communal rites and local festivals which Yamashika told her he had participated in as either a celebrant or a performer of tales in a ritual space. In addition to *harai* and *watamashi*, they include *yogomori* (or *o-komori*), annual performances at small shrines, the Ganjōju (fulfilment of wishes) festival after the conclusion of rice-planting in Nankan, and the Bishamon-san and Sarutahiko-san festivals in a district of Yamaga (Ga 1972, 29–31).

As for engagements for the benefit of individuals, Kimura Rirō has recorded that Yamashika was sometimes requested to perform rites for healing illness through ritual appeasement of a *kami* that had been angered. The common *kamado-barai* performed before the oven was essentially a rite to request Kōjin's protection, but a different rite was called for in cases when it was considered that a deity's wrath had already been incurred. When first requested to do an exorcism or healing rite for people suffering from multiple sicknesses, Yamashika refused, saying, "I've done *jibarai* and rites for newly built houses, as well as the *kamado-barai*, but I don't know how to ask for Kōjin-san's protection in this sort of situation" (Kimura 1994, 97).

It is not clear whether Yamashika was expected to play biwa for these engagements. It seems he was asked to perform such ritual acts simply by virtue of being one among the variety of professional ritualists—*yamabushi*, *mōsō*, *zatō* and the like—who had served regional communities in the past. The persistence of belief in the *biwa hiki* as a kind of multi-purpose agent of the sacred is also evident in the fact that Yamashika was charged in 1967 with care of the *go-shintai* (symbols of the deity) from the local Inari shrine in Nankan and held it as one of the sacred objects in his house from then on. A few years later Inari cult believers started coming to him to ask for help with matters such as illness, finding things they had lost and prayers for their offspring's success in exams.

All of the above rites are documented incompletely in sources on *mōsō* and *higobiwa*, but it is clear that their form and contents varied regionally. Kimura Yūshō noted, for example, that the *watamashi* was said to be a longer and more complicated event in the Amakusa islands than in northern Kumamoto Prefecture, but he died without having had a chance to witness the Amakusa version (Kimura 1994, 157–158). Yasuda corroborated this in documentation of Hashiguchi Keisuke's accounts of his apprenticeship and professional experiences in Amakusa in the 1930s: The "full" *watamashi* ceremony there was a rare event affordable by only wealthy households, so after building a new dwelling most made do with a *Kōjin-barai*. What is more, the latter was usually requested when a *biwa hiki* happened to come around doing *kadozuke* rather than by way of a formal request in advance (2001, 30). To judge from some of Yamashika's anecdotes about travelling with other biwa professionals, the *harai* and *watamashi* in northern Kumamoto Prefecture, too, were events often decided upon at short notice because a *biwa hiki* happened to be in the area.

A final but important point about the ritual work of *biwa hiki* in Yamashika's time is that inaccurate knowledge of the pronunciation or meaning of terms in the texts chanted was apparently widespread. When giving an account of how he had learned the *watamashi*, Yamashika spoke of his frustration at other players' inability to explain referents in the ritual text (see chapter 4). While transmission of words whose meaning is unknown is a common feature of blind oral performance traditions that incorporate elements from written texts, Yamashika's difficulty accessing knowledge of these ritual items and their wordings—solved only when he learned the correct terms and their meaning from a certified *mōsō*—may reflect the general reduction in *biwa hiki* ritual work by the early twentieth century that Yasuda and others have noted.

* * *

This chapter has presented the grounds for and the current state of knowledge of the narrative and ritual traditions that Yamashika Yoshiyuki engaged in. As suggested earlier, to categorise the repertory and performance activities of *biwa hiki* as either secular or sacred is to misrepresent the nature of many performances in which tales, songs and even comical gags were important for the completion of a ritual event, or were carried out as a core ceremonial act. Again and again in writings on Yamashika and other *biwa hiki*, researchers have sought to justify giving priority to either ritual or secular narrative as the definitive distinguishing characteristic in the identity of this performance tradition, but the fact remains that Yamashika Yoshiyuki, Ōkawa Susumu, Tanaka Tōgo, Hashiguchi Keisuke and others all differed in terms of the relative importance of ritual and entertainment activities for their livelihoods as professional *biwa hiki*. Much the same applies to what we know of their teachers, who were active in the first decades of the twentieth century. With regard to the final one hundred years of the active tradition (ca. 1870–1970), then, no definitive statement can be made as to the function of *biwa hiki* in religious life in central Kyushu. Prior to that, during nearly two centuries when the *tōdō-za* exerted its authority so effectively that *mōsō* effectively vanished from public records in Higo Province, *biwa hiki* had carried out not only the rites required by membership of a Myōon Kō under nominal control of the *tōdō-za* but also the *harai* and other ritual events that elsewhere were performed by *mōsō* and *yamabushi* priests. As such they long fulfilled the dual functions that are central to ideas of the *biwa hōshi*. From the time in 1907 when the two *mōsō* sects, newly established as *hōryū* entities within Tendai Buddhism, defined performance of songs and tales as activity inappropriate to the duties of their member priests, it was inevitable that *biwa hiki* of the former Higo region, who continued to perform old tales while occasionally serving as celebrants of rites, would come to be regarded as twentieth-century relics of *biwa hōshi*.

It is ironic that as *biwa hiki* older than Yamashika and ones of his own generation passed away—together with audiences who were appreciative of biwa narrative performance skills and knowledgeable of tales—Yamashika found himself to be the centre of attention in a wave of documentation and research activity. This was driven by scholars' concern for *higobiwa*'s significance in the construction of theories of national music and literature history and by bureaucrats' and the media's concern to present to the public and declare the importance of a local endangered art form. Their numerous tellings of Yamashika's life and music are the subject of chapter 3.

This page is intentionally left blank.

3

IMAGINING, ENCOUNTERING AND DOCUMENTING YAMASHIKA

> I really understood only about half of what he asked me! And I think the professor left without understanding a lot of what I tried to tell him, too.
>
> (Kimura 1994, 113)

The density of materials presented in chapters 1 and 2 comprises evidence that, as a blind professional biwa player in the twentieth century, Yamashika Yoshiyuki was located within a complex nexus of socio-historical practices and images from folklore and literature. Those elements yielded multiple and interrelated images with which he and others could construct his identity variously, at different times and in changing contexts. In this chapter, I will examine diverse modes in which scholars and ethnographers, film-makers and photographers, Japanese and foreigners sought to document Yamashika's life and music and represent him to the public. I will also problematise the nature of the relations that obtained between Yamashika and some of his interlocutors—including myself—and look at how these may have conditioned the ways he told his story to each of them. I will consider at most length the thickest of the layers of cultural texts that envelope Yamashika, the life history authored by Kimura Rirō, wherein interview material has been transformed in the production of an authenticity of voice that addresses a national readership. I propose that it be properly viewed as Kimura's work not only in the construction of the textual detail of Yamashika's first-person narrative but also in the selection of materials according to Kimura's own areas of interest. At the same time it is an intersubjective document that presents discussion by Yamashika of many topics not touched upon in other sources due to the friendship and quasi-familial relationship between him and Kimura.

In surveying these diverse representations of Yamashika ten years after his death, I seek both to deepen my own understanding of a man whom I encountered for sustained periods between 1989 and 1992 and to assess ways in which images yielded by history figured in late-twentieth-century perceptions of him as a performer and individual. Issues of multi-vocality and intersubjectivity in the construction of life-history texts have drawn much attention in anthropology and ethnomusicology (including recent contributions by Stock [2001]; Arnold and Blackburn [2004]; and Babiracki [2008]). In recognition of this and the complex role that interpretive agendas play in portrayals of an individual's life and character, I do not privilege any of the representations I discuss as comparatively more faithful to a unitary, core truth of Yamashika's identity. I do, however, suggest that representations grounded in data about his work in a local setting provide a depth of perspective lacking in ones that portray him as a living relic of the distant past. Moreover, I note that discrimination against blind performers until recent times, although among the most important issues thrown up by consideration of Yamashika's localised experience, is a matter that is all but absent from texts on *biwa hiki* until the mid-1990s.

Documentation of "The Last *Biwa Hōshi*"

Among both populist and scholarly representations of individual practitioners of the blind biwa traditions, documentation and writings about Yamashika have been the most numerous and broadest in their reception. Yamashika has been a central figure in many of the representations of the Kyushu biwa traditions, and his identity—a multi-contextual and multi-layered construction at the hands of many—is often as "the last *biwa hōshi*." Depictions of Yamashika can be thought of as concentric formations of representation which have as their centre the primary matter of his own performances and utterances. Writings and portrayals of historical *biwa hōshi* and blind biwa players of regional Kyushu occupy formations at the periphery, but at the same time their contents touch the inner set of representations, for they have produced knowledge and images of the blind biwa traditions that inform the ways Yamashika has been perceived and presented.

Academic Documentation

The most extensive documentation of Yamashika is in writings by Tanabe Hisao (1963b, iv), Ga Machiko (1972), Murayama Dōsen (1978 and 1986), Narita Mamoru (1985a), Hyōdō Hiromi (1991) and Yasuda Muneo (2001). With the exception of some of Tanabe's and Murayama's writings, all of these portraits appeared in academic journals or books for scholarly readership.

Tanabe Hisao's account of Yamashika is contained in his narrative of a four-day trip to Kumamoto to hear and record *higobiwa* players. Written in five instalments from August to December 1963 for *Hōgaku no tomo*, a periodical read by practitioners and lovers of traditional Japanese music, the tone of Tanabe's text shifts between that of a colourful travel diary and a scholarly documentation. The trip was made possible by Kimura Yūshō and the *chikuzenbiwa* player Hirata Kyokushū (who travelled with Tanabe) as well as various officers of the Kumamoto Prefectural Government and the Kumamoto division of the national broadcaster NHK (1963b, ii, 19–20). Musicians were "summoned" to where Tanabe was staying, as was not unusual in fieldwork by Tokyo scholars at the time, and Yamashika was requested to play for him at a hot springs *ryokan* near Tamana. Tanabe was impressed by Yamashika's performance to the extent that he recommended in a report that Yamashika be designated a bearer of a cultural asset (*bunkazai hoji-sha*) and wrote that his music was "close to the correct lineage of pure *higobiwa*," but at the same time he was concerned that Yamashika's intonation in both singing and biwa-playing often strayed (1963b, iv, 18–19).

Ga Machiko's 1972 article *"Higobiwa saihōroku"*[1] was based on a graduation thesis written under the supervision of the narrative literature specialist Fukuda Akira. It is a detailed presentation of interview data and text transcriptions for seven living *biwa hiki*, with very little subjective commentary. Yamashika, who was around seventy years old at the time of the interviews, is documented at most length, as Ga stayed in nearby Yamaga for a week, visiting him each day.[2] There is extensive data about whom Yamashika had learned repertory

---

1. The title as published includes "hōsairoku," but this is a misprint caused by reversal of two characters in the word "saihōroku."
2. Oral communication, May 2006.

from and about the kinds of work with the biwa he had typically done during the 1950s and 1960s.

Murayama Dōsen is a folklorist who, apparently by choice, has worked on the fringes of academia. His first writing about Yamashika was a three-page portrait, based on a 1974 interview, within a long essay on Japan's biwa traditions published in a 1978 issue of *Aruku miru kiku* (Walk, Watch, Listen), a journal of writings on diverse countries' folklore and traditional culture, for a non-specialist readership. In 1986 an article devoted to Yamashika appeared, "A record of the *higobiwa* tradition," in which almost all of the 1978 material is incorporated, with slight revisions. With the exception of appendix materials on instruments and the structure of tales in *higobiwa*, the article comprises a concise version of Yamashika's professional history presented in four sections: Apprenticeship, *Kadobiki* Experiences, Expanding the Repertory, and Activities as a Biwa Professional.

In contrast to Kimura's 1994 text, which contains modified transcriptions that render Yamashika's accounts in first person speech, Murayama's text is in the third person with occasional direct quotes from Yamashika. In an "in conclusion" segment, Murayama's subjective view of Yamashika is clearly expressed: In putting forth his theory of a research methodology that puts "the performer's own view of the act of *katari*" at the centre and makes "a basic contribution to the continuation of the tradition" as living narrative performance (*ikita katari*), Murayama states that he has written about Yamashika's life because he was "deeply impressed by both his narrative performances and his way of living (*ikizama*)" (1986, 441–443).

Narita Mamoru is a Tokyo-based scholar of historical *katarimono* texts known for his authoritative work on *oku jōruri* (Narita 1985b), a tradition that can be seen as a counterpart of *higobiwa* in northern Japan, as it was practised by male blind biwa and *shamisen* players (*bosama*) and drew upon a narrative repertory originally transmitted from central Japan (Hirose 1997, 116). He visited *biwa hiki* and *mōsō* in Kyushu over a period of several years, and the pages of his 1985 book that portray and quote Yamashika document conversations held (with Yamashika and later Kimura Rirō)[3] in the early 1970s. Narita positions

---

3. Kimura Rirō, personal communication, December 2004. Kimura is not named in Narita's text, however, and he expressed annoyance at the lack of such acknowledgement of secondary sources in Narita's writing on Yamashika and the

Yamashika within "the *mōsō* tradition" (*mōsō no denshō*) but calls him a "*biwa hōshi* of Higo" from the first and focusses upon the points of similarity between the texts for particular segments of Yamashika's ritual repertory and those of *saimon* recited in folk ritual in other parts of Japan (Narita 1985b, 64–70). He argues that the *Kikuchi Kuzure*, as recited by Yamashika, served as a placatory *chinkon* narrative for the spirit of the Hizen warlord, Takanobu, and that repertory of this sort was transmitted by Higo-region biwa players who preserved the functions of medieval-period *biwa hōshi* (187–199).

Hyōdō Hiromi refers to Yamashika in many of his writings on *katarimono* since the mid-1980s, but the first of his three-part series "*Zatō(mōsō)biwa no katarimono denshō nitsuite no kenkyū*" (Studies of the zatō[mōsō]biwa narrative performance tradition; 1991) is centred on Yamashika's practice as a basis for retrospective speculation on the historical nature of the *Heike* narrative performance tradition. Hyōdō is explicit about his reasons for having made Yamashika the focus of his research: firstly, because of his vast repertory ("even if one looks back to the early part of Shōwa, one cannot find a performer of Yamashika's stature") and secondly because only Yamashika continued to engage in oral composition in performances of the 1980s (1991, 16–18). Hyōdō provides a very compact but dense profile of Yamashika's training and professional activities, then lists forty-five tales as ones Yamashika was still capable of performing in 1991. The bulk of the article thereafter is devoted to exposition of the *fushi* system and its acquisition in the Tamagawa line through successive study of *hauta* and two single-*dan* tales, *Ono no Komachi* and *Dōjōji*, during the first two years of apprenticeship. Hyōdō presents a comparative analysis of ten different performances of *Dōjōji*,[4] in terms of variation in *fushi* structure and the performative articulation of narrative scenes, then turns to extrapolatory commentary on the structure of the *Heike monogatari* in its many different versions.

As a chronicler of the history of Higo-region biwa traditions, Yasuda Muneo has often referred to Yamashika in passing, but writes about him at most length in the opening chapter of his 2001 book, *Higo no biwa-shi*. Here he gives a three-page profile, which "as far as

---

"*Higo no mōsō*" tradition.

4. The rendering and *fushi* scheme for one of the ten performances given in Hyōdō 1991 is the basis for my own presentation of *Dōjōji* in chapter 4.

possible avoids overlap with the several extant reports on Yamashika" (19). The profile contains information about Yamashika's training and professional life that supplements but in some cases contradicts data given by Hyōdō, Ga and Murayama. Yasuda devotes far more of his text to Hashiguchi Keisuke, who completed an eight-year apprenticeship in Amakusa from the age of thirteen, followed by professional work in the same region, and therefore could be said to have "a more orthodox professional profile than Yamashika" (23).

In 2004 there appeared a book of writings on the theory of *monogatari* by Fujii Sadakazu, the Tokyo University academic who had led a fieldwork project on Kyushu biwa traditions funded by the Toyota Foundation in 1981 and 1982. Yamashika is introduced during several pages on the subject of oral composition and formulaic text in Japanese historical narrative, and on page 90 there is a suggestive visual juxtaposition of Yamashika holding his biwa at a similar angle to the *gusle* fiddle held by a blind Serbian narrative singer (*guslar*) in the adjacent cover image from Albert Lord's *The Singer of Tales*. This reinforces Fujii's claim that "the Kyushu *biwa hōshi* were none other than [Japan's] *guslar*" (90), which he makes in the course of arguing for the importance of the research that has been done since the 1980s on performance techniques of figures like Yamashika.

Representations for the Broader Public

Apart from these academic portrayals, several publications and media productions for a general audience have referred to or focussed upon Yamashika. He is included as one of the fresco of "itinerant" performers in books such as Ozawa Shōichi's *Nihon no hōrōgei* (Japan's itinerant performing arts; 1982 [1974]); he was the subject of a book-length photographic essay, together with his last wife, Misao (Miyagawa 1983); and he appeared in newspaper and magazine articles, as well as in television and film documentaries. The majority of popular press articles are brief, rather shallow treatments that draw upon stereotypic images of *biwa hōshi*, in particular the frightening figure of Mimi Nashi Hōichi. In just a few, the space between those very images and the reality of Yamashika's life and art is tentatively probed—exceptional in this regard is Yamamoto Izumi's article on Yamashika in *Hōgaku Journal* (Yamamoto 1992), based on several visits with Yamashika over a period of some months—but in most instances simple stereotypes stay firmly in place. For example, a portrayal of Yamashika based on a three-day stay at his house for the purpose of "witnessing the artform in the environment where it had usually been practised," published in the music magazine *Noise* ends with the following:

> The phantom image of Mimi Nashi Hōichi becomes visible through the medium of Yamashika. Yet one has to be prepared to stay overnight to hear him play, and from that one comes to feel the huge gulf there is between us, who live day and night a life so far removed from the world of his tales, and the lives of those fallen Heike who anticipated Hōichi's performances. (Kamijima 1991, 100)

By staying with Yamashika, the writer had been able to observe his highly regulated, strict approach to a daily routine while living alone at age ninety and remarked that this may also tell us something about Yamashika's approach to his narrative art. Notwithstanding, the piece ends with the above statement, a rather trite expression of the writer's sense of distance from Yamashika's lifestyle, which conjures the cliché that the *biwa hiki* was somehow part of the world of his tales.

By contrast, the 1986 thirty-minute television program *Tsuchi ni utau: biwa-shi no Yamashika Yoshiyuki* (Singing for the earth: The biwa master, Yamashika Yoshiyuki) is an example of a Kumamoto-produced documentary that depicts Yamashika almost solely in terms of his local and Kyushu identity. In it he is described as both a *mōsō* and a *biwa-shi* (biwa master) rather than a *biwa hōshi* and emphasis is given to his ritual activities, including performance of sutras and biwa for a *watamashi* and exorcism of harmful spirits by chanting sutras while striking individuals' bodies with a book of Buddhist texts. This focus on Yamashika's ritual work accords well with sequences of him working in the fields and the program's overall theme, that his closeness to the local community and the land are inseparable from the "simple, unadorned" tone of his vocal recitations and the power of his performances.

While the majority of texts produced by local writers and artists tend to assume a greater degree of familiarity with regional history and geography and do not treat *biwa hiki* as exotic, remote figures, exceptional representations of the latter sort have also been produced by local organisations: The 1994 documentary made by NHK Television's Fukuoka division, *Saigo no biwa hōshi Yamashika Yoshiyuki* (Yamashika Yoshiyuki, the last *biwa hōshi*), for example, emphasises the distance between modern-day people of Kumamoto Prefecture and a figure such as Yamashika and plays time and again on the trope of his miraculous survival as "the last" *biwa hōshi*. Significantly, this contrasts with another program produced a year earlier by the same organisation but with a different production team, "*Ninjō biwa hōshi ikiru*" (A living *biwa hōshi* of human feelings), shown in the weekly half-hour *Wonderland Kyushu* series. Here Yamashika's former role in the life of his community, Kobaru, is emphasised, so that the "*biwa hōshi*" in the program's title is embedded in a past familiar to many people in the Fukuoka-Kumamoto region who know the life ways of its smaller villages.

An important visual record was produced in 1983 by Miyagawa Mitsuyoshi, a photographer based in Ōmuta, a town not far from Yamashika's home in Nankan. In content this photo-essay book stands midway between the two kinds of representations I have been discussing. *Higobiwa meoto sanka: Yamashika Yoshiyuki fūfu no seikatsu kiroku* (A song of praise for *higobiwa* and matrimony: A record of the daily life of Yamashika Yoshiyuki and his wife) intersperses images of many kinds of daily activities with photos of rituals, narrative and song performances, transcribed text extracts from biwa repertory, and short essays by Tokyo researchers and a local cultural bureaucrat.[5] Primarily for distribution in Kyushu bookshops, the choice of black and white images and the wording of explanatory captions highlights the fact that Yamashika and his fourth wife, the *shamisen* player Misao, lived in seemingly archaic social and material circumstances far removed from those of most modern-day Japanese. In this regard, and in the inclusion of many images that portray the old couple as cute and endearing, the collection presents them through hackneyed means. Kimura Rirō (1994, 144) points out that relations between Yamashika and Misao were far from good, so Miyagawa's presentation of nothing but images of the couple working together and enjoying themselves is quite deliberately selective. The prevailing light-heartedness and "cuteness" of his portrayal is reflective of the gentle nostalgia of so

---

5. The researchers are the literary historian Fujii Sadakazu and the folklorist Murayama Dōsen.

many representations of rural folkways in Japanese media of the 1980s. Yet despite stereotypic features that place Yamashika and Misao at a distance, some of the book's images and captions provide detail about their lives of a highly specific kind. Portrayal of Yamashika's skills in finding and digging up edible large bamboo roots and a description of the inconvenience of not being able to go outside on rainy days (due to the danger of slipping over on wet surfaces that they can't see), for example, are elements of an account that results from years of acquaintance with the couple.

Among representations produced by Tokyo-based individuals and organisations, the 1992 film, *Biwa hōshi Yamashika Yoshiyuki*, written by director Aoike Kenji, is important because of its breadth of circulation in Japan after winning the documentary category of the Mainichi Newspaper annual film award competition in 1993 as well as gaining approval by the then Ministry of Education for use in school curricula. Since then it has been the sole means by which Japanese schoolchildren have had access to knowledge of Yamashika and his performance tradition.[6] Aoike's film is not an ethnographic documentary, for it offers viewers relatively little historical and social contextual information and says nothing of the film-makers' interaction with Yamashika between November 1991 and October 1992 or of their own agency and effect upon what is seen. Rather, it emphasises the singularity of both Yamashika's professional life and his personal circumstances by interweaving segments of sacred and secular performances with interviews with Yamashika and footage of his daily routine. On the whole, the film was made with minimal staging and manipulation of Yamashika and others who appear in it but the director's editorial inclusion of much footage devoted to Yamashika's homelife (including several scenes of Yamashika in his cups) and a sequence of photos from Miyagawa's book that suggest Yamashika's memories of domestic life before Misao entered an old people's institution, all contribute to the summary impression of Yamashika as a decidedly lovable old

6. I should say that I was marginally involved in an aspect of the film's production and am named in its credits as one who provided assistance or "cooperation" (*kyōryoku*): I first voiced—in another context—the idea of organising a 1992 Tokyo performance by Yamashika, and, together with Kimura Rirō, succeeded in gaining Yamashika's agreement. He was thus prepared for a similar proposal put to him some weeks later by the film's director. The resultant concert performance in the Mokubatei Theatre, Asakusa, Tokyo, constitutes the climax of the film.

man. This is pithily expressed in prominent phrasing on fliers made by Aoike's production company for the newly completed film's publicity: "'jittchan' to yobare ai-sarete iru biwahiki-san no futsū no seikatsu" (the everyday life of a *biwa hiki* known as "jittchan").

The film's emphatically rose-tinted image of Yamashika's life also results from the fact that viewers are not told that some of the performances filmed would not have taken place if not for the film crew's instigation. In particular, the rite of *yogomori* inside a local Shinto shrine had not taken place since 1989, yet even then it had been sponsored by a Kyushu television producer.[7] The June 1992 concert performance in a theatre in Tokyo which forms the climax of the film, moreover, was almost unthinkable during the previous winter, when Yamashika's strength seemed to be rapidly waning. Yet viewers are given no hint that this was both an extremely rare and a risky undertaking.

One can speculate on Aoike's reasons for taking poetic licence in these matters. Firstly, since the film was a commercial venture which Aoike financed from his own pocket, he had to ensure the public appeal of his final product. More significant, however, is the fact that the film's construction obscures distinctions between Yamashika's circumstances within his rural community at that time and in former times. In this sense the performances shown can be viewed as illustrations of the director's images of past practice rather than exemplifications of the current situation. Depiction of the locale in which Yamashika lived as more remote and serene than it in fact is and of Yamashika himself as, first and foremost, someone "cute and lovable" serves to project a poetic vision of the past that valorises the old ways of life in the *furusato*,[8] the traditional rural village. This wistful view of the agrarian past has been the norm in Japanese popular cultural texts since the 1950s (although it existed as an important mode of representation of rural life throughout most of the twentieth century) and expresses a kind of Japanese "pastoral allegoric"[9] response to the onslaught of

7. The film's voiceover script says that the *yogomori* performance shown was the first one in four years but does not state that film-makers had requested and sponsored both the 1989 and 1992 performances.

8. For an analysis of the concept of the traditional furusato and its hold upon modern urban Japanese ideals of living environment and community life, see chapter 1, "Nostalgic praxis," of Robertson 1991.

9. See James Clifford's "On ethnographic allegory" in Clifford and Marcus (1986, 98–121).

modernity. It should be recognised that Aoike's responses to Yamashika are complex and cannot be grossly characterised as merely "nostalgic," but nevertheless he has consciously played upon this trope in the film and its publicity statements. Indeed, his original intention of addressing the film to the general public, as part of an ongoing debate on late-twentieth-century Japanese identity, is apparent from a statement he made to the regional press at the time the filming began:

> Yamashika's way of life is that of ordinary Japanese in former times. I want this film to be more than just an introduction of the last bearer of the *higobiwa* tradition; I want to put the question 'What is a Japanese?' (Nishi Nihon Shinbunsha 1991)

Soon after Aoike's film was completed in 1992, there appeared in the *New York Times* (International Edition, November 16th) and the *International Herald Tribune* the only non-scholarly printed text in English about Yamashika and the blind biwa traditions of Kyushu, written by David Sanger. As the journalist was at the time stationed in Tokyo, he probably learned of Yamashika either from Aoike's film, which had been released just prior to when Sanger paid a visit to Yamashika, from Hyōdō Hiromi (whose comments are quoted), or from an article of mine published in a Tokyo English-language daily, the *Japan Times*, on June 21, 1992. Sanger's piece appeared as "Nankan Journal," an instalment in a long-running column of reportage from locales all over the world. Writing for readers with absolutely no knowledge of the subject matter, his approach is to explain Yamashika's importance for Japanese academia and media while stressing his age and physical deterioration and the contrast between his humble material circumstances and the arrival of researchers and "film makers toting truckloads of recording equipment" in his remote village. From the first, Sanger identifies Yamashika as a "*biwa hōshi*, or lute priest," and as a man believed to be the last of his kind. He gives basic information about the contexts for Yamashika's ritual and entertainment activities, then turns to Hyōdō's explanation of the old man's significance: "No other person in Japan can recount so many tales." The article concludes with information on Yamashika's training and his views of why it is that no one is willing to put in the time sufficient to learn the narratives in his repertory, offset by an expression of apparent nonchalance about the fate of his tales.

Finally, Yamashika and *higobiwa* have been represented on the internet in a number of websites. One is in English: The photograph collection *Asia Grace* includes an image taken by Kevin Kelly at Yamashika's house in 1972. The same image—which presents the unidentified musician as if he were a living relic from the past of rural Japan[10]—can be viewed on a website about the book. In searches for the term *"higobiwa,"* however, a webpage in Japanese generally comes up first: Katayama Kyokusei's site entitled (in romanisation as given on the site) *"Chikuzen-biwa, higozatoh-biwa."*[11] Most of the information on the site concerns Katayama's own performance activities, but it also contains a page about Yamashika, the *higobiwa* repertory he taught Katayama and the learning process itself.

Yamashika and His Interlocutors

> I don't know how it's happened, but these days university students and professors come to visit me. And foreigners come here to talk with me—it's the truth! (Kimura 1994, 113)

In the first section of this chapter, I have divided extant writings on Yamashika into academic and populist representations. While such a grouping carries implications about approaches, methods and intentions in documentation activities, it tells us nothing about the sorts of relations that exist between biwa players and the producers of texts in various media. On one occasion I asked Yamashika about his own experiences with researchers and his strategies for dealing with them. He said of his interlocutors that only "one in ten of them" would ever tell him the reasons why they wished to interview him—in other words, the objectives of their work and the subjects of concern to them. He found this annoying, as he didn't know what they wanted of him and would have to find out for himself by indirectly "interviewing" them! He also complained that few researchers seemed to realise that he had become a biwa player out of sheer economic necessity and would have done something else to earn a living had he had a reasonable choice.[12]

---

10. In the printed book (published privately by Kelly in 1982), Yamashika was not identified as the individual in the photo. The *Asia Grace* website gave his name only from late 2004. Kelly is one of the co-founders of the American magazine *Wired*.

11. http://artist.musicinfo.co.jp/~kyokusei.

12. Interview of November 5, 1991. In the same interview he implied that he had

Scholars

In the last three decades of his life Yamashika had a lot to do with people engaged in professional scholarship. A few, such as Yasuda Muneo and his student Uda Yasushi, came from nearby, but the majority came from the distant centres of economic and cultural power in Japan: Tokyo, Osaka and Kyoto. Most held positions at renowned educational and research institutions, and their fieldwork with Yamashika and other biwa players was funded as part of their professional activities. Had Yamashika still been busy on a daily basis with performance and ritual work after 1970, he might have refused some of those who came to observe and talk about his life and art. Yet he was not, and the fact that he had very little income from that time on meant that he was liable to view researchers as people who might help by creating publicity and opportunities to generate income. As Kimura puts it, with reference to photographers who came to document Yamashika's lifestyle,

> He can't very well dare to say no to these things, because it's all publicity: he believes that if the fact that "*biwa hiki* are still alive" becomes better known through such photos, then some of the people who see them will come to hear him perform. That's because he's a professional. (1994, 148)

Those expectations were fulfilled to a certain extent, for Yamashika was occasionally engaged to perform in public venues, including the National Theatre in Tokyo in 1976, was written about in many forums, and became the recipient of awards from various cultural foundations, some of which provided a sum of money. Scholarly documentation of his abilities as a biwa practitioner could doubtless be shown to have contributed to his income and well-being from 1975 until his death in 1996. From the time I met him in 1989, moreover, I gained the impression that he enjoyed the company provided by those who came from distant places to hear him play and talk. He would insist that those who came alone or in a group of two should stay the night if they wanted to hear him perform; this was a strategy that provided him not only with an opportunity to "interview" the interviewers but also with company for the evening meal and *sake*.

---

had no choice in the matter of his profession—that in the end his parents had made the decision to apprentice him as a *biwa hiki*.

An important aspect of Yamashika's relations with researchers during his last years, when he felt he could no longer perform to his own satisfaction, was an awareness that their work would yield what people might know of him and biwa recitation in the future. On several occasions he expressed his lack of surprise that no one wished to do a *biwa hiki*'s work any longer (even if there had still been sufficient call for that sort of work), but in discussion he also speculated about whether some young people might be able to learn his style from recordings and the possibility of their developing something new from it.

What did Yamashika make of the things scholars wrote about him? Was he aware of errors in some of what went into print? Did he care that Tanabe Hisao had characterised ritual work and comic recitations as aberrant activities that had not been part of the "original" work of Higo-region *biwa hiki*? And to what extent were his own conceptions and explanations of his work influenced by ideas suggested in prior discussions with researchers? These questions are not easily addressed, as Japanese protocol places severe constraints on the airing of criticism against anyone from whose actions one has benefited or with whom one might yet have ongoing relations. By the end of my own fieldwork with Yamashika, however, I had broached such issues often enough to reach the conclusion that he was both aware of misrepresentations in some widely circulated writing about him and annoyed by people who had come with presuppositions about the nature of his art. His comments to Kimura about his 1963 interview with Tanabe reflect just such a critical attitude:

> I was asked lots of questions by Professor Tanabe at that time, but I understood very little of it, and just told him things I *did* know, recited a few pieces, and came straight home afterwards. I really understood only about half of what he'd asked me! And I think the professor left without understanding a lot of what I tried to tell him, too. In my work there are established conventions and procedures, but if you try to explain them logically, most people can't understand. (1994, 113)

Yamashika's skepticism about the validity of the term "*higobiwa*" (evident in statements like "I wonder what '*higobiwa*' really is. Perhaps someone made it up," Kimura 1994, 114), suggests that he would not readily adopt the terminology or explanations of those who came to interview him, regardless of their social standing. As I have argued in chapter 2, Yamashika's sense of tradition was grounded in personal experience, the truth of which could hardly be dislodged from his discourse.

The Kimuras

Numerous people were interested in Yamashika as a research and documentation subject over the last three decades of his life, so those who approached him earliest had the relative "advantage" of developing relations at a time when he had little idea of the nature of research activity or its potential consequences for his reputation and livelihood. This can be compared to later periods when—as is evident from his statement about having to "interview" the interviewer—he developed strategies for dealing with researchers in such a way as to anticipate some of their expectations and control the amount and kinds of information yielded to them. But the depth and extent of materials reflected in writings on Yamashika by Kimura Yūshō and his son Rirō is not only a product of their having had contact with him before other writers; it is also a reflection of their having known him on a wholly different basis than most others. Importantly, they were able to speak with him in local dialect, and consequently establish a quality of familiarity impossible for researchers from elsewhere who spoke substantially different standard Japanese. However, people who came from Kumamoto or Fukuoka were also able to speak and understand dialect to varying degrees, so of greater significance than language facility was the Kimuras' physical proximity in the town of Yamaga; this enabled them to see Yamashika often and regularly over a span of decades, and on many occasions to play an active role in helping him carry out both professional and domestic tasks. This kind of personal engagement with Yamashika is of course deliberately reflected in Kimura Rirō's text, in its inclusion of appreciative quotes such as the following:

> Let me tell you, the person who knew most about all this was your father [Kimura Yūshō]. He was dedicated—he taught me some things I didn't even understand myself![13] (1994, 113)

13. Kimura Yūshō would sometimes read texts to Yamashika, and tell him things—

Kimura's selection of such statements for his edited text can be interpreted as the result of a desire to emphasise the fact that his father was the person who made Yamashika known to people beyond Nankan and the areas in which he had worked. Yet the nature of the relationship between the Kimura family and Yamashika is something I heard verified both by Yamashika himself and in discussion with others who lived in Kobaru (Yamashika's village within the township of Nankan) between 1989 and 1992. It is clear that Kimura Yūshō and, in turn, Kimura Rirō and his wife Chiemi would come (as often as not with their own children) to take Yamashika to the doctor's and even to cook, clean and work in the field or garden with him. While this sort of activity is now extolled as unexceptional in manuals on ethnographic field work, as far as I could tell only the Kimura family and one other, an (unrelated) photographer named Kimura Yoshio, were treated with a familiarity that allowed them to engage in such activities with and for Yamashika during their acquaintance with him. Kimura continues the relationship by sponsoring memorial events for Yamashika, including ones that would normally be organised and financed by a family member.[14]

In characterising the Kimuras' relations with Yamashika as closer than those of other researchers and documentors, I am not valorising their position. I emphasise this qualitative difference of relationship as something that is fundamental to understanding the nature of Kimura Rirō's text.

Foreigners

In the quote at the head of this section, Yamashika proclaims the astonishing fact that foreigners come to talk with him. As the dates for the various individual discussions from which Kimura's text has been woven are not given, there is no telling which foreigners were being

---

for example, about historical figures in various *gedai*—which could only be learned from books and people in the literate world. Kimura Rirō, oral communication, July 1999.

14. As Yamashika's surviving son was effectively out of contact from soon after his father's death, Kimura took it upon himself to arrange for ritual observances marking the seventh year after death and related events. The rites and events took place on July 20, 2002, at the Kobaru temple where Yamashika's ashes are housed and at a hotel in Yamaga.

referred to. There is one documented meeting between a foreigner and Yamashika in the early 1970s: The American Kevin Kelly was in his own words, "hitchhiking around Kyushu about February 1972 [and] staying in youth hostels" when he met a young student whom he "accompanied on a few of his cultural outings," one of which was to Yamashika's house in Nankan.[15] Given that Kelly found his way to Yamashika via a nearby youth hostel, it is certainly possible that other foreign travellers did the same in the 1970s and 1980s.

It is likely that the person Yamashika referred to was a Sardinian man named Doriano Suris. A resident of Fukuoka since the 1970s, Suris was a trained classical guitarist who had apprenticed himself for several years to a *chikuzenbiwa* maker and had met Yamashika soon thereafter. He was so struck by Yamashika that he came to visit him as often as possible for several years, often spending the night there before heading back to Fukuoka. He took particular interest in aspects of the construction of biwa played by Yamashika and other surviving *biwa hiki* and offered to do repairs on them when necessary.[16] It was probably Yamashika's acquaintance with Doriano Suris over many years that made it easier for him to agree to my visiting him often over a ten-month period in 1991 and 1992.

My Own Engagement with Yamashika

Self-reflexive writing in ethnography is always open to the charge of irrelevance and indulgence, but in a text of this sort I believe that limited adoption of that mode is justified; as the remainder of this book concerns Yamashika and what is known of his experiences as a *biwa hiki*, it is important that the bases for my own first-hand knowledge of him be made clear. Our interaction between 1989, when we first met, and mid-1992 was conditioned both by my being a foreigner and someone who had not lived in the region (unlike Doriano Suris) and by the enabling framework for my fieldwork, as a person funded to research biwa traditions by a division of the Japanese government.[17]

15. Kelly, email of December 18, 2004.
16. In December 1991, at a performance I and others organised near Kumamoto, when it seemed there was a problem with one of the tuning pegs just before Yamashika was to start, it was Suris who stepped from the audience to make on-the-spot adjustments!
17. My work from 1991 to 1992 was funded by the Japan Foundation, which at that time was administered within the Foreign Ministry.

At the same time, the circumstances of Yamashika's domestic life as a blind person living alone meant that in order to talk with him about his work as a *biwa hiki* I had to spend considerable periods of time—often several days and nights in succession—doing many things with him, including cooking, domestic tasks, listening to sumo broadcasts, eating, drinking, and, above all, listening and responding to him. What had begun as a formal relationship became far more complex by the last few months before I left Kyushu in June 1992.

Like Murayama, Hyōdō and many others, I was introduced to Yamashika by Kimura Rirō. In early March, 1989, he drove me and a friend from my *satsumabiwa* study group in Tokyo to Yamashika's house in Nankan. On our first visit, Kimura's presence made things much easier, for he knew the pace at which Yamashika liked to get acquainted and talk of various topics and when it might be appropriate to ask him to perform for us. The fact that Yamashika gave a tremendously energetic forty-five minute recitation of the first *dan* of *Shuntokumaru* was also in large part due to Kimura's knowledge of what foods and *sake* to provide for him and at what rate to serve them. Yamashika's mixture of early-twentieth-century forms of both Higo and Chikugo dialect—spoken with the use of just a few teeth—was at that time almost incomprehensible to me, so Kimura's presence was vital for maintaining communication. Because of the dialect problem, even when I returned to do sustained fieldwork in 1991, Kimura's expression in the vernacular of my intentions was at first the *only* means whereby Yamashika could form an idea of what it was that I was doing there, of why I wished to come and spend entire days at his house, and why I should want to hear him perform at length even when, in his own view, he could no longer play the biwa nor recite with real skill. I found that, as the months went by and I came to be able to converse with him more freely, he would keep harking back to Kimura's explanation of my intentions, namely, to learn about differences between "the same" *fushi* patterns in different tales, how particular *fushi* might change in accordance with characters or situations within a tale, and also how a tale was shortened, lengthened or otherwise changed in response to performance conditions. He would sometimes ask why I now seemed to be seeking different things from him.

Yamashika had turned ninety by the time I began to visit him on a regular basis from September 1991. By his own account, he had been unable to perform to his satisfaction for several years prior to that. Nevertheless, to judge from the evidence of his performance at our first meeting, in March 1989, his voice had at that time hardly diminished in strength or degree of control from recordings made at the start of the 1980s. I was shocked to see the deteriorated state of his health when I arrived in 1991 and to hear in his performance a marked loss of control and strength of vocal tone by comparison with when I had visited him briefly a second time in May 1990. From that time I felt keenly the inequity of power between Yamashika and *all* of his interlocutors: His physical condition was such that it took a great effort for him to play biwa and recite and even to concentrate his attention on questions for more than thirty minutes at a stretch. In my case, as a foreigner who at first could understand little more than half of what Yamashika said when not speaking in standard Japanese, I had to make even heavier demands upon him than other researchers. Yet I was all too aware that he was most unlikely to refuse to cooperate with a scholar paid by the Japan Foundation to work with him. My provisional solution to this sense of inequity was to try to demonstrate to him both my willingness to persevere in learning a short recitation from him (something that proved to be impossible in the end), and my desire that my work should somehow benefit him within his own society. To this end, I spoke about Yamashika in media interviews, wrote articles for newspapers, introduced persons to him whose writings and photographs later appeared in national journals and participated in organising performances in both Kumamoto and Tokyo (see de Ferranti 1992a and 1992b).

Yamashika was highly skeptical of my interest in his performance techniques and my wish to understand ways in which *fushi* are sung in different tales and performances. Firstly, he felt that a period of eight to ten months was far too short for this kind of work; a full period of several years' apprenticeship was more appropriate. Should I wish to take up the latter option, however, he sadly informed me that he felt he was now incapable of effectively teaching the rudiments of performance technique, for his body had grown too weak with age; my research would probably be largely a waste of time, whichever way I decided to proceed! Having told me this, he was extremely welcoming, encouraged me to come to talk with him as often as possible and at various times during the following ten months even tried to obtain an instrument with which I might practice.[18] Perhaps because of his experiences with Tanabe Hisao and other scholars whose representations of him had circulated widely in books and journals, Yamashika also exhorted me not to make mistakes in what I wrote and to tell him about it while he was still alive.[19]

I soon found out the difficulty of making "efficient" use of time spent with Yamashika (in terms of fulfilling research objectives) and tried to resign myself to the fact that data of the sort I hoped to gather would only emerge fragmentarily and in far smaller quantities than I had hoped during the course of many days devoted to helping Yamashika do household chores and simply keeping him company. The only way to ensure sustained periods of directed discussion was to stay overnight at his house for several days. Most of what I did learn from Yamashika during 1991 and 1992 was not about the subject I had set out to address, text-music patterning and its variability, for two reasons: Yamashika had little interest in telling me about the ways *fushi* were used to render different texts—he felt that such talk was futile if I didn't actually know how to perform his *fushi* in rudimentary pieces first, and he was no longer well enough to teach me in what he felt was an appropriate manner.[20]

---

18. I eventually borrowed one from Ōkawa Susumu, of Izumi-chō, Kagoshima Prefecture, which I used for lessons with Hashiguchi Keisuke and to play to Yamashika what I had been able to imitate of his *Dōjōji* on the basis of a recording. On the occasion of our last meeting, at a *ryokan* in Tokyo the day after his second performance at the Mokubatei Theatre in Asakusa, in June 1992, he was still concerned that I obtain an instrument with which to continue practising and feigned scolding me for not having brought along a delapidated four-stringed *chikuzenbiwa* I'd recently obtained through an antique shop in California.

19. While in Kyushu I wrote two newspaper articles (1992a and 1992b), which were Japanese and English-language versions of the one text. I responded to Yamashika's request by ensuring that the Japanese version was read to him. He subsequently said nothing about it to me. Two English academic articles that concern Yamashika (de Ferranti 1994 and 1995) were written later, but all I was able to do was briefly describe their contents when speaking with him by telephone (for the last time, in October 1993). They were pieces framed by theoretical concerns of ethnomusicology (the role of text-melody models in the process of oral composition) and cultural studies (the politics of representation), respectively, and Yamashika's response to my descriptions was, from memory, one of indifference. Whether that was due to the nature of the contents, the insufficiency of my explanations, his own greatly reduced state of health or a combination of all those factors, I cannot say. The call ended with an invitation to come see him again soon.

20. I did, however, learn some of the *fushi* set and most of the *te* of Hashiguchi

Yamashika was the topic of two articles I wrote soon after the period of fieldwork, but my 1997 doctoral thesis was largely devoted to analysis of music and text in performances by Ōkawa Susumu. This decision was taken because Ōkawa had been able to explain at length (and for the most part in standard Japanese) the use of *fushi* in recordings he had made in the 1970s, when still well enough to perform. The subject of this book, which I started writing some ten years after the fieldwork period of 1991–1992, is closer to the concerns that came to occupy me after I realised that I probably would not learn substantially more from Yamashika about his performance practice and text-music patterning than Hyōdō and other researchers already had.

Kimura's *Kikigaki* Life History of Yamashika

Higo biwa hiki Yamashika Yoshiyuki yobanashi (Fireside tales of a *biwa hiki* of Higo, Yamashika Yoshiyuki) was published in Tokyo in 1994 under the authorship of Kimura Rirō. The text is situated in the broad space between academic and populist writing that is highly significant in Japanese intellectual life. It constitutes a fundamental resource for much of the information about Yamashika's training, professional work and experiences that I present in chapter 5. Accordingly it should be subjected to source criticism in the sense of an examination of both the structure and constructedness of the text and its value as a source of information about Yamashika and the profession of *biwa hiki* in the period it covers, the first half of the twentieth century.

Among the many scholarly books, articles, and essays on the blind biwa traditions that I have described above and in chapter 2, Kimura's text is the most detailed about Yamashika, best known of the Higo-region *biwa hiki*. It draws on material from interviews with him from the late 1970s through to the mid-1980s. To return to the metaphor used at the beginning of this chapter, this is the "thickest" of the multiple layers of cultural texts that envelope Yamashika and the one which occupies a space closest to the metaphoric core, Yamashika's own words and actions. This is not to say that Kimura's text wholly envelopes the core so that nothing of it can be discerned: Most of the first-person narrative material in the text undoubtedly has the sound

---

Keisuke in lessons over five months, using the biwa loaned to me by Ōkawa Susumu.

and feel of Yamashika's way of talking, even though the interview material has been transformed to produce an authenticity of voice that is both persuasive and comprehensible for a national (as distinct from a Kumamoto or Kyushu) readership.

Kimura Rirō and His Various Writings on Yamashika

Before discussing the life history text, we should consider Kimura Rirō's background and his other writings on Yamashika. As Kimura Yūshō's son, he had known Yamashika since his childhood in the 1950s. Rirō was still only in his teens when his father died in 1965 (aged 45); later he studied European literature and worked for some years in Tokyo before returning to Kumamoto in the early 1970s, taking a position as a cultural affairs specialist with the Yamaga Municipal Council's Education Office (where he eventually became director). He soon took up his father's work with some of the few *biwa hiki* then still living but concentrated his energies on Yamashika from 1974. The period in which he most frequently visited Yamashika was the late 1970s through to the mid-1980s; by the late 1980s he had recorded approximately 120 cassette tapes of conversations between them (1994, 142). From around 1980, most researchers who sought access to Yamashika did so through the auspices of Kimura at the Yamaga Municipal Council.

In addition to editing some of his father's notes and essays and writing texts on resources for the biwa traditions (see chapter 2), Kimura has written transcripts of texts from performances by Yamashika with commentaries (Higobiwa Hozonkai 1991, 133–137, 167–202).[21] In 1981 he wrote an article that contains key information about his intentions in writing down his talks with Yamashika Yoshiyuki: He had been visiting Yamashika from the mid-1970s but began interview work in earnest in 1979 in response to essays by Yasuda Muneo and by his father, Yūshō, which call for close investigation and detailed documentation of information offered orally (*shōsai na kikigaki*) by those performers still living.[22] This article also questions the validity of

---

21. Of these, the transcripts of *Kikuchi Kuzure, Ono no Komachi* and two *hauta* are reproduced in the appendices to Kimura 1994 but without commentary or explanation of the textualisation processes.

22. Kimura says, in one of two essays that comprise the "Finale" (*shūmaki*) segment of his 1994 text, that he started visiting Yamashika regularly in 1974, but in "*Higo o*

the characterisation of music performed by the surviving *biwa hiki* in Kumamoto Prefecture as a distinctive Higo tradition (ibid., 61-62). Kimura's 1997 article "*Zatōbiwa no katari*" (Zatōbiwa narrative), in a volume of the *History of Japanese Literature* Iwanami Kōza series, includes material on Yamashika not published elsewhere. The article was written after the publication of his 1994 book at the invitation of the volume editor, Hyōdō Hiromi, and it returns emphatically to the skepticism of the 1981 piece with regard to the status of *higobiwa* as a clearly definable, unitary historical performance tradition. Yamashika's accounts are referred to at some length in arguing that he and other players from the former Higo region had always been received in other regions of Kyushu not as *higobiwa* performers but simply as *biwa hiki* who had travelled from Kumamoto. In the course of critiquing the idea that biwa players in the Higo region had originally been *mōsō*, Kimura gives various reasons why Yamashika himself sought and gained membership of a *mōsō* sect in 1973, the same year as the *higobiwa* tradition was designated an Intangible Cultural Asset. Kimura implies that the wording of the Office of Cultural Affairs' document, which refers to Higo-region blind musicians as former *mōsō*, was one influential factor in Yamashika's decision to join the Fukuoka-based Gensei Hōryū sect.

Little of the direct questioning of *higobiwa* as a historical construction that Kimura engages in in his 1981 and 1997 articles appears in *Higo biwa hiki Yamashika Yoshiyuki yobanashi* beyond inclusion of a partial version of Yamashika's own musings on the origin of the term and a single sentence at the end of Kimura's first commentary between sections of Yamashika's first-person narrative (35). The question of whether *higobiwa* players had originally been *mōsō* is not touched upon. In a segment of commentary and additional resources headed "About *higobiwa*," Kimura apologises for his own lack of expert knowledge of the history and nature of the tradition (153), then presents a set of extracts from his father's writings on the subject (154–163).[23]

---

hazushita biwa no kenkyū o," of 1981, he wrote that he had been carrying out the *kikigaki* project in earnest for two years. Yasuda's article was published in *Higobiwa dayori* No. 17 in 1981 but apparently had been written in the mid-1970s (Higobiwa Hozonkai 1991, 60), while Kimura Yūshō's writings had first appeared in various local newspapers in the early 1960s.

23. These writings are given in full on pages 6 and 7, and 42 to 45 of Higobiwa Hozonkai 1991.

The Text and Its Construction

The decision to include in the 1994 book only fragments of Kimura Yūshō's early 1960s writings rather than any new research on the regional biwa tradition, nor even references to more recent writings by scholars such as Yasuda and Hyōdō, reflects both the nature of this work and its intended readership. The final word of the book's title, *yobanashi*, is indicative of the work's genesis in conversations with Yamashika but also reflects Kimura's engagement in the processes of listening, questioning, transcription of recorded utterances and selection and re-wording of materials. This word also sets the tone for the book's contents, for *yobanashi* are stories told in the evening among friends and family, most likely while drinking. "Fireside tales" is perhaps the English expression that best conveys the intimacy of setting and comfort implicit in *yobanashi*. Although the term was suggested by the editor (as Kimura told me in 1998), he accepted it as fitting his own conception of the impression readers should receive. It is a document of the first half of Yamashika's life—of his childhood, training and experiences during the period when he was most active as a professional *biwa hiki*—by the writer who was personally closest to him. It is not presented as a definitive study or research text on the traditions of blind biwa players in Kumamoto nor Kyushu at large.

The book is structured so as to affirm the priority of the individual and his performance tradition's localised realm of meaning, over the broader concerns that have given rise to most research writings on biwa music. Accordingly the bulk of the text is composed of *kikigaki*, that is, an oral history compiled from many conversations and interviews. *Kikigaki* have taken many forms as a medium for documentation of the historical experience of individuals in circumstances for which few written documentary sources exist—third-person narratives constructed from the words of speakers are common, as are transcripts of interviews and *zadankai*, discussions among a group of people. A form of documentation that emerged from practices in both Japanese and Euro-American ethnography in the first half of the twentieth century, *kikigaki* are nonetheless comparable with earlier forms of Japanese self-narrative: *jiden* or *jijoden* (autobiography), *kaisō* (memoirs), *geidan* (writings by performing artists, or by those who listened to and transcribed what they said, about their professional lives and related experiences), *nikki bungaku* ("diary literature," an important ancient and medieval genre of personal narrative) and *shishōsetsu* ("I" novels of the modern era). While *geidan* have been written since as early as the fourteenth-century *sarugaku* noh-actor Zeami's time, full *jiden* by performing artists are hardly known before the end of the nineteenth century.[24] In this sense, *jiden* of Japanese musicians (whether written by the musician or a writer such as Kimura) are a modern narrative genre.

Structure

Kimura's book is a *jiden*, but one that is transparently structured by the writer (and editor) and framed by his commentary; materials from many years of recorded interviews are presented as a first-person narrative in a voice that emulates Yamashika's. Responses and questions put by Kimura in discussion are not even obliquely represented, but the narrative is arranged into sections, each of which is several pages long and has a title indicative of its principal topic. In the table of contents, the following material appears (followed by various appendices of repertory texts and source materials, which I omit here):

kōjō (maeoki)		Prologue (introduction)
ichiban-kuchi	First talk	
aima—hitoiki irete		*time out*—take a breath
niban-kuchi	Second talk	
aima—koko de ippuku		*time out*—a little rest here
sanban-kuchi	Third talk	
shūmaki (tsuika no hanashi)		Finale (additional discussion)

Kimura's commentary frames the first-person speech text and divides it into three segments by means of two short "time out" texts that provide background and explanation of various points. Each of the three segments consists of a series of anecdotes and episodes which Kimura has extracted from his talks with Yamashika and characterised by a title. As a partial life history, the overall contents are

24. See *Temae miso* (Nakamura 1944, 677–678).

chronological—from Yamashika's childhood to middle age—but the content of each of the first two "talks" is only roughly chronological, while that of the third is mostly non-chronological. In the first, on childhood and youth, the initial materials pertain to conditions in Yamashika's family, so that readers gain an idea of the financial inhibitions that prevented him from obtaining medical treatment for his eye condition, the tremendous quantity of farmwork he had to do for his father and the latter's selfishness and negativity. Episodes about a faith-healing retreat and encounters with a water sprite (*kappa*) suggest the contemporary depth of folk belief in Yamashika's community. Yamashika's attempts to earn money for himself and to take part in the usual activities of his society are expressed in sections entitled "Delivering papers" and "The Youth Association." Together with an episode about going for a conscription examination, which closes the first "talk" segment, those sections also suggest ways in which Yamashika's youth was affected by societal institutions of the time. The second "talk" is almost entirely devoted to Yamashika's apprenticeship, but contains several passages and one whole section descriptive of life in Amakusa, including many expressions of Yamashika's fondness for the place. There is also a brief section about the fact that he had his first sexual experiences there, while sleeping in small rooms with many people packed close together. The long episode that concludes the second segment, "Relations between the teacher and his apprentices," conveys the extent of financial scrutiny exercised among professional biwa players and suggests the root cause for Yamashika's early return from Amakusa. The contents of the non-chronological third "talk" (which is twice as long as the others) are far more diverse and include conditions and experiences of professional life, discrimination, stories of origin, marriage and personal life, instruments used by *biwa hiki*, and an account of the last days of the Second World War in Yamashika's experience.

Turning to Kimura's commentary sections, the first is an introduction that begins with an imagined speech by Yamashika as if he were introducing himself before performing the narrative that comprises the first segment of the book. For this reason, the title of the introduction is *Kōjō (maeoki)*. *Kōjō* (literally, a prologue) is one of the words that Yamashika used for the greeting (*aisatsu*) and "warm-up talk" he would often give as the first part of a performance (see chapter 4). The language of the *kōjō* is mostly standard modern Japanese but contains enough quasi-archaic and dialect forms to be reminiscent of Yamashika's style in performance. Accordingly, when the text switches from Yamashika's imagined *kōjō* to commentary in Kimura's own "voice," most of what he says has to do with Yamashika's use of language in performance and daily life and the fact that his conversation in old-style dialect has had to be modified so that readers can understand.

The first of the two "time out" commentary sections by Kimura presents historical information pertinent to understanding Yamashika's accounts of his childhood and youth as well as geographical information about districts in and near Nankan. The second commentary section discusses possible reasons for Yamashika's having decided not to return to complete his apprenticeship, the difficulty of starting professional work without having been fully trained and the broader context of Japanese nationalism and imperialism that shaped the society of the late 1920s when Yamashika started to earn a living as a *biwa hiki*.

After segment three, Kimura comments on his approach to selecting materials from transcribed conversations with Yamashika then simulates how Yamashika would end an evening's discussion—in effect, the close of the *yobanashi*. He then provides information about Yamashika's homelife, in particular his life with his fourth wife, Misao, who was also blind, and the activities of a typical day and speculates on both the impact of Yamashika's profession on domestic relations and the psychological damage wrought on him by his father's cruelty. After this highly personal commentary, he turns briefly to the matter of Yamashika's willingness to develop whatever skills he needed and even to join the Gensei Hōryū sect in order to maintain a clientele for his music and thus continue to support his family and himself. In light of this important characteristic of Yamashika's professional profile, Kimura criticises the tendency of both scholars and the media to ignore the contemporary settings for the practice of traditional arts such as music of the Kyushu *biwa hiki*:

> Researchers are always lamenting the deterioration of the authenticity of Japanese traditional performing arts, and they tend to treat those arts still being practised as things isolated from contemporary realities. The mass media likewise represents only an array of picturesque "rapidly disappearing performing arts." But actual practitioners of those arts

are more resilient than we usually imagine, and continually respond to their own awareness of their precarious situation. (147)

Constructedness and Subjectivity

While most of Kimura's text is composed of Yamashika's first-person narrative, the selection and distribution of transcribed materials, the structure of paragraphs and the wording of individual sentences are ultimately the work of Kimura and his editor at the Tokyo publishing house San'ichi Shobō.

The recorded talks which Kimura and his wife transcribed (1994, 224) as source material for the text began in 1979, when Yamashika was already 78 years old, and went on for nearly a decade thereafter. As Kimura implies by his choice of statements for the very start of the narrative and explains further elsewhere in commentary, most of the talks took place when Yamashika was drinking in the evening. Under such circumstances, the old man's way of talking was not only couched in the depths of local dialect but was also inevitably repetitive, elliptical, and full of diversions and partial incoherencies. In deciding to present Yamashika's words not as responses in a dialogue, but as a coherent, accessible first-person narrative that retains Yamashika's *kuchifuri* (way of talking), Kimura had to substantially change the wording (142). He termed this a "reorganisation" of the recorded speech (*saiwa kōsei*),[25] a procedure that involved multiple levels of transformation of Yamashika's utterances, including insertion of sentence subjects where they had been provided by Kimura in dialogue, replacement of dialect forms with standard Japanese or else watered-down forms that could be understood by readers not familiar with Higo and Chikugo dialects; removal of digressions, and re-ordering of ideas so as to give their presentation shape as a narrative.

Nonetheless, Kimura has used persuasive techniques to create a narrative style that conveys not only Yamashika's *kuchifuri* but also the setting in which Kimura heard all of what is "told" by Yamashika in the text. In the first segment, for example, Yamashika's account of childhood memories begins with an exhortation to drink, so that the listening—and the telling—will be easier. This is not only a rhetorical gesture; it is performative in the sense that it establishes a frame for

---

25. This term appears on the title page of the typed manuscript Kimura sent to the San'ichi Shobō publisher, of which I received a partial copy.

the subsequent act of narration. It is moreover in keeping with the informal mode of narrative (as distinct from dialogue or conversation) and intimate setting implied in the title of Kimura's book.[26]

The bulk of Kimura's text is based on recordings that are documents of his interaction with Yamashika over many years, but the decision to render the material as first-person narrative transforms it from an intersubjective document into a performative construction of a subjectivity presented as Yamashika's. That being said, Kimura's framing commentary includes enough ethnographic information (about his own relations with the musician and the way in which Yamashika's words have been altered) for readers to hold in mind the distance between what they read in the narrative segments and the ways in which such events and experiences may actually have been communicated by Yamashika.

Content

Kimura sought to convey not only the *kuchifuri* but also "the plain face" (*sugao*) of Yamashika (142). This implies not only his way of talking and presenting his memories but also something of his character and personal experiences. The principal strategy employed to this end is a selective presentation of topics, many of which are not touched upon in other sources. Their discussion was enabled only by the friendship and quasi-familial relationship between Yamashika and Kimura. Kimura acknowledges the relationship as having been not unlike that with a grandfather because he knew Yamashika from the time of his earliest memories. Inevitably this had important consequences for the kinds of information he chose to include in Yamashika's narrative segments and in his own commentary sections:

> To sufficiently communicate to others one's intimate experience of a person is truly difficult; I ask for readers' understanding of the fact that my personal feelings have inevitably played a part in this task. (142–143)

26. In my own experience, Yamashika drank *sake* with and after his meal every night and would always try to ensure that I and any others present drank steadily along with him. All lengthy discussions at night were both enabled and delimited by the quantity of *sake* available. What is more, as the drinking progressed, Yamashika's responses would as often as not turn from short replies to narratives that might be dramatised through a range of voice-types and onomatopoeic syllables.

Among topics discussed that reflect the intimacy between Kimura and his "subject" are Yamashika's father's cruelty, certain of his childhood memories, his relations with women and his experiences of discrimination. On all four of these matters, Kimura's book is a unique source. By graphically conveying the exploitative, neglectful and perhaps even sadistic behaviour of Yamashika's father, in combination with accounts of the family's privations, we gain an impression of the strength of Yamashika's motivation to become financially independent. By including accounts of sexual experience, love and friendship, Kimura imparts a personal depth to Yamashika's character that is lacking in all other sources on blind musicians in Kyushu.[27] By broaching the matter of discrimination against itinerant performers, the blind and *biwa hiki* in particular, in both Yamashika's narrative and his own commentary, Kimura opens up territory that is hardly touched upon in the many other documents about Yamashika and the Kyushu biwa traditions.

In view of the broad wave of reformist social activism and academic interest since the 1970s in remnant prejudice against *burakumin* (the modern Japanese term for various groups in Japanese society regarded as essentially defiled and subject to discrimination since the mid Edo period[28]), one would expect those matters to figure importantly in documentation of Yamashika and other *biwa hiki*. In chapter 5, I present data about Yamashika's and others' personal experiences of discrimination because of blindness and their professional engagement in *kadozuke* performance, but, beyond my own discussions with *biwa hiki*, that data comes from only two published sources: Kimura 1994 (in particular pages 105 to 109) and a single paragraph in Yasuda 2001 (19). If discrimination against blind biwa players is conspicuous by its absence from most documentation of Yamashika, this may be because such treatment had continued to a certain extent until recent times. Persistence in regional Kyushu of discriminatory practices and attitudes towards people regarded as of *burakumin* or otherwise "tainted" origins may have inhibited publication of accounts that could be interpreted

---

27. Kawano's 2001 book on the Miyazaki-region *mōsō* Nagata Hōjun is comparable in the way it considers his marriage to a sighted woman but keeps a formal distance in tone, perhaps because of Nagata's status as a practising priest in Nobeoka and environs.

28. Groemer (2001a, 352) argues that it was only from this time that the people referred to as *eta* or *hinin* were treated as "essentially" polluted and therefore outcasts.

as implying such origins with respect to living or recently deceased individuals. Only Kimura's text, published in the last two years of Yamashika's life, deals with the issue directly and at length.

There is a degree of nostalgia that surfaces often in Kimura's book—perhaps as much nostalgia for Kimura's own experiences of eliciting Yamashika's accounts of his life over a decade of visits to his home, as for the distant way of life described therein. As is so often the case in the body of twentieth-century writings and cultural texts (including many ethnographic documents) that articulate a "pastoral allegoric" view of the *furusato* world and its inhabitants, that world is one the author himself did not live in:

> By documenting the daily experiences of a living biwa player, I wanted to achieve some sort of understanding of the nature of an age I'd not experienced. (153)

By comparison with many of the texts described in chapter 2 and earlier in this chapter, however, Kimura's is not one in which nostalgia reduces Yamashika and other *biwa hiki* to stereotypic figures of a lost golden age. The degree of detail and the range of topics that Kimura includes in portraying Yamashika's experiences ensure that readers gain a sense of the complexity of making a living as he did as well as the conflict and difficulties he faced. At the same time, certain kinds of material that figure in other sources have been omitted, perhaps because the nature of Kimura's relationship to Yamashika led him to avoid matters that may have reflected poorly on his character. For example, in the section entitled "Relations between the teacher and his apprentices," the account of a dispute between his teacher, Ezaki, and an older pupil ends without any hint of the anger at Ezaki which Yasuda (1991, 21) claims was the principal reason Yamashika cut short his apprenticeship. Likewise, in the third segment of first-person narrative (*sanbankuchi*), Kimura omits any reference to Mori Yoichi, a figure of importance in Yamashika's professional development, without whom he may not have been able to acquire sufficient skills and repertory to continue as a *biwa hiki*. Mori was a *biwa hiki* from a place called Kamiuchi within Miike (either a village just south-west of Nankan, or the Miike area just outside Ōmuta[29]), whose professional name

---

29. The localities specified in Murayama 1986 and Kimura 1994 are Miike and

was Tamagawa Kyōzan. Ga Machiko was told by Yamashika that over the course of a year between Yamashika's return from Amakusa in 1925 and his naming ceremony on January 6, 1927, Mori had taught him important repertory pieces such as *Ichi no Tani*, *Ko Atsumori*, *Azekakehime*, *Shuntokumaru* and *Oguri Hangan* (Ga 1972, 28; see also Murayama 1986). Yet there is no mention of this in Kimura's book, and indeed a date is given for the naming ceremony (Kimura 1994, 74) that is two years earlier than that given by both Ga and Yasuda.[30]

Kimura's own interests and preferences are also reflected in the choice of materials from his transcribed conversations. He undoubtedly emphasises *kamigoto* in his portrayal of Yamashika, at the expense of information about secular repertory. Yamashika's anecdotes about ritual performance and knowledge fill many pages of the book, but the titles and contents of the non-ritual narratives that have been the principal subject of research writings on Yamashika are mentioned just a handful of times.[31] This bias toward the sacred would appear to be an aspect of Kimura's own nostalgia for a time when local belief in the powers of *kami* such as Kōjin, Suijin and Jijin underpinned maintenance of agrarian rituals such as the *kamado-barai*, *suijin-barai* and *watamashi*.

*   *   *

Soon after finishing fieldwork in Kumamoto in 1992, I wrote the following:

> Not all of the many voices which speak of Yamashika have equal authority or persuasive force, for their reception is largely a matter of

Kamiuchi, respectively, but a Taisho 2 (1913) map of the area (Kokudo Kōtsūshō 1926) shows that Kamiuchi was a place within an area called Miike near Nankan. A second area called Miike existed to the south-west, however; this was the infamous Miike coal-mine region near Ōmuta. Note that Ga (1972) and Yasuda (2001) both give the Ōmuta vicinity as Mori's place of residence.

30. The only reference to Tamagawa Kyōzan is as one of two *biwa hiki* chastised by the senior member of the Tamagawa-*ha*, Tamagawa Sekijun, at celebrations after Yamashika's naming ceremony (Kimura 1994, 82). It is possible that Kyōzan was not otherwise referred to in the set of tapes that Kimura and his wife transcribed in preparing the book manuscript.

31. The appendix texts for the *Kikuchi Kuzure* and several *hauta* (188–223) are exceptional in this regard but are not referred to beyond a commentary written by Kimura's father.

the extent to which the power to confer cultural legitimacy is vested in the respective "speakers," a power in its turn conferred in accordance with a hegemony which shapes Japanese academic and intellectual discourse. (de Ferranti 1994, 48)

With hindsight and further experience of academic and intellectual life in Japan, this seems a too-broadly conceived, even simplistic, way to portray the operation of power and the reception of cultural texts. It remains true to say, however, that "the negotiation of authority over 'the last *biwa hōshi*' is part of a larger arena of struggle for cultural authority over accounts of Japanese performing arts history, social history, and national identity" (ibid., 65). From the perspective of that struggle, the texts about Yamashika (and other blind biwa players) that I have surveyed can be divided into those which address him as a member of the national community—"Japan" and its people—and those which locate him firmly within the historically distinct culture of Higo. The same holds for representations of the *mōsō* traditions, which in some cases (Nakayama 1934; Narita 1985a; Hirose 1997) are framed so as to incorporate them into popular and academic discourses about national histories of religious institutions, the performing arts, and the blind, and in other cases place emphasis on regionally framed identity and meanings (Murata 1994; Nagai 2002; Kawano 2001). Yet the range of materials I have discussed provides examples of *both* kinds of texts produced by *both* local and Tokyo-based groups and individuals. This is evidence that those who have addressed Yamashika and the biwa traditions have not been "cultural insiders" merely by virtue of their residence in Kumamoto or Kyushu and that, conversely, some who have no particular ties to regional Kyushu (for example, Suwa Atsushi, the Tokyo director of the 1983 documentary *Satsuma mōsōbiwa*) have portrayed biwa players as individuated subjects whose music has been acquired and performed for the most part in specific local contexts with little or no emphasis on its relations to the established canon of Japanese musical history or to stereotypic images of the past. Whereas some of those who lived "next door" to *biwa hiki* actively incorporated them into hegemonic constructions of national cultural schema and identity, others who lived far from Kyushu have resisted casting Yamashika and other *biwa hiki* merely as relics of *biwa hōshi*, at the same time seeking localised frameworks of understanding and meaning for their portrayals of blind musicians.

Like that between local and Tokyo voices, the divide between academic and populist representations of Yamashika and the biwa traditions is not a merely theoretical one, for it reflects circumstantial and ideological factors that shape the production and reception of writings and cultural texts. Nonetheless the divide is spanned by common elements that cannot be disregarded. Scholarly texts are created as the daily produce of the academic profession and reflect their producers' involvement with particular issues and developments in scholarship, but they are not necessarily free of stereotypes and hegemonic representational forms. On the other hand, although suffused with a gentle nostalgia and undoubtedly constructed in accordance with their makers' personal agendas and preferences, texts such as Kimura's and Suwa's present Yamashika and the Satsuma *mōsō* Fukijima Junkai as contemporary individuals in richly detailed local settings rather than as men reduced ahistorically to the ghosts of *biwa hōshi*.

In the space between the many accounts of his music and performances, his professional and daily life, Yamashika's identity is highly contested, but it remains elusive and ultimately resistant to simplification. With his final illness, the performance tradition of blind *biwa hiki* in effect ended. From well before then, however, knowledge of the tradition and of living *biwa hiki* had become the sum of these many representations in a variety of media.

4

TALES IN PERFORMANCE

> As for performance and storytelling, they were ruined by that war. Before the war our art still had some standing—there were even plenty of amateurs who learnt biwa, and there were audiences who knew how to listen and enjoy the tales.... When people were able to pay attention to the close details of a story, you just couldn't perform carelessly, you know. Nowadays you can do it however you like—just any old way, and no one will say a thing!
>
> (Kimura 1994, 140)

Yamashika Yoshiyuki performed in many contexts in his professional life. The importance of his activities as a ritual celebrant has been acknowledged in chapters 2 and 3, but performance of narratives and songs for entertainment made up the great bulk of his work. For that reason, exposition of the performance process in this chapter concerns *danmono*, the central body of repertory of Yamashika and other *biwa hiki* whose practices were documented during the 1970s through 1990s. The approach adopted here is multi-faceted but can be characterised as formal analysis of textual, performative and musical elements informed by comments about practice that Yamashika and others made, by the observations of several researchers who conducted fieldwork with Yamashika and other *biwa hiki* and by my own observations of performances between 1989 and 1992. The framing of this chapter reflects my conviction that only a combination of such tools and methods can do justice to the complexity of the narrative performances for which Yamashika was renowned locally and nationally.

Performance Contexts and Procedures

Actual experience of performance by blind biwa players was already rare by the time I began intensive fieldwork in 1991, although five men in various parts of Kyushu remained able to play: Yamashika Yoshiyuki and Hashiguchi Keisuke in Kumamoto Prefecture, Takagi Seigen in the Kunisaki peninsula of Oita Prefecture, Fukijima Junkai in Kagoshima Prefecture and Nagata Hōjun in Miyazaki Prefecture. The youngest of those five, the Tendai-sect priest Nagata Hōjun (b. 1935), continued in 2007 to perform rites with biwa for parishioners near his temple in Nobeoka (see chapter 6), but by the early 1990s most performances by blind biwa players were at the request of researchers and cultural bureaucrats. This was a situation in which the conditions of past performances described by Yamashika and others were utterly disparate from those of the few performances still taking place. It follows that the content of tales produced through oral composition may also have been different to that in past performances.

Settings and Audiences

Since about 1970,[1] *biwa hiki* have performed secular narratives mainly at the instigation of researchers, aficionados of local folklore and culture, or under the auspices of public bodies such as the Higobiwa Preservation Society, and these performances took place occasionally in public halls and lecture rooms or recording studios and more rarely in private homes. Audiences were for the most part small, but heterogeneous in terms of audience members' places of origin and the degrees of their familiarity with narratives that had once been the most commonly performed items of biwa singers' repertories. In these respects, and in the fact that the lifestyles of the audience members were unfamiliar to the performers, they have been quite unlike the typical audiences of the pre- and immediate post-war eras.

In the pre-war era, no more than a hundred people would have attended a performance in a *zashiki* (formal room in a house or inn). Most of the audience would have been from a single locale and would have shared a lifestyle well known to the musician, who consequently felt confident of his ability to establish a rapport. As a purely oral tradition in which text fixity was rarely observed in practice, many aspects of a given piece in performance were determined by the

---

1. From Ga's interview work done in 1971, it is clear that Yamashika had still performed frequently until the late 1960s, and other *biwa hiki* had continued work until the early 1960s (Ga 1972, 26).

nature of the relation between singers and their audience. Time and again *biwa hiki* players told me that to perform well one must know something about who is listening; at the very least one should know where they are from and what sort of work they do, for this will help both in choosing a recitation and in deciding what passages to recite in detail, to simplify or perhaps to omit.

During a performance, the quality of response from the audience would often determine the actual length and make-up of segments within the narrative. Yamashika expressed the performer's former reliance upon audience response in order to shape his tale in the following statement: "*Biwa hiki* register their audience's response as they recite, you see, but today people don't understand the stories well, so there *is* no response! This makes it very hard to perform at all" (quoted in Uda 1991, 85).

Kadobiki and *Zashikibiwa*

Harai ritual work became less common in the early twentieth century, so *biwa hiki* came to rely on secular narrative performance for a greater portion of their income. The two principal contexts for secular narrative performance were *kadozuke* (or *kadobiki* in the vernacular), in which a *biwa hiki* would wander from house to house performing short songs and excerpts from narratives, and *zashikibiwa*, which was a pre-arranged performance of longer excerpts and entire tales, usually given in the *zashiki* of a private house.

Kadobiki and *zashikibiwa* performances each had characteristic narrative repertories as well as shorter songs; there were pieces that would be performed only for *kadobiki* or *zashikibiwa*, respectively, as well as a group of common tales presented in shortened form in *kadobiki*. In both contexts the *zatō*'s first concern was to interest listeners to the extent that they would offer some form of remuneration. In *kadobiki* this had to be done without overly depleting the musician's own energies and resources, while in *zashikibiwa* a chief concern was to neither bore nor offend listeners, who at any time were able to leave without paying. It was only through the astute exercise of diverse performance strategies and responsiveness to patrons' moods and tastes that *biwa hiki* were able to make a living.

The functional distinction between the *kadobiki* and *zashikibiwa* repertories was based not only on the disparity in timeframe for performance but also on considerations of the kinds of people who were likely to make up an audience: As *kadobiki* could be done only during the day (with the exception of evening *yonagashi*, described below), when it was safe for a blind person to walk from one village to the next, those most likely to hear the biwa player were children, women nursing babies and the elderly—in other words, those who could not work in the fields. Of these, the women were in control of money and grains given as payment to itinerant musicians. Accordingly, biwa players sought to please them by presenting abbreviated versions of tales in which experiences of particular concern to women were highlighted. For example, an especially favoured theme was that of the domestic torment of a young woman by her mother-in-law, which figures in *Azekakehime* and other narratives that were among the most frequently performed tales for *kadobiki*. Some *biwa hiki* would try to win additional remuneration by entertaining the children of a household with various comic routines and tricks (*kyokubiki*), among which the *hachinin-gei* (eight-person show) was most common.[2]

When doing *kadobiki* performances the biwa player's first task was to draw the attention of patrons to the quality of his skills. This was done in one of two ways: Usually he stood outside a house, playing and calling out or singing a short fragment until he attracted the attention of someone who gave him rice, barley or money immediately and asked him to move on, or invited him inside the gate to play more. Having secured the invitation of a householder, the musician would usually sit and play for between two and ten minutes in the entrance hall, or on the *engawa* verandah. On rare occasions, however, he would be invited inside the house to perform for up to half an hour. In both circumstances he was concerned to preserve his voice, for after one *kadobiki* performance was over, he had to go on to another house to play for a new group of listeners. A common way to avoid straining the voice was to present either a *hauta* song or a condensed version of a tale using only two sorts of melody pattern: a kind of "ground" melodic recitation pattern called *katari*, *kotoba(-bushi)* or *okuri* (in the

---

2. See the section on *charimono* in chapter 2.

biwa hiki Hashiguchi Keisuke's terminology); and occasional passages of the *nagashi*, a distinctive musical pattern that could be delivered with relatively little effort but pleased listeners because of its poetic register, its prominent use of melisma and its sustained regular beat.

In the event that he was invited to play inside the house for longer than the usual period of time a *biwa hiki* had to carefully gauge the minimum length of performance likely to be acceptable to his patrons. For this purpose, he developed a stock of fixed-text passages from each of his most popular tales such that he could "leap into" the middle of the narrative, starting his performance from a passage that everyone knew and taking the tale on in quick succession to a favourite or climactic scene. Such fixed-text passages were useful as markers emblematic of the tale as a whole (Hyōdō 1993, 61–62) through which listeners could be immediately drawn into the excitement and "flow" of a narrative they already knew well. The performer thus presented his patrons with only excerpts that he felt they most wanted to hear—and which, from the performer's perspective, could be rendered in as short a time possible.

While doing *kadobiki* in an area with which he was unfamiliar, it was considered more efficient for the *biwa hiki* to simply walk around a village playing and singing simplified versions of the pattern called *nagashi* until he received alms or was invited to stop at a house. When this was done in the evening in the amusement district of a town, it was called *yonagashi* and involved singing and playing ear-catching passages until some drinkers asked the *biwa hiki* to stay on and perform more. As music for people at play, Yamashika believed it called for a deliberate strategy of presenting diverse kinds of material:

> In *kadobiki* there should be a difference in the way you play for *yonagashi*. There are people who do just the same things as they would during the day, but those people mostly do popular songs [*hauta* and the like] anyway—they do things that will lighten people's spirits. (Kimura 1994, 128)

In contrast to *kadobiki*, *zashikibiwa* performances were usually given in the evening on occasions for celebration and affirmation of community, such as the rice and barley harvest festivals, and new year festivities, or else as entertainment after the conclusion of a *harai* or other ritual performed by the *zatō*. *Zashikibiwa* could also take place on days of no particular note, and sometimes approached the form of a concert in which two or more *biwa hiki* who travelled together, or simply happened to be working in the same area on a given day, performed in succession.[3] In such events each *biwa hiki* usually appeared with their own banner bearing their performer's name (figure 4.1).

Figure 4.1. Yamashika performing while seated on a chair behind a banner bearing his professional name, Tamagawa Kyōen (-shi). Photograph by the author (November 1991).

Considerations that had bearing on the choice of narratives for a given *zashikibiwa* performance included the locale and the occasion, and whether persons of authority were present. A tale of local Kyushu history might be appropriate for a particular locale—for example, *Tamayohime* in Tamana, as it tells of the woman who gave the town its name—and on auspicious occasions a particular tale might be chosen; for example, at New Year festivities the comic piece *Tai no mukoiri*

---

3. Ōkawa Susumu told me of often having done this, both by himself and together with other *biwa hiki*, such as Morita Takashi, with whom he had travelled. See also Hashiguchi's accounts of doing *kadozuke* in small groups, in Yasuda (2001, 28).

(The *tai*'s wedding) might be presented because of the *tai*'s (sea bream) association with prosperity and abundance. When people of high social standing were present, a tale of appropriate dignity had to be told, about warriors of the Heike and Genji clans or other samurai-class figures whose narratives were in the most formal category of repertory.

Zashikibiwa provided opportunities to perform several segments or even all of some well-known tales in the *danmono* category, some of which required more than five hours to perform in full. On festival days, and in particular *nijūsan-ya*, the night of the autumn equinox, a performance might last longer, until at least one or two in the morning, so that all or the bulk of longer tales could be performed (Ga 1972, 29). Just prior to the performance, members of the audience would often make specific requests for favoured tales or *dan* episodes therein, but the *biwa hiki* had licence to decline such requests.

In *zashikibiwa* a performer would tune his instrument, then first address the listeners in speech rather than in song or recitation. He had several objectives in doing such *aisatsu* (introductory greetings) or *kōjō* (prologue or "warm-up" talks): to clear his throat before singing; to test the acoustic of the performance space; to introduce himself and gain the listeners' confidence; to say something about the narrative he will sing, should it need explanation; and to effect a transition from lived reality to imaginative experience by means of a parallel transition from the register and forms of everyday speech to those of recitation. In Yamashika's practice the *aisatsu* varied in length from about three to ten minutes in accordance with time constraints and the setting of the performance and regularly formed a three-part scheme, as follows:

1. Greetings and self-deprecating comments, usually in the form of elaborate apologies for his own lack of skill as a performer.
2. Jokes about the occasion or the audience's task of listening.
3. Introduction of the name of the tale to be recited, accompanied by a shift to a more mannered style of delivery and adoption of literary forms of speech, including some rhetorical formulas which mark the end of the talk.

While even in recordings of the 1970s Yamashika would belittle his own talents when introducing himself, as his strength waned by the mid-1980s such comments took on a tone of seriousness due to his keen awareness of his vocal and instrumental techniques' deterioration with age. Apart from his own infirmities, for Yamashika a common source of humour in introductory *aisatsu* was the extremity of change in post-war Japan and especially the effect that this had had on listeners' abilities to understand his tales. For example, in a warm-up talk for the second *dan* of *Ichi no tani* in a performance of November 1991, Yamashika reminded his audience that the traditional occupation of farmers had been "gathering shit" from both humans and animals to make fertiliser, but as animals were now no longer involved in farm work, even country folk didn't know the meanings of old terms for parts of animals' bodies, such as *koma no sanzu* (a horse's rump). By means of this explanation he caused much laughter among the audience and also ensured that they would understand the expression *koma no sanzu* when it occurred in a crucial episode towards the end of the tale.

In response to what he knew of the nature and mood of the *zashikibiwa* audience, a *biwa hiki* would decide whether or not to perform short *charimono* comic pieces between longer recitations. Yamashika emphasised the importance of these pieces for his livelihood:

> At night the audience likes to drink. During the summer festivals they even start drinking in the middle of the day. At those times there'd often be requests for "something interesting," which meant something funny. If you didn't have some pieces like that, you couldn't make money when you were engaged to play for people who were drinking. (Kimura 1994, 128)

The *biwa hiki* would also judge whether it was appropriate to use the performance technique called *chari (o ireru)*, which refers to the introduction of humorous asides or short comic scenes during the course of a tale, in stark and immediate contrast to their surroundings (see further de Ferranti 1996a). *Chari* seems to have been an important characteristic of performance under appropriate circumstances, but if the *biwa hiki* was mistaken in his decision to introduce humour of this sort, his audience was usually quick to show their displeasure.

A rare variant practice in *zashikibiwa* performance was to illustrate elements in the tale in another medium, dance:

> Up in Ōmuta they even used to bring in a dancer with the stories! Compared to places like that, back around Yamaga the audiences' needs were easier to satisfy. (Kimura 1994, 128)

Given that *biwageki*, biwa recitation with simultaneous dramatic portrayal of the narrative, was a form of performance that some *chikuzenbiwa* and *satsumabiwa* performers engaged in during the early decades of the century, this recollection suggests that among blind *biwa hiki*, too, there may have been a variety of mixed-media modes of performance.

Other Contexts: Myōon Kō, *Nabiraki* and *Yogomori*

Once a year, after the observance of the Myōon Kō ceremony (see chapter 2), there would be a concert (*taikai*) of several hours' duration on a stage, preferably outdoors, in which all Kō member musicians would compete for the local community's pleasure and their own renown.[4] As will be described in chapter 5, a new professional's name-taking event (*nabiraki*) also involved a ceremonial performance by local members of the teaching lineage group (*ha*) in which he had been trained; they were in effect public concerts in which many *biwa hiki* appeared in succession.

The *yogomori* (or *o-komori*) was an important performance context that continued to yield Yamashika occasional income into the 1980s. It involved performance of *gedai* repertory inside small shrines from evening well into or throughout the night on festival dates. The belief that the shrine's deity was absent—as well as the surrounding community's desire for entertainment—prompted the expectation that a *biwa hiki* should perform for as long as he could, with few breaks. The presentation of entire multiple-*dan gedai* was common, so *yogomori* performances tested the *biwa hiki*'s stamina and oral compositional skills.

Concert Performances Since the 1960s

By the mid-1960s, when the Tokyo musicologist Tanabe Hisao first publicised the survival of a biwa narrative tradition in central Kyushu, *biwa hiki* had all but ceased doing *kadobiki*, both because of their advancing age and because the number of people willing to give money for such performances was far fewer than in pre-war years. Engagement

---

4. See Uda (1992, 28) for Hashiguchi Keisuke's vivid account of such a concert which took place in 1929 or 1930 at Minamata.

to do *zashikibiwa* performances had also fallen in frequency, although they were not yet rare. Largely in response to Tanabe's writings, a flush of interest by local scholars, media and cultural bureaucrats led to the organisation of concert-style performances in public facilities (including halls designed for Western musical concerts), in which two or more musicians would each present a *hauta*, a *danmono* comprising only a single *dan*, such as *Dōjōji*, or even a *dan* from a longer tale. During the 1970s such concerts were held regularly under the auspices of the Higobiwa Preservation Society and might include as many as six *biwa hiki*, but thereafter there was a rapid depletion in the numbers of those still able to perform, and media interest also abated. By the mid-1980s only two *biwa hiki* were able to perform publicly, and only one, Yamashika, did so with any frequency.

I was able to attend several performances by Yamashika during 1989, 1991 and 1992, under the auspices of various scholars and film producers. The first aspect of the new performance conditions to which Yamashika had to adjust was the unfamiliar, heterogeneous nature of his audiences. Yamashika's solution to the challenge of facing an audience of anonymous listeners was to question those looking after him at length about the people who would listen to his performance. As I observed on two occasions when I was with Yamashika immediately prior to a concert-hall performance, in most cases his choice of a narrative to perform would be made only after he had learned as much as possible about the audience.

A second problem faced by *biwa hiki* was the limited performance time available for each participant in a concert. During the 1980s Yamashika responded to frequent requests for brief appearances of twenty to thirty minutes by presenting the single-*dan* tale *Dōjōji* as a stock-in-trade piece for such occasions. He was not always allocated the minimum of twenty minutes required for his version of the story to be presented, however, and there is at least one recorded performance in which Yamashika suddenly apologises for having to cut the tale short, wishes his audience good health and promises to recite the rest of the story for them if he ever gets a chance![5] Notwithstanding, on most occasions *Dōjōji* or another well-known single-*dan* tale fitted well into the time allocated for Yamashika's performances.

---

5. Performance of October 10, 1989, recorded and transcribed by Hyōdō (1991, 49–50).

On those occasions during 1991 and 1992 when Yamashika was given a period of some hours in which to perform—in other words, a period similar to that which had been the norm in *zashikibiwa* events— he had to cope with the fact that his own physical condition was hardly what it had been in the past, so his voice was liable to weaken or give out much sooner. His way of dealing with this problem was to present large sections of the narrative in declaimed heightened speech or syllabic pitched recitation (*kotoba*), a style of vocal delivery that is far less taxing than the conventional use of various *fushi* patterns that require diverse forms of vocal delivery, including melismatic song.

Formal Elements in Narrative Performance

Analysis of musical performance first of all must address the question of discrete items or "pieces" in the repertory performed. Other than *hauta* and relatively short items always performed in their entirety without a break, most tales (*gedai*) in the *biwa hiki* repertory were *danmono* that could be broken down into the shorter units of *dan*, which were given either in isolation or as a sequence of performance items with breaks for the musician and audience in between.

Framing Tales

After the *aisatsu* introductory talk had ended and a *biwa hiki* began his performance of a tale, what expectations did the audience hold about the way he would present a tale for them? In other words, what were the formal principles of narrative text structure in performance? The following points summarise the textual framing of a tale from the *danmono* repertory. They reflect performances I witnessed or have listened to and the contents of texts that have been transcribed from Yamashika's repertory.

1. Tales about very well-known figures and episodes, such as Minamoto no Yorimitsu ("Raiko") and Taira no Atsumori, would often begin with a brief set of introductory phrases to give the narrative setting or even with none at all (for example, in the case of the well-known *Dōjōji* tale). For example, a tale about one of

Raiko's vassals who is struck blind, *Zentai Heike*,[6] begins with the following three lines:

> *Minamoto no Yorimitsu kō tote*
> Lord Yorimitsu of the Minamoto
>
> *hana no miyako ni goza wo sue*
> resided in the capital
>
> *amata no kerai o izanaite tsukihi o kurasetamau*
> passing his days surrounded by his many vassals.

Yamashika then launches into the first events of the narrative, describing Yorimitsu's fondness for collecting birds, and a *mejiro* in particular (a bird in the care of someone who becomes one of the main characters of the tale):

> *itatte Yorimitsu-kō wa monosuki na hito de*
> Without doubt Lord Yorimitsu was a man who
>   delighted in possessions.
>
> *ko-tori o atsume o-tanoshimi nasaru*
> He enjoyed collecting small birds,
>
> *ichiban ki ni iru sono tori wa mejiro de atta*
> and the bird he liked most was the *mejiro*.

2. In other cases the tale itself would be prefaced by a short sung text, called the *makura* ("pillow text"), *kingen* ("words of gold"), or, less commonly, *daigo* (meaning unknown).[7] Ōkawa, Yamashika and Hashiguchi all told me of this special practice of an introductory text at the start of longer tales presented in *zashikibiwa* or *yogomori* performances. As the term suggests, the contents of *kingen* were

---

6. According to Kimura (oral communication, December 2005), the title of the tale might be *Zen Taiheiki*, for when he took down the text, Yamashika varied his pronunciation of the title and did not explain its meaning. For the full text transcription see Higobiwa Hozonkai (1991, 226).

7. In discussions with Yamashika, Ōkawa, Hashiguchi and Morita Shōjō in the early 1990s, *makura* was used both to refer to this, and to what I have called the prologue or "warm-up talk." The word's principal referent, however, was this reflective sung introduction. Ōkawa also said that what he called the *daigo* was called a *makura* in *naniwa-bushi*. It may be that the word reflects influence from *gidayū-bushi* practice, in which the first scene (*shōdan*) of the first act of a *jidaimono* play is called the *daijo* (大序).

didactic, so as to suggest a kind of solemn reflection upon the joys and torments of the events to be described in the story to come. The *kingen* was usually marked off from the first *dan* by a full or abbreviated form of a short biwa prelude played at the start of most pieces. The following *kingen* is from an April 1989 performance of the first *dan* of *Ichi no Tani* (the performance shown on the cover of this book):

Yo hisokani omoi miru ni	If we think over for ourselves the ways of the world,
ue o mireba kagiri nashi	the limitless heights above us,
shita o mite mo	and below,
doko made shita ka wake ga wakaranu	the bottomless depths.
satemo yama kara nagareru tani no mizu	The waters of the valleys flow down from the mountains
yuku sue sue made mo	and go all the way to their ends.
nagarete iku sansui mo	The flowing mountain streams, too,
shibashi konoha no shita kuguru	pass for a while under the leaves—
taikai to naru hi made mo	until the day they become part of the great ocean,
iwa ya konoha no shita o kuguru	they must pass under rocks and leaves.

The texts of some of the *kingen* known to *biwa hiki* were common, including the following, as sung by Yamashika and Hashiguchi (Ga 1972, 36):

mizu wa hōen no ki ni shitagau	As water is shaped by its vessel
hito wa zen aku no tomo ni yoru	people are shaped by the moral worth of their friends—
toka ya kore wa kojin no tatoe nari	so say the proverbs of the ancients.

3. After the *kingen* had been sung, the first narrative events would be marked by a verbal formula that emphatically framed a narrative temporal space, most commonly *aru hi no koto ni* ("one day"/"on a certain day"). Another common formula was that used after the *kingen* given above, in the 1989 performance of the first *dan* of *Ichi no Tani*, *kore wa koko ni* _____ ("Here before us is _____ ").

4. Each *dan* would unfold as a sequence of scenes or episodes, played out as first-person dialogue framed with third-person description and commentary. Temporal continuity between episodes was generally self-evident, but in cases of temporal shift, so as to

describe events coincident with or which preceded ones already presented, marker expressions such as *hanashi ga kawaru* (in context meaning "the story changes here") were used.

5. In items of two or more *dan*, the tale as a whole exists as a fixed sequence of primary events or scenes, but the content of individual *dan* is fluid; both the number of *dan* required to narrate a "complete" tale and the relative contents of each *dan* (as distinct from the sequence of narrative events that comprise the entire tale) were highly variable. In most cases the break between *dan* would occur at a *yama* ("peak") narrative point, that is, a point of excitement from which listeners would anticipate the impending fortunes of key figures in the tale. Accordingly, Yamashika's stock phrases for marking the end of a *dan* included ___ *no on-mi no ue, kanzenu hito wa nakarikeri* ("No one could be unmoved by the circumstances of ___") and *ima ga yo made mo* ___ *no na ga nokoru* ("The names of ___ live on in the world, even today").

6. The end of the performance—which was not necessarily the end of the tale, unless all *dan* or only the final *dan* of a lengthy tale had been presented—was marked both musically and verbally. The latter usually included a formulaic phrase to say that the story was over, such as ___*no monogatari* ___ *mazu kore made* ("The tale about ___, ___ ends here, for now"). Often included, too, were one or more phrases that broke the "frame" of performance by referring to the *biwa hiki* himself, for example: *nagaku o-jama ni narimashita* ("I've troubled you for long enough"), and *o-somatsu deshita mazu kore made* ("My performance was poor but I'll end it here").

Sonic Elements of Performance

As a musicologist, in my fieldwork with *biwa hiki* I focussed upon understanding the simultaneous oral composition of narrative text and musical patterning. In discussions with Yamashika and other *biwa hiki*, on the whole I sought to avoid using terms for music and narrative structure that were not familiar to the musicians themselves. Yet when explaining to each of the three men I interviewed just why I was there and what I hoped to understand with their help, I inevitably would use the general word for music, *ongaku*, often preceded by *katarimono*, as a general term for genres of narrative performance with musical instruments. In Yamashika's case, this soon brought the response that what he had done for a living was in no sense performance of *ongaku*, but something more like *sekkyō*, that is, the performance of tales for the purpose of edification. He stressed thereby that although he played biwa, the focus of his work was always the act of *katari*, the telling of stories that would engage an audience. While another former *biwa hiki*, Ōkawa Susumu, showed comparatively more interest in "musical" aspects of performance technique (and indeed recited with far more consistent melodic pitch than Yamashika), he too stressed that the ground of a *biwa hiki*'s income was entertainment, so skill in matching repertory to occasion, shortening and lengthening tales and episodes as appropriate, was far more important than musical technique.

Although Yamashika maintained that what he performed was not music, performance nevertheless involved two sonic resources, the voice and the biwa. Yamashika and some other—if not all—*biwa hiki* used facial expressions to heighten the impact of certain passages within tales, but a spectrum of different kinds of vocal delivery and styles of biwa playing were the media through which tales were performatively framed and experienced. The fundamental significance of these elements cannot be overemphasised: When people who have no knowledge of the contents of biwa narrative repertory listen to recordings or attend performances, the tales themselves are often difficult to follow, but there is a vivid impression of movement through a range of vocal styles and instrumental patterns.[8]

Instrumental Elements

In biwa narrative, where the reciter-singer is at the same time the instrumental performer, the bodily movements required to make the biwa sound are themselves indispensable elements of performance, without which the text fails to appear fluently; Yamashika often stressed that as his fingers grew numb with age so that he could no longer control them on the biwa, so too did his recitation falter without its enabling framework of instrumental *te*, punctuating strokes or phrases on biwa. This is because phrases and individual strokes on the biwa both frame and punctuate vocal rendition of the narrative.

8. This has been so even for listeners with no understanding of Japanese to whom I have played *biwa hiki* recordings.

Among all biwa traditions, only the ritual repertory of *mōsōbiwa* is performed with continuous instrumental sound beneath the voice. In Yamashika's *hauta*, *danmono* and most sections of *kamigoto* ritual performance, the biwa part comprises two elements: isolated tones and brief figures that punctuate the course of text delivery and full melodic phrases and patterns that last up to thirty seconds, which are played at the start of the performance and between text segments. *Nori*, a pattern that is the most rapid and dynamic in the course of a performance, may be begun in such a way as to temporarily overlap with the voice. The same can be said of certain parts of *nagashi*, a pattern conspicuous for its poetic content and melodic mellifluousness, but such moments of overlap are exceptional. Melodic phrases and longer biwa patterns associated with a particular vocal pattern are generally played before the voice begins, so that the biwa part introduces the principal pitches of the ensuing vocal phrases, including the voice's starting pitch. From the perspective of a listener familiar with the performance tradition, these introductory biwa patterns signal the type of *fushi* that is to come, so that the development of the performance can be anticipated to a certain extent by those knowledgeable of correspondences between *fushi* and content type.

Vocal Elements

As the majority of Japanese historical music traditions involve the voice, the establishment of genres has involved their characterisation by distinctive modes of vocal performance. The musical narrative traditions—genres such as *utai* chanting in noh, *Heike* recitation and performance of puppet theatre narratives with *shamisen*—are of course distinguished first of all by their performance media, but each is immediately recognisable by two sonic elements of performance: sets of patterns (*fushi*) that have aurally conspicuous melodic and rhythmic profiles and vocal delivery technique. Both these elements have been theorised by musicologists, but far more attention has been given to identification and definition of patterns than to description of ways of shaping vocal sound quality through delivery technique. This reflects the fact that discourse about performance in the canonical *katarimono* traditions, whose documentation constitutes a substantial body of musicological research (for example, Yokomichi and Omote 1960; Bethe and Brazell 1978; Inobe et al. 1984–1985; Tokita 1997; Tokita and Komoda 2002; Komoda 2003a), has involved extensive naming of vocal (and instrumental) patterns as the building blocks of repertory composition and transmission, with a fair degree of consistency; yet performers' discourse about vocal technique and sound quality, while rich and varied, has been far harder to contain in analytical exegesis.

Performance patterns (*fushi*)—Common to the analysis of all musical narrative in Japanese tradition is identification of *fushi*, performance patterns specified by name, which exist to varying extent as identifiable performance segments in most genres of Japanese historical music. They are highly stereotypical in melodic and text form, context and function across the repertory of a given tradition. For the most part they are units singled out in performers' terminology because of distinctive music-textual characteristics. (I hyphenate to emphasise the inseparability of these elements.) I use the general term *fushi* to denote these patterns because it is the word used by the *biwa hiki* I knew, but they are also referred to as *kyokusetsu* (literally "musical joints" but also translatable as "tunes within pieces") or *senritsukei* ("melodic patterns") in Japanese musicological writings.[9]

The first concern of *senritsukei* theory has been to derive, for a given tradition, the full set of named patterns from the various sources available. This has been done on the basis of both written text-scores and the oral terminology of current performance practice. Kindaichi, for example, derives forty distinct patterns for *heikebiwa* from comparision of four text-score sources (1973, 116–119), while Yokomichi's scheme of pattern-types in noh draws upon the oldest writings on performance and compositional practice, by the fifteenth-century playwright Zeami, but also on terminological innovations of recent practice that are not a standard element in text-scores. Most patterns are given the names they have in these sources, but it has not been uncommon for researchers, in their attempts to make sense of what performers do, to

---

9. *Senritsukei* patterning as a general principle across Japanese oral narrative performance genres has yet to be presented at length in English, but for individual genres some studies include detailed exposition; see de Ferranti (1991, 1995 and 1997) and Tokita (1999, chapter 6). See Tokita (2000) for a comparative study of patterning in *heikyoku* and *shamisen* narrative genres. In Japanese, the 2002 anthology edited by Tokita and Komoda is invaluable.

propose new names for patterns that do not bear any name in a given tradition.[10]

In *heikebiwa*, noh and other genres associated with literate practitioners in the Edo period, *fushi* pattern segments were set down in treatises associated with high-ranked performers and in text-scores for amateurs.[11] In non-elite genres the names of patterns and their distribution against narrative or song texts generally existed only in oral tradition until such time as practitioners adopted written media or researchers produced documentation. While the early-twentieth-century sighted practitioners of *higobiwa* described in chapter 2 produced some written sources for *biwa hiki* repertory (as well as their own new compositions), no such text-scores were associated with blind performers.

How does one talk about *fushi* as the structural building blocks of narrative performance, and, moreover, "composition-in-performance," in Yamashika's case? It is this fundamental difficulty, I believe, that Yamashika was referring to when he told Kimura Rirō that

> I think the professor [Tanabe Hisao] left without understanding a lot of what I tried to tell him, too. In my work there are established conventions and procedures, but if you try to explain them systematically, most people can't understand. (1994, 113)

In his own view, Yamashika's attempts to explain the "conventions and procedures" of his performance practice to Professor Tanabe failed. Tanabe was extremely knowledgeable of performance principles in Japanese song and narrative traditions, but the reason for ineffective communication on this matter may have been that he sought from Yamashika articulation of a musical system for which notations provide evidence in many traditions, but which blind *biwa hiki* could only demonstrate through actual performance of repertory items. Unlike segments fixed in text-scores, which can be discussed in isolation from the surrounding performed narrative, none of Yamashika's *danmono*

---

10. For example, Yokomichi notes that some patterns (such as the one he named *jo no ei*) have no designation in traditional *utai* notations of noh plays (Yokomichi and Omote 1960, 15).

11. Explanations for the existence of such sources in the blind *tōdō-za* performance tradition are numerous, but the teaching of *heikebiwa* to sighted amateur students of the art during the Edo period was one important context for having written scores and documents made.

repertory comprised fixed narrative texts with fixed *fushi* "settings." Even for short, single-*dan* items of relatively high textual fixity, such as *Dōjōji*, the tale's *fushi* scheme could vary greatly in different performances.[12]

Elicitation of Yamashika's set of *fushi*, then, required more extensive fieldwork than Tanabe was able to do in his brief 1963 visit to Kumamoto, as was demonstrated by later researchers. Yamashika's *fushi* types were highly variable in performance, and changes from one type to another were often not clear-cut, for he would move rapidly among two or more types (and among modes of vocal delivery, as described in the section to follow) in a short space of time. Melodic and stylistic dimensions of much of any given performance by Yamashika had a kaleidoscopic aspect when compared to the practice of some other *biwa hiki*—something that may have been perplexing to Tanabe. This characteristic "slipperiness" of vocal delivery is already evident from the opening passages of a performance; transcription of the start of a performance of *Dōjōji* requires much use of non-pitch-specific notational devices to represent the way Yamashika's delivery moves freely from near-spoken chant to pitched recitation and employs vocal glides in which pitch content is undetermined (as evident in appendix 2).

Analyses by fieldworkers, in particular those of Murayama (1986) and Hyōdō (1991, 1993), show that Yamashika's set of terms for *fushi* was small by comparison with many other narrative performance traditions. There are just seven general types—*kotoba*, *serifu*, *nori*, *urei*, *nagashi*, *okuri* and *kiribushi*. These *fushi* types are the basis for table 4.1, a summary table of Yamashika's set of performance patterns, with their typical contents, function, text and rhythm forms. (Note that the narrative function terms *kotoba* and *chūshin* are explained below, in reference to *shōdan* units.) I have included in the table a term apparently devised by Hyōdō, *kotoba-bushi*,[13] and the two principal forms of *okuri*, *urei-okuri* (*ō-okuri*) and *ko-okuri*.

---

12. In this respect there was marked contrast between Yamashika's practice and that of Ōkawa Susumu, apparently because of the prominent place of a sighted, literate teacher in the latter's lineage. See further de Ferranti (2003).

13. Hyōdō claimed (1991, 170) that Yamashika himself would use the term *kotoba-bushi* to distinguish *rōshō* (pitched or intoned) *kotoba* from *ginshō* (declaimed) *kotoba*. In my fieldwork (1991–1992) with Yamashika I tried on many occasions to confirm this but concluded that he did not recognise the term.

Table 4.1. Profiles of Yamashika's primary *fushi* set.

pattern	dramatic content	narrative function	text forms	rhythmic forms
kotoba	explanation/ speech	often within *kotoba-bushi* segments (*kotoba/chūshin*)	third/first person	
kotoba-bushi	description/ explanation	initiates new narrative units	third person; 7–5 mora units predominate	syllabic, with some longer values at ends of mora groups
serifu	speech	dialogue/monologue (*chūshin*)	first person	
nori	exciting action, especially fighting	climactic events of each *dan* (*chūshin*)	7–5 units in sequence	mostly syllabic, often within 8-beat phrases
urei	grief	may follow "*-kakari*" form in *kotoba* part of *shōdan* (*chūshin*)	7–5 mora units predominate	8-beat phrases common; pulse derived from preceeding *te*
nagashi	transitions in time and space	marks changes of scene (*chūshin*)	7–5 (two, three or four lines)	pulse-value from biwa *te*'s 'triplet' figure
okuri				
urei-okuri (*ō-okuri*)	suffering	at start of *shōdan* (special)	7–5 (1 line)	no pulse value
ko-okuri	various	start/end of *dan*	7–5 (1 line)	pulse only during *te*
kiribushi	summation of tale	ends *dan* (includes initial *ko-okuri*) (special)	some 7- and 5 mora units	initial *ko-okuri* breaks preceding segment's pulse value

Hyōdō has argued that both the small number of Yamashika's *fushi* and their fluidity of conception were to his advantage in oral compositional practice: "The looser and less standardised the definitions of *fushi* types, and the broader the scope of variation afforded to each one, the freer and more responsive to the individual tale the performer's style can be" (1991, 37). I would add that an increased ability to respond to the circumstances and audience of each performance was also afforded by the indefinite nature of his performance patterns.

Vocal delivery—Vocal delivery is a complex issue at the core of *katarimono* analysis, for in several genres a range of different styles of delivery are used to differentiate character types and the expression of emotion in context. To describe this variety of styles, three modes of vocal delivery in Japanese music have been employed as points of analytical orientation: *ginshō*, *rōshō* and *eishō*. In application to *katarimono*, these abstract terms may be translated and defined as follows (Hirano 1990, 35–37):

- declamation (*ginshō*)—syllabic vocalisation of moras without stable pitch or temporal value, as a form of heightened speech
- intoned recitation (*rōshō*)—mostly syllabic vocalisation with stable pitch content and moras of mostly equal duration
- song (*eishō*)—mostly non-syllabic vocalisation, with stable pitch content and moras of various durations, such that melodic phrases are formed by melismatic motion.

While useful for analysis, this tripartite distinction is not always reflected in the naming of patterns—for example, in my experience Yamashika made no consistent distinction between declaimed (heightened speech) and recited (sung) versions of the syllabic ground pattern, *kotoba*. In most vocal performance traditions there are patterns that contain passages in more than one mode of delivery. Nonetheless, performance in these three modes (as well as in medial styles that move among and between these modes) is common enough for Hirano's model to be adopted as a basis for describing vocal style and characterising pattern-types.[14]

Yamashika stressed that the fundamental point of difference between the *chikuzenbiwa* and *satsumabiwa* styles and his own biwa narrative was that the former were sung or recited throughout in a single vocal style, while his repertory involved mastery of many different voices.[15] Diversity of vocal styles (in particular for segments in first-person speech) and a general fluidity of delivery style within

---

14. Hirano's model is tested and critiqued by some papers in Tokita and Komoda (2002).
15. The claim somewhat misrepresents *chikuzenbiwa* vocal practice, in which short passages of declaimed text sometimes occur.

fushi segments must be recognised as basic traits of Yamashika's performance practice; he often shifted between heightened speech, recitation and singing in the course of a single *fushi* segment.[16]

As documented by Hyōdō, Yamashika expressed the importance he attached to modulation of vocal delivery style as follows: The descriptive *kotoba* passages are "just said" (*tada iute iku*), while in *serifu, urei* and *nori* he "becomes that very character" (*sono mi ni natte kataru*; 1991, 168). In my own experience Yamashika used the term "*kotoba*" to denote both declaimed "*kotoba* in heightened speech" (*ginshō kotoba*) and clearly pitched "recited *kotoba*" (*rōshō kotoba*). What was of primary importance for him, therefore, was the distinction between "plain" narrative delivery and an animated delivery style that renders the experience of a character with immediacy and intensity; distinction between unpitched declamation and pitched delivery was of far less concern.

Pitch and Mode as Elements of Performance

In performance, narrative text-phrases are articulated by means of punctuating vocal pauses and biwa figures. As stress accent is not a feature of the delivery of text (because it is not a significant feature of spoken Japanese), mora groupings of 7, 5 and variant lengths are usually melodically marked. This is almost always so for recited patterns and often so for sung patterns. For example, in the following two text phrases from Ōkawa Susumu's *Shiga Dan Shichi*, the performer articulates a metrical scheme by raising and lowering the syllabic recitation pitch:

```
         ga no ichiryu-
Shi-                    u / Dan Shichi wa         7 + 5

fuka-amigasa de         / me-
                            n-tei kakushi         7 + 7
```

Although pitch changes here occur either one mora before or after the start of a new mora group, the effect is a melodic reinforcement of metrical structure.

---

16. Recordings are not available in sufficient numbers to allow any general statement about consistency between Yamashika's practice and that of other Tamagawa-*ha* members. Yet this fluidity of vocal delivery is a significant point of contrast when one compares recorded performances by Yamashika with those of musicians such as Hashiguchi and Ōkawa who claimed affiliation with other *ha*.

Metrical units can also be marked melodically by exposure of the penultimate or final mora, or both moras, by singing at a lower pitch or by rendering them non-syllabically—that is, melismatically. (Both techniques are evident in phrases of the *kotoba bushi* segment of appendix 2, a partial transcription of a performance of *Dōjōji*.)

In all three forms of vocal performance, pauses and biwa punctuation are performative markers of text-phrases. In sung segments this can produce melodic phrases that are non-congruent with the text's metrical units. For example, the passage from Yamashika's 1975 performance of *Kikuchi Kuzure* cited above comprises an initial 4-mora word ("*isogeba*"), followed by three regular metric units of 7 (or in one case 8) + 5 moras, but in performance only the first three of these 7 + 5 mora units is articulated in accordance with the metric framework. Biwa figures and melodic phrasing divide the text as shown below:

> *Isogeba*
> *Kikuchi no Nobu-ko to*
> *kagiri nashi*
> *hi kazu mikka ni ataru*
> *hi wa Kikuchi*
> *Wai-fu ni tsuki ni*
> *keru*

The 7 + 5 metre is operative nevertheless as a regulatory principle in the text and its composition in performance.

There was no system of absolute pitch in *biwa hiki* practice; the instrument was tuned high or low in accordance with the register of a musician's voice and his physical condition. In all of Yamashika's *fushi* the relative pitches of the biwa's four open strings—transcribed as E', A', and E (the third and fourth strings at a unison)—and their octave equivalents are prominent and stable. These pitches function as pillar tones in tetrachordal formations of vocal melody, and constitute most of the sustained tones and phrase-ending pitches. Other tones that are relatively stable in the vocal melodies are the pitches produced at the biwa's second, third, fourth and fifth frets on the unison third and fourth strings: G - A - B - d. In playing instrumental passages (*te*), Yamashika rarely applied more left-hand pressure at the frets than was required to produce these pitches. At the fifth fret, by contrast, he used pressure to produce several pitches, e - f - f#, and a range of microtonal inflections between them. These pitches are often correspondingly unstable in the vocal line (as is evident at *omoinaku sono ori ni*, in the appendix 2 transcription). At other times, however, a clear distinction is made in the vocal melody between f-natural and f#. Such distinction comprises a form of modal articulation of certain *fushi* types, namely, *nori* and the pattern I will refer to as *urei-kakari*; in the former, f# is clearly intoned, while in the latter, f-natural only is sounded.

In general terms, the modal character of performances by Yamashika and other *biwa hiki* recorded since the 1960s is similar to much Japanese narrative music in modern practice, in that the melodies of both the voice and the *biwa* contain pitch formations that correspond to three of Koizumi's four tetrachord types (the exception being the Ryūkyū tetrachord, with its internal major third). Of the *miyako-bushi* (si - do - mi), *ritsu* (do - re - fa) and *minyō* (re - fa - sol) tetrachords, the first two are most common, while the *minyō* type occurs prominently only in some instrumental passages. At various points, there is marked aural contrast between successive *fushi* that are for the most part *ritsu*-type and *miyako-bushi*-type in modality. This must be recognised as an important structural aspect of any performance, one that contributes to the listener's comprehension of narrative form.

Example 4.1 summarises tetrachordal profiles for all of Yamashika's *fushi* (note that this example refers to vocal melody only; tetrachords including d would be added to this scheme if pitches of the instrumental passages were also taken into account): In this summary scheme, what distinguishes tonal configurations in various *fushi* is the presence of an upper tetrachord on A or B and consistent use of a whole or half-step above E and a whole step below each of the pillar tones, A and E (G below A, and D below E). Those *fushi* whose modal profiles are distinct from all others are *urei, urei-kakari*,[17] *nori* and *nagashi*. By contrast, the sung form of *kotoba* (*kotoba-bushi*), *ō-okuri* and *ko-okuri* can easily be confused with other *fushi* if factors other than mode, such as rhythm, metre and vocal delivery style, are not taken into account.[18]

---

17. Hyōdō (1991, 169) devised "*kotoba-bushi* (*urei-kakari*)" (usually abbreviated to "*urei-kakari*") as a sub-category of *urei*.

18. In the case of the sung form of *kotoba*, however, modally-articulated distinction from "*urei-kakari*" is important. The pattern is also distinguished by melodic form, for it has a greater variety of melodic phrase types than *urei-kakari*.

Example 4.1. Tetrachordal formations in all Yamashika's *fushi* types. (Auxilliary pitches are shown as smaller notes.)

kotoba-bushi*   urei   urei-kakari   nori   ō-okuri   ko-okuri   nagashi

* Note: The *kotoba-bushi* segment in *shōdan* 1 of *Dōjōji* (appendix 2 transcription) is atypical, adding B-e above the A, with d as an auxiliary pitch.

Many of these characteristics are evident in a transcription of the start of the first section of a performance of *Dōjōji* (appendix 2). Movement among more stable pitch levels by means of microtonal pitch glides of various kinds is shown in graphic form at "... *shitaute Kiyohime*...," "... *damashita ka ano Anchin-bō*..." and elsewhere. I have also sought to represent two kinds of irregular pitch phenomena:

1. Pitches represented by "x" noteheads, which are lightly or "half-voiced," in that they are sounded as minor elements within tones that are predominantly guttural and "breathy" (as in "*hayaku koko o tōrisugita*").

2. Pitches that are considerably sharper or flatter than the pitches represented in standard Western notation. I have employed quarter-tone sharp signs and arrows to represent this, as at "... *shitaute*..." and "*kore yori isoide mairan to*."

It should be noted that the clarity of modal articulation in the extant recordings of *biwa hiki* performances is quite variable. Its importance as a technique for structuring narratives in performance therefore is also variable. In the performance tradition as documented since the 1960s, rendering of distinct vocal delivery styles was given priority over stability of vocal pitch—just as Yamashika's characterisations of performance style suggest.[19] This was especially so for Yamashika,

---

19. To judge from the range of recordings I have heard, by the latter half of the twentieth century, consistent modal distinction between *fushi* types may have characterised the practices of only a minority of *biwa hiki*, among them Nishimoto Tsuneki and Ōkawa Susumu.

with his tendency to move freely from speech to near-spoken chant to pitched recitation. Even in recordings from the 1970s and early 1980s, when Yamashika was in relatively good health, there is considerable instability, both in the sense that individual tones are sung sharper or flatter within the bounds of discrete patterns and that some tones sounded together with "equivalent" tones on the biwa are not in unison with the latter.

Tales in Performance: The Oral Compositional Process

Extension and reduction (and, on some occasions, inclusion or omission) of the materials that make up a single *dan* was carried out by oral compositional processes, such that the basic framework of the tale remained unaltered but particular segments were omitted or embellished. It is important to recognise that a *biwa hiki*'s ability in oral composition-in-performance varied with circumstances and health. Kimura Yūshō noted, for example, that comparison of Yamashika's renditions of parts of the *Kikuchi Kuzure* in 1953 and 1963, respectively, suggested a significant diminishment of skill: "[Unlike before] he repeated the same phrases again and again until one grew tired of them, and he mixed up formal and colloquial styles of speech" (Higobiwa Hozonkai 1991, 130). In light of Yamashika's own comments about the importance of audience knowledge of repertory, it may be inferred that even by the early 1960s he no longer felt a need to produce narrative text of the richness he had formerly been capable of.

Performance and Narrative Units: The *Shōdan* Model

Before examining performances of a tale by Yamashika, it remains to explain the mechanism whereby *fushi* segments articulate narrative and performance units at a higher level of the structural hierarchy.

Fushi appear in succession in accordance with an enchainment mechanism that produces narrative and performance units that are fundamental to the oral compositional process. The term *shōdan* denotes those units in many analyses of *katarimono* performance traditions. It has changed in application since the 1960s when employed by the musicologist Yokomichi Mario to refer to named vocal and instrumental pattern segments in noh plays. Yokomichi proposed *shōdan* (literally "small *dan*") as structural units one level below the five *dan* (sections) that the actor, playwright and theorist Zeami (1363–1443) had stipulated as the fundamental compositional and narrative units of a play. Below the *shōdan* are several levels of division relevant to particular pattern types, and above it the following levels of structure (Yokomichi and Omote 1960, 15):

nō ichiban	a full noh play
ba	the first or second half of a play
dan	a narrative scene, made up of several pattern segments
shōdan	a single, named pattern unit

While the *shōdan* is a distinct performative unit, it is the importance of the *dan* (made up of several *shōdan*) that was stressed by Zeami. This is because it is at the primary level of narrative division and therefore is the largest of the playwright-composer's imaginative blocks for the internal structure of a play. It is around this narrative-scene unit—also referred to as a "paragraph" (*danraku*) unit—that most analyses of musical narrative genres have been arranged since Yokomichi's seminal work, and much musicological analysis (for example Inobe 1969; Motegi 1988; Komoda 1993; Tokita 1997, 1999) has been concerned with adapting elements of this model to genres that involve the voice of an individual singer-reciter and instrumental accompaniment rather than the diverse performative media of noh.

Before going on, we should recognise that structural analysis at this level of abstraction is not ethnographically grounded in the way that exposition of performance patterns at the level of *fushi* is. The latter are named performative entities that practitioners often refer to, but Yokomichi's term *shōdan* was devised to suggest the functionality of patterns within a higher-level formal unit (the narrative-scene unit called *dan* in noh). Unlike in noh, for the majority of *katarimono* genres to which this model has been applied there is little or no evidence that a narrative-scene unit formed by chains of *fushi* or named pattern segments is recognised or verbally acknowledged in traditional practice. This is certainly the case in the narrative tradition of *biwa hiki*, in which even musicians who classified *fushi* in greater detail than

Yamashika did not identify a performative or narrative unit between the levels of pattern segments and full performance items (*dan*, two or more of which comprise a piece in most of the *danmono* repertory). Nonetheless adaptations of the *shōdan* model have been tools for elucidation of the text-music structure of diverse performances and thereby shed light on the oral compositional process.

To return to the development of this model: In an influential 1989 article, Gamō Mitsuko surveyed the occurence of regular sequences of musical and textual features within several medieval *katarimono* genres. She demonstrated that in all of those traditions there exists what she called a *dan* unit, at a structural level where "musical and textual 'paragraphs' correspond very closely" (1989, 124). In most cases the unit comprises an initial pattern segment in declaimed style followed by one or more segments in recited or sung style.[20] Gamō calls the former *kotoba* and the latter *fushi*, so that together these make up two elements within a formal template for the central narrative and performative paragraph unit in medieval *katarimono*:

KOTOBA pattern segment + FUSHI pattern segment(s) = 1 DAN unit

In the 1980s Komoda's analyses of *Heike* introduced new terms and levels of division. The aspect of her work that in turn became most significant for analysis of the narrative repertory of Yamashika and other *biwa hiki*, as expounded by Hyōdō since 1991, is the concept of introductory and "main" *fushi* segments within each of the *dan* or text-music "paragraphs" in a *Heike* repertory item. In his interpretation of oral compositional procedure in the narrative tradition he called *zatō(mōsō)biwa*, Hyōdō correlates this concept with Gamō's *kotoba* + *fushi* template for the central narrative scene unit of performance in *katarimono* of medieval origin. An important terminological point of difference, however, is that Hyōdō opted to call the text-music paragraph unit *shōdan* rather than *dan*. This is because Kyushu *biwa hiki* used the term *dan* to denote each of the several long, discrete performance items within a complete *danmono* tale. Accordingly, for each narrative and performative paragraph within a *dan*, wherein *fushi*

---

20. Gamō's term for such segments is *kyokusetsu-kei* (1989, 107). She does not distinguish between the two delivery styles, but her definition of *fushi* makes it clear that both recited (*rōshō*) and sung (*eishō*) styles are included (1989, 114).

pattern segments are organised in regular formations, Hyōdō adopted the term *shōdan* ("small *dan*").

Two broad functional categories of pattern types, the *kotoba*-type (declaimed *kotoba*, its corresponding sung form *kotoba-bushi*, and a small number of functionally equivalent patterns) and the *chūshin*-type (main-position) patterns form the basis for Hyōdō's formulation of the narrative and performative paragraph unit (*shōdan*). He proposes that such *shōdan* always contain the following sequence (1991, 32):

KOTOBA-type (or equivalent) segment + 1 or more CHŪSHIN-type segments = 1 SHŌDAN

It is this *shōdan* unit that mediates between the levels of individual *fushi* patterns and *dan* in the music of Yamashika and other *biwa hiki*. The evidence of comparative analysis of multiple performances of repertory shows the unit to be fundamental to the performative procedure whereby a piece is produced anew each time in response to unique contextual factors.[21]

Fixity and Variability: Yamashika's *Dōjōji*

> When I do the "same" piece, I do it differently each time, so different people would say different performances were my best. (Kimura 1994, 125)

It is through comparison of multiple performances of a tale that the question of composition-in-performance can be addressed. What are the common elements in each performance, what differences are there, how do they occur and why? In examining this problem, one is not trying to establish any "standard" or definitive form of the piece but to establish how different versions of the piece come about.

The experiences of researchers who have sought to establish the contents and number of *dan* in particular repertory items (*gedai*) of *biwa hiki* suggest that the *dan* unit was not characterised by fixity. Tales were reconstituted in different performances as different numbers of *dan* of varying length by using extendable chains of *shōdan* to construct each *dan*. For Yamashika's practice, Hyōdō's schematic

---

21. In de Ferranti 1997 (chapters 4 and 5), I examine the operation of the *shōdan* in performances of the tale *Shiga Dan Shichi* by Ōkawa Susumu and compare it to Yamashika's practice.

comparison of recorded performances of the short single-*dan* tale *Dōjōji* over the course of a decade is the most extensive data of this kind available (1991 and 2000).[22]

The *Dōjōji* tale (also called *Anchin Kiyohime*) exists in many versions in a multitude of performance and literary genres and dates back at least to the late-eleventh- or early-twelfth-century collection *Konjaku monogatari-shū*. For Tamagawa musicians this was an especially important piece because in training it was used to consolidate what they had learned of *fushi* types; it had to be mastered before they could go on to expand their repertory by learning as many *gedai* as possible. *Dōjōji* held this function because it is a relatively short item in which all of the principal *fushi* patterns are included. Yamashika referred to it as a *gei-katame* or *fushi-katame* item (a "test piece" that rounds out one's skills or knowledge of *fushi*).

Dōjōji is a story that was known to the majority of Japanese until the second half of the twentieth century because of its presentation in so many theatrical and oral media. In performance, therefore, audience attention would be focussed not on the unfolding of the story but on the *biwa hiki*'s treatment and elaboration of details in individual scenes such as the transformation of a young woman into a raging snake-demon, the demon's pathetic realisation of her own ugliness and the search for her former lover inside a temple compound. Hyōdō identifies a sequence of eight narrative scenes as common to Yamashika's *Dōjōji* in multiple performances:

1. Kiyohime has been tricked by her lover, the acolyte Anchin-bō, and is rushing toward where she believes she will find him. She reaches the Hidaka River at dusk.
2. She asks the ferryman to take her across, but he says she must wait until morning.
3. She presses the urgency of her need to cross. He recalls a young priest's warning against allowing Kiyohime to cross the river after him, and refuses her passage.
4. Weeping, she implores him, but he laughs at her plight.

---

22. Note that the version of Hyōdō 1991 included in Hyōdō 2000, an anthology of diverse writings, is considerably shortened and lacks much of the data included in the original article.

5. Despairing, she jumps into the river and swims across, and transforms into a snake spewing flames from its mouth.
6. Seeing its own reflection, the snake-demon Kiyohime resolves to kill Anchin-bō, and rushes on toward the Dōjōji temple.
7. She enters the temple compound and coils herself around a large bell under which the priests have hidden Anchin-bō. The bell heats up and begins to melt.
8. The acolyte dies, aged 23.

The following text transcription and translation with *fushi* segments and *shōdan* markings is for the performance of October 14, 1989, which took place at Yamashika's home without an audience other than the ethnographer himself. Hyōdō's description of it as "the most standard performance" (*mottomo hyōjunteki na ensō*; 1991, 36) therefore reflects his concern to understand formal principles of the oral compositional process, rather than ways in which it was reflective of typical performance settings. Of ten recorded performances whose content Hyōdō compares, this performance undoubtedly displays most agreement between narrative content (the eight scenes or narrative paragraphs) and performance structure (eight *shōdan*).

Figure 4.2. Depiction of Kiyohime in distress on the banks of the Hidaka River. Chikanobu Toyohara, *The Boatman*, 1898. Triptych from the Bamboo Knots (*Take no hitofushi*) series. (http://commons.wikimedia.org/wiki/File: Chikanobu_The_Boatman.jpg)

Dōjōji

See Hyōdō 1991 and 2000 for the Japanese-script text transcription. This romanised version differs only in the omission of dashes that Hyōdō uses to show elongation of syllables in performance, and in the indication of breaks between text-phrases by movement to a new line; occasionally my assessment of the performative articulation of text-phrases produces different groupings. The recorded performance is included on the CD *Rites and Tales with Biwa: Yamashika Yoshiyuki, Blind Musician of Kyushu* (Nihon Dentō Geinō Shinkō Zaidan 2007) and its companion booklet (Kimura and de Ferranti 2007) also gives the full text.

shōdan 1
ko okuri
ato o shitaote Kiyohime ga
Following behind, longing [for him], Kiyohime . . .

kotoba-bushi
Anchin-bō o kyō ka asu ka to
"The priest Anchin, [will he come] today or tomorrow?"
matedomo kurasedomo
Though she waits, though she waits all day long,
kaette mairanu mō wa sankei mo
he doesn't return. Already his pilgrimage
sunde iru hazu
ought to be finished.
yūbe atari ni kaeru ka to omoeba ikkanai ka na kage mo katachi mo miezu
She thought he'd come back last night. No shadow, no trace of him.
omoinaku sono ori ni
While weeping at the thought of this,
kaze no uwasa de kikeba sono bōsan wa
she heard a rumour—that priest
hayaku koko o tōrisugita ga to kiku yori mo
had hurried on by! Hearing this:
haa, ware o damashita ka ano Anchin-bō
"Ah, he fooled me, that priest Anchin!
kore yori isoide mairan to
Now I have to hurry!" [she says, and]
waga ya o idete
Sets out from her home.

nagashi
ato o
Following behind,
shitaote
longing [for him],
isogiyuku
as she hurries
Hidakagawa no watashi-
to the Hidaka River crossing—
ba ni yōyō
place, at last—
tadori tsuki ni
arrived at last.
keru
[arrived]

shōdan 2

kotoba-bushi
haruka mukō o nagamureba
Looking into the far distance
haruka mukō no kishine ni kobune mo
way over at the base of the far riverbank
yō de funaosa ga kasamukete nemuri-iru
the drunken ferryman is settling in to sleep, with his hat over his eyes.
ureshi ya kono kawa koeyukeba
"Good!—if I cross this river
Dōjōji made wa hitoashi to
Dōjōji won't be far off!"
koe o kagiri ni kore mōshi
Then at the top of her voice, she calls out,
mōshi funaosa domo
"Hello Mr Ferryman!
hayō kono fune o watashite tabe
Quickly! Bring the boat over!
hayō hayō to yobu koe ni
Quickly! Quickly!" she cries.
[chūkan-teki (transitional style)]
nemimi ni bikkuri funaosa ga
Startled from his sleep by the sound, the ferryman,

serifu[23]
me o surikosuri busshōzura
rubbing his eyes, his face all unkempt
attaka shimashi nanzoi nō
"[You must be joking!] [?]
tatta hitori no funa-chin torite achira kochira to fune mawashi
I'm not going to move my boat about all over the place for just one fare.
kata ga tamaranu daiichi nemutai
My shoulders never stop aching, so I want nothing more than some sleep!
yo ga aketara watashite yarō
I'll take you across in the morning."
umai saichū ketatamashiku okosarete
angrily cursing
adabu ga warui to
[in foul temper?]
tsubu yakeba
and spitting.

shōdan 3

ō-okuri
sore wa
That is
anmari
too much
tsuyoku na
for her.

urei-kakari
dōzo kono kawa hayō
"Please, this river, quickly
watashite okure
take me over!
watashi wa yukaneba narimasen hayaku ikitai
I must go across, I want to go soon
Dōjōji made wa yukitai hayō
I want to get to Dōjōji quickly.

---

23. *Serifu* (literally "lines" in first-person speech) is functionally equivalent to spoken *kotoba*.

hayō watashite okure
Take me across, quickly!"

serifu
nanja?
"What's that?
Dōjōji e yukitai to mōsu ka
'Want to get to Dōjōji,' you say?
uohō, sore de wakatta
Oh—now I see!
shō ni watashita kano yamabushi no tanomi ni wa nō
That *yamabushi* who came past here early this evening asked me to do something for him.
ato yori jūrokushichi no jochū ga tazunete kuru de arō
He said there'd probably be a young woman of sixteen or seventeen following him, and told me,
sō yū jochū ga kita toki wa
'When such a woman comes along,
kanarazu kono fune wa watashite kure na
by no means give her passage!
moshimo watasaba sottchaba ga nandai
If you take her across, it will be terrible for me.
ōte wa inochizuku ni mo oyobubeshi to
She will probably threaten my life!'
kuregure
He specifically
tanonde iyattara
asked this of me.
nanbo matte mo watashi wa sen
So wait as long as you like, but I won't take you across!
naran
No!
sannen, sangatsu matte mo naran zo
You can wait for three years or three months, but no!
watasanu, naranu, naranu to
I won't take you, no, no!"
tsubu yakeba
and he spat on the ground.

shōdan 4

ō-okuri
koko ni
At this,
aware wa
poor
Kiyohime
Kiyohime!

ō-okuri
sore wa no
That is
anmari
too much
tsuyoku na
for her.

urei
tatoe watashite kudasatte mo
"Even if you were to take me across,
sona san ni
[even so?]
toga mo
My sin
nangi mo kakurumai
nor my suffering, I won't hide.
watashi wa yukaneba kogarejini
If I don't go there I'll burn to ashes [die as a *kogarejini*]
omou otoko o hito ni netorare
The man I love may be taken by another—
zehi ya nasake ja zengon ni
please have pity!
kono fune dōzo watashite okure
Take me across in this boat
kōja kore ja kō kō kō yū wake
It's this way; it's, it's, it's like this—
zehi ni watashite kudashanse
Please, by all means take me across!
funaosa-dono kono tōri
Ferryman, Sir, I beg you."

te o awase
She wrings her hands
uramitsu wabitsu
in regret and sorrow,
mi o modaenaki
and writhing in her torment,
sakebu koso dōri nari
she weeps bitterly.

kotoba
funaosa kiku yori
Hearing this, the ferryman says to her,

serifu
nani
"What?
Dōjōji e yukitai to mōsu ka
'Want to get to Dōjōji,' you say?
onna no kogarejini o itasu to mōsu ka
You'll die a *kogarejini* from love, you say?
fufufufufufufu
Hahahahahaha...!
ware mo rokujū amari no oibori jaga na
I'm an old fellow of about sixty now,
nagaraku
and I've had a long life
watashimori wa shite iru soregashi mo
working as a ferryman.
kogarejini to yū hanashi wa kiitaru koto wa nido-sando
I've heard tell of '*kogarejini*' a few times,
hanashi ni wa tabitabi kiite mo
yes—I've heard about it often enough,
kogarejini o mitaru koto wa sara ni nashi
but I've never seen one.
tatoeba watasaneba sottchaa shinuru ki ka
Are you all set to die if I don't take you across?
shinuru tsugou de aru nara yoshi
If that's how you feel, then well and good,
hatsume ni hitome mite yaru
I'll get to see it for the first time.

sono atari de kogarete miyare yo
So why don't you go ahead and burn away right where you are!
nenagara
While I'm lying down here,
waga kenbutsu sen to fune hara ni sune funzurase
I'll watch the show!" Having said this, he went back into the boat,
nigaguchi iu mo kawagoe
abusing her—[and back and forth] across the river,
kenka shikake to
it seems this argument
mienikeru
will go on.

shōdan 5

urei-kakari
a kore made tazunete
"Ah, [I've] asked this much for his help
kitaru mizukara mo
and come this far by myself, too.
tatoe watashite kuren tote
If he won't take me across,
tada yamiyami to nan no kaerō ka
then how can I just go home dejectedly?
ika naru koto ga aru tote mo
Whatever happens,
onna no omoitattaru nenriki de kono kawa o
As a woman, by sheer willpower, this river
watatte misen nan de
I WILL cross! What's this?
watashite kurenu mono tote
Says he won't take me across it?
kono kawa watararenu koto ga arubeki ka to
I'll damn well get across this river!"
sate mo isshin ni omoikondaru
How utterly determined she is!
[chūkan-teki]
onna no ikioi
The power of a woman
osorosha
is terrifying!

nori
kami wa
Her hair
zanbara ni furimidashi
dishevelled and flying about,
watatte misen to mizu kurui
"I will get across!" she cries, and into the raging waters
kawa ni zanbu to tobikondari
of the river she jumps with a splash!
satto tobichiru mizu kemuri
Suddenly steam flies up and scatters all around,
nukite o kitte essassa
as she swims overarm, [splish-splash],
hanetate
[one stroke
ketatete oyogishi wa
after another] swimming,
shini myōho ga gotai o kogasu
her whole body burning with wrath,
kuchi yori haku heki henhentaru
and flames spewing from her mouth,
honō o
flames
fukikake ha o narashi yoman yosen no
blowing, and gnashing her teeth, and with her myriad
uroko o gyaku tatete oyogishi arisama wa
scales upturned—the ways she swims,
miru mo osoroshi ya
the sight of it is horrifying,
tora no ikioi ryū no sei
the strength of a tiger, the force of a dragon!
funaosa miru yori wananakigoe
Seeing this, the ferryman lets out a cry.
are osoroshi ya
"Eh? Oh no!—
Kiyohime ga oni ni natta, ja ni natta
Kiyohime's become a demon, a snake-demon!
magomago shite wa kuwaruru kuikorosarete ichidaiji to
If I get into a panic, I'll be eaten, eaten alive!" He acts quickly,

fune o norisutete tobiagaru
jumps out of his boat, abandons it,
tsutsumi ga hara o yokogiri ni
cuts across the river bank
inochi karagara nigete yuku
and runs for his life.

shōdan 6

kotoba-bushi
ato ni nokoroshi Kiyohime wa
Kiyohime remains there,
tsuno o furitate ha o narasu
waving her horns about and gnashing her teeth,
uroko o gyakutatete oyogishi arisama
scales upturned—this is how she swims.
sate mo Kiyohime tadahitosuji ni
She goes straight across:

nagashi
shin ni kōsei
In her true form,
taimatsu sarazu
[like a] great flaming torch
nannaku kishine ni oyogi-
without difficulty, to the far riverbank she swims,
tsuku teru tsuki kage ni mizu kagami
the moonshine reflected in the water [as in] a mirror.

urei-kakari
mireba hitai ni wa
Looking at her reflection, she sees on her brow
futatsu no tsuno
two horns.
kono yoshi o nagamete Kiyohime
Staring at them, Kiyohime thinks
aa kore wa waga mi no sugata ka
"Ah, is this really what I look like?
miru mo osoroshi ya
I'm horrifying to look at!

wagami nagara mo aiso ga tsukiru asamashi kono sugata
Though it's me, all my fairness is gone from this wretched form,
kono kawa koeta bakari ni
just from having crossed this river,
kō yū asamashi ya sugata ni naru kara wa
I've become this miserable thing.
tazunete ite mo
Even if I ask him now
nan no nishiki no mae ni
how can he cherish me?
kō yū warawa o nan de nobenobe to sowashō nesashō ni
how can he embrace and sleep beside this thing that I now am?
waga sowarenu ue kara wa
But if I'm not beside him,
hito o sowasene wa naran
then someone else will be there!
waga sowanu ue kara wa
Without me beside him,
nan no hito o
who will be there,
nishiki no mae ni sowashō nesashō
cherished by him, sleeping beside him?"
sore o omoeba Anchin-bō
Thinking of Anchin-bō like this,
kawaisa amatte nikusa ga hyakubai
her hatred grows a hundred times stronger than her fondness for him!
waga mono ja waga tonogo to omoinagara mo
"He's mine, he's my fine man," she thinks,
sowarenu ue kara wa
"but if he won't have me beside him,
kore yori izuko dokodoko made niguru to mo
then no matter where he may escape to after this,
nan de Anchin nigasubeki ka
I won't let him get away!
dokodoko made mo okkakete
I'll pursue him everywhere.
torikorosai de okubeki ka to
I should catch him and kill him!"
urami o kasane
Resentment

nikumu Kiyohime
and hatred fill Kiyohime.
sate mo onna no tada hitosuji-gokoro
So, the single-mindedness of a woman—
omoikondara yaruse mo nai
once she's thought of something, there's really nothing for it.
kono ue kara wa mazu okkakete yukan to
"Now I must go after him!"

nagashi
matta kake-
Again, she starts
idasu zorizuka
running—Zorizuka[24]
hitomura
through the village
shigeru moriba-
and a dense wood
yashi Dōjōji ni mi-tera to isogiyuku
hurrying toward Dōjōji, to the temple.

          shōdan 7
kotoba-bushi
haruka mukō no kata ni wa rokushaku takahei wa
Way off in the distance, a wall six feet high,
shirojiro to mieru
its whiteness makes it visible.
kore wa izuku to mite iru uchi ni
"Where is this?" she wonders as she sees it.
chikayori mireba
Coming closer and looking at it again,
kore ga iraka narabeshi Dōjōji
[she sees] the buildings of Dōjōji standing side by side.
a uresha kore zo to hashiri yoru
"Ah, good, this is it!" she thinks, and running on
mon no to o kewashiku mo
to the door of the temple gate, she ferociously

---

24. This may be a place-name.

kotoba
chatto hirakete hirakete hirakete okure to
knocks, saying, "Open! Open it! Please open up!"

kotoba-bushi
yobedomo sakebedomo
She calls and yells,
nan no kotae mo
but there is no answer—
sara ni nashi
none came.

kotoba
ō akenu hazu wa tōsanu hazu
"Oh, it seems they won't open it, they won't let me in.
hito o kakumau oku kara wa
There's someone hiding inside—
tōshite kurenu hazu ja
that's why they won't let me in!
ō kono ue kara wa ika ni itashite
Oh, if that's the situation, then what can I do
tera no uchi ni hairō ka kukkyō no funbetsu to
to enter this temple [discreetlyf],"
happo ni manako o hairi
and she looks all about her.
[chūkan-teki]
achira kochira to mimawasu uchi
As she looks here and there, [she sees]
hitoki ni tsuitaru wa monmae no
attached to a tree before the gate
hitoki no matsu ni wa tsutakazura
a vine clinging to a pine tree.
ō uresha kore zo to hashiri yoru
"Oh! Good, [I'll use] this!", and runs over to it.

nori
iu yori hayaku tobiagaru Kiyohime wa
Quicker than it takes to say, Kiyohime leaps up onto
edda o
and around the vine [branch],

makitate makinoboru rokushaku takahei o
coiling around, and over the six-*shaku* wall—
dotto uchikoete massakasama ni ochiru to mietarishi ga
over she goes, and it seems she falls upside down, landing with a thud!
shudō no tsurigane nari wataru
The red bronze bell sounds throughout the temple compound
GOON-ON GOON-ON
"donnnng–donnnnng"
sate mo kane no hibikishi arisama o
Now, hearing the bell's sound,
tare shirumai to omoishi ga
thinking, "Who can that be?"
tera no bōsan no renchū
the priests of the temple
hatto bakari ni odoroki tamau
are thoroughly surprised:

kotoba (nori-kakari)
iyaa mō ano onna ga kitaru ka Kiyohime ka
"Oh no! Is that woman here already—is that Kiyohime?
yo ni mo nikkuki ikaga wa sen
What in the world shall we do?
kono mama sutete oku naraba Anchin-domo
If we leave him to her, Anchin
ano Kiyohime kara kuikorosarete ichidaiji ikaga wa sen
will be slaughtered and eaten by Kiyohime! It's an emergency, what shall we do?"
sate mo gorokumei no bōsan ga
So, five or six priests—
dō shita nara no ga sō ka nogare yoka to
what could they do to save the situation?
shian o itashi yōyō no koto ni ki ga tsuitaru wa
Thinking it over, then after a while someone notices—
tsurigane-dō ano tsurigane shita ni yō maki yō toware
the bell chamber! "Under that bell—
tsurigane naka ni kakusu nara
if we hide him inside the bell,
kore koso daijōbu dewa gozaranu ka to
he'll be alright, won't he?"

sate mo sono ba no kata ni
So the men who are there,
go-rokumei no bōsan-gata ga katsugidasu
the group of priests hoists one of them
tsurigane ni noboriagatte suddaitaru[25]
to climb up the temple bell [and ?]
shudō no tsurigane o
The red bronze bell
oroshi Anchin-bō o sono tsurigane naka ni
they lower—and that bell, putting Anchin-bō inside,
kakushi kō shite oitara jū yokarō de gozarō to
hiding him. "It'll be good enough to leave him like that," they say,
sono mama tera no hitoma ni tojikomoru renchū wa
then shut themselves away in one room of the temple.
teranai hisso to
All is quiet in the temple.
koe mo ishidatazu iki mo shinobasete
No one speaks, and all hold their breath.
kokorobosoku mo nogareyo to
There's but a slim chance they'll get through this.

kotoba
sate mo yōyō hitoiki
Then at last they drew their breath.
ōki na ikitsuite wa narumai to
Not a big breath, but,
sate mo daijōbu to omowareshi ga
"Well, it's alright now," they think.
[chūkan-teki]
kawaru
Then everything changes!
sono hiwa no Kiyohime
Just then Kiyohime
kusai tadotta no ka
seems to be following the smell of him.
ika naru shiwaza ka jū no ikiyoi sei na mono
By some means, with the power of a dragon,

---

25. This may be a local dialect word. I have been unable to determine its meaning.

nori
shidai ni sō ni noboru kuru nawabari
gradually she climbs up to where the bell is.
sate wa kusai de satoru ka
So perhaps she has understood—from the smell!
kokozo to omoi
"Here it is!" she thinks,
yaa isogiyoru shudō no tsurigane o makitate
and rushes to coil herself around the bell.
[chūkan-teki]
makitate maite wa nanamaki-han
Coil upon coil, seven and a half in all.
ryūtō kuwaete nanamaki-han ni to
Seven and a half coils, including the dragon's head!
maite ō-bachi de
Coiled like that, with her tail as a beater,
shudō no tsurigane o tataku nara
she strikes the red bronze bell.
sono onna no nenriki ka
By the will of that woman—

urei
oitawashi ya tsurigane
how piteous!—the temple bell
yudama to natte taratara to
turns to liquid metal, and drop by drop
nagareru tokuete
becomes a molten current.
nagareru tsurigane no
The bell melts—
nogare mo naranu
no escape [for him].
sate mo akuma kara niramaretaru
And so, having provoked a demon
obō-san mo
the priest—

***shōdan* 8**

[chūkan-teki]
oitawashi ya toshi no koro
what a piteous age [to die at]:

ō-okuri
nijū-san sai o
Twenty-three years,
ichiki toshi
this one life
tsui ni
at last,
munashiku
in vain,
kieta mo
gone.

urei
aware wa
Piteous
hakanaki mo Anchin-bō
poor Anchin-bō—gone,
onna fuzei kara uramarete
hated for disliking a woman!
tatsu yō ni asa no tsuyu to y mono ka
Just like dew in the morning sun,
iio no tsuyu ni kiete iku
vanished, like the last drop of dew.

kiribushi: norikakari
iriai-zakura kanemaki Dōjōji
Sunset blossoms, the bell-coiling [at] Dōjōji,
Anchin Kiyohime no monogatari iriai-zakura no kanemaki
the story of Anchin and Kiyohime, the sunset blossoms, the
    bell-coiling [at]
Dōjōji Anchin Kiyohime tsurigane-dō to
Dōjōji, Anchin, Kiyohime and the bell chamber
ima ga yo made mo
even today in the world

na o nokosu
their names are still known.
[kiribushi] ko-okuri
Hidakagawa kanemaki Dōjōji
"The Hidaka River—the bell-coiling [at] Dōjōji!"

*   *   *

In his analysis of *Dōjōji*, Hyōdō demonstrates the operation of his template for *shōdan* units in comparative analyses of ten performances (1991, 23–26, 33–34, 47–54). He proposes three further criteria that contribute to *shōdan* unit articulation in Yamashika's practice and finds *shōdan* divisions wherever two or more of the following elements occur after a *kotoba–chūshin*-type pattern sequence:

1. The opening *kotoba* pattern of a unit may be preceded by a *kotoba no te* biwa pattern.
2. One of several falling cadential melodic figures may be sung at the end of a unit. Hyōdō refers to these figures by the name of the pattern they conclude followed by the suffix *-otoshi* (for example, *nori-otoshi*). For each of these there are "large" *ō-otoshi* and "small" *ko-otoshi* forms.
3. At the start of some units the *ō-okuri* pattern is sung instead of a *kotoba* (or *kotoba-bushi*) pattern. The *ō-okuri* is one of a small number of fixed formulaic text phrases that express grief but at the same time signal a change of scene or speaker. (1991, 32)

The *fushi* and *shōdan* structure of the performance is summarised in Table 4.2.

Table 4.2. *Shōdan* articulation in "*Dōjōji*" (performance of October 14, 1989). *Fushi* and *shōdan* segments as shown in Hyōdō 1991, 52–54. Only *te* that mark the beginnings and ends of *shōdan* are included.

shōdan	fushi segments	kotoba/ chūsin/ special	narrative text	te	Ō-/ko-otoshi
1	ko-okuri	S	Kiyohime pursues Anchin.	t (initial *te*)	ko
	kotoba-bushi	K	Explanation of Anchin's having tricked her.		
	nagashi	C	She reaches the Hitakagawa.		ko
2	kotoba-bushi	K	She sees the ferry man. She calls to him. Entreats him to take her across.	t (*kotoba no te*)	ko
	serifu	C	He says he'll take her in the morning.		Ō
3	ō-okuri	S	"Sore wa anmari tsuyoku na" (commentary line: "That was too much for her!")	t (*ō-okuri no te*)	
	urei kakari	C	She stresses the urgency of her need.		ko
	serifu	C	He recalls the *yamabushi* priest's request, and refuses.		Ō
4	ō-okuri	S	"Koko ni aware wa Kiyohime (commentary line: "At this, pity Kiyohime!")	t (*ō-okuri no te*)	
	ō-okuri	S	Sore wa anmari tsuyoku na"	t (*ō-okuri no te*)	ko
	urei	C	Account of grief.		ko
			Final imploration.		Ō
	serifu	C	Ferryman laughs.		Ō
5	kotoba-bushi (urei-kakari)	K	Kiyome despairs.	t (*kotoba no te*)	
	nori	C	She jumps into the river, becoming a demon. The ferryman escapes.	t (*nori no te*)	Ō (*nori-otoshi*, sung over start of *te*)
6	kotoba-bushi	K	Kiyohime is left there alone.		
	nagashi	C	Swims across the river.		
	kotoba (urei-kakari)	K/C?	Sees her reflection by moonlight. Apalled by her condition.		ko
	nagashi	C	Resolves to kill Anchin-bō. Heads towards temple.		ko
7	kotoba-bushi	K	Kiyohime knocks at the temple gate.	t (*nori no te*)	Ō
	kotoba	K	She thinks to herself.		
	nori	C	She climbs a vine to enter the compound.		ko
	nori-kakari (kotoba)	C	Priests hide Anchin under the bell.		
	nori	C	Kiyohime coils herself around the bell.		
	urei	C	The bell begins to melt.		
8	ō-okuri	S	"Koko ni aware wa Anchin-bō" (commentary line: "At this, pity Anchin-bo!")	t (*ō-okuri no te*)	
	urei	C	Anchin-bō dies, aged 23.		
	kiribushi (nori-kakari ko-okuri)	S	Conclusion.		Ō

A comparison of four of the ten performances summarised by Hyōdō, using the October 14, 1989, performance's structure as a frame of reference (as shown in Table 4.3), shows that there is freedom to omit certain elements of narrative content within scenes and flexibility in the choice of *fushi* for presentation of a limited number of elements. For example, either of the first two elements of scene 2 (Kiyohime seeing the ferryman then calling out to him) can be omitted, and forms of the *nagashi* pattern are used instead of *kotoba-bushi* to render these elements in two of the four performances; similarly, the first two elements in scene 5 (expressions of anguish by Kiyohime) are lacking in two performances, and the fifth element in scene 7 (the snake-demon coiling herself around the bell) is rendered with either the *kotoba* or *nori* pattern.

Table 4.3. Narrative events and *fushi* structure in four performances of *Dōjōji*. (Adapted from chart in Hyōdō 1991, 33–34. Note that solid **bold** lines show *shōdan* divisions articulated by *fushi* sequences. Broken vertical lines denote a division not confirmed by Hyōdō's criteria.)

Narrative Scene	1	2	3
content	a. "Ato o shitaute Kiyohime ga" b. Explanation of Anchin's having tricked her. c. She reaches Hitakagawa.	a. She sees the ferryman b. She calls to him. c. She asks him to take her across. d. He says he must sleep, and will take her in the morning.	a. "Sore wa anmari tsuyoku na" b. She stresses the urgency. c. He recalls the *yamabushi*'s request, and refuses.
89.10.14	a. kō-okuri b. kotoba-bushi c. nagashi	a. kotoba-bushi b. kotoba-bushi c. kotoba-bushi d. serifu	a. ō-okuri b. urei-kakari c. serifu
90.3.12	a. ko-okuri b. c. (ko-okuri)	a. nagashi b. nagashi c. kotoba-bushi d. serifu	a. ō-okuri b. urei-kakari c. serifu
83.11.12	a. ko-okuri b. kotoba-bushi c. (ko-okuri)	a. kotoba-bushi b. c. urei-kakari d. serifu	a. ō-okuri b. urei c. serifu
82.7.27	a. ko-okuri b. c. nagashi	a. b. ko-nagashi c. kotoba-bushi d. serifu	a. kotoba-bushi b. urei-kakari c. serifu

Tales in Performance 227

Table 4.3. (continued)

	4 a. "Sore wa anmari tsuyoku na"/ "Koko ni aware wa Kiyohime" b. Account of grief. c. Final imploration. d. Ferryman laughs.	5 a. "Koko ni aware wa ..." b. "Sore wa anmari ..." c. She despairs. d. Jumps in the river and becomes a demon. e. The ferryman escapes.	6 a. "Ato ni nokorishi ..." b. Swims across river. c. Reflection in water. d. Apalled by what she sees. e. Resolves to kill Anchin. f. Heads towards temple.
89.10.14	a. ō-okuri b. urei c. urei d. serifu	a. b. c. kotoba-bushi (urei-kakari) d. nori e. nori	a. kotoba-bushi b. nagashi c. nagashi d. kotoba-bushi (urei-kakari) e. urei f. nagashi
90.3.12	a. ō-okuri b. urei c. urei d. serifu	a. ō-okuri b. ō-okuri c. urei-kakari d. nori e. nori	a. kotoba b. nagashi c. nagashi d. urei-kakari e. urei-kakari f. nagashi
83.11.12	a. ō-okuri b. urei c. urei d. serifu	a. b. c. kotoba-bushi (urei-kakari) d. nori e. nori	a. kotoba b. nagashi c. d. urei e. urei-kakari f. nagashi
82.7.27	a. ō-okuri b. urei-kakari c. urei d. serifu	a. kotoba-bushi (urei-kakari) b. c. urei-kakari d. nori e. nori	a. kotoba b. nagashi c. urei-kakari d. urei-kakari e. urei f. nagashi
	7 a. Knocks at the temple gate. b. Thinks to herself. c. Climbs a vine to enter temple compound. d. Priests hide Anchin under the bell. e. Kiyohime coils herself around the bell. f. The bell begins to melt.	8 a. "Koko ni aware wa Anchin-bō." b. Anchin dies, aged 23. c. Conclusion.	
89.10.15	a. kotoba-bushi b. kotoba c. nori d. nori-kakari e. nori f. urei	a. ō-okuri b. urei c. kiri-bushi	
90.3.12	a. kotoba-bushi b. kotoba c. nori d. nori e. kotoba f. urei	a. ō-okuri b. ō-okuri c. kiri-bushi	

Table 4.3. (continued)

83.11.12	a. kotoba b. kotoba c. nori-kakari d. nori-kakari e. nori f. urei	a. ō-okuri b. urei c. kiri-bushi
82.7.27	a. kotoba b. kotoba c. nori d. nori e. kotoba, nori f. urei	a. kotoba b. o-okuri c. kiri-bushi

At the same time, across all four performances *shōdan* structure is highly stable, and for the most part consistent with that articulated in the October 14, 1989, performance. There are two points of contrast: (1) the start of the second *shōdan* is delayed by presentation of the first two events of scene 2 through forms of the *nagashi* pattern in the 1982 and 1990 recordings; (2) in two performances (1983 and 1990) the boundaries between *shōdan* 3 and 4, and 6 and 7, respectively, are not clearly articulated because of a lack of the usual markers, *ko-* or *ō-otoshi* vocal cadences and *te* in the biwa.

Comparison of multiple performances by Yamashika was carried out by Hyōdō as part of his broader project of deriving the nature of oral composition of the so-called national epic, *Heike monogatari*, from the procedures of *biwa hiki* in the late twentieth century. In so doing he greatly increased knowledge of Yamashika and the Kyushu biwa traditions among scholars of Japanese literature and performance by placing them at the heart of a new theory of the structure of early *Heike* narrative.[26] At the same time, in his analysis Hyōdō tended to portray Yamashika's performance style in such a way that there appears to be a higher degree of distinction between *fushi* types than is apparent when one listens closely to actual performances and to characterise certain *fushi* in ways that are not fully in keeping with the evidence of their deployment in actual performances. There are several ways in which Hyōdō's model and analysis of *shōdan* formation in *Dōjōji* could be modified to better account for the evidence of recorded performances

---

26. In de Ferranti 1997 (72–75, 355–357) and 2003 I have discussed the apparent derivation of Hyōdō's methodology from the Parry-Lord project of retrospectively deriving compositional techniques of the Homeric epics from the formulaic practices of Yugoslav *guslar* singers.

(de Ferranti 1997, 312–316), but perhaps most important is to emphasise that the boundaries of narrative scenes are redrawn, within certain formal limits, in each performance of a tale rather than in relations of agreement or "irregularity" (*hensokuteki na*; Hyōdō 1991, 36) with a form articulated in a single "most standard" (*mottomo hyōjunteki*) performance.

Despite a tendency to oversimplify and obscure the actual extent of formal ambiguity in Yamashika's practice, Hyōdō's account of the performance process in *Dōjōji* effectively demonstrates the oral compositional mechanism whereby great variability of text—the wording of the tale—is offset by the stability of narrative content and scenes whose integrity is for the most part performatively maintained and marked through conventional *fushi* sequences, cadence and instrumental *te* forms.

*   *   *

Analysis of the formal characteristics of music of oral tradition and the mechanisms of oral composition by individual performers can be reflective of both social and psychological dimensions of music-making—the social and experiential realms of music's meaning—if documented and interpreted with an awareness of the panoply of factors that bear upon the act of performance. In the second half of this chapter I have focused upon elements in the formal mode of musical and oral narrative experience. I would argue that this mode should not be overlooked merely because of its apparent high degree of abstraction and that it be acknowledged as an important source of music's effect on both performers and listeners. It is always interrelated with other modes of experience and meaning and conditioned by contextual factors such as those described in the chapter's first half. More broadly speaking, formal processes and mechanisms in an individual's performance of oral narrative are shaped by the intersection of historical and contingent personal factors. Having explored the richness of Yamashika's oral compositional skills, it is appropriate now to return to such factors and consider in detail the circumstances in which Yamashika honed those skills and acquired other forms of knowledge that enabled him to make a living with the biwa in rural twentieth-century Kyushu.

This page is intentionally left blank.

5

THE LIFE OF THE ROAD
Yamashika Remembers

Shōbai wa michi ni yotte shinakereba omoshiromi ga nai.
This sort of work's only interesting if you respond to
where the road takes you.
(Yamashika, interview by author, November 5, 1991)

All three of the principal jobs that sustained *biwa hiki*—*kadozuke, zashikibiwa* and *kamigoto*—required that they frequently travel far from their homes and stay away for days or even weeks at a time. They could accurately be described as "itinerant" performers only when doing *kadozuke*, which involved seeking a new place to stay every few nights as they worked through the residences in one district after another. Nonetheless Yamashika Yoshiyuki was a musician who spent most of his working life travelling to or seeking engagements in many locales across Kyushu.

There are few sources for knowledge of the professional lives of *biwa hiki*, *goze* and other performers who earned income doing *kadozuke* in Kyushu at that time. Unlike sighted professional performers of *jōruri*, *naniwa-bushi* and other narrative arts, they rarely if ever worked at places that kept records of performance programs, such as theatres or small variety halls in towns (*yose*). The detailed accounts given to various researchers by Yamashika and Hashiguchi Keisuke remain the primary resources for what we can know of the lives of *biwa hiki* in the twentieth century.

The first half of this chapter is an account of Yamashika's entry to the profession: the factors that led to his decision to train as a *biwa hiki*, the conditions of apprenticeship, the training process, the circumstances in which he left his apprenticeship after barely half of the agreed period of five years had elapsed and the means whereby he eventually began professional life. In the second half I turn to Yamashika's (and at times Hashiguchi's) accounts of experiences doing *kadozuke* and other kinds of performances around central and southern Kyushu. The material therein, which includes encounters with both discriminatory and charitable treatment, as well as memories of collaboration among diverse kinds of performers, affords consideration of the status of blind and itinerant musicians in rural Japanese society of the mid twentieth century.

Becoming a *Biwa Hiki*

> I went to learn biwa when I was 21, but before that I wondered a lot about how I'd ever be able to support myself in life. My father just used me for his own purposes, but never gave me even a *sen*. I'd thought about leaving home, but I knew I'd have to get some sort of skill so that I could feed myself. I certainly thought that, but I never even considered becoming a *biwa hiki*. (Kimura 1994, 38)

It is clear that Yamashika did not want to become a biwa singer; he came to the decision to train as one only after other options had been exhausted. In rural Kyushu of the 1920s there were few ways for a blind youth from a poor background to become self-sufficient, but the profession of *biwa hiki* to Yamashika was one of the least attractive. Other genres of musical and narrative performance, including the tremendously popular genre of *naniwa-bushi*, seemed to offer at least a chance of both a larger income and an escape from a life of dependency in rural villages. Yet they were new, potentially unstable, professions by comparison with the long-established trade of the *biwa hiki*, and in rural Kumamoto the traditional pre-modern professions of the blind were still the norm. Yamashika was unable to find a way towards any of those other possible vocations, and in the end his lack of education and the influence of his grandfather (who loved to do *jōruri* recitation as an amateur) figured strongly in the decision for him to be apprenticed as a *biwa hiki*.

Yamashika's Choice of Vocation in Context

In the early 1920s, when Yamashika made his decision to apprentice himself to a *biwa hiki*, the choice of vocation was not yet an especially rare one for a blind youth in rural Kumamoto Prefecture. That much is clear from the responses of his family, the fact that there were still a good number of biwa players active in the region, some of whom were not much older than Yamashika and statements such as, "With biwa I never thought I'd have a problem earning a living . . ." (Kimura 1994, 42). Yet five to ten years later, when Yamashika was trying to establish himself as a professional, the demand for entertainment by *biwa hiki* may have been affected strongly by the spread of access to radio and affordable players of SP records. In rural Kumamoto, moreover, belief in the efficacy of the *biwa hiki*'s ritual services was already much depleted by comparison with belief in rites carried out by certified *mōsō* in some other regions of Kyushu (Yasuda 1991, 12). Yamashika was one of the last people to opt for such a profession and to enter a formal apprenticeship. Among factors important for his decision were the conditions of agrarian poverty in Kyushu during the period 1900 to 1920, the framework of care for those with disabilities, means whereby blind people could attempt to make a living and the range of musical narrative performance genres to which a young person in a rural village was exposed at the time.

Nankan and Its Rural Poor

Yamashika's family owned land and a small house in the village of Ōhara (now called the Kobaru area).[1] During the early twentieth century Nankan was a farming village that produced rice, barley and vegetable produce for the markets of Ōmuta, Tamana, Yamaga and other towns whose economies derived from their positions as ports, transportation hubs, and attractive natural and leisure resources (appendix 1, map 2). Proximity to those towns meant that Nankan inhabitants would gain news of national affairs by word of mouth or—for the few who could read fluently—from information broadsheets or town newspapers. Yet until at least the 1920s the material benefits and innovations evident in daily life in Tokyo and Osaka at the time were all but unknown to village families, whose lifestyle was in many respects little changed from that of a century earlier during the last decades of the Tokugawa Shogunal regime. Like all agrarian communities, Nankan's economy was always subject to not only the effects of weather but also to national policy on produce distribution, taxation

---

1. Ōhara and the villages of Sakashita, Yonetomi and Kenboku were incorporated into Nankan-chō in 1955.

and labour. As Yamashika's youth and early professional life coincided with Japan's period of imperialistic expansion, the country's wars with Russia, China and America, and in general the prominent place of the military in national life, all had direct impact upon him and his family. At the very beginning of his narrative, Yamashika states that at the time he first had trouble with his eyes at age three his father was "away fighting the Russians." What's more, in retrospect he believed that that absence had been a primary reason for him not receiving treatment for his eyes from the time they began to hurt, as the following reiteration of his mother's words shows:

> There's no money 'cause his father's away. If he has to go into hospital, we'll have to go there to nurse him. And what about the charge for him being there? (Kimura 1994, 12)

As remembered by Yamashika, his father had often complained of there not being enough labour on hand for the farmwork. So it is likely that he was a conscript for the requisite three years, not a volunteer soldier. That is all the more likely as the conscription system honed during the 1894 war with China was well established by the time of the war with Russia in 1904–1905.

Poverty and even instances of starvation were far from rare in rural Japan of the twentieth century's first four decades. Famine is documented as having occurred in a large area of northern Honshu during 1934 (see Hane 1982, 114–117). While Kyushu and south-west Japan were generally less subject to rice crop failure, the lives of rural tenant farmers were extremely hard, with a routine of labour that varied seasonally but was rarely less than twelve hours daily and yielded just enough for a poor, monotonous diet.[2] Yamashika's father was not a tenant farmer but instead owned a small plot, as the family was able to contemplate selling a field to pay medical expenses. Nonetheless it is clear from the way Yamashika describes the amount of labour his father made him do and the lack of variety in his family diet (which he came to feel acutely after experiencing more varied meals in his Amakusa teacher's house), that the environment in which he grew up was only marginally less severe than that of a tenant family home.

---

2. The graphic accounts of rural poverty of the Meiji, Taisho and early Showa eras given in Hane 1982 (29–49) can be usefully compared with Embree 1939, a study of a single community in southern Kumamoto Prefecture in the mid-1930s.

Like most people of poor farming families, Yamashika's childhood and youth was spent in very crowded conditions: the house comprised three rooms[3]—a kitchen and bathing area, and two rooms, each of six *tatami* mats, or less than three metres square—in which lived three generations, in all eight people after Yamashika's younger siblings were born. The household had insufficient money for medical care beyond ordinary needs (which were probably met with Chinese *kanpōyaku* medicines and various indigenous remedies), but the possession of a few small fields and a family plot beside the house meant that even in the worst of times there had been a source of food. That remained the case throughout Yamashika's life, although the acute reduction (perhaps even complete disappearance) of demand for the services of *biwa hiki* during the Second World War, coupled with regulations concerning donation of produce toward the war effort, meant that he was reduced to living with insufficient sustenance for some years (Kimura 1994, 107–108).

Blindness, Disability and Medical Care

People with disabilities born into poor families generally face tremendous hardship—difficulties rivalled perhaps only by those of the family that must find a way to look after them. Yamashika's eye problems began at the age of three and apparently became acute over the ensuing three to four years (to judge from the fact that he could barely make out his own shoes from others' when he started school at age six). His family's response to the crisis was at first simply not to acknowledge it but to treat it as a problem that might be temporary, and which in any case they couldn't afford to remedy. Let alone hospitalisation, the boy was not even taken to a doctor; as for treatment, his family would merely wash the boy's eyes with hot water. Some years later, as his mother came to realise that her son might have a lifelong disability, she responded by taking him to undergo simple exorcism rites at local temples and in turn to participate in a retreat over several days at a Shingon temple (*O-Daishi-san*) under the guidance of a nun. Although such ritualistic or faith healings were in the end ineffectual, they probably assuaged Yamashika's mother's sense that she must try to help her son by whatever means were available to her.

3. Yamashika enlarged his house in the 1970s so that a new room was dedicated to images and altars for various deities.

From the way Yamashika's family talked of the expenses for hospitalisation, it is clear that they knew of and perhaps had been to hospitals in large regional towns such as Ōmuta, a few hours' journey away, or perhaps even in the prefectural capital, Kumamoto. Even if physical access to treatment at a hospital was feasible, however, it seems that the costs were prohibitive, both in terms of monetary expense and labour days lost through a family member having to stay at or near the hospital. The mere cost of having a doctor examine the boy was also spoken of as prohibitive by family members.

The medical system in Japan in the last years of the Meiji period was undergoing rapid change, as the national government—in part in response to calls from the military for maintenance and improvement in the health of its potential conscripts—began to develop policies to deal with health problems that had been the responsibility of prefectural and even local administrations since the start of Meiji. A nationwide ratio of one doctor to every three hundred households, documented in the 1920s, meant that most rural villages in fact had far higher ratios; in many villages there were no doctors at all (Hane 1982, 47). Embree's 1939 report of conditions in the mid-1930s shows that this was still the case in Kumamoto Prefecture nearly three decades after Yamashika's childhood (255). Various government and private surveys of the health of rural villagers in the 1930s and 1940s moreover demonstrated that lack of facilities as well as widespread ignorance about modern medical care persisted until the Occupation era (Kano, Tsurumi and Nakayama 1997, 29).

One may speculate that the inability of Yamashika's family to provide him with medical care stemmed not only from the difficulty of obtaining funds but also from a combination of a culturally bequeathed sense of helplessness in the face of visual disability as well as his father's negativity, selfishness and apparent inability to think and plan logically. As has been mentioned in earlier chapters, "the blind" (*mōjin*) was a term that embraced all people with visual impairment that affected their ability to function in society, and the various social institutions whereby some *mōjin* were enabled to make a living included many members who were far from blind in the modern-day understanding of the term. For poor, uneducated people, the understanding of blindness and disability as karmic phenomena, embodied in much Buddhist lore, contributed to a sense that the condition was unlikely to improve. The possibility that Yamashika's eye problems would persist, regardless of treatment, may have been enough for most of his family to resign themselves to his being a *mōjin*. Yamashika's retrospective view was that his father had taken that attitude from the first and reacted to the situation vindictively: "My father treated me cruelly, as he thought of me as a hindrance" (Kimura 1994, 105), and "I often heard him say 'He's blind, so he'll never amount to anything'" (ibid., 45). At the same time, there were means available to obtain the necessary funds: if only his father had been willing to follow the logical steps of obtaining a doctor's opinion about the boy's eyes then going ahead with the sale of a field if it seemed that hospital treatment would be effective. The likelihood that Yamashika's eye problems could have been ameliorated is further reflected in the comments of an old woman in the Kobaru neighbourhood, who spoke ill of Yamashika's father for spending money on his own clothes while neglecting the boy and expressed the conviction that "he should get his son some medical care for his eyes" (ibid., 30).

Means of Making a Living among the Blind in Rural Kyushu

Among all blind people other than those of warrior status, the most common professions during the Edo period were music, massage, acupuncture and moxa therapy. Ritual work, such as that of the *mōsō* and the Tōhoku-region *itako* female mediums, was also common in some regions. Half a century after the end of the Shogunate, alternatives to these traditional means of sustenance for the blind were beginning to appear in Kyushu, at just the time that Yamashika made his decision to learn biwa. Notwithstanding, Yamashika's discussions with his family about a means of livelihood, in which relatives proposed that he learn *jōruri*, biwa or acupuncture, indicate that the traditional trades of the blind were still the norm in rural Kumamoto:

> One September, Mum couldn't bear the problem [of my future] any longer, so she went to talk with her people at Kenboku. "The boy will be helpless if he goes on like this. I don't know what he'll end up doing, but he says he wants to learn to do *naniwa-bushi*. His grandfather says he ought to learn *jōruri* or biwa—what should we do?" Her father said, "He doesn't have to do that sort of thing—he can learn acupuncture. I'll have a talk with him about it."

> I told him, "There's a skilled acupuncturist in our village, but even so, no one comes to get treatment from him. You can't make a living from that. You don't want me to do *naniwa-bushi*, and I don't really like *jōruri*, so I may as well learn biwa. Even though biwa players have to do *kadobiki*, I'll learn that." (Kimura 1994, 41)

In the early decades of the twentieth century the nationwide popularity of certain forms of entertainment centred on musical narrative made it possible for blind youths—for whom music was always considered as a possible occupation—to fantasise about training and making their way as professional performers and teachers. Foremost among these was *naniwa-bushi*, a style of dramatic storytelling with *shamisen* accompaniment that had developed during the 1870s through 1890s and achieved tremendous popularity across Japan by the time Yamashika was in his teens:

> At that time *naniwa-bushi* was the most popular style of music, so without thinking about it a lot, I decided I'd like to learn that. It's not as if I'd ever done any of it—I was just dreaming, really. With biwa I never thought I'd have a problem earning a living, but I really didn't like the idea of doing *kadobiki*. *Naniwa-bushi* players don't have to do *kadobiki*, you see. (ibid., 42)

Despite his reservations about *kadobiki* (*kadozuke*), clearly Yamashika had confidence in the ongoing demand for the services of *biwa hiki* in his region. While reasons for this are not offered in Kimura's text, a claim in Murayama's *Higo biwa denshō-shi* (A record of the Higobiwa tradition) suggests that there was still sufficient call for the various rites that *biwa hiki* had performed for centuries. This was apparent even to Yamashika's father:

> His father ... insisted that he train as a professional biwa player, as he felt that "even if the tales (*gei*) lose their audience, there'll always be ritual (*harai*) work for you." (Murayama 1986, 430–431)

The Effect of Yamashika's Personal Circumstances and Preferences
Yamashika emphasised again and again in conversations with Kimura that during adolescence he was in continual conflict with his father, who he felt had rejected him because of his disability. He spoke of how on various occasions neighbours and relatives were shocked to see that his father provided no money for medical treatment of his son's eyes,

nor any for buying him new clothes, while he bought himself garments in a style younger than his years. Yamashika also described running away several times after episodes of verbal abuse, and memories that indicate his father's negligent attitude.

As expressed in the quote at the head of this section, before starting his apprenticeship at twenty-one, Yamashika had worried for years about how best to acquire skills that would enable him to live without being dependent on his parents. Yet potential dependence on his siblings was also a cause of anxiety to him:

> The thing is, with all those times I ran away from home, I just felt if I could do something other than farmwork, anything at all would do. I knew one thing for sure: I'd be very unhappy being a dependant of my younger brother. So I did nothing but think about how to get away from home.
> . . . When I asked my father about it, he said, "That won't be necessary—you'll be alright farming, boy. You'll be right, 'cause your two younger sisters will marry and go elsewhere, and you've two brothers here." But I thought, "When my brothers bring wives here, it won't be as my father thinks. I simply have to earn my own living doing something." (Kimura 1994, 38)

In contrast to his father, Yamashika's paternal grandfather, who lived under the same roof then died while Yamashika was doing the first year of his apprenticeship in Amakusa, seems to have been a benevolent figure who loved musical narrative and could do a little *jōruri* recitation himself. He both helped and influenced his grandson.[4] With regard to Yamashika's decision to learn biwa as a profession, Murayama stresses the influence of Yamashika's grandfather:

> His grandfather loved *jōruri*, and when performers who made a living from *kadozuke* came (as they often did from the Chikugo and Miike regions), he'd ask them to stay the night, then gather old folks from the neighbourhood to hear a tale. At those events sometimes he himself even performed a curtain-raiser piece for the *jōruri* professional.[5] (Murayama 1986, 430–431)

While Yamashika himself did not enjoy *jōruri* enough to want to learn it as a profession, it was perhaps his grandfather's enthusiasm for

---

4. As Yamashika told Kimura, "My grandfather knew about two *dan* of a story called *Orio Yanagi*" (1994, 118).

5. On the great popularity of *jōruri* among amateurs across the country in the early twentieth century, see Gerstle (1999, 122–123).

performance that led him to an interest in *naniwa-bushi*, and in turn to agree to train professionally in biwa singing. As he himself stressed, however, until pressed by circumstance and the lack of apparently viable options, he had "never even considered becoming a *biwa hiki*."

Apprenticeship

At the end of 1922, at the age of 21,[6] Yamashika at last became an apprentice in the *biwa hiki*'s trade. The ensuing two and a half years provided him with the basic skills needed to begin earning income with biwa, but also with a sense of how much more he would have to learn for that income to be sustainable or sufficient for him to start a household back in Nankan. To a certain extent this would have been the case for any apprentice, but Yamashika decided to curtail his training by nearly half the agreed period (for reasons I will explore) and so faced serious insufficiencies in the first years of his professional life.

Historically, apprenticeship was the framework for transmitting Japanese trades, many of which either were never taught through formal education or were not introduced to schools or technical colleges until the late twentieth century. In cases where a trade was to be carried on by the child of a practitioner, a formal apprenticeship was not required, but if learners came from outside the artisan's immediate family, a term of apprenticeship was contracted. Common to both apprenticeship and less formal frameworks for training was—and to a large extent still is—the acquisition of skills and knowledge over an intensive training period of several years, during which little or no theoretical or analytical exposition was given. Apprenticeships are undertaken in various circumstances, but those who are *uchi-deshi* (live-in apprentices), as Yamashika was, perform labour of various kinds for the teacher and thereby not only acquire the technical skills of a trade but also learn about the day-to-day lifestyle of a practitioner and the effects of the trade on a family's livelihood. In this sense, Yamashika's thirty months in the house of an Amakusa *biwa hiki* taught him much about the life he could expect to lead in future.

---

6. He was twenty-two years old by the method of counting used at the time, according to which one was one at birth, and two at the next New Year.

Figure 5.1. Yamashika outside his teacher's house in Amakusa.
Photograph by Kimura Rirō (used with permission).

Terms of Contract

As in all historical performing arts at the time, Yamashika's professional training involved a contract between the teacher and the trainee's family. The extent to which, among *biwa hiki* of the Kumamoto region, such contracts were documented in writing is unclear, but Yamashika said that in his case none of what was decided was written down:

As had been decided when I was indentured, *kimono* were the responsibility of my family. There was no document or proof of that agreement—it was all done verbally. (Kimura 1994, 70)

Given that both teacher-professionals and apprentices were either blind or impaired in their vision, it is likely that in most cases the detail of contracts was entered into verbally, with witnesses to the agreement.[7] An element of trust and goodwill was essential, so negotiations went most smoothly when there were already social relations between the biwa teacher and people known to the prospective apprentice's family. This need for indirect acquaintance with the teacher-to-be was the principal reason why Yamashika was apprenticed to Ezaki Shotarō, a biwa player from the distant Amakusa islands who had trained near Nankan and sometimes came back to perform there. Yamashika's maternal grandfather knew that the Amakusa *biwa hiki* was doing work in the area when Yamashika and his mother came over to consult about his future and suggested that negotiations be initiated immediately. He served as one of the intermediaries together with the father of a friend of Yamashika's who had already entered an apprenticeship with Ezaki:

> Hori Matami . . . who became an apprentice before me, used to hang around at our place before he went off to Amakusa, so I knew him pretty well. He was three years younger than me, and he went away to do a seven-year apprenticeship at the age of fifteen. (ibid., 42)

Apprenticeship at the time required that the teacher provide a living space and sustenance,[8] so the agreed duration and costs were fundamental elements of the contract. Terms of apprenticeship do not appear to have been regulated by the performers' associations of professional affiliation (*kō*) but were set by the individual teachers who offered them. The duration of an apprenticeship was determined by a student's age. Most began to learn in their early to mid teens, but as blindness also rendered older youths incapable of an ordinary profession, some *biwa hiki* apprentices were over twenty years old.

---

7. A written document may well have been drawn up later for the teacher, Ezaki, as he later successfully sued Yamashika's father for breach of contract in the Takase court (Kimura 1994, 79). Attempts to view any remaining documents filed at that time have been unsuccessful.

8. While this was usually so, Yamashika's teacher Ezaki also had one student who was a local Amakusa youth and lived in his own family home nearby.

An indentured period of seven or eight years was standard for most teenagers, while men over twenty were usually apprenticed for four or five years (Yasuda 1991, 5). In Yamashika's case, his family's first request that he be taken on as an apprentice met with refusal because he was already considered too old at twenty-two (Yasuda 2001, 20). Subsequently it was agreed that he would be apprenticed for five years only because of his age. As compensation to the teacher for the shortened period, it was normal for several months of rations to be given, but in this case Ezaki reduced it to one month's worth in exchange for Yamashika providing labour in his rice and vegetable fields:

> If you do the work for me in the fields first, we can calculate your pay at 20 *sen* per day, so in a month you'll have paid 6 yen 25 *sen* worth of rations. That'll be alright instead of the eight months' ration payment. (Kimura 1994, 43)

Yamashika's labour was also promised as a means to obtain a discount of another 50 yen (being five times 10 yen per year) down payment that was due to the teacher (Yasuda 2001, 20). A total of 30 yen was decided as cash fee: 10 yen as "thanks" to local *biwa hiki* around Hondō in Amakusa (presumably because they would lose some of their custom when Yamashika started to do *kadobiki* as a trainee in the area), 10 yen for food costs and another 10 yen for various other purposes. This too, seems to have been a discount arrangement worked out informally:

> The formal agreement had been that we'd pay for two years of tuition and five years of accommodation with the teacher, but informally deals were often cut; in my case, so long as I worked in the fields, and my family provided clothing, the teacher said he didn't need any fee for accommodation.[9] (Kimura 1994, 70)

The contract apparently did not specify just what performance skills or repertory the apprentice would be taught nor how much or on what regular basis the teacher would give lessons. Yamashika's later comments to several interviewers reflect the fact that he was disappointed at the infrequency of lessons and the small quantities of knowledge imparted to him at first, which he could do nothing about:

9. In conversation, Yamashika explained this to me in more detail: Money for rations was required only when the apprentice was over twenty, in which case the cost would be 30 *sen* per month, but in his case this was waived in exchange for labour (interview of November 5, 1991).

I had my first biwa lesson on the first of November. All I did was learn how to hold the plectrum and pluck the strings. I had lessons in the mornings and evenings for the next 4 or 5 days, but after that he didn't teach me at all. I'd ask him, "When will we have another lesson?" and he'd reply, "When we plant the barley [*mugishino*] and rice [*taue*] and when we cut the barley [*mugitsukuri*], they're the only times. There'll be ten days during *mugishi* and *taue*, and about a week during *mugimaki*." I'd just say, "Oh" in resignation, but then he'd say, "What's this 'Oh'? That's as much as they'll teach you wherever you go!" I'd say, "Oh" again, and he'd blow up at me. I said to his wife, "I hear I'll only be taught for 17 days in the whole year! How am I going to learn anything properly?" . . .

But the truth is he would only teach me for 17 days in the year. When he'd taught just a little, he'd say, "Go over it yourself! Practice it as much as you can. It won't be any good unless you practice until your voice goes hoarse—and I'm not joking!" He'd say that, then go off to work by himself. OK, it's fine to sing until your voice goes hoarse, but who could practise properly? You can practise if you've been told just what it is that you should do. We'd only just begun, so even if the biwa was in tune to begin with, we had no way of telling when it had gone out of tune! (ibid., 53–54)

The Training of *Biwa Hiki*

Data available on the apprenticeships of three *biwa hiki*—Yamashika, Ōkawa Susumu and Hashiguchi Keisuke—indicate that training followed a common general course, with some adjustment for the shortened period of study accorded to older students:

1. Memorisation in fixed form of *hauta* texts and other short items frequently performed in *kadobiki*, during short lessons given once every three or four days (though far less frequently for Yamashika).
2. Acquisition of vocal melodies for the basic set of *fushi*, by singing the above items with the teacher, who when necessary would sound a beat with a *sasara-dake*, a large whisk made of bamboo slivers.
3. During the second year, acquisition of fundamental biwa left-hand and right-hand performance techniques, then the two *te* used most often in repertory for *kadobiki*, *kotoba(-bushi)* and *nagashi* patterns (all *te* were acquired while singing their *kuchi-shōga*, mnemonic vocable versions).

4. During the second and third years, acquisition of a group of short "*iro-ha*" (ABC) narratives, so that *kadobiki* could be carried out alone.
5. During the third or fourth year, acquisition, to the teacher's satisfaction, of a single *gei-gatame* item (a "test piece"), in which all of the teacher's *fushi* and *te* were presented (Hyōdō 1991, 23), so that thereafter, to learn a new piece, a performer had only to learn its story and perhaps some text passages considered as highlights, which tended to occur in fixed or near-to-fixed form.
6. Acquisition of such further repertory items as the teacher wished to transmit, including some full-length *gedai* and, in some cases, the texts for the *kōjin-barai*, *suijin-barai* and *watamashi* rituals. All other repertory was to be learned by listening to performances by the teacher and others.

In the case of a full-length apprenticeship of seven or eight years, the biwa would not be touched until the second year. Hashiguchi and Ōkawa did not begin to learn their *iro-ha* tales (which included *Azekakehime* for Ōkawa and a short version of *Ishidōmaru* for Hashiguchi) until well after the second year of indentureship. During Yamashika's five-year apprenticeship, however, steps 1, 2 and 3 were undertaken concurrently in the first year (Hyōdō 1991, 18). Some sources suggest, moreover, that Yamashika was able to make his progress even faster by asking more experienced students to teach him both the short single-*dan* item *Ono no Komachi* and the longer *Dōjōji* by the end of his second year rather than waiting for the master to teach it to him. According to Hyōdō, Yamashika learned *Ono no Komachi* from his teacher after about one year of apprenticeship (1991, 20), but Yasuda asserts that Yamashika may have learned both biwa *te* (instrumental patterns) and *Ono no Komachi* not from his teacher but from an older pupil (2001, 21).[10] The second single-*dan* narrative Yamashika acquired, *Dōjōji*, was a longer item that served as the *gei-gatame* because it contained all of the typical *fushi* and biwa patterns of the Tamagawa-*ha*. Yamashika would usually

---

10. Such discrepancies between data of the various people who documented Yamashika's professional life abound. The reason that Ezaki had taught Yamashika very little biwa technique by the time he left the apprenticeship, Yasuda claims, is that the first two years of tuition had been devoted to memorising the words and some *fushi* of songs and short narratives (2001, 21).

have had to wait until the second half of his contracted five years to study *Dōjōji*, but claimed to have been so eager to learn it that at the end of his second year he persuaded the senior apprentice, Hamaguchi Kamesaku, to teach him while Ezaki was away (Hyōdō 1991, 17; Ga 1972, 28). It was perhaps out of a sense that he had already acquired the basic skills he would need that Yamashika was able to decide to leave his apprenticeship early.

The content of step 6 in the above scheme was highly variable, according to the teacher's breadth of repertory and attitude toward his students. While Hashiguchi said that he was not formally taught the *kōjin-barai* nor all the sections of the *watamashi* ritual, Ōkawa Susumu did learn ritual pieces from his teacher. In Yamashika's case, ritual material would perhaps have been taught later in his apprenticeship, had he completed it.[11] Both Yamashika and Ōkawa claim to have learned a greater amount of material from their teachers than does Hashiguchi. Hashiguchi says that he acquired pieces by *kikioboe* (listening to others' performances until he could put together his own version of a piece) after the fourth year of his indentureship but appears not to have expanded his repertory after completing the apprenticeship. Ōkawa also told me of his own efforts to gain new repertory by *kikioboe* after learning what he considered a small number of *gedai* directly from his teacher (see de Ferranti 1997, 170–172; 2003).

Living Conditions and Training Experiences

As a live-in apprentice, Yamashika worked Ezaki's fields almost daily for at least the first year of his indentureship. Much of the time his teacher was away doing jobs or *kadobiki* with the senior apprentice. Despite maintaining the conventional personal distance required of a contracted "guest," he got on well with the teacher's family and later spoke nostalgically of how at ease he had been while living in Amakusa.

Relations between Yamashika and his teacher were formal. He recalled that the infrequent lessons were the only times when Ezaki spoke forcefully to him:

11. It is unclear whether Yamashika knew any ritual pieces at the time he left his apprenticeship. According to Uda (1991, 78), he was taught none by his teacher, but it is possible that he was taught by a more senior student. Kimura (1994, 89–98) says that he had not learnt the *watamashi* and some other rituals.

The lessons weren't so often, but my teacher was very strict when he taught them. The rest of the time he was very polite to me. (Kimura 1994, 56)

Yamashika was fortunate that his teacher had been "strict" but had nonetheless restrained himself from mistreating students, for at the time violence and abuse of apprentices were far from uncommon. Yamashika was well aware of this even at the time, for he recounted at length to Kimura these and other anecdotes about teacher-student physical abuse that he learned of while in Amakusa:

> There are a lot of people who've been slapped in the face or hit on the head by their teacher, but our teacher would only hit us on our knees. He told us, "You mustn't hit an apprentice when you're teaching. I can hit my wife's head, 'cause I own it, after all, but apprentices are other people's children who I'm just looking after, and I'll have to return them to their family when they've been trained."
>
> There was an old *shamisenbiki* woman in Takase. My teacher stayed at her house once, and after dinner some of the locals came for their lessons. They paid her a kind of monthly fee called a *fudageiko*. The *shamisen* player kept time by hitting the mats with a *kiseru* [a tobacco pipe]. Sometimes she'd say, "You haven't learnt it!" and hit them on the head with the pipe. If the student was a girl, she'd cry out, "Ouch, that hurts!" and the teacher would hit her again, saying, "Ah, so it *does* hurt, does it?" My teacher told her, "That's terrible—don't do that! Her head'll be damaged if you injure her! It's up to you how you teach them, but they're paying you for the lessons, so you have to put up with the fact that they won't always be very good. I know it's a bother, because I teach, too." By saying that, he shamed the *shamisen* teacher and put a stop to it, but she complained, "You always treat your students too well!" (ibid., 55–56)

When Yamashika's, Ōkawa's and Hashiguchi's apprenticeships are compared, a common characteristic is that none of their teachers attempted to pass on to the student all, or even more than a small part, of his repertory. What was transmitted during apprenticeship was a basic set of biwa performance skills, the texts and *fushi* for a small number of *hauta* and short *kadozuke* pieces, and the resources required for the young *biwa hiki* to expand his repertory by *kikioboe*, both during the final years of apprenticeship and the following period of beginning work as a professional. The extent to which the individual musician undertook expansion of repertory by *kikioboe* was highly variable, in accordance with professional and personal circumstance.

The tuition that Yamashika received from Ezaki during his foreshortened period of training is only fragmentarily described in the published sources (and indeed in my own recorded conversations with him). Basic technique for holding and plucking the biwa was first learned by direct physical guidance:

> We'd learn the biwa *te* first by the teacher sitting behind us and grabbing our hands directly to guide them. After we got used to it, he'd transfer to his own instrument and we'd play along with him. (Kimura 1994, 54)

The process described here is the same that takes place at the start of tuition in non-blind biwa traditions today because it rapidly gives the student a feel for how best to hold, position and move the plectrum. Because the requisite amount of pressure to apply between frets with the left-hand fingers to produce correct pitch is something that cannot be well described, the fingers need to be physically guided to appropriate angles and degrees of tension while the student is learning to hear pitches within biwa phrases accurately.

> For *te*, you have to press with your fingers just the right amount. I didn't get the point for a long time. I'd just press with my fingers, and it'd hurt—and of course the right pitch didn't come out. So my teacher would press down directly on top of my fingers (until I got the right pitch), and that would hurt even more. "Here, this is the right sound" he'd say, but it was so difficult to do by myself. I'd try doing it over and over again, but I just couldn't understand how to get the right sounds from those frets. I'd do this so many times that the skin on my fingers would break, and they'd bleed. . . . By persevering like this for long enough, little by little the sounds I'd make on the instrument became more stable. (ibid., 57)

Another strategy for learning pitches within biwa patterns, as well as memorising the patterns themselves, was to sing them in *kuchibiwa* syllables (also called *kuchibiki*):

> When you play biwa, there's a downstroke and an upstroke. We'd sometimes go through a *gedai* without the instrument, using *kuchibiki* ("*chinchiri*" and other syllables) for the biwa part. . . . I couldn't say them well—I'd become uncertain in the middle. The syllables were sung in a way that gave you some idea of the amount of finger pressure on the strings, but early in my training I'd no idea how that worked.[12] (ibid., 56–57)

---

12. *Kuchibiwa* are a form of *shōga*, vocables for singing parts (or in some traditions,

After a certain elementary confidence in placing pitch was achieved, the teacher started to play on his own instrument so that the student could play along and imitate. For the long phase of learning in which he would exactly imitate Ezaki's performance, Yamashika was required to sit with knees touching the blind teacher's:

> The teacher and I would sit facing each other with our knees touching, and he'd place one hand on my knee. If I moved the knee away, he'd hit it and get mad. He told me, "I'm blind, so I don't know whether you're facing me or in the other direction. If we keep our knees together, I know you'll learn the thing properly." (ibid., 55)

While the skills of biwa-playing and memorisation of texts for core song and rudimentary narrative repertory were separated out for practice and acquisition, the melodies of *fushi* and various styles of vocal delivery were gradually internalised only in the course of learning to sing or declaim beginners' items, then actual repertory, exactly following the teacher's model.

To acquire the basic succession of pitches in vocal *fushi*, the student would do *tsurebushi*, that is, sing the words and *fushi* of a rudimentary piece together with the teacher. The first pieces used for this purpose were *hauta* songs,[13] which mostly required only the basic recitational forms of *kotoba* or *katari* but also served as a means of learning the florid and most complicated of *fushi*, the *nagashi*. In Yamashika's case, three *hauta* were studied in succession,[14] then the single-*dan* items *Ono no Komachi* and *Dōjōji* were acquired. Yamashika would practise these pieces by himself to consolidate and reinforce his memory of how *fushi* segments were distributed against the words, but their structure was far more complex than the rudimentary *hauta*:

> I'd practise a piece over and over with the *fushi* placed just where my teacher had put them, but even ten times through wasn't enough. I'd go through it fifteen or twenty times, and still make mistakes.

all) of repertory, in which performance techniques are encoded. In *satsumabiwa* and *chikuzenbiwa* practice there is a consistent encoding of relative—not exact—pitch with vowel sounds. See further Guignard (1986), Fujita (1986) and de Ferranti (1989).

13. Yamashika, interview by author, November 9, 1991.
14. Hyōdō names *Kiyotanigawa*, *Ume wa Nioide*, and *Ikka Hiraite* (1991, 181) but Ga (1972, 26) gives *Kiyotanigawa*, *Ginitsubane* and *Ano Yamakage* as the three songs learned.

The first part of the piece was alright, but after that I'd get lost, and the teacher would yell at me, "Look—you've got caught up again!" (Kimura 1994, 54)

Given the nature of *danmono* repertory performance by competent *biwa hiki*, which requires not only a broad range of distinct voice-types for dialogue but also ability to shorten, elide, lengthen and embellish episodes in a tale in response to performance conditions and audience make-up, the above skills acquired during Yamashika's apprenticeship were the bare minimum that would enable him to begin work. It may be that in response to the promise shown by Yamashika, his teacher would have gone on to impart to him more advanced performance techniques, including ways of improvisationally elaborating upon the versions of core repertory he'd learned during his two and a half years as an apprentice or indeed fleshing out the "bones" of other narratives. Ezaki might also have gone on to teach Yamashika the few *kamigoto* ritual pieces that he knew. Circumstances intervened, however, to bring Yamashika back to Nankan, and in turn to cut short his five-year apprenticeship little more than halfway through. Part of the background to those circumstances was experience of a competitiveness that crept into financial relations between Ezaki and one of his advanced apprentices.

Financial Relations between the Teacher and His Apprentices
A biwa professional's income came from a variety of activities, and apprentices who had reached proficiency in performance represented a form of labour that their teacher was entitled to exploit in the course of their further training. In the early years of apprenticeship, students were required to accompany the master on *kadozuke* and to carry his belongings and any produce received as payment. After at least two years of training, they were able to perform *kadozuke* themselves or together with other apprentices, but all money and goods received thereby were to be turned over to the teacher (Yasuda 1991, 5). Accordingly, incidents of pupils concealing income and even absconding with it were not uncommon.

In his talks with Kimura about working in Amakusa during the latter two of his years there, Yamashika mentioned the following as performance modes in which his teacher had worked: *kadobiki*, *momimorai* (performance in exchange for *momi*, unhulled rice husks), *ochabiki* (performance at the time of the tea harvest, in exchange for leaves, either dried or undried), *kamigoto* (although not *watamashi*, which Yamashika said he never experienced in Amakusa)[15] and *zashikibiwa*. After learning the required elementary repertory, Yamashika accompanied and assisted both his teacher and the most senior of his apprentices on jobs in the first three modes, beginning with *kadobiki* work about a year after he had arrived in Amakusa.

Yamashika received very little for assisting in *kadobiki*: "Whenever I did work with the teacher, he'd only give me a little money when it pleased him, saying, 'Here's your tobacco money!'" Moreover any money or produce earned while working with the senior apprentice was handed over to the teacher:

> While I was an apprentice, I gave all my earnings to the teacher. If I had to go out to do something, I'd sometimes use just a little of the earnings for that purpose. Apart from gifts during the Bon festival and at New Year, the teacher gave me no money. (ibid., 69–70)

The convention that apprentices' earnings were handed to the teacher is confirmed by Hashiguchi's accounts of his own apprenticeship in Amakusa (Yasuda 2001, 26). It was called into question, however, by an incident that Yamashika recounted at length to Kimura (1994, 66–70): While the teacher was away on another job, Yamashika and the senior apprentice had been engaged to entertain for two nights by a group of farmers, who remunerated them generously in both *momi* and cash. The senior apprentice, an Amakusa local who lived with his family and paid Ezaki only for lessons, felt entitled to keep the earnings, not even dividing it with his junior assistant, Yamashika. The teacher was furious on both counts, and a full-scale argument developed between him and the parents of the senior apprentice. After an intermediary resolved the dispute, Yamashika concluded that

> it made me see my teacher as a difficult man, because the apprentice was actually justified in his argument. It's normal for all the money a live-in apprentice earns to be given to the teacher, but the senior apprentice wasn't living in, and only paid for individual lessons, so he ought to have had to give up only a part of his earnings. (ibid., 69)

---

15. Yamashika said that his teacher did "hardly any" *kamigoto* work but in another talk with Kimura discusses the fact that when his teacher did *kamigoto* in Amakusa, the rites were little different to those of the Nankan area (1994, 61).

In October of Yamashika's third year in Amakusa, a message came asking him to come home because his father was sick. Securing his teacher's permission, Yamashika returned to Nankan for what was to have been a short stay. Yet he never went back to resume his apprenticeship, for reasons that he himself later said were not substantial ones. Yet the incident about the senior apprentice's earnings may well have figured strongly in his deliberations about the future.

Participation in Local *Biwa Hiki* Groups and Acquisition of a Professional Name

> After I had to come home because of Dad's illness, my teacher in Amakusa came up to do biwa work around Nankan twice, but I didn't meet him here. I'll talk about this later, but there were reasons why he didn't want to see me. (Kimura 1994, 72)

On January 16, 1927,[16] Yamashika took a performer's name by holding a *nabiraki* (celebratory performance using the name for the first time) and started working as a biwa player in the Nankan area without the permission of his teacher—in effect cutting short his contracted apprenticeship period by more than two years. This was possible because the profession of *biwa hiki* was a highly unregulated one in the early twentieth century. In chapter 1, I discussed the *tōdō-za* guild's achievement in the late seventeenth century of Shogunal support for its efforts to control groups of blind musicians in Kyushu and to separate *harai* rituals with biwa from performance for entertainment. Many blind professionals continued to do both kinds of performance and did not comply with guild regulations even if they were made to join. This centuries-long background of complex relations between *biwa hiki* and institutions that tried to order their activities was compounded in the Meiji period when the *tōdō-za* itself was banned, and even *kadozuke* was prohibited for a time. In these turbulent circumstances, it seems that many *biwa hiki* sought to continue the *kō* (specifically, Myōon Kō) model of association that had begun under the *tōdō-za*, as a geographically based unit of organisation. At the

---

16. Kimura gives 1925 as the year (1994, 76), but is contradicted by Yasuda, Hyōdō and Ga. This can only be accounted for by the fact that Yamashika's talks with various researchers yielded contradictory information on a range of points.

same time, new means of association came into being, such as those described in chapter 2. The *ha* (school or line of practice) grouping of performers who were taught by a prominent musician, or by students of or players descended from that teacher, also continued to operate as a manifestation of the artistic "house" or family (*ie*) model that exists in most Japanese historical artforms.

Yamashika's Participation in the Tamagawa-*ha*

Yamashika called himself and was considered a Tamagawa-*ha* biwa professional simply because his teacher in Amakusa had been a Tamagawa player trained by the founder of the *ha*, Hori Kyōjun of Nankan. The fact that Yamashika discontinued his apprenticeship early and did not receive any certificate from his teacher appears to have been irrelevant for his status as a Tamagawa-*ha* performer. The most senior musician of the Tamagawa-*ha*, Sekijun, even helped Yamashika to plan his naming festivity and encouraged him to informally learn more from him—a fact that suggests there was rivalry among teacher-performers of one and the same lineage at this time:

> When I went to consult him about how to do the *nabiraki*, he said, "Why on earth did you go off to learn in such a strange place as Amakusa? I was Kyōjun's top student, so why didn't you come to me?" Sekijun was a distant relative of mine, and senior to my teacher in Amakusa, so that question was a crucial one! "Is it because I'm old?" he asked me, but I explained the truth of the situation politely, and he understood. After that, Sekijun in effect became my second teacher. (ibid., 80)

While Yamashika saw Sekijun in this way, no researcher has listed any *gedai* that Yamashika claimed to have learned from Sekijun. The relationship clearly involved mentorship, but evidence in several sources points to the conclusion that it was Mori Yoichi (Tamagawa Kyōzan), not Sekijun, who served the crucial role of providing Yamashika with supplementary repertory. Yamashika told some researchers (but not others) that before his *nabiraki* he had spent a year doing *kadobiki* in the company of Mori, and was able to learn new *gedai* from him (Hyōdō 1991, 15; Ga 1972, 28; Murayama 1986, 432). Yasuda even claims that Tamagawa Kyōzan, not Sekijun, was the main person responsible for organisation of Yamashika's naming ceremony (2001, 22).

A possible explanation for why Yamashika was able to receive new repertory from Mori rather than Sekijun is suggested by Mori's apparent disregard for some key matters of protocol as a Tamagawa-*ha* member. He was an ally of the offender, Kōgetsu, in the following anecdote about a dispute at Yamashika's naming festivity:

> Kōgetsu had originally not been a Tamagawa-*ha* player, but he'd participated in the memorial gathering for Kyōjun, and thereafter used a Tamagawa name. Sekijun told him, "What have you been doing? Keeping quiet all this time about the fact that you've slyly taken a Tamagawa name? You're unfit to sit here and drink with us! You shouldn't be allowed to eat our food either! *Mikajime sen*! Why don't you have a proper naming event?" (Kimura 1994, 82)

Yamashika recalls that Kyōzan (Mori) in fact had "given" Kōgetsu a Tamagawa name for a bottle of *sake*. This episode shows that membership of a *ha* was solely based on training lineage; if one claimed membership through illegitimate use of a *ha*'s signature name without having been trained by a player of the *ha* nor held a *nabiraki*, one was subject to the censure of bona fide members. It may be that Sekijun, as the senior Tamagawa-*ha* musician, was constrained from teaching *gedai* to a novice who had formally been the apprentice of another Tamagawa player, while Mori felt free to ignore such constraints.

As suggested in chapter 2, neither the antiquity nor the exact terms of distinction between *biwa hiki* groups in the former Higo region, even in relatively recent practice, are well understood. The following is a summary of the characteristics of the *ha* which emerged from my discussions with Yamashika and other *biwa hiki* in the early 1990s:

1. Each *ha* was initially formed around an individual musician and teacher of renown and moreover was confined to *biwa hiki* who were resident within a circumscribed area in proximity to that of the head musician. In this way, the *ha* of the three musicians whom I interviewed in the 1990s—Tamagawa (Yamashika's), Miyagawa (Ōkawa's), and Hoshizawa (Hashiguchi's)—seem to have existed in northern Higo, southern Higo, and in the Amakusa region, respectively.
2. Membership of a particular *ha* was denoted by the practice, common to many forms of traditional performing arts, of

individuals receiving an artistic name (*geimei*), the constituent elements of which were the *ha* name (Tamagawa, Miyagawa and Hoshizawa, among others) and a personal name in which at least one character was common to the names of many, if not all *ha* members. Despite such unequivocal group identification through professional naming practices, it seems that formal means of association were very few, and there was—at least in the cases of Yamashika, Hashiguchi and Ōkawa—little obligation on the part of individual singers to associate or communicate with other *ha* members, except at meetings which were in some areas held in association with the Myōon Kō ceremony and at occasional *nabiraki*.

3. Distinctions in performance style along *ha* lines were acknowledged by *biwa hiki*, but the extent of their importance is hard to discern. All three *biwa hiki* interviewed in the 1990s spoke in terms of particular *fushi* and performance techniques which characterised the art of members of their own *ha*. Notwithstanding their verbal emphases of such differences, the abilities of the singers to recognise the *ha* affiliation of other recorded performers were not consistent. For instance, Ōkawa Susumu was able to say emphatically that, judging from the *fushi*, a player named Nishimura Kyōzan (Sadaichi) was a member of his own Miyagawa-*ha* within twenty seconds of my starting to play an old recording by him, but Yamashika was quite unable to suggest any particular *ha* affiliation after listening to a 1975 recording of Ōkawa's singing.[17]

Yet the *ha* had little or no control over individuals' professional actions; in this respect the institution was unlike the Myōon Kō, whose senior performers had power to enforce a professional behavioural code on members at meetings associated with the annual group rites. It is clear that members of different *ha* were free to travel around together, do *kadobiki* and even perform one after another in *zashikibiwa* events.[18]

17. This may well be because Yamashika's base area of professional activity had been in the northern part of Kumamoto Prefecture as well as in Amakusa and the nearer reaches of Fukuoka Prefecture. It is possible that he had never had occasion to hear a Miyagawa-*ha* musician's performance.

18. Both Ōkawa Susumu and Hashiguchi Keisuke, of the Miyagawa-*ha* and Hoshizawa-*ha*, respectively, told me that they had travelled together with friends who

While Yamashika recalled the argument at his *nabiraki* caused by Kōgetsu's illegitimate use of a Tamagawa name, his own willingness to travel to Miyazaki with another *biwa hiki* who used the name without having been trained by a Tamagawa-*ha* teacher (Kimura 1994, 130) suggests that it was not an organisation that demanded stringent forms of loyalty.

Acquisition of Professional Status and a Performer's Name

Yamashika's account of the way the senior musician in the Tamagawa-*ha* in the early 1920s had berated a *biwa hiki* for illegitimately using the name Tamagawa Kōgetsu ends with Sekijun's exhortation for the man to "have a proper *nabiraki*." As a formal declaration of one's professional status under a given professional name, this public event was considered important for legitimate membership of a *ha*. While the conclusion of an apprenticeship usually yielded an actual certificate from one's teacher, the successful conclusion of a *nabiraki* was in effect the means by which *biwa hiki* acquired their professional licence in the eyes of their fellow musicians and the patronage communities that would sustain them.

A *nabiraki* required financial backers. For Yamashika's festivity, his surviving (maternal) grandfather asked a group of friends to join him in that important role (Kimura 1994, 78). With financial support in place, the next step was to ask local biwa players to participate by each performing a piece. For Yamashika's ceremonial event, seven local *biwa hiki* came to play. All except one were Tamagawa-*ha* musicians, and they agreed to appear for a token fee that was less than they would usually receive for performing; the highest fee, of 7 yen 50 *sen*, was paid to the most senior player, Sekijun. Despite the token fees, the backers could not possibly break even:

> Those fees were supposed to come from money given by people, as a gift [*o-hana*] to me, but when it wasn't enough, my father had to cover it. I got about 20 yen of gift money together by going around to 40 houses in the upper parts of Kobaru and Miya. The most people gave was 30 *sen*, and the least about 5 *sen*. But that wasn't enough. My father was supposed to top it up, but he didn't give much. The overall

---

were of the Tamagawa-*ha*. For Hashiguchi, Yasuda has documented in some detail relations with other *biwa hiki*, both within Amakusa and during travels elsewhere (2001, 27–35).

expenses were about 40 yen—what with the *sake* and fish we had to have for people who'd given *hana* money and all—so we came out in the red. (Kimura 1994, 80)

In-kind support came from various sources, including relatives and community members who knew Yamashika and his family:

The *o-hana* may have been a bit small, but I had some fine banners made for me, and I was helped out in many ways. People in my neighbourhood made me a big banner to hang behind me, and another for the front. Someone else gave me a table banner. I heard the banners cost 13 yen altogether. The Miya people were determined not to be outdone, so they gave me yet another big banner. (ibid., 80)

As explained above, a professional name denoted one's lineage through the *ha* (Tamagawa, in this case) and usually included one of the characters of one's teacher's name. Hence Tamagawa Sekijun had used the syllable *jun* (順, meaning "order or obedience") in the name of his teacher, the Tamagawa founder Hori Kyōjun, while Yamashika used the sound *kyō* (教, meaning "teaching"), which had also been in his Amakusa teacher's name, Kyōsetsu, and is pronounced the same as the syllable *kyō* (京, meaning "capital") in the founder musician's name. The choice of another syllable and character for the second word in the name was left up to the individual, who selected something meaningful for himself: Sekijun's "Seki" was an alternative reading for the second character (関, meaning "gate") in Nankan. Yamashika explained that he'd decided upon *en* (縁, meaning "connection") because "I had a connection (*en*) with Kyōjun in becoming a *biwa hiki*" (ibid., 81) but decided to spell it with a character that means to display or perform. His professional name therefore became Tamagawa Kyōen (玉川教演).

Notwithstanding Yamashika's compliance with the convention of using one of the characters in his teacher's name, in response to an invitation to attend the event, Ezaki wrote from Amakusa that "You'll be ashamed of yourself, because you're not adequately trained yet." He did not come to the *nabiraki* and he initiated proceedings against Yamashika's father in the District Court of Takase to recoup losses caused by the foreshortened apprenticeship.[19]

19. Kimura gives Taisho 13 (1924) as the date for this court action but January 1925 for the *nabiraki* itself. Perhaps the court proceeding was only initiated in 1924, after it became clear that Yamashika wouldn't go back to continue his training in Amakusa.

Yamashika gave this vivid account of the communal event, his own performance, and Sekijun's encouraging words:

> On the day of the *nabiraki*, the place we'd prepared was filled to overflowing with people who'd heard there would be biwa, food and grog. We had to let them sit out in front of several houses along the street! I performed a single *dan* first of all. Then the seven participating *biwa hiki* performed in order, with Sekijun's *Sumidagawa* last, then another *dan* by me, *Kugami Gassen*, at the end. I did the flower-viewing scene on Flower Garden Mountain, when Princess Hoshikawa Nagahide is carried off into the sky by a demon. (I can't remember what happens in the first *dan* of that story—I only remember the *dan* that I performed that day.) Sekijun was pleased: "You picked a good section to perform. You will probably take off like an angel in your career." I'll never forget his praise. (ibid., 82)

Making a Living as a *Biwa Hiki*

> Well, that's how it was — I managed to study certain things while I was working to make my living. It was mostly half-baked, and done pretty carelessly, I have to say. I think it's because *biwa hiki* have stopped doing proper training (just as I did) that they've gradually become unable to earn a living at all. (ibid., 94)

In the 1920s the profession of *biwa hiki* remained one that some visually impaired youths and their families considered a viable alternative to dependency. The best among older musicians, who had started their careers in the last decades of the nineteenth century, still made a decent living from biwa, as Yamashika indicates in a comment about the senior Tamagawa-*ha* player, Sekijun:

> At the time I did my naming ceremony, he lived in Itakusu, and his wife made *tōfu* and ran a sweet shop over there. Of course, he was good enough to have supported them both just from playing biwa. (ibid., 79)

By mid century Yamashika was to find that even a good player could not support his family solely from biwa performance, but when he started his career in the late 1920s there was still reason for optimism— provided that he commanded all three of the *biwa hiki*'s traditional modes of work: *kadobiki*, *zashikibiwa* and *kamigoto*.

Acquisition of Skills and Repertory from Other *Biwa Hiki*

This retrospective comment by Yamashika indicates that for all the talent and confidence he showed in holding a naming event and ceremonial performance after having trained formally for little over two years, he was well aware that his skills remained deficient and that he would have to make up for the fact that his training was incomplete; for several years to come he would have to keep "studying" while he was working. Yasuda points out (2001, 21) that from 1927 until 1933, Yamashika continued to help out on a part-time basis with his parents' farmwork. If he was not solely dependent on biwa work until then, this may have facilitated his ability to spend time learning new pieces and styles.

At the time that Yamashika publicised his self-proclaimed professional status through a *nabiraki*, he had already gained a fair amount of experience of offering biwa songs and narrative performance; he had frequently done *kadobiki* with the teacher and the senior apprentice around Hondō (in Amakusa) over the course of a year and a half, and had done short items in *zashikibiwa* performances for gatherings on festive and important occasions. While *kadobiki* for various forms of payment was the staple work that *biwa hiki* could—and in most cases had to—engage in whenever funds were depleted, the importance of *zashikibiwa* engagements could not be overlooked. This is underlined by comments made by Yamashika about his teacher's training and specifically the fact that Ezaki had changed teachers in order to be able to learn repertory appropriate for *zashikibiwa*. Ezaki had originally learned from a man who specialised in ritual and gained most of his income doing *kadobiki* but therefore could not teach any of the full *gedai* needed for *zashikibiwa* work. Ezaki sought and received permission to switch teachers to Hori Kyōjun so that he would gain a better chance of becoming self-sufficient (Kimura 1994, 58–59).[20]

Like other *biwa hiki*, Yamashika was taught relatively few songs and tales by his teacher. He sought to acquire more from older apprentices or other *biwa hiki* even before he left the apprenticeship (Hyōdō 1989, 181), then continued to expand his repertory of *gedai* through a variety of strategies during the early stages of his career.

20. By the time Yamashika was apprenticed, Ezaki was in his early fifties and the bulk of his living came from a combination of *zashiki* engagements, the yield of his land, his students' fees and his wife's income from occasional midwifery (Hyodo 1991, 38).

The most important of these was the relationship he developed with the older musician of long experience, Mori Yoichi (Tamagawa Kyōzan). The *gedai* Yamashika said he had learned from Mori were to be tremendously important for his earning capacity: *Ichi no Tani, Ko-Atsumori, Azekakehime, Shuntokumaru,* and *Oguri Hangan*. All were among the most often performed tales in Yamashika's repertory, but the circumstances for their acquisition remain unclear: With the exception of *Azekakehime*, during *kadobiki* these tales would have been performed only in very concise versions or as sequences of excerpted highlights. Even if requests for extensive performances of certain of these *gedai* were made, acquisition of the longer tales (one of which, *Oguri Hangan*, is over six hours long in performances that include "all" *dan*) from hearing only occasional performances of certain sections would have been effectively impossible. If Mori did teach these *gedai* to Yamashika, his willingness to transmit such key repertory outside a formal teacher-apprentice relationship is puzzling, given the competition among narrative performers for diminishing patronage in rural Kyushu. As already noted, Mori was something of a maverick. It may be, moreover, that he was near the end of his working life and responded to Yamashika's talent and dedication by ensuring he learned items that audiences would request.

Subsequently Yamashika sought new materials from all sorts of performers—not only biwa players, but also *naniwa-bushi* and *jōruri* professionals[21]—either openly or secretly by listening to their performances and constructing a version of his own from memory. When other performers taught him a piece, he would reciprocate by teaching them a tale unknown to them from his own repertory. Sometimes he would even pay money to musicians he met so that they would teach him new pieces he believed would help attract and retain audiences (Murayama 1986, 437–438). His stock of humorous pieces (*kokkeimono*) and *chari* "light-relief" episodes for insertion into standard tales was mostly acquired from a player renowned for his skill in *chari*, Takezawa Kōgyoku, with whom Yamashika travelled for three weeks (ibid., 435–436).

21. Ga 1972 (28–29) gives a list of the names of six more performers from whom Yamashika acquired repertory—and the items acquired—after his apprenticeship and time with Mori Yoichi. See also Hyōdō (1991, 16).

Something Yamashika had no experience of at the time he began professional work was engagement by householders and community groups to perform *kamigoto* repertory, specifically those for *harai* rites. I have presented evidence in chapter 2 that the relative quantity of ritual engagement in the *biwa hiki*'s work had decreased significantly by the early twentieth century. It seemed to Yamashika, however, that such work was still essential if he was going to make an adequate living from biwa. Therefore in the years immediately after his *nabiraki* he persistently strove to acquire the necessary *kamigoto* repertory and ritual skills, while earning income through *kadobiki* and *zashikibiwa* work. Kimura records in detail how Yamashika eventually acquired the text for *watamashi* only by persistent enquiry and checking the content of what he'd heard, and sections of this account are worth quoting at length:

> I think it was in August of my first year of work, when I was going around in Chikugo:[22] There was a place called Mizoguchi—it's now part of Chikugo City—which had 4 or 5 houses. Someone there asked me, "Won't you stay here tonight?" so I had a place to sleep. Then the same person told me, "Our house has been built fairly recently and still hasn't got a gate. We haven't done a *watamashi* here yet, so please stay and play biwa in the house." I hadn't learnt it, so I declined the offer. "I can't do a *watamashi*."
>
> "That's OK. If you don't know it, it's enough just to play biwa here for us."
>
> "Well, in that case..."
>
> ...Along the way [home], I dropped in at Ishibashi-san's in Motoyoshi. He wasn't going out working that day. "Oh, you've come around early!" he said. I told him of what had happened the night before, and asked him to teach me *watamashi*. He said he couldn't teach it to me, because he'd only learned it himself by *kikioboe*.
>
> ... "That's OK—will you teach me what you know, anyway?" I asked.
>
> "No, I won't do that, but you should come around with me. Tomorrow I think I'll go toward Shiragi. There might be a request for *watamashi* along the way. If you listen to that, you can pick it up."
>
> I decided to go with him because I wanted to learn the thing, no matter what it took. So the next day we went off together to a weaver's workshop, and straight away they asked him to do a *watamashi*. "You've come at just the right time. We haven't had a *watamashi* since

---

22. Yasuda claims that the Chikugo region (of southern Fukuoka Prefecture) became Yamashika's principal area of professional activity from 1933 (2001, 20–22) but it seems Yamashika had worked in Chikugo occasionally before then.

the workshop was built. Please do one tonight, and stay over here afterwards." So I was able to hear the *watamashi* ritual for the first time. Listening to the words Ishibashi chanted, I understood most of it, but there were still a lot of words I wasn't convinced about. For instance, I asked Ishibashi what god "the *kami* of the first pillar, Ittenshi?" really was, but he'd just say "Ittenshi is just Ittenshi." I also asked Takezawa, and the *kengyō*-san at Kita no Seki, but none of them knew. Even though I thought that was strange, I learnt the *watamashi* that way, anyway.

Later on I learnt the ways of cutting the *gohei* that are needed for *watamashi*. There was a *biwa hiki* that the Takenoe no Inari shrine attendant knew, who agreed to teach me if I stayed there and cooked for him for two days....

Once I visited Takezawa in Hongo, Setaka-machi, when a *kengyō*-san named Sakamoto Saichi was there. I asked him about that peculiar Ittenshi.

"It's rude of me to ask you this as it's the first time we've met, but ..."

"Wha-t? There's no such god! The gods of the first house pillar are 'Nichitenshi' and 'Gatsutenshi'—the sun and the moon gods."

So the puzzle was solved—and after that I was able to learn *watamashi* properly from Sakamoto. (Kimura 1994, 89–92)

All of these memories and anecdotes of how Yamashika acquired skills and *gedai* show that he was well aware from the first that the size and scope of his repertory as an entertainer and ritual celebrant would determine his ability to be self-sufficient. As someone who decided to become a *biwa hiki* in early adulthood, even during his apprenticeship Yamashika saw the need to learn much more than his teacher was willing to impart. His decision to leave midway through the apprenticeship put him at some risk, but he responded with resourcefulness and determination, in time compiling a repertory larger than any other *biwa hiki* whom researchers documented from the 1960s on.

Kadozuke and Discrimination against *Biwa Hiki*

In chapter 4, I described *kadozuke* as one of two contexts for secular narrative performance and gave a detailed account of Yamashika's typical strategies and procedures for gaining the patronage of householders while conserving his own energy. I will now reconsider *kadozuke* in terms of a broader set of concerns that overcomes distinction between "religious" and "secular" activity, categories that result from consideration of repertory alone rather than contexts for acts of performance.

As discussed in chapter 1, performers who presented in public outdoor spaces (*daidō geinin*) and those who performed in front of houses for various forms of remuneration (*kadozuke geinin*) were both accorded marginal status from the medieval era on, and in many contexts were associated with the discriminated classes (*senmin*). In many regions forms of *kadozuke* performance were an important part of seasonal agrarian rites; itinerant performers bestowed blessings upon and purified households through their visits. It must not be forgotten that responses to itinerant performance were also conditioned by Buddhist traditions, in which performing and begging for a living were activities adopted by holy figures from the times of earliest records, and merit resulted from giving alms.

Within these conceptual frameworks, *kadozuke* can be viewed as a syncretic cultural practice, whereby "strangers" who performed from door to door could receive food or money for four reasons: for specific ritual services they rendered in protecting the living environment (for example, the *Kōjin-* and *Jijin-barai* services offered by *biwa hiki*) for the inherent—if not always consciously acknowledged—sacred significance of their visit, for the merit gained from giving alms and for the brief entertainment they usually provided.[23] At the same time, they were figures to be treated with caution.

Biwa hōshi, *biwa hiki* and *goze* musicians had in common their blindness and diverse degrees of association with the sacred. The negative interpretation of blindness in Buddhist tradition if anything reinforced the low status associated with itinerant "begging" and contributed to the potential for discriminatory treatment of the sort reflected in literary and iconographic depictions of *biwa hōshi*. For *goze* of the Tōhoku region, the importance of blind female shamans (*itako*) in regional belief and ritual practice accentuated an ambig-

---

23. This last element should not be thought any less important than the others, for all forms of *kadozuke* involve performance—in many cases of a ritual that involves lively song and dance or of a solemn ritual text followed by song or storytelling, or song, dance and storytelling alone.

uous sanctity associated with performance for alms,[24] while for *biwa hiki* in Kyushu and in parts of western Honshu a similar effect resulted from the practice of engaging blind biwa players as one of several kinds of celebrant of local *harai* rites.

Kadobiki performance was done in different areas, depending on the time of year. As it was important for biwa players to find people at home, the optimal times for them to visit a village were on festival days and days of rest after the new year, and when harvests of barley, rice or tea had been finished. Hence *biwa hiki* would keep a schedule in their minds of the dates of such events in villages throughout the areas they travelled. In periods when income was likely to be small in their vicinity, they would have to travel further afield. The biwa played in *kadobiki* would have to be dismantled for carrying in a bag on the back then re-assembled at the outskirts of a village. The repertory was mostly *hauta* that involved only two kinds of performance pattern (*fushi*) but also included short forms and extracts from favourite tales, including ones specifically tailored to appeal to the young women with children, who would be the sole people at home at certain times of year, as well as gags for entertaining children. *Kadobiki* was often done in pairs or even small groups of several *biwa hiki*,[25] and because of their visual impairment it was common for performers whose wives could see to be guided by them. Hence it also happened that a *biwa hiki* doing the rounds near home might be followed by his children!

> When you're going around in the villages, it's best to go with just one, or at most two others, as you'll have trouble staying anywhere with more than that. It's hardest to find a place to stay when you've had to take children with you. (Kimura 1994, 131)

Biwa hiki and their travelling companions would either sleep in the houses of patrons who were particularly fond of their tales (in which case they would perform at night for their hosts and interested neighbours by way of thanks), in cheap flophouses (*kichinyado*) used mostly by performers or be put up by other *biwa hiki* in the area. On the whole it was preferable to work in and around rural villages rather than towns:

---

24. Suzuki Shōei has written at length about the sacred and *goze* performance (1996, 2005).
25. Hashiguchi had often done this (Yasuda 2001, 27–28).

In those days, it wasn't profitable to do *kadozuke* in the larger towns. You'd stand playing under some house's eaves, but you'd be refused at ten houses in a row. Then one would ask you to play, and then another ten would refuse you. In the villages, however, if you'd been refused at one house, the next would almost surely help you out. (ibid., 130)

Discrimination and Its Persistence

Even a cursory reading of the memoirs of blind musicians of the Tōhoku region who did *kadozuke* for a living shows that all suffered exploitation, abuse and humiliation as itinerant performers (Takahashi 1983; Groemer 1999). It seems things were marginally better for biwa players in Kyushu:

> *Biwa hiki* had a lot less hierarchy to deal with than people who did other kinds of *kadozuke* performance. In those days the people who did *naniwa-bushi* and *ukarebushi*[26] had to sit down in the *genkan*, while the people listening to them sat at the *shimoza* position inside.[27] But with biwa, it wasn't always like that. (Kimura 1994, 116)

I would suggest that in pre-war Kyushu there was still a general recognition that *biwa hiki* were bearers of *harai* ritual skills and that for this reason they were often treated with more respect than blind *kadozuke* performers of *shamisen*-accompanied narrative genres of more recent origin, who were considered beggars pure and simple.

What were the bases for such harsh treatment of men and women with a visual disability? I have described traditional attitudes to blindness in some cultures imbued with Buddhist thought, with an underlying tendency to see individuals as implicated in their own plight on account of evil deeds in a former life. Yet the principal basis for discriminatory treatment of *biwa hiki* and *goze* would seem to have more to do with the social meanings of *kadozuke* than with any general tendency to mistreat the blind. In Edo-period Japan, blind

---

26. A narrative tradition considered to have been one of the formative elements in *naniwa-bushi*.

27. The *genkan* is the entrance hall where one removes outside shoes before stepping up to the level of inner rooms. *Shimoza* (literally, the "lower seat") is the position in a house's *zashiki* room for those of lower status relative to others.

males and females were subject to the social and legal constraints upon their class; regulatory exemptions were not given to the blind as a matter of course but varied according to status and obligation (Katō 1974, 31–34). Under the Tokugawa regime, people who moved around to make their living—that is to say, itinerant workers—were subject to rigorous regulation, but active discrimination was reserved for those who were both itinerants and beggars:

> In Edo [and]... in other urban areas, anyone—blind or sighted—who made a living as a street performer was likely to be associated with *hinin*, although not necessarily registered as such. (Groemer 2001a, 354)

The stipulation "in other urban areas" notwithstanding, the persistence of historical views of outdoor performers as akin to groups of people treated as outcasts (*hinin*, literally meaning "non-human") yielded a stigma that still affected practitioners of *kadozuke* in twentieth-century rural Kyushu.[28]

Yasuda has documented the use in Kumamoto Prefecture until the mid twentieth century of severely discriminatory terms such as *kanjin biwa* ("biwa for donations") and *monomorai biwa* ("begging biwa") to refer to the occupation of *biwa hiki* (2001, 19). Yamashika spent much of his late teens contemplating how he could eventually gain independence from his father and siblings, and must already have known of such local expressions. As the mainstay of a *biwa hiki*'s income was money or in-kind payment received through door-to-door performance, Yamashika's view of *kadobiki* was decidedly negative at the time he was weighing up whether to train as a performer. In this context, things he had been told by his paternal grandfather may have influenced his thinking:

> *Kadozuke geinin* were always made to sit lower than the people listening to them. "You're a lowly person, so don't come any further than that!" is what they used to say to them. Even in my grandfather's time they'd say that pretty harshly: "Stay at the *shimoza*!"[29] That's just how things

---

28. Nakayama Tarō suggests that ascription of *hinin* status to blind *biwa* players started as early as the medieval period, on the grounds that the suffix "*hōshi*" was applied to them (1934, 78–79).

29. This and the succeeding comment suggest that when his grandfather was a young man in the early years of Meiji, *kadozuke* performers who were invited into a house were not allowed to proceed far beyond the *shimoza* (literally, the "lower seat")

were once. I guess you'd call it discrimination now, but at the time that was standard behaviour. (Kimura 1994, 116–117)

His grandfather had learnt some *jōruri* when young, and Yamashika recalls that he once told him:

> "When I learned that tale, any kind of performance had to be done at the *shimoza*. Now it's the *kamiza*, but it was *shimoza* up until Meiji." So he said that's how it was up until Meiji 10, but I really don't know whether that's the truth . . .[30] (ibid., 118)

While Yamashika did not refer directly to a fear of discriminatory treatment, he did say "with *biwa* I never thought I'd have a problem earning a living, but I really didn't like the idea of doing *kadobiki*," and had told his relatives "even though *biwa* players have to do *kadobiki*, I'll learn that" (ibid., 41). Clearly he had felt apprehension about begging with the biwa as one of the central activities of his livelihood.

The effects of discrimination and marginalisation on Yamashika and his family can themselves be considered a part of the legacy of historical treatment of blind *kadozuke* practitioners. In his rendering of Yamashika's words and commentary, for the most part Kimura only hints at those effects, but they are unequivocally evident in the following passage:

> At the time, my eldest son was at that school. Other kids used to say things to him like, "Hey, there's a *biwa hiki* hanging round your place." He couldn't just be quiet and bear it, so he'd yell back, "That's not true, don't say those lies!" and start fighting with the others. He was generally reprimanded for that, and for a while he stopped going to school altogether . . . My son suffered a lot on account of the sort of work I did. (ibid., 109)

---

near the entrance of a *zashiki* room, but that this means of discrimination had largely disappeared by Yamashika's youth at the beginning of the twentieth century.

30. This recollected comment implies that there had been improvement in the status accorded performers in rural Kumamoto during his grandfather's lifetime (which presumably began in the last decades of the Shogunate, some fifty to sixty years before making such comments to his grandson), for when engaged to play in the main room of a house they no longer had to sit at a position reserved for people of inferior status and instead could perform at the *kamiza* (literally, the "upper seat").

During fieldwork in 1991 to 1992, I encountered at first hand the remnants of stigma against blind biwa players in various forms of "resistance" to research on *higobiwa*. While the *biwa hiki* I worked with were for the most part uninhibited in their talk and generous with their time, some people associated with them and with deceased biwa players were reluctant or absolutely unwilling to cooperate. Ōkawa Susumu's family had turned away all researchers who sought to talk with him for ten years or more. The grandson of Nagamatsu Daietsu, the celebrated sighted performer of the 1920s and 1930s, owned a set of his disc recordings (which in 1963 Tanabe Hisao had described as the single most precious sonic resource for documentation of *higobiwa*; see chapter 2) but refused to allow researchers to listen to them. A retired professor of archaeology had obtained the original open-reel tape of a recording of Yamashika made in the 1950s but had told no-one at the Higobiwa Hozonkai of it and was extremely reluctant to let me dub it onto digital audiotape (DAT) for the sake of preservation. The papers and documents pertaining to *higobiwa* of the estate of Hirakawa Kōji, a central figure in the Preservation Society in the 1970s and author of several articles on the history of *higobiwa*, were not available for viewing even by distinguished local researchers such as Yasuda Muneo. Also, an individual researcher's fine recording of Yamashika performing before a local audience in the early 1970s could only be dubbed on condition of legal affidavit and payment of a large fee.

These experiences mirror a pattern in evidence since the beginning of research and documentation of the blind biwa traditions in central Kyushu. During the 1970s and 1980s families of former *biwa hiki* were highly reluctant to allow their participation in concerts organised by the Higobiwa Hozonkai for fear that their relative's former occupation would become widely known (Yasuda 2001, 19). In the late twentieth century, past association with the low-status or outcast groups called *burakumin* in the post-war era[31] could still lead to subtle but tangible discrimination in Japan, so suspicion of strangers' scrutiny of the performers of *kadozuke* arts was not uncommon.[32] I

---

31. Historically many terms have existed for these groups (including *hinin*, as explained above), but in Edo-period usage "*eta*" was most common.
32. A comparable fieldwork project on *kadozuke* performers is that of Jane Marie Law on the puppeteers of Awaji; she has described how in the 1980s she often met with resistance to her enquiries about itinerant performers of ritual puppetry (1997, 169).

suspect that such protective behaviour may have been caused by many factors but in particular by discriminatory treatment of *biwa hiki* and other beggar-musicians in pre-war Kyushu.

Unequivocal assertions that *biwa hiki* and other beggar-musicians were regarded as outcasts are almost impossible to find in sources, perhaps because the stigma had not disappeared by the 1990s, so statements to that effect would potentially harm the families of people known to have been *kadozuke geinin*. I have located only two such claims in print: In the novelist Ishimure Michiko's chronicle of stories heard from people in the Minamata region during the 1960s and 1970s, *Seinanyaku densetsu*, "*Rokudō Gozen*" contains an account of a *goze* described as "*rokudo ga baba to iwarete, biwa hiku tsure mo motan jorori hinin ja ga*" (1980, 233). The contextual meaning of this phrase in local vernacular is that the woman called Old Lady Rokudo (or Rokudo Gozen) was a "*jōruri hinin*"—an itinerant, outcast-status performer of old tales—but one who travelled around without a companion *biwa hiki*.[33] The second published reference of this kind are passages in Matsushita's study of historical documents on discriminatory practices in Kyushu, concerning the treatment of particular groups of *mōsō* and *goze* as low-status persons (1985, 11–12 and 252, respectively).

In my fieldwork, I was warned by Kimura and others that in the Kumamoto region most people over the age of seventy would associate biwa performance by the blind with begging and that relatives of deceased *biwa hiki*, in particular, would often be reluctant to talk of their parent's or grandparent's work. My first experience of this was when I played *satsumabiwa* on "*Keirō no Hi*" (Respect for the Elderly Day, which until 2003 was September 15) at a gathering of some two hundred octogenarians in the coastal town of Tsunagi, near Minamata in southern Kumamoto Prefecture. With the help of the mayor, I distributed eighty-five questionnaires on the local biwa players as they remembered them. As we waited for the responses to come in, the mayor of Tsunagi told me that many people had expressed embarrassment and reluctance when he distributed the sheets to them, for—as he put it—the topic of *biwa hiki* was still a distasteful one for them. He predicted—quite accurately, as it turned out—that

33. In this case *jōruri* (*jorori*) probably denotes tales in general. As I was told by Ōkawa Susumu and his wife, a former *goze* in the Izumi-chō area south of Minamata, many used to travel with their *biwa hiki* husbands or partners.

no person over the age of sixty would willingly admit that any relative or acquaintance of theirs had played biwa for a living. Only about thirty people responded in any detail, with just a single admission that anyone had "known" a *biwa hiki* as a friend. I learned a lot from these responses, however, including the fact that the usual term for biwa singers around Tsunagi had been one which singled them out as people of low status: *biwa-don*.[34] Five people called them "strange" or "rather frightening" figures.

I experienced the shame that attached to the *biwa hiki*'s profession most vividly, however, when I stood at the door of the former professional biwa player Ōkawa Susumu's house and caught a glimpse of him in the room behind his daughter-in-law, who seemed embarrassed by his appearance and refused me permission to speak with him. I later succeeded in meeting him but during one discussion experienced the expression of his own sense of shame at having been a blind beggar in his youth: He was happy to talk on topics such as the tales in his repertory, the way he had learned them, the various melody patterns and their usage, the fine singers he remembered and what had been good about their performances, and the like, but he categorically refused to answer when I asked him to describe in detail his *kadozuke* activities. Instead, he said, "Well, how about I ask you a question for once! Can you tell me why you university folk want to know about such things? It was a long time ago, but it's painful for people like me to remember it, let alone talk to you about it!" Still living, as he did, in the area where he had done much of his "begging" and having been too sick for some years to practise his second profession of acupuncture, it seems that his experiences of social discrimination as a *biwa hiki* were still very close to him.

Working Regions and Remuneration

Biwa hiki for whom data is available all had experience of working in several regions of Kyushu, regardless of where they had been apprenticed or their standing as a musician in the vicinity of their home. Whether in the company of their teachers during training, or

---

34. *Don* is a term of respect in Satsuma dialect, but historically a discriminatory term (*sabetsu yōgo*) in Higo dialect.

with friends or acquaintances among fellow biwa players, or on their own, they travelled to wherever it seemed there would be a reasonable return for their labour through money or in-kind payment. For the most part this meant doing *kadobiki* and picking up occasional ritual work along the way in villages and small towns no more than a few days' walk from home. Yet in the 1920s and 1930s Yamashika, Hashiguchi and Ōkawa all had occasion to go further afield. In the necessity for them to "do the rounds" in distant parts for weeks or even months at a time in order to earn enough to sustain their families, their situation was similar to that of many blind *bosama* players of *shamisen* in Tōhoku during the same period, who would often spend all of the summer and early autumn working in Hokkaido before returning with (or as often as not, without) funds that would see them through the winter to come (Groemer 1999, 214–216).

Areas of Work

How did *biwa hiki* decide upon areas to work in? While no clear answer can be given, most data is available for the Amakusa islands, for that is where both Yamashika and Hashiguchi were trained. In Amakusa, blind musicians existed in sufficient numbers for the Myōon Kō to be operative as a professional organ of association until the 1940s. It held an elaborate annual ceremony[35] and *taikai*, a public concert at which all members would play their best repertory (described by Yasuda on the basis of Hashiguchi's recollections; 2001, 31–34), regulated several aspects of professional activities of members of its three *kumi* (subgroups, one each for the "upper" [*kamigumi*], "middle" [*nakagumi*] and "lower" [*shimogumi*] regions of the island chain), and was able to ensure that non-member *biwa hiki* earned little income from *kadobiki*. Yet according to Hashiguchi's account the Myōon Kō did not set any

---

35. The annual ceremony, also called Myōon Kō, varied regionally, although in all cases it was a simplified imitation of the *tō-e* rite conducted each year on the sixteenth day of the second month by *tōdō-za* leaders in Kyoto. From the little evidence available—descriptions of the rite as remembered by Yamashika and Hashiguchi, and documents of the last Kō groups in Amakusa, the Nankan and Udo areas—we know that the preparation and performance of this rite took up the greater part of a gathering of group members over several days. See Ga (1972, 37–38) and Yasuda (2001, 31–33) for excerpts from Hashiguchi Keisuke's and Morita Takashi's vivid accounts of Amakusa region Kō ceremonies in the 1930s.

nawabari (boundaries) to restrict the *kadobiki* work of individual member musicians (ibid., 27).[36]

Yamashika's account confirms that membership of the *Kō* in a given area was decisive for a blind musician's ability to do *kadozuke* there; he said that because his teacher had not been a member of any of the *kumi* of the Amakusa Myōon Kō in the 1920s, he had only been able to do door-to-door work "in places where his wife had worked as a midwife" (Kimura 1994, 63).

Although trained in Amakusa and the districts near his hometown, Nankan, by musicians whose lineages were Higo-based, during his career Yamashika was often active as a biwa player inside what had been the province of Chikugo until the modern era:

> My work was concentrated in Nankan and Tamana county, but I also worked in Kurume, Miike, Saga, Yanagawa and around Yamaga, and I even went as far as Miyazaki sometimes. (ibid., 128)

As appendix 1, map 2 shows, Yamaga is near Nankan, but Kurume, Miike and Yanagawa are all located in the southern reaches of Fukuoka Prefecture, that is, the former Chikugo. The other two places Yamashika mentions, Saga and Miyazaki, were further away. While Saga City (in the southern part of Saga Prefecture) could probably have been reached on foot from Nankan in little more than a day, a journey even to the westernmost reaches of Miyazaki Prefecture required use of various modes of transportation (but mostly walking, to judge from Yamashika's accounts) over some one hundred or so kilometres.

Journeys beyond Nankan, Tamana and other nearby places were made for a variety of reasons: to make the most of harvest periods for produce in certain regions, or conversely the periods between intensive farm labour, when many people would be at home and have time to listen to performances; for festivals on a grand scale at famous shrines and temples, which would attract during both day and evening large potential audiences for itinerant performers; requests to perform on the occasion of particular ceremonial events; requests for

---

36. In one of the few accounts of the Myōon Kō beyond Amakusa, Ga (1972, 31) states that there were twenty-two members of an Omuta-region Myōon Kō that Yamashika joined but says little about the extent to which the organisation regulated working areas; while she claims that "there were boundaries" (29), she says nothing of how they were established or maintained.

the performance of a *harai* or other rite, which according to Yamashika sometimes came "by bicycle or on foot from places as far away as 7 *ri* [ca. 28 kilometres]" (Ga 1972, 29); and *o-mairi* (devotional visits) to shrines of importance for the blind, such as the Ikime Jinja in Miyazaki (see chapter 1).

Payment
Much, perhaps even most of what a *biwa hiki* earned was not in cash but in kind. Only *zashikibiwa* performance was done in the expectation of payment in currency alone. As farming was the profession of the majority of households in areas where *kadobiki* was done, remuneration was generally received in the form of produce: unhulled rice, barley, soybeans, tea, small root vegetables and even salted or dried fish. White, polished rice was generally received only for *harai*, in which case the payment was often divided into rice from the *kumotsu* offerings on the altar and cash for the entertainment offered after a *watamashi* (Ga 1972, 30).

The form of payment not only depended upon the season and locale but was also physically delimited by what could be carried by a visually impaired man walking the roads with a bag containing a musical instrument and other essential items. One might imagine it was almost impossible for anything more to be carried by such men but Yamashika has graphically described how youthful *biwa hiki* or apprentices would carry heavily loaded sacks of sweet potatoes (*karaimo*) when need be:

> Now *karaimo* are heavy, and none of the other *biwa hiki* wanted to haul them around, but [when he was young] my teacher accepted them, so he came to be called "*Karaimo biwa.*". . . People who'd been working the fields would ask him, "So can you play a little for us?" and he'd play something so they'd give him about a *kan* [3.75 kg] more of *karaimo*. Then he'd go on to another place and the take would add up to about three or four *kan*. On a good day he could receive between 250 and 300 *kin* [150–200kg]. When he sold those *karaimo*, the money didn't add up to much, but my teacher used to tell me it was a lot better than walking around all day for nothing. (Kimura 1994, 59–60)

Harvest periods, when particular produce would be most plentiful, were crucial for earning income through *kadobiki*. Apart from the rice harvest throughout autumn, barley was received in April through

May and soybeans in June. *Biwa hiki* had terms to specify various kinds of *kadobiki*, which differed according to the type of produce sought (see "Financial Relations between the Teacher and His Apprentices" above). Each required appropriate preparation for carrying the produce:

> *Ocha-biki* is *kadobiki* at the time of the tea harvest. We'd make 60 or 70 bags from raw paper (*kizuki*) for holding the tea. We had to separate it because the tea from different places was dried to different extents—some of it was dried once, some twice, and some three times. Some people would be good enough to tell us, "Our tea isn't *aracha* [undried leaves]." So we had to put it all into separate bags, and sort it into like and un-alike after we got home. In two days we received three *tō* of tea.[37] (ibid., 62)

Hashiguchi recalled that for *kadobiki* performance in Amakusa in the 1930s, most households would give either a small, shallow bowlful (*teshio*) or a single teacupful of rice or barley (Yasuda 2001, 27). The produce received had to be either carried home or stored, then exchanged for currency. No research on the Kyushu biwa traditions has documented how this was done but in most agrarian districts there were buyers of produce who then took it to sell to distributors and at town markets. It is likely that the buyers made a considerable profit by giving *kadozuke* musicians a minimal exchange rate then selling the produce at or above the market rate.

Kadozuke geinin were widely viewed as beggars to whom one should offer alms, but of a minimal quantity. If currency was given, it was usually one *sen* per *biwa hiki* from each household (ibid., 27).[38] On the basis of fieldwork in southern Kumamoto Prefecture in the 1930s, Ella Wiswell gives an account of five *sen* having been regarded as far too much currency to give to a *kadozuke* musician who played *tategoto* (a small portable *koto*; Wiswell and Smith 1982, 260).

For *zashikibiwa* performances, listeners were expected to reward the musician in currency, which was placed in a tray passed around at the end. Hashiguchi claimed "from five to ten *sen*" was a typical amount given by each listener at a *zashikibiwa* event in the early 1930s.

37. Thirty *kin*, or just under twenty kilograms.
38. The following statement by Yamashika (Kimura 1994, 131) gives an idea of the relative purchasing value of one *sen*: "The places we stayed at were mostly *kichinyado*. If they had a good rice allowance, they'd be about 25 *sen* for a night. If you paid 40 *sen* you'd get three square meals there."

In this way, between 1.5 and 2 yen would usually be earned if a *biwa hiki* performed all the pieces on his own (Uda 1992, 31). Yamashika indicated, however, that this may have been a fairly poor rate of pay:

> After I'd done my *nabiraki*, I was soon engaged to do *zashiki* performances all over the place. My sister went to Sakashita (village) as a bride, and there were lots of patrons around there. I'd always go at New Year. I've forgotten what pieces I performed, but I always got 2 or 3 yen for the night. There was a fellow named Azono no Kyōteru, from Kawabe, who used to say he'd never play for less than 5 yen, and who once got about 8 yen. What's more, he used to have people come and transport his instrument and him, then take him home when he was finished! I was cheap compared to that. (Kimura 1994, 84–85)

As a supplementary or perhaps substitute payment—and at the same time a form of alms—at certain times of year villagers would also offer the *biwa hiki* sustenance:

> When I'd go out to work I'd only take *onigiri* [rice balls] with me as something to eat. I didn't take any water container. In spring I took no food at all, because in the villages I'd always find something to eat. Without fail, there'd be something. When I went there, I'd be given food even if I didn't want it! (ibid., 126)

*   *   *

These memories speak to one of the broader concerns of chapter 1, societal responses to the figure of the *zatō* or *biwa hōshi* through history. Only those who had trained and lived for years as *biwa hiki*—Hashiguchi, Ōkawa and most of all Yamashika—were able to talk at length about their work as performers, and even for them, the topic of *kadobiki* at times brought great discomfort. Yet the life of the road was one led by many musicians and performers in twentieth-century Japan. There is no way to tell what proportion of those people were blind or had visual impairment, but to judge from the accounts of itinerant performers in northern Japan (for whom documentation is plentiful) and those of *biwa hiki*, few blind men and women freely chose to enter such a profession. They became biwa or *shamisen* players and singer-reciters by sheer force of circumstance and used all and any resources available to them to make their living in this way until a national legal framework for a physically disabled people's welfare system (*Shintai Shōgaisha Fukushi Hō*) was established in 1949. After that *kadozuke* work was no longer essential to maintain income, and in any case it became less effective as interest and community support for all forms of performance considered part of the pre-war social order all but disappeared. It took two decades until *kadozuke geinin* began to be rehabilitated in the public eye as valuable bearers of folkways, in the late 1960s and 1970s. It was only from that time that *biwa hiki* and other rural *kadozuke* performers could be viewed through the rose-tinted lens of a nostalgia for "vanishing" traditions rather than as strange, even loathsome musicians whom the road brought to one's doorway, then mercifully carried away.

6

BLIND BIWA SINGERS FORGOTTEN, REMEMBERED AND REHABILITATED

Fragmentary memories written down by those who answered the questionnaire I distributed to people over the age of seventy in the coastal town of Tsunagi suggested the extent to which, in rural Kumamoto Prefecture in 1991, *biwa hiki* were still thought of by the oldest generation as strange and even shameful figures on the margins of local society. Their brief responses told little of the significance of the biwa singers' repertory of tales or ritual skills for the lives of community members. None of the answers mentioned *harai* or any other kind of rites, and less than ten of the respondents remembered local *biwa hiki* well enough to say anything about the sorts of *gedai* that had been performed. ("*Heike*" and "*jōruri* stories" were the terms used to characterise repertory by those who answered.) What can be inferred from this is that in southern Kumamoto Prefecture it had already been rare for *biwa hiki* to perform *harai* rites by the 1930s and that those working the area had virtually disappeared by the middle of that decade, when all the respondents had been old enough to understand the content of recited tales.

On another occasion two women, somewhat younger than those who responded to the questionnaire, were willing to tell me what they recalled of visits by *biwa hiki* when they were children: They had grown up in a coastal village north of Tsunagi during the 1930s and 1940s, and both had learned *chikuzenbiwa* in nearby Minamata from about the age of ten. Accordingly, they had been interested in the blind players of biwa who occasionally came by, even if their art was very different from that of the urbane, refined *chikuzenbiwa* style. For that reason—and perhaps because they had been children—these women seemed to lack any of the sense of loathing for the musicians that was apparent in the responses of many Tsunagi people. They spoke of some blind musicians who had lived in or near their village and others who would come on foot from elsewhere at festival times. Most would stand outside the houses plucking the biwa and singing briefly, just until a coin or some rice was given; only if one had a good voice and an engaging style of presentation would he be asked inside to sing. The women described the typical *biwa-don*'s[1] singing style as *damigoe*, a thick, low tone, which they associated particularly with men's drinking songs. They could remember listening intently but did not recall what tales or songs were sung.

Try as I might, I was unable to find any people other than these two women who were both willing to talk and familiar with biwa singing to the extent that they could describe the behaviour of musicians in "the old days." In other regions—most of all the Amakusa islands, where *biwa hiki* and *goze* sustained Myōon Kō associations until the 1940s—such musicians may have been remembered with far greater clarity. Yet during my fieldwork the September 1991 gathering on "Respect for the Elderly Day" in Tsunagi was the best opportunity I had to elicit such memories from people in rural Kumamoto. Most other attempts met with gentle rebuffs that reflected a lack of interest, embarrassment about so much having been forgotten, and perhaps an ongoing discomfort with talk about performing "beggars" and other shameful matters of times past.

Such people maintained the attitudes and prejudices of their youth. The reappraisal of the traditions and legacy of Japanese blind itinerant musicians that had begun in the 1960s, with researchers' and the media's efforts to document living performers in several regions, meant little or nothing to them. Beyond the human proclivity for habitual learned behaviour, I can only speculate that this reticence (like that of Ōkawa Susumu's family, in their reluctance to let me meet him) stemmed from a belief that, even in 1991, public knowledge that someone's parent or grandparent had been a "*jorori hinin*" (to use the term for performers of old tales documented for the Minamata region by Ishimure Michiko) could bring about harm, in unspecified ways that were never mentioned to me.

---

1. These women used the discriminatory term *biwa-don* (see footnote 34, chapter 5) probably because they acquired it from their parents.

Effects of the Social Re-positioning of *Biwa Hiki*

Under the scrutiny of scholarship and the terms of regional and national government cultural affairs policy from the early 1970s, the few surviving *biwa hiki* were socially "rehabilitated"; having been only marginally better than beggars in the eyes of common society, they suddenly were lauded as bearers of a vanishing folk performance tradition, which authoritative experts called *higobiwa*. The musicians' skills and life experiences were now considered important links with cultural history. As living repositories of historical traditions of importance for constructions of regional identity and in the history of canonical performing arts, they were required to make public demonstrations of their art form. Those still able to perform were engaged to do so again, but in conditions that had previously been unknown to them, on concert stages in public halls and auditoriums, and even urban music clubs (*raibu hausu*), before relatively large, heterogeneous audiences.

Presentation of the *biwa hiki* as respected bearers of cultural history embedded in oral narrative traditions moreover effected an important transformation of the status of the biwa singer: Before largely unknown audiences the musician no longer had to negotiate the favour of patrons whom he knew saw themselves as his social superiors, and who could leave without offering any payment. The change in audience–performer relations had consequences for performance style and strategies of the sort discussed in chapter 4. A purist's understanding of tradition would represent the new performance conditions of the 1970s to 1990s as a distortion of a pristine art form whose "natural" condition had been that of pre-war *kadobiki* and *zashikibiwa* in the Kumamoto region. It may be, however, that presentations of biwa narrative organised by scholars and bureaucrats contributed to the life of the tradition rather than its purported "death." When the cameras and tape recorders of researchers and the media were turned on Higo-region *biwa hiki*, they responded as professional performers to the needs of these new patrons and the audiences they generated, gauging the appropriate choice and length of repertory items just as they had done for other patrons in earlier times.

Fragmentary Transmission of Yamashika's Repertory

Public re-positioning of blind biwa singers yielded support from both the national and Kumamoto Prefectural governments which enabled the Higobiwa Preservation Society to fund a program from the mid-1970s for a small number of sighted, literate people to take up lessons with Yamashika Yoshiyuki. The program had mixed success; while some students persevered with occasional lessons for years, others stopped coming after just a few months. The local media presented at least one person—a woman who had already trained in *nagauta shamisen*—as a potential successor to the *higobiwa* tradition that had been designated an Intangible Cultural Asset in 1973. Yamashika even granted some of the students Tamagawa-*ha* professional names (perhaps as much as anything to encourage them to keep practising). Yet none continued to be active in performance beyond appearing at events organised infrequently (at best annually) by the Preservation Society.

On several occasions Yamashika himself told me that he felt none of the students who had attempted to learn repertory from him in the 1970s and 1980s had achieved competence, chiefly because they were unable to command the range of vocal production styles needed to carry a tale in performance. The centrality of distinction between *fushi*, based on characteristics of both melody and vocal production, as discussed in chapter 4, is something that Yamashika was unable to convey to those who attempted to learn his performance style.[2]

Yamashika's last student was a man from Osaka who had already acquired a professional name as a *chikuzenbiwa* player before beginning lessons with Yamashika in 1990. Katayama Kyokusei came from the Kansai region each month to receive tuition over a period of several years. By mid-1992 Katayama was able to perform the *hauta Ono no Komachi* well enough for Yamashika to agree to him singing it in his final Tokyo performances at the Asakusa *yose* theatre, Mokubatei (an event organised by film director Aoike Kenji, Hyōdō Hiromi and

---

2. It is also noted in chapter 4 that while Yamashika's style itself was characterised by a fluidity and ambiguity of *fushi* boundaries, the distinguishing features of a core set of *fushi* are unambiguous. In my own experience of trying to learn the first part of a *gedai* with Yamashika, the fact that he in no way simplified or clarified his performance style for teaching caused difficulty. It may be that this was an ongoing problem for all those who learned from him.

others).[3] By the time Yamashika was no longer well enough to teach, in 1994, Katayama had acquired a set of introductory pieces. Although he had learned no *danmono* from Yamashika apart from the relatively short, single-*dan* tale, *Dōjōji*, he went on to be engaged by a Kumamoto municipal organisation[4] to give monthly tuition to a small group of interested community members from 2000 to 2004. Katayama made his own text-scores (*daihon*) for the repertory he had acquired, based on transcriptions from Yamashika's recorded performances and partial demonstrations during lessons, and in turn used them to teach. The texts were presented in printed form for the first time in a source book published with funding from the Kumamoto Municipal Council to mark the end of the five-year tuition project that it had funded (Kumamoto Shimin Kaikan 2004).

In this way, since Yamashika's last performances in the early 1990s, the body of traditional oral narrative maintained by *biwa hiki* in central Kyushu has passed out of the hands of blind musicians, and the few repertory items acquired by sighted players have come to be treated as fixed-text narratives.[5] Of the many biwa players identified by scholars and the Preservation Society since the 1960s, it is only *Yamashika's* repertory and performance style that has been textualised and transmitted in this way. Katayama Kyokusei has presented himself as a performer of the "*Higo zatōbiwa*" tradition as transmitted by Yamashika Yoshiyuki,[6] and posters and fliers for his performances invariably mention Yamashika. For example, an advertisement Katayama made for a performance of June 23, 2002, near Osaka, includes the following text:

3. At the time, Yamashika considered Katayama's vocal style to be little different to that acquired during his prior *chikuzenbiwa* training (interview of May 7, 1992). It may be that the event's producers sought his participation as part of a strategy for presenting Yamashika's art as one that would not be lost after his death. Katayama also bears the performer's name Kyōkai 教海 yet acquired this not from Yamashika but informally from Kimura Rirō in 2004 (Kimura Rirō, personal communication, April 2005). The name had been given Kimura by Yamashika in recognition of the fact that he wrote and taught about biwa, but did not perform.
4. Kumamoto Shimin Kaikan Bunka Jigyō Kyōkai (Kumamoto Civic Centre Association for Cultural Enterprise).
5. Since April 2006 one member of the group that learned with Katayama, Kumabe Shūhei, has himself performed *Ono no Komachi* occasionally at traditional performing arts showcase concerts in Kumamoto Prefecture.
6. http://artist.musicinfo.co.jp/~kyokusei.

Katayama learned *Higo zatōbiwa* from the man who was called the last *biwa hōshi*, Yamashika Yoshiyuki, and himself is said to be one of very few biwa players who can transmit Yamashika's *fushi* and performance style.

The wording of the final sentence here acknowledges the fact that in the 1970s and 1980s, others also learned a few pieces from Yamashika; as none of those others are active performers or teachers, however, they are not named. The Kumamoto Shimin Kaikan's 2004 source book is also part of the effort to salvage and perpetuate some of Yamashika's repertory. Recordings of performances by a range of *biwa hiki*, some of whose vocal techniques produced clearer pitches and melodic phrases strikingly different to Yamashika's, are in the possession of the Kumamoto Municipal Museum and the Shimin Kaikan archives. They could be made available to Katayama or anyone else deemed skillful enough to learn elements of their narrative recitations. It is apparent from the evidence presented in this book that Yamashika and most other *biwa hiki* documented since the 1960s shaped their individual style by learning from and imitating a range of other musicians. For a *higobiwa* revivalist to incorporate elements of the styles of two or more past performers as documented in archive recordings would therefore be in keeping with this aspect of past practice. Yet no one has yet attempted to do so; priority has been given to the act of face-to-face transmission of a handful of short pieces, from Yamashika to Katayama, and in turn from him to others.[7]

Another "Last" *Biwa Hōshi*

Apart from a handful of presentations of his two-*dan* signature piece *Kuzu no Ha* in the mid-1990s, Hashiguchi Keisuke was not in sufficient

---

7. The partial record of the biwa traditions of central Kyushu that is constituted by extant audio and audio-visual recordings may or may not ever contribute to a revival of longer narrative items or a greater selection of the repertory. Both the proper preservation and the publicisation of that record are of fundamental importance if such a thing is to be possible at all. During its existence the Higobiwa Hozonkai did a great deal to draw public attention to the repertory and skills of Kumamoto-region blind biwa players, but its track record in archiving and protecting recordings was poor; it is possible that many important recordings held by the Hozonkai were lost through inappropriate storage methods and conditions.

health in the years after Yamashika's death to perform biwa narrative and thereby draw attention to his status as the last surviving former *biwa hiki*. From the mid-1990s it seems that efforts were begun to pass the mantle of "the last *biwa hōshi*" not to Hashiguchi but to the Miyazaki-based *mōsō* Nagata Hōjun (b. 1935). Scholars and the regional and national media have turned their attention to Nagata because he is the only blind biwa player who continues to engage in *harai* and other rites for householders. As a member priest of the Jōrakuin Hōryū and performer of *mōsōbiwa*, Nagata has never commanded a repertory of non-ritual narratives of the sort that Yamashika did, but he is skilled in *shakumon*—didactic Buddhist tales about the deeds of Shakyamuni and various characters from folklore, one of which relates the sacred origins and powers of the biwa—and performs them in certain of his ritual duties. His robust health, outgoing character, deep resonant voice, engagingly melodious recitation and lively biwa accompaniment style have ensured adequate sales of the CD and DVD recordings that scholars have made of him, and since his receipt of the prestigious Pola Foundation *Dentō Bunka Chiiki Shō* (Regional Traditional Arts Award) in October 2002, regular performances have been organised in Tokyo, Osaka and other major cities. When I attended a concert performance by Nagata in June 2006, I was struck by the way the event combined elements of ritual and entertainment: Nagata sat on a dais in splendid priests' robes with some Tendai Buddhist ritual tools set around him, began his performance using *juzu* prayer beads as a percussive source and intoning the Heart Sutra over strokes on a hand-held gong, then after a first recitation with biwa, addressed the audience in a suave but familiar manner, actively eliciting more than a few laughs. During his pieces, many of the audience sat forward in their chairs, upright with eyes closed, so that they appeared to be meditating. This is not behaviour that I ever witnessed at a Yamashika concert performance (although some of those watching Yamashika's *kamado-barai* rite in April 1989 lowered their heads in apparent reverence). What it suggests is that Nagata's unequivocal identity as a blind Buddhist priest who serves parishioners in rural parts of "distant" Miyazaki Prefecture has enabled one of the elements of the *biwa hōshi* image, sanctity, to take precedence for his growing number of supporters in cities across Japan. In 2007, to many Nagata is "the last *biwa ōshi*," but one of quite a different kind to Yamashika.[8]

8. The Nagoya-based blind *heikebiwa* (*heikyoku*) Imai Tsutomu Kengyō (b. 1958) could be said to be yet another kind of modern-day *biwa hōshi*, in the image of the

Contemporary *Biwa Hōshi* and Public Demand

Public reception of this biwa music has been utterly free of the stigma that until recently was foremost in the minds of elderly Kyushu people whenever blind *biwa hiki* were mentioned. In Katayama Kyokusei's case, the repertory he learned from Yamashika is presented in the context of formal concerts of biwa music in which both *chikuzenbiwa* and *higobiwa* items are framed as "classical" (*koten*) styles of narrative recitation on historical themes. Similarly, in the ten or so years during which Nagata Hōjun has been portrayed with increasing frequency in a range of texts and media, an emphasis upon his lifestyle as a priest serving a modern-day community has brought him closer to the settings of middle-class Japanese lives than Yamashika ever was. *Kadozuke* "begging" and the poverty and suffering of *biwa hōshi* shown in many historical depictions have both been erased, and in their place are images of Nagata heartily walking the backroads of northern Miyazaki to serve his parish of several hundred homes and farms with seasonal *harai* rites, or else relaxing at home in an average-sized, orderly house attached to a well-appointed temple.[9] It seems that the potential weight of the legacy of the *biwa hōshi* has been fully grasped by those who market Nagata and his music, so that at one and the same time they direct attention to his sanctity and his "normality"—on the one hand, his skills in ancient rites and esoteric sacred lore of the sort associated with *biwa hōshi* and on the other his fondness for a coffee-break with his wife at their favourite café in front of Nobeoka Station (see Kawano 2001, 6). In this way, the negative elements of the *biwa hōshi* image are diluted—even neutralised—and the rehabilitation of Kyushu blind biwa players continues in the early twenty-first century.

Yamashika responded to public demand throughout his professional life, from his early determination to acquire *kamigoto* skills and *naniwa-bushi* narratives, to his 1972 request to be granted special membership of the *mōsō* organisation, the Gensei Hōryū—and, indeed,

---

Edo-period high-ranking *tōdō-za kengyō*, who played and taught *koto*, *shamisen*, and *kokyū* as the bases for their income and performed *heikebiwa* mostly in ceremonial contexts. Yet it is not this kind of blind professional biwa player that has passed into the popular imagination; it is the image of the medieval-period *biwa hōshi*, the itinerant ritualist-entertainer, that has persisted.

9. See, for example, photographs in Kawano (2001) and in Kawano, Kojima, Komoda and Nakayama (2005).

his subsequent decision to let his membership lapse because it had failed to yield any noticeable increase in his income. His willingness to be filmed, photographed and recorded by so many professionals and amateurs who came to his home and to perform in concert-style events quite unlike those he had been used to were also part of his efforts to continue to make a living. Carried into the public eye by the wave of nostalgic interest in traditional lifeways of rural Japan that arose in the 1970s, Yamashika reacted to the circumstances of a new kind of marketplace in which there was demand for "living relics" of the medieval *biwa hōshi*. Seasoned by the search for non-institutional, individuated forms of spiritual experience that Japanese urbanites engage in no less than the inhabitants of Euro-American metropolises in the early twenty-first century, this demand now yields Nagata Hōjun concert audiences in Tokyo, Osaka and other cities.

The roles that Yamashika and other blind biwa players have played in their actual and imagined (local, regional and national) communities since the 1960s have been largely determined by the particular aspects of their complex identities that have been deployed in presentation of their professional skills and in representations for public consumption. The contemporary market for musicians reminiscent of *biwa hōshi* both perpetuates and is sustained by this process of selective representation. The figure of the *biwa hōshi* has enduring cultural meaning in modern Japan. Woven from multiple strands of national, regional and personal history, that meaning is embedded in the many portrayals of Kyushu blind biwa players that I have addressed.

*   *   *

Yamashika's performance style may not have fully conformed with that of his Tamagawa-*ha* teacher in Amakusa, and some of the means by which he acquired professional competence and built up repertory after curtailing his apprenticeship may have been unorthodox even in the broader context of practice among *biwa hiki* in central Kyushu. What sets him apart from Nagata Hōjun and any other blind performers of biwa who may yet put themselves before the public,[10] however, is the scope of

---

10. Given that in late 2007 Nagata has no successor to the position of a priest who plays biwa in serving his parish in Nobeoka, it seems unlikely that another "last *biwa hōshi*" will appear from those quarters.

his repertory of songs and tales and his skill in oral composition—a skill he acquired by doggedly pursuing ways to survive as a *biwa hiki* at a time when new media and alternative forms of entertainment were eroding the audience for biwa singing even in rural Kyushu. Regardless of how many "*biwa hōshi*" ultimately emerge in twenty-first century Japan, Yamashika was without doubt the last performer to command such professional skills and knowledge—and the great bulk of Yamashika's narrative repertory was neither recorded nor transmitted to the few who learned some songs and short tales from him as fixed texts. It is in this sense that Hyōdō Hiromi, in a text penned years after his other writings on Yamashika (and just as this book was being finished), rhetorically refers to him as "certainly the last *biwa hōshi*."[11]

With reference to the imminent loss of his vast repertory of tales, at the age of ninety-one Yamashika himself exclaimed to the *New York Times* journalist David Sanger, "If they are gone, they are gone..." (Sanger 1992). In so doing he defiantly and performatively declared his own consciousness of being the last *biwa hiki*—the last biwa singer.

---

11. Hyōdō's introductory note to Kimura and de Ferranti 2007, a booklet with the three-CD set of recordings "Rites and Tales with Biwa: Yamashika Yoshiyuki, Blind Musician of Kyushu" (Nihon Dentō Geinō Shinkō Zaidan 2007).

ACKNOWLEDGEMENTS

Acknowledgements are a tale in themselves—of the roads one has walked to reach the point of closure on the day when the final sentence of a manuscript seems right. (And as often as not beyond that, to the point at which one's publisher will allow no further changes!) Tales about the teller can easily go on too long, but in this case the journey itself has been remarkably long, so my thanks to those who have helped me along the way should not be foreshortened.

First of all, the kindness and patience shown me by Yamashika Yoshiyuki during the years when I visited and stayed with him, and during 1991 and 1992 by the former *biwa hiki* Ōkawa Susumu and Hashiguchi Keisuke, enabled me to learn much of what is documented in this book. My introduction and ongoing relations with Yamashika were made possible by Kimura Rirō, and he and his family continued to help during my period of extensive fieldwork. Even as I was dissecting Kimura's 1994 book on Yamashika in exasperating detail, he was generous in explaining the text and its process of construction, helping me obtain several important images and eventually agreeing to my proposal that we locate and document archive recordings of performances by Yamashika for a CD compilation.

In Kyushu I also benefitted greatly from the advice of Yasuda Muneo, the historian of *mōsō* Nagai Akiko, and the assistance and camaraderie of Yasuda's former student Uda Yasushi, during visits in the 1990s. My extensive period of fieldwork in and around Kumamoto Prefecture would not even have begun without the generosity of Iyama Tadayuki and Yoshiko, who took me into their home to recover from illness at the very beginning of the research trip. Iyama's house and studio atop a hill near Tsunagi then became the launching site for my visits to Ōkawa's home in nearby Izumi as well as for jaunts in search of traces of *biwa hiki* in places as distant as the Nichinan Coast and the eastern reaches of Kagoshima Prefecture. On one of those trips I was joined by the photographer Shibata Yōsuke, whose experience in putting elderly subjects at ease helped us talk at length with some former biwa players.

I had important, illuminating conversations with Hyōdō Hiromi during my fieldwork in 1991 to 1992 and after, and I owe him particular thanks for access to his many recordings of performances by Yamashika and other *biwa hiki*. His text transcriptions and analyses were the starting point for my earlier work on the practice of Ōkawa Susumu, and the analysis of *Dōjōji* presented in chapter 4 of this book is a slightly revised presentation of his initial rendering of the tale in a 1991 piece. Japan's leading scholar of the history of biwa music, Komoda Haruko, was also generous in sharing her knowledge of a range of matters that I doggedly pursued with her in person, on the telephone and by email. My colleague in narrative music studies and Japanese music research, Alison Tokita, terrorised me by requesting that I give the opening presentation in Japanese at a Nichibunken seminar that yielded much of the material for the seminal anthology she later co-edited with Komoda (Tokita and Komoda 2002). Over the years since then Alison has often prompted me to clarify important issues in my work on the Kyushu biwa traditions, and that fruitful collegial dynamic continues in our current collaboration on a research project about music and modernity in inter-war Osaka.

Allan Marett exercised both his remarkable intellect and his generosity of spirit to help me shape the initial fieldwork materials into my 1997 Sydney University doctoral thesis. (Much of the thesis content has been revised and presented elsewhere, but some of it informs sections of this book.) I am sure Allan's insightful comments on issues of mutual concern will continue to stimulate my thinking for years to come.

After the 1991 to 1992 fieldwork in Kyushu, I became a postgraduate exchange student at the University of California, Berkeley, where Bonnie Wade kindly read and criticised drafts for my early publications on the music of blind biwa singers. While written over a decade later, some parts of this text build on ideas that first emerged in those discussions at Berkeley. San Francisco was also where the composer and pianist Ketty Nez lent her superior pair of ears to double-check my transcriptions of *biwa hiki* performances (including one of the opening section of a performance of *Dōjōji*, included as appendix 2 in this book) and shared her tremendous facility with notation software. I will never forget the premiere in Berkeley of her 1992 work dedicated to Yamashika Yoshiyuki, "Contrasts—Wind Over Distant Seas" (for voice, *shō* and *shamisen*).

The following colleagues and friends all have generously lent their skills and expertise at various times when I approached them for help with verification of particular points, references, Chinese readings and even proofreading: Andrew Alter, Fujita Takanori, Gerald Groemer, Sylvain Guignard, Joseph Lam, Susan Matisoff, Yang Mu, Steven Nelson, Robert Sharf, Jason Stoessel, Hitomi Tonomura, Sato Van Aacken, Yamaguti Osamu and Cuncun Wu.

After Karen Brazell and the Cornell East Asia Series accepted my manuscript, the final preparation of the text, images and appendices was made possible by the consummate skills and selfless generosity of Rowena Smith and Lindsay Rowlands, in Armidale, and by the encouragement and professionalism of CEAS Managing Editor, Mai Shaikhanuar-Cota, half a world away in Ithaca.

There are numerous other individuals whose friendship and collegiality have helped me over the years that I've worked on this project. While I can't name them here, I look forward to offering each of them thanks in person.

At various times the research that led to this book has received support from the following bodies, university divisions and support schemes: The Japan Foundation; The Fulbright-Hayes Commission; The National Museum of Ethnology (Minpaku, Osaka); The Andrew W. Mellon Foundation; The Department of Music, Sydney University; The Center for Japanese Studies, University of Michigan (Ann Arbor); the University Research Grants scheme and other research funds deployed by Professor Peter Flood at the University of New England; and the School of Arts and Discipline of Music at the University of New England.

Academic careers are generally pursued at the expense of homelife. Perhaps that has always been so, but in the current era of a corporate academia that is everywhere driven by compulsion to monitor the dollar-yield of each day's labour, the interests of partners and family are too often marginalised in the struggle to make time for research. Shizuko Yamagishi is the one who has sacrificed most on account of this book, and deserves my thanks beyond all others.

Armidale, May 2009

APPENDICES

APPENDIX 1

Map 1. Kyushu, showing prefectures and their approximate correlation with pre-Meiji provinces.

Map 2. Principal places in central Kyushu that are mentioned in the text.

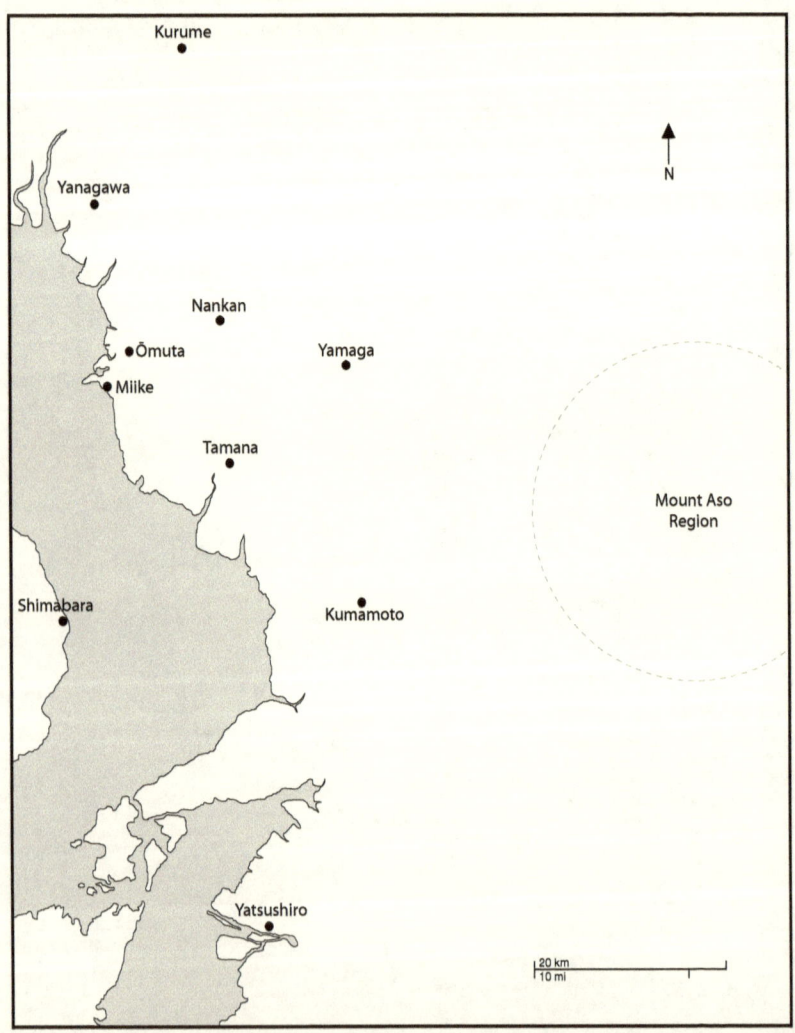

APPENDIX 2

First *shōdan* of *Dōjōji* (Yamashika Yoshiyuki; performance of October 14, 1989).

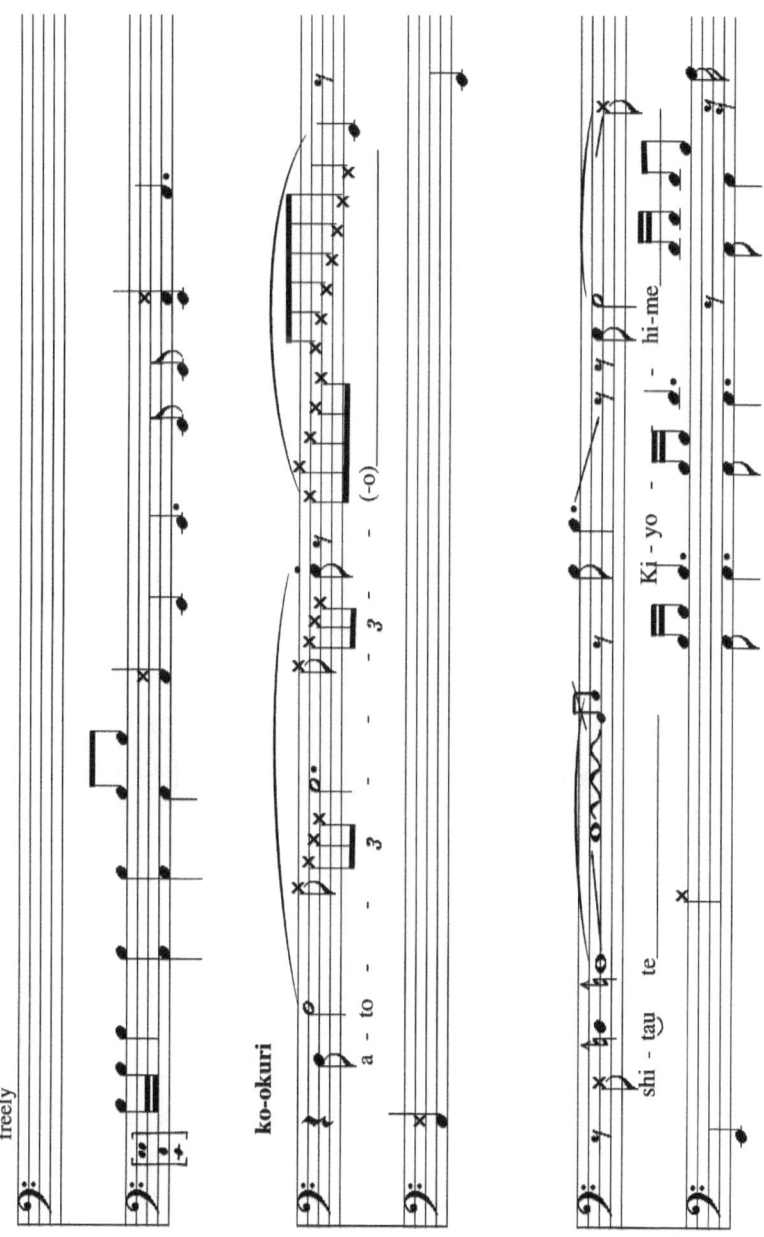

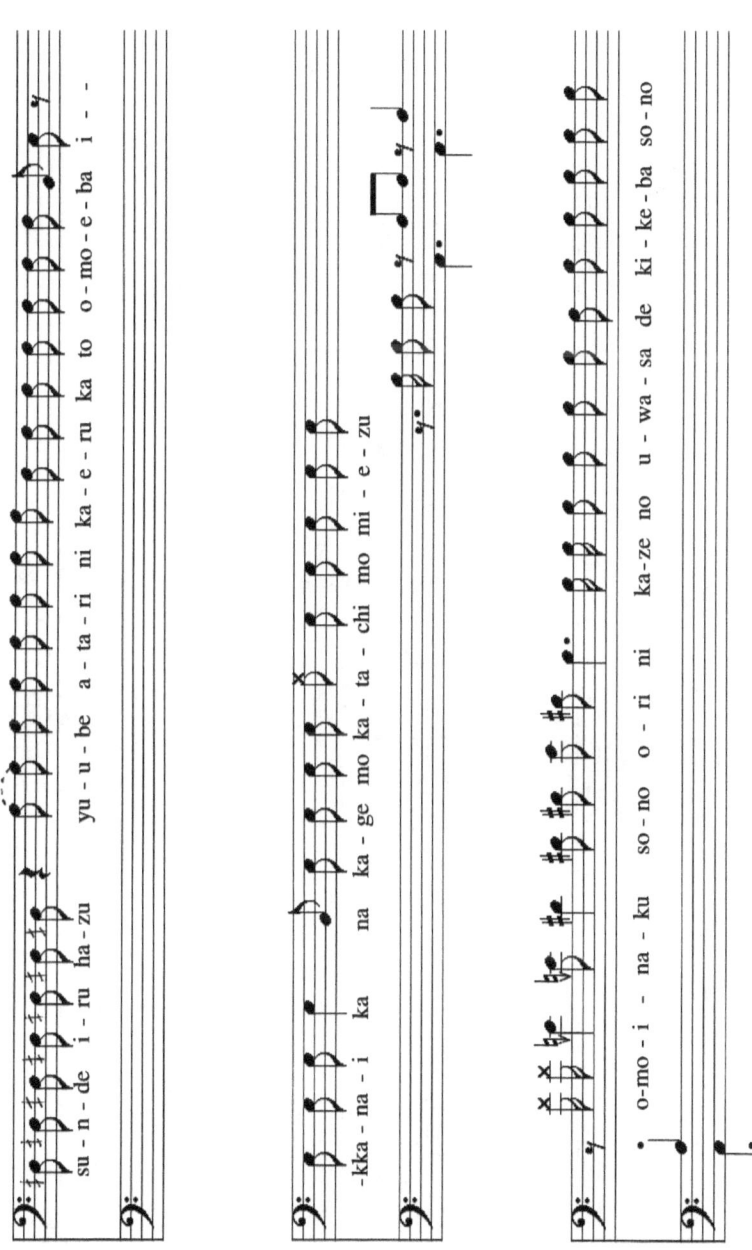

BIBLIOGRAPHY

Araki Hiroyuki and Nishioka Yōko, eds. 1997. *Jijin mōsō shiryōshū denshō bungaku shiryō shūsei* 19. Tokyo: Miyai Shoten.

Araki Hiroyuki and Fukuda Akira, eds. 2000. *Fugeki mōsō no denshō sekai, dai isshū*. Tokyo: Miyai Shoten.

Arnold, David, and Stuart Blackburn, eds. 2004. *Telling Lives: Biography, Autobiography and Life History*. Bloomington: Indiana University Press.

Atsumi Kaoru et al., eds. 1984. *Tōdōza heikebiwa shiryō: okumura-ke zō*. Kyoto: Daigakudō Shoten.

Babiracki, Carol. 2008. "Between life history and performance: Sundari Devi and the art of allusion." *Ethnomusicology* 52 (1): 1–30.

Bakan, Michael. 1999. *Music of Death and New Creation: Experiences in the World of Balinese Gamelan Beleganjur*. Chicago: University of Chicago Press.

Bakshi, Dwijendra Nath. 1979. *Hindu Divinities in the Japanese Buddhist Pantheon: A Comparative Study*. New Delhi: Benten Publication.

Bethe, Monica, and Karen Brazell. 1978. *Nō as Performance: An Analysis of the Kuse Scene of Yamamba*. Ithaca, NY: China–Japan Program, Cornell University.

Bialock, David. 2000. "Nation and epic: *The Tale of the Heike* as modern classic." In *Inventing the Classics*, ed. Haruo Shirane and Tomi Suzuki, 151–178. Stanford: Stanford University Press.

Biwa Shinbun. 1912. "*Kojiki biwa no shinnyū*." no. 33, 1/1/1912.

Butler, Kenneth. 1966a. "The textual evolution of the *Heike Monogatari*." *The Harvard Journal of Asiatic Studies* 26: 5–51.

Clifford, James, and George Marcus, eds. 1986. *Writing Culture: The Poetics and Politics of Ethnography*. Berkeley: University of California Press.

Danielson, Virginia. 1997. *The Voice of Egypt: Umm Kulthum, Arabic Song and Egyptian Society in the Twentieth Century*. Chicago: University of Chicago Press.

de Ferranti, Hugh. 1989. *Seiha Satsumabiwa no kifuhō to sono kinō*. Master's thesis in Musicology, Tokyo National University of Fine Arts.

———. 1991. "Composition and improvisation in Satsuma biwa." *Musica Asiatica* 6: 102–127.

———. 1992a. "*Ikite iru katari gei*." *Mainichi Shinbun*, Kyushu edition. April 16.

———. 1992b. "Last of traditional bards keeps art alive." *The Japan Times*, June 21.

———. 1994. "Speaking of Yamashika: 'The last *biwa hōshi*' and his many voices." *Repercussions* 3 (1): 47–76.

———. 1995. "Relations between music and text in Higobiwa." *Asian Music* 26 (1); theme issue on music in oral narrative, ed. Scott Marcus and Dwight Reynolds: 149–174.

———. 1996a. "Licensed to laugh: Humour in the *zatōbiwa* narrative tradition of Kyushu." *Musicology Australia* 19: 1–15.

———. 1996b. "Thinking of Yamashika, the 'last *biwa hōshi*.'" *The Japan Times*, June 23.

———. 1997. *Text and Music in Biwa Narrative: The Zatōbiwa Tradition of Kyushu*. Doctoral thesis. Department of Music, University of Sydney.

———. 2000. *Japanese Musical Instruments*. Oxford University Press.

———. 2002. "*Senzaiteki ni tekusuto ni motozuite iru ōraru konpojishon*" (Residual textuality in oral compositional practice). In *Nihon no katarimono: kōtōsei, kōzō, igi* (Japanese narrative performance traditions: orality, structures, meanings), ed. Alison Tokita and Komoda Haruko, 63–86. Kyoto: International Research Center for Japanese Studies.

———. 2003. "Transmission and textuality in narrative traditions of Japanese blind musicians." *Yearbook for Traditional Music* (Journal of the International Council for Traditional Music) vol. 35: 131–152.

———. 2006. "The Kyushu biwa traditions." In *The Ashgate Research Companion to Japanese Music*, ed. Alison McQueen Tokita and David W. Hughes, 105–126. Aldershot: Ashgate Publishing Ltd.

Dunn, C.J. 1966. *The Early Japanese Puppet Drama*. London: Luzac and Company, Ltd.

Embree, John. 1939. *Suye Mura*. Chicago: University of Chicago Press.

Fritsch, Ingrid. 1991. "The sociological significance of historically unreliable documents in the case of Japanese musical guilds." In *Tradition and its Future in Music: Report of SIMS 1990 Osaka*, ed. Tokumaru Yosihiko et al., 147–152. Tokyo: Mita Press.

———. 1996 *Japans Blinde Sänger: im Schutz der Gottheit Myôon-Benzaiten*. Munchen: Iudicium Verlag GmbH.

Fugeki Mōsō Gakkai Kaihō. 1991. "*Mōsō o kiku*." *Fugeki mōsō gakkai kaihō*, no. 4: 3–5.

Fujii Sadakazu. 2004. *Monogatari riron kōgi*. Tokyo: Tōkyō Daigaku Shuppankai.

Fujii Sadakazu et al. 1983. *Jijin mōsō no katarimono denshō (sekkyō-saimon) ni kansuru yobiteki kenkyū*. Unpublished grant report. Report reference number 81-3-108. The Toyota Foundation.

Fujita Takanori. 1986. "*Kuchishōga*: The vocal rendition of instrumental expression in the oral and literate tradition of Japanese music, with emphasis on the *nohkan*." In *The Oral and the Literate in Music*, ed. Tokumaru Yosihiko and Yamaguti Osamu, 239–251. Tokyo: Academia Music.

Fukuda Akira. 1981. "*Setsuwa to katarimono*." *Kokubungaku kaishaku to kanshō* 8: 107–115.

Fukuda Akira and Yamashita Kin'ichi, eds. 2003. *Fugen-mōsō no denshō sekai, dai 2 shū*. Tokyo: Miyai Shoten.

Fukuoka-ken Kyōiku Iin Kai 1983. *Chikuzen no kōjin biwa*. Two volumes, appendix volume entitled "*Kuzure*" *Shisho*. Fukuoka: Fukuoka-ken Kyōiku Iin Kai.

Fukushima Kunio. 1987. "*Geinō to kami: mōjin geinōsha to dōshigami*." *Kokubungaku kaishaku to kansho* 9 (5): 71.

Ga Machiko. 1972. "*Higobiwa saihōroku*." *Denshō bungaku kenkyū* 13: 26–43.

Gamō Mitsuko. 1989. "*Chūsei seigaku no ongaku kōzō*." In *Nihon no ongaku, ajia no ongaku*, 5 *(Ongaku no kôzô)*, 106–128. Tokyo: Iwanami Shoten.

Gerstle, Andrew. 1999. "*Takemoto Gidayū* and the Individualistic Spirit of Osaka Theatre." In *Osaka: the Merchants' Capital of Early Modern Japan*, ed. James McClain and Wakita Osamu, 104–124. Ithaca, NY: Cornell University Press.

Bibliography

Golay, Jacqueline. 1973. "Pathos and farce: Zatō plays of the Kyōgen repertoire." *Monumenta Nipponica* 28 (2): 139–149.

Gorai Jū. 1972. "*Mōsō biwa*." Commentary and text transcriptions in *Nihon shomin seikatsu shiryō shūsei*, vol. 17: 109–253. Tokyo: Sanyosha.

Groemer, Gerald. 1999. *The Spirit of Tsugaru: Blind Musicians, Tsugaru-jamisen, and the Folk Music of Northern Japan.* Warren, MI: Harmonie Park Press.

———. 2001a. "The guild of the blind in Tokugawa Japan." *Monumenta Nipponica* 56 (3): 349–380.

———. 2001b. "The creation of the Edo outcaste order." *Journal of Japanese Studies* 27 (2): 263–293.

———. 2007. *Goze to goze-uta no kenkyū.* Nagoya: Nagoya Daigaku Shuppankai.

———. 2008. "Visual disability, religious practices, and the performing arts during the Edo period in northern Japan." *Chiikigaku* 6: 1–32.

Guignard, Silvain. 1986. "Structure and performance of a melodic pattern, *haru nagashi*, in chikuzen-biwa." In *The Oral and the Literate in Music*, ed. Y. Tokumaru and O. Yamaguti, 273–287. Tokyo: Academia Music.

Gu lu. 1999. *Qing Jia Lu.* Nanjing: Jiangsu Gujuchubanshe.

Hane, Mikiso. 1982. *Peasants, Rebels, and Outcastes: The Underside of Modern Japan.* New York: Pantheon.

Haraguchi Nagayuki. 1973. "*Higobiwa no rekishi*." *Nihon dangi* 275: 7–24.

Harich-Schneider, Eta. 1959. "The last remnants of a mendicant musicians' guild: The goze in northern Honshu (Japan)." *Journal of the International Folk Music Council* 11: 56–59.

Harootunian, Harry. 2000. *History's Disquiet: Modernity, Cultural Practice and the Question of Everyday Life.* New York: Columbia University Press.

Higobiwa Hozonkai. 1991. *Higobiwa.* Kumamoto: Higobiwa Hozonkai.

Hirai Yoshinobu. 1966. "*Mōsō to biwa no fukaikō joron*." *Wayō kokubun kenkyū* 4 (10): 36–43.

Hirakawa Kiyoshi. 1991a (originally 1978). "*Higobiwa chōsa no keika (I)*." In *Higobiwa*, Higobiwa Hozonkai, 1991: 21–28. Kumamoto: Higobiwa Hozonkai. Reprinted from *Higobiwa tayori* no. 12.

———. 1991b (originally 1979). "*Higobiwa chōsa no keika (II)*." In *Higobiwa*, Higobiwa Hozonkai, 1991: 29–38. Kumamoto: Higobiwa Hozonkai. Reprinted from *Higobiwa tayori* no. 13.

Hirano Kenji. 1975. "*Mōsōbiwa no katarimono*." In booklet with *Biwa—sono ongaku no keifu*. Nippon Columbia CLS-5205~10, Hirano Kenji and Tanabe Hisao (compilers), 35–37.

———. 1989. "*Mōsōbiwa*." In *Nihon ongaku daijiten*, 441. Tokyo: Heibonsha.

———. 1990. "*Katarimono ni okeru gengo to ongaku*." *Nihon bungaku* 39 (6): 33–43. Reprinted in *Heikebiwa—katari to ongaku*, ed. Kamisangō Yūko, 195–212. 1993. Tokyo: Hitsuji Shobō.

Hirano Kenji and Tanabe Hisao (compilers). 1975. Booklet with *Biwa—sono ongaku no keifu*. Nippon Columbia CLS-5205~10.

Hirose Kōjiro. 1997. *Shōgaisha no shūkyō minzokugaku*. Tokyo: Akaishi Shoten.

Honda Yasuji. 1962. *Nihon koyōshū*. Tokyo: Miraisha.

Hosokawa Han Seishi Kenkyūkai. 1985. *Kumamoto Han chōsei shiryō ichi—sōgetsu gyōji kiroku nukigaki ichi*. Kumamoto: Hosokawa Han Seishi Kenkyūkai.

Hyōdō Hiromi. 1985a. *Katarimono josetsu*. Tokyo: Yūseidō.

———. 1985b. "Shinkō ni okeru jisha: kyōka no ideorogii." In *Taikei bukkyō to nihonjin 1: kami to hotoke*, 97–132. Tokyo: Shunshūsha.

——— 1991. "Zatōbiwa no katarimono denshō nitsuite no kenkyū (I)." *Saitama daigaku kiyō* 26: 13–60.

———. 1993. "Zatō(mōsō)biwa no katarimono denshō nitsuite no kenkyū (II)." *Saitama daigaku kiyō* 28: 35–76.

———. 1999. "Zatō(mōsō)biwa no katarimono denshō nitsuite no kenkyū (III): moji tekusuto no seiritsu to katari no henshitsu." *Seijō kokubungaku ronshū* 26: 101–207.

———. 2000. *Heike monogatari no rekishi to geinō*. Tokyo: Yoshikawa Hiroshi Bunkan.

———. 2001. "Katarimono ni okeru moji tekusuto (daihon) no kinō." In *Nihon no katarimono: kōtōsei, kōzō, igi* (Japanese narrative performance traditions: orality, structures, meanings), ed. Alison Tokita and Komoda Haruko, 87–102. Kyoto: International Research Center for Japanese Studies.

Hyōdō Hiromi, ed. 1997. *Iwanami kōza Nihon bungakushi*, vol. 16: "Kōshō bungaku." Tokyo: Iwanami Shoten.

Iba Takashi. 1928. *Nihon ongaku gairon*. Tokyo: Kōseikaku Shoten.

———. 1934. *Nihon ongaku-shi*. Tokyo: Gakugeisha.

Inobe Kiyoshi. 1969. "Katarimono ongaku ni okeru katari to bansō." In *Nihon, tōyō ongaku ronkō*, ed. Tōyō Ongaku Gakkai. Tokyo: Ongaku no Tomosha.

Inobe Kiyoshi et al. 1984–1985. *Gidayū-bushi ni okeru Yōshika Tenkai no kenkyū*. Tokyo: Academia Music.

Iseki Keiichi. 1982. *Heikyoku monogatari*. Tokyo: Bunwa Shobō.

Ishii Masami. 1986. "Tenpō monogatari-ron." In *Monogatari kenkyū: tokushū katari soshite inyō*, 145–169. Tokyo: Shinjidai Sha.

———. 1988. "Mōsō no hayamonogatari." *Gakugei kokugo kokubungaku* 22: 18–29.

———. 1996. "Biwa hōshi no zushōgaku." In *Heike monogatari kenkyū to hihyō*, ed. Yamashita Hiroaki, 145–161. Tokyo: Yūseidō.

———. 1997a. "Biwa hōshi no enshō (Biwa hōshi no zushōgaku [2])." In *E to katari kara monogatari o yomu*, 118–136. Tokyo: Daishūkan Shoten.

———. 1997b. "Biwa hōshi to inu." In *E to katari kara monogatari o yomu*, 88–117. Tokyo: Daishūkan Shoten.

Ishimure Michiko. 1980. *Seinanyaku densetsu*. Tokyo: Asahi Shinbunsha.

Ivy, Marilyn. 1995. *Discourses of the Vanishing*. Chicago: University of Chicago Press.

Iwahashi Koyata. 1922a. "Biwa hōshi—sono 1." *Fūzoku kenkyū*, no. 7: 14–17.

———. 1922b. "Biwa hōshi—sono 2." *Fūzoku kenkyū*, no. 8: 3–6.

———. 1923. "Biwa hōshi—sono 3." *Fūzoku kenkyū*, no. 9: 13–16.

———. 1926. "*Mumyō hosshō kassenjō*." In *Keiki shaji kō*, 157–176. Tokyo: Yūzankaku.

———. 1951. *Nihon geinōshi: Chūsei kabu no kenkyū*. Tokyo: Gei En Sha.

———. 1975. *Geinōshi sōsetsu*. Tokyo: Yoshikawa Hirobumikan.

Iwasa Miyoko, ed. 1989 *Bunkidan*. Tokyo: Kasama Shoin.

Jackson, Michael. 1998. *Minima Ethnographica: Intersubjectivity and the Anthropological Project*. Chicago: University of Chicago Press.

Kamijima Toshiaki. 1991. "*Rō biwa sōsha to maboroshi no Mimi Nashi Hōichi*." *Noise*, no. 8 (Winter 1990–1991): 100–101.

Kamisangō Yūkō, ed. 1993. *Heikebiwa—katari to ongaku*. Tokyo: Hitsuji Shobō.

Kanetsune Kiyotsuke. 1913. *Nihon no ongaku*. Tokyo: Rokugō Kan.

Kanō Masanao, Tsurumi Shunsuke and Nakayama Shigeru, eds. 1997. *Minkangaku jiten*. Tokyo: Sanseido.

Katō Yasuaki. 1974. *Nihon mōjin shakaishi kenkyū*. Tokyo: Miraisha.

Kawano Kusumi. 2001. *Biwa mōsō Nagata Hōjun: gendai ni hibiku yongen no fu*. Tokyo: Nihon Hōsō Shuppan Kyōkai.

———. 2005. *Saigo no goze, kobayashi haru, hikari o motometa 105-sai*. Tokyo: Nihon Hōsō Shuppan Kyōkai.

Kawano Kusumi, Kojima Tomoko, Komoda Haruko and Nakayama Ichirō, eds. 2005. *Hyūga no biwa mōsō Nagata Hōjun*. Biwa Mōsō Nagata Hōjun o Kiroku Suru Kai.

Keister, Jay. 2004. *Shaped by Japanese Music: Kikuoka Hiroaki and Nagauta Shamisen in Tokyo*. New York: Routledge.

Kelly, Kevin. 1982. *Asia Grace*. Published by the author.

Kikkawa Eishi. 1965 and 1986 (2nd ed.). *Nihon ongaku no rekishi*. Tokyo: Sōgensha.

Kikkawa Eishi, ed. 1984. *Hōgaku hyakka jiten*. Tokyo: Ongaku no Tomosha.

Kimura Rirō. 1981. "'*Higo' o hazushita biwa no kenkyū o*." In *Higobiwa*, Higobiwa Hozonkai, 1991: 61–62. Kumamoto: Higobiwa Hozonkai.

———. 1994. *Higo biwa hiki Yamashika Yoshiyuki yobanashi*. Tokyo: San'ichi Shobō.

———. 1997. "*Zatōbiwa no katari*." In *Iwanami kōza Nihon bungakushi*, vol. 16: "*Kōshō bungaku*," ed. Hyōdō Hiromi, 67–87. Tokyo: Iwanami Shoten.

Kimura Rirō and Hugh de Ferranti. 2007. Explanatory notes in booklet with Nihon Dentō Geinō Shinkō Zaidan 2007 (see Audiography).

Kimura Yūshō. 1963a. "*Higobiwa-don*." *Kyūshū bungaku*. Shōwa 38, June edition.

———. 1963b. "*Higobiwa o hozon shiyō*." *Kumamoto nichinichi shinbun*, Thursday August 1 (evening edition): p. 2.

Kindaichi Haruhiko. 1973. "*Heikyoku no dai-senritsukei no shurui*." In *Nihon ongaku to sono shūhen*, ed. Koizumi Fumio, Hoshi Akira and Yamaguti Osamu, 99–142. Tokyo: Ongaku no Tomosha.

Kishibe Shigeo. 1936. "*Biwa no engen—koto ni shōsōin gogenbiwa nitsuite*." *Kōkōgaku zasshi* 26 (no. 10 and no. 12).

———. 1944. "*Ōbei-jin no biwa saihou kigen setsu to sono hihan*." In *Tō-a ongaku-shi kō*, 247–278. Tokyo: Ryūginsha.

Kisliuk, Michelle. 1998. *Seize the Dance!: BaAka Musical Life and the Ethnography of Performance*. New York: Oxford University Press.

Koizumi yakumo jiten. 2000. Tokyo: Kōbunsha.

Kokudo Kōtsūshō. 1926. *Kyūhan chizu*, Yamaga. Tokyo: Kokudo Kōtsūshō.

Kokuritsu Gekijō (National Theatre of Japan). 1970. *Kōjinbiwa*. Kokuritsu Gekijō dai 3 kai chūsei geinō kōen (concert program).

———. 1990. *Nihon ongaku sōsho*, vol. 5: *Kayō*. Kokuritsu Gekijō.

———. 2004. *Hōgaku kanshō kai—biwa no kai, shakuhachi no kai*. Kokuritsugekijō Dai 128-kai Hōgaku Kōen.

Komoda, Haruko. 1993. "*Heikyoku no ongaku kōzō*." In *Heikebiwa—katari to ongaku*, ed. Kamisangō Yūkō, 161–193. Tokyo: Hitsuji Shobō.

———. 1999. "*Hi-mōjin shakai ni okeru heikyoku no kyōju to gakufu no kyōgō*." In *Iwanami kōza niohon no ongaku, ajia no ongaku*, vol. 4 (*Denshō to kiroku*): 99–124.

———. "*Gagaku-biwa kara mōusōu-biwa e—gakki no keifu*." (*From the gagaku-biwa to the mōusōu-biwa—an instrumental genealogy*). Paper presented at the Fugeki Mōusōu Gakkai annual conference on the 11th of May, 2002.

———. 2003a. *Heike no ongaku—tōdō no dentō*. Tokyo: Daiichi Shobō.

———. 2003b. "*Nihon no biwa, gakki no shurui to hensen*." In *Nihon no gakki, atarashii gakkigaku e mukete*, ed. Tōkyō Bunkazai Kenkyūjo, 61–70. 2003. Tokyo: Tōkyō Bunkazai Kenkyūjo.

———. 2004. "*Oto de tadoru biwa no keifu—kakite kara merodi e*." In *Hōgaku kanshō kai—biwa no kai, shakuhachi no kai*, Kokuritsu Gekijō, 2–4. Kokuritsugekijō Dai 128-kai Hōgaku Kōen.

Kumamoto Han. 1966. *Hanpōshu*. Tokyo: Sōbunsha

Kumamoto Shimin Kaikan. 2004. *Higobiwa o kataru*. Kumamoto Shimin Kaikan Bunka Jigyō Kyōkai Higobiwa Saisei Jigyō Kentō I-inkai.

Lancashire, Terence. 2002. "*Kagura*—A 'Shinto' dance? Or perhaps not." *Asian Music* 33 (1): 25–58.

Law, Jane Marie. 1997. *Puppets of Nostalgia*. Princeton, NJ: Princeton University Press.

Lord, Albert. 1991. *Epic Singers and Oral Tradition*. Ithaca, NY: Cornell University Press.

———. 2000 (1960). *The Singer of Tales*. Cambridge, MA: Harvard University Press.

Ludvik, Catherine. 2001. *From Sarasvati to Benzaiten*. Doctoral thesis, Centre for the Study of Religion, University of Toronto.

Malm, William. 1959. *Japanese Music and Musical Instruments*. Tokyo and Rutland, VT: Charles E. Tuttle.

Marcus, George. 1999. *Ethnography Through Thick and Thin*. Princeton, NJ: Princeton University Press.

Matisoff, Susan. 1978. *The Legend of Semimaru, Blind Musician of Japan*. Columbia University Press. Updated edition with new preface 2006, Boston: Cheng & Tsui Company. Citations are to the Columbia University Press edition.

Matsuoka Minoru. 1987. "*Horobiyuku mōsōbiwa*." *Fugeki mōsō gakkai kaihō*, no. 3: 1–2.

Bibliography

Matsushita Shirō. 1985. *Kyūshū hisabetsu buraku shi kenkyū.* Tokyo: Akaishi Shoten.

McCullough, Helen (trans.) 1988. *The Tale of the Heike.* Stanford: Stanford University Press.

Miyagawa Mitsuyoshi. 1983. *Higobiwa meoto sanka.* Ōmuta, Fukuoka Prefecture: private publication.

Miyake Hitoshi. 2001. *Shugendō: Essays on the Structure of Japanese Folk Religion.* Ann Arbor: Center for Japanese Studies, University of Michigan.

Motegi Kiyoko. 1988. *Bunraku: koe to oto no hibiki.* Tokyo: Ongaku no Tomosha.

Murata Hiroshi. 1974. "*Jijin shinkō to mōsō.*" *Matsuri,* no. 26 (special issue on *mōsō* and *goze*): 5–14.

———. 1994. *Mōsō to minkan shinkō.* Tokyo: Dai Ichi Shobō.

Murayama Dōsen. 1978. "*Biwa: wasurerareta oto no sekai.*" *Aruku miru kiku,* no. 135: 4–35.

———. 1986. "*Higobiwa denshō-shi*" ("A record of the *higobiwa* tradition") In *Bukkyō minzokugaku taikei 2: Hijiri to minshū.* Tokyo: Meicho Shuppan.

Nagai Akiko. 1997. "*Mōsōbiwa no katari.*" In *Iwanami kōza Nihon bungakushi,* vol. 16: "*Kōshō bungaku,*" ed. Hyōdō Hiromi, 88–109. Tokyo: Iwanami Shoten.

———. 2002. *Nikkan mōsō no shakai-shi.* Fukuoka: Ashi Shobō.

Nakamura Nakazō. 1944. *Sandaime Nakamura Nakazō jiden "Temae Miso."* Tokyo: Hokkō Shobō.

Nakano Hatayoshi, ed. 1993. *Mōsō.* Rekishi Minzokugaku Ronshū 2. Tokyo: Meicho Shuppan.

Nakayama Tarō. 1934. *Nihon mōjin shi.* Tokyo: Shōwa Shobō.

———. 1936. *Zoku Nihon mōjin shi.* Tokyo: Shōwa Shobō.

Narita Mamoru. 1985a. *Mōsō no denshō.* Tokyo: Miyai Shoten.

———. 1985b. *Oku-jōruri no kenkyū.* Tokyo: Ōfūsha.

Nelson, Steven. 2001. Unpublished paper on *Heike* and *kōshiki* (delivered at 2001 Association for Asian Studies annual conference in Chicago).

Nihon koten bungaku daijiten. 1998. Tokyo: Meiji Shoin.

Nihon minzoku daijiten. 1999–2000. Tokyo: Yoshikawa Kōbunkan.

Nihon minzokugaku jiten. 1981 (reprint, first published 1941). Tokyo: Meicho Fukyū Kai.

Nihon ongaku daijiten. 1989. Tokyo: Heibonsha.

Nijō 1973. *The Confessions of Lady Nijō [Towazugatari],* trans. Karen Brazell. Stanford: Stanford University Press.

Nishi Nihon Bunka Kyōkai, ed. 1993. *Fukuoka kenshi: bunka shiryō hen: mōsō, zatō.* Fukuoka: Fukuoka-ken.

Nishi Nihon Shinbunsha. 1991. "*Kiroku eiga roke hajimaru.*" Kyushu edition, November 30.

Noda Tarō. 1935. "*Higobiwa no hanashi.*" *Inaka,* no. 11 (March 15): 24–32.

Nomura Machiko. 2007. *Higobiwa katari-shū.* Tokyo: Miyai Shoten.

Orikuchi Shinobu. 1924. "*Kokubungaku no hassei (dai ikkō)—jugen to jojishi to*." In *Nikkō* 1/1. Reprinted in *Orikuchi Shinobu zenshū*, vol. 1, ed. Orikuchi Hakushi Kinen Kai, 1954, 63–75. Tokyo: Chūō Kōronsha.

———. 1926. "*Kokubungaku no hassei (dai yonkō)—shōdōteki hōmen o chūshin to shite*." *Nihon bungaku kōza* 3, 4 and 12. Reprinted in *Orikuchi Shinobu zenshū*, vol. 1, ed. Orikuchi Hakushi Kinen Kai, 1954, 124–216. Tokyo: Chūō Kōronsha.

———. 1954. "*Iki minkan denshō saihōki*." In *Orikuchi Shinobu zenshū*, vol. 15, ed. Orikuchi Hakushi Kinen Kai, 413–478. Tokyo: Chūō Kōronsha.

———. 1995. *Orikuchi Shinobu zenshū*. Tokyo: Chūō Kōronsha.

Ozawa Shōichi. 1982 (first published 1974). *Nihon no hōrōgei*. Tokyo: Kadokawa Shoten.

Plutschow, Herbert. 1990. *Chaos and Cosmos: Ritual in Early and Medieval Japanese Literature*. Leiden: E.J. Brill.

Raz, Jacob. 1983. *Audience and Actors: A Study of their Interaction in the Japanese Traditional Theatre*. Leiden: E.J. Brill.

Reed-Danahay, Deborah. 1997. *Auto/Ethnography: Rewriting the Self and the Social*. Oxford and New York: Berg.

Robertson, Jennifer. 1991. *Native and Newcomer*. Berkeley: University of California Press.

Ruch, Barbara. 1977. "Medieval jongleurs and the making of a national literature." In *Japan in the Muromachi Age*, ed. Toyoda Takeshi and John W. Hall, 279–309. Berkeley: University of California Press.

Ruiz-de-Medina, Juan. 2001. "*Kirishitan fukyō ni okeru biwa hōshi no yakuwari ni tsuite*." *Tōkyō daigaku shiryō hensanjo kenkyū kiyo* 11: 172–187.

Sakata Ken'ichi. 1992. *Chikugo rōkyoku shi gaisetsu*. Published by the author.

Sanger, David. 1992. "Such stories to tell, but he's 91 and in no hurry." Article in *New York Times* and *International Herald Tribune* (Paris edition), November 16: A7. Available through New York Times on-line archive, www.nytimes.com.

Satō Mitsuaki. 1982. " '*Higobiwa no hajimari' ni tsuite*." In *Higobiwa*, Higobiwa Hozonkai, 1991: 63–65. Kumamoto: Higobiwa Hozonkai. Reprinted from *Higobiwa dayori* no. 19.

Satō Teruo. 1973. *Rōran no uta to Heike monogatari*. Tokyo: Chūō Kōronsha.

Shimazu Tadashi. 2000. *Edo izen no satsumabiwa uta*. Tokyo: Perikan Sha.

———. 1997. *Meiji izen no satsumabiwa shi*. Tokyo: Perikan Sha.

Shintō daijiten 1977 (reprint, first published 1937). Kyoto: Rinsen Shoten.

Stock, Jonathan. 2001. "Toward an ethnomusicology of the individual, or biographical writing in ethnomusicology." *The World of Music* 43 (1): 5–19.

Strong, John S. 1983. *The Legend of King Asoka: A Study and Translation of the Asokavadana*. Princeton, NJ: Princeton University Press.

Suzuki Shōei. 1996. *Goze: shinkō to geinō*. Tokyo: Takashi Shōin.

———. 2005. "*Goze no shūkyō-sei to miko*." *Fugeki mōsō gakkai kaihō*, no. 17: 1–5.

Takahashi Chikuzan. 1983 (first published 1975). *Jiden: tsugaru-jamisen hitoritabi*. Tokyo: Shinshokan.

Takami Hirotaka. 2006. *Kōjin shinkō to jijin mōsō—Yanagida Kunio wo koete*. Tokyo: Iwata Shōin.

Takamure Itsue. 1971 (first published 1956). "*Higobiwa*." In *Takamure Itsue zenshū*, vol. 9. Tokyo: Risōsha.

Takeda Shūrō. 1925. *Nihon nangoku monogatari*. Tokyo: Shunyōdō.

Tamagawa Kyôsei. 1990. "*Higobiwa nōto*." *Rekishi Tamana*, no. 3: 61–67.

Tamamuro Fumio. 1997. "On the suppression of Buddhism." In *New Directions in the Study of Meiji Japan*, ed. Helen Hardacre and Adam Kern, 499–505. Leiden: E.J. Brill.

Tamana-shi Kyōiku Iinkai. 1974. *Tamana-shi no bunkazai; sōshū-hen*. Tamana: Tamashi-shi Kyōiku Iinkai.

Tanabe Hisao. 1941. "*Tōyō ongaku-shi*." In *Tōyō-shi Kōza*, vol. 14. Tokyo: Yūzankaku.

———. 1947a. *Nihon ongaku no arikata*. Kyoto: Kyōto In Shokan.

———. 1947b. *Nihon no ongaku*. Tokyo: Chūbunkan Shoten.

———. 1963a. Unpublished report on *Higobiwa* submitted to the Bunka-chō, the Education Ministry's Cultural Affairs Division.

———. 1963b i-v. "*Higobiwa*." Series of five articles in *Hōgaku no tomo*, nos. 99–103 (August–December issues).

———. 1963c. *Nihon ongakushi*. Tokyo: Tōkyō Denki Daigaku Shuppanbu.

———. 1964. *Nihon no gakki*. Tokyo: Sōshisha Shuppan.

Tateyama Zennōshin. 1911. *Heike ongaku-shi*. Tokyo: KimuraYasushige.

Terauchi Naoko. 1996. *Gagaku no rizumu kōzō*. Tokyo: Dai Ichi Shobō.

Tokita, Alison. 1997. "*Katarimono no ongaku bunseki*," *Iwanami Koza: Nihon bungakushi*, vol. 16, ed. J. Kubota et al., 299–321. Tokyo: Iwanami Shoten. Second edition 2001.

———. 1999. *Kiyomoto-bushi: Narrative Music of the Kabuki Theatre*. Basel and London: Barenreiter.

———. 2000. "The nature of patterning in Japanese narrative music: Formulaic musical material in *heikyoku*, *gidayu-bushi* and *kiyomoto-bushi*." *Musicology Australia* 23: 99–122.

———. 2003. "The reception of the *Heike Monogatari* as performed narrative: The Atsumori episode in *heikyoku*, *zatō biwa* and *satsuma biwa*." *Japanese Studies* 23 (1): 59–85.

Tokita, Alison, and Komoda Haruko, eds. 2002. *Nihon no katarimono: kōtōsei, kōzō, igi* (Japanese narrative performance traditions: orality, structures, meanings), co-edited by Komoda Haruko and Alison Tokita. Kyoto: International Research Center for Japanese Studies.

Tōkyō Bunkazai Kenkyūjo, ed. 2003. *Nihon no gakki, atarashii gakkigaku e mukete*. Tokyo: Tōkyō Bunkazai Kenkyūjo.

Tsao Penyeh. 2002. "Narrative song: Southern Traditions—Suzhou Tanci." In *The Garland Encyclopedia of World Music*, vol. 7, *East Asia: China, Japan and Korea*, ed. Robert Provine, Yosihiko Tokumaru and J. Lawrence Witzleben, 261–265. New York: Routledge.

Uda Yasushi. 1991. "*Kinsei irai ni okeru higobiwa no hensen*." In *Higobiwa*, Higobiwa Hozonkai, 75–88. Kumamoto: Higobiwa Hozonkai.

———. 1992. "*Hoshizawa tsukiwaka no katari-gei: Amakusa ni okeru biwa-shi no kiseki*." *Kita Kyūshū daigaku kokugo kokubungaku kai*, no. 6: 23–34.

Wakita Haruko. 1978. "*Sanjoron*." In *Buraku-shi no kenkyū, zenkindai hen*, 51–88. Kyoto: Buraku Mondai Kenkyūjo.

Walton, Susan Pratt. 1996. *Heavenly Nymphs and Earthly Delights: Javanese Female Singers, their Music and their Lives*. PhD dissertation, University of Michigan.

Wiswell, Ella Lury, and Robert J. Smith. 1982. *The Women of Suye Mura*. Chicago: University of Chicago Press.

Wu Ben. 1992. "*Pipa yinyue jiqi shehui Beijing*." *Zhongguo yin yue xue* 2: 57–67.

Yamamoto Izumi. 1992. "*Saigo no biwa hōshi, Yamashika Yoshiyuki*." *Hōgaku Journal*, no. 71: 14–21.

Yamamoto Kichizō. 1976a. "*Kuchigatari no ron: gozeuta no baai (jō)*." *Bungaku* 44 (10): 1365–1386.

———. 1976b. "*Kuchigatari no ron: gozeuta no baai (chū)*." *Bungaku* 44 (11): 1470–1478.

———. 1977. "*Kuchigatari no ron: gozeuta no baai (ge)*." *Bungaku* 45 (1): 89–107.

———. 1988. *Kutsuwa no ne ga sazameite—katari no bungeikō*. Tokyo: Heibonsha.

Yamashita Hiroaki. 1993. *Heike monogatari no seiritsu*. Nagoya: Nagoya Daigaku Shuppan-kai.

———. 1994. *Katari to shite no Heike monogatari*. Tokyo: Iwanami Shoten.

———. 1995. "*Biwa hōshi no Heike monogatari*." *Kokubungaku* 40 (5): 14–22.

Yamazaki Tomoko. 1972. *Sandakan hachiban shokan: teihen josei-shi josho*. Tokyo: Chikuma Shobō.

———. 1999. *Sandakan Brothel No. 8: An Episode in the History of Lower-Class Japanese Women*, trans. Karen Colligan-Taylor. Armonk, New York and London: M.E. Sharpe.

Yanagita Kunio. 1946. *Monogatari to katarimono*. Tokyo: Kadokawa Shoten.

———. 1947. *Kōshō bungei-shi kō*. Tokyo: Chūō Kōronsha.

———. 1998. *Yanagita Kunio zenshū*. Tokyo: Chikuma Shobō.

Yasuda Muneo. 1981. "*Higobiwa hozon nitsuite*." In *Higobiwa*, Higobiwa Hozonkai, 1991: 60. Kumamoto: Higobiwa Hozonkai.

———. 1991. "*Higobiwa no denshō*." *Minzoku geinō kenkyū*, no. 14: 1–14.

———. 1993. "*Futatabi Higobiwa nitsuite*." *Nihon minzokugaku*, no. 195: 28–56.

———. 1994. "*Higobiwa no keifu*." *Kumamoto daigaku bungakubu ronsō*, no. 44: 3–16.

———. 2001. *Higo no biwa-shi*. Tokyo: Miyai Shoten.

———. 2004a. "*Higobiwa ni tsuite*." In *Higobiwa o kataru*, 1–8. Kumamoto Shimin Kaikan. Kumamoto Shimin Kaikan Bunka Jigyō Kyōkai Higobiwa Saisei Jigyō Kentō I-inkai.

———. 2004b. "*Kindai Kumamoto no biwakai: Meiji-Taishō-ki Kumamoto no biwa kankei shinbun shiryō kaidai ni kaete*." In *Higobiwa o kataru*, 476–452. Kumamoto Shimin

Kaikan. Kumamoto Shimin Kaikan Bunka Jigyō Kyōkai Higobiwa Saisei Jigyō Kentō I-inkai.

Yokomichi Mariō and Omote Akira. 1986. *Nōgeki no kenkyū*. Tokyo: Iwanami Shoten.

———. 1960. *Yōkyoku shū* (Parts I and II). *Nihon koten bungaku taikei*, vols. 40–41. Tokyo: Iwanami Shoten.

Yonemura Kōji. 1973. "Higobiwa gaikan." *Nihon dangi*, no. 275: 1–6.

———. 1976. *Kumamoto geinōkai monogatari*. Tokyo: Nihon Dangisha.

Yūki Ryōgo. 2005. *Lorenso Ryōsai*. Nagasaki: Nagasaki Bunken Sha.

AUDIOGRAPHY and VIDEOGRAPHY

Audio recordings

de Ferranti, Hugh (depositor). Recorded perfomances by and discussions with Yamashika, deposited with the PARADISEC digital archive (paradisec.org.au, persistent identifier HDF1-YY).

Hirano Kenji and Tanabe Hisao (compilers). 1975. *Biwa—sono ongaku no keifu*. Nippon Columbia CLS-5205~10.

Japan Gramophone. 1963. *Nihon biwagaku taikei*. Polydor Japan SLJM -1031/37.

Kawano Kusumi. 1997. *Ima o ikiru biwa mōsō no sekai*. (NK-1997).

Kawano Kusumi and Takagi Kesako. 1997. *Hotoke no sato no biwa mōsō* (KK3ST).

Misumi Haruo (compiler). 1977. *Kunisaki no biwa hōshi*. CBS-Sony 22AG-201.

Nihon Dentō Geinō Shinkō Zaidan (Japan Traditional Cultures Foundation). 2007. *Higo no biwa-hiki Yamashika Yoshiyuki no sekai—katari to kamigoto*. (English title: *Rites and Tales with Biwa—Yamashika Yoshiyuki, Blind Musician of Kyushu*) Three CD set. Victor Entertainment VZCG 8377~9.

Nippon Columbia. 1975. *Biwa—sono ongaku no keifu*. CLS-5205~10. Hirano Kenji and Tanabe Hisao (compilers).

Nomura Machiko. 2007. CD included in Nomura 2007 (see Bibliography).

Audio-visual recordings, films and television programs

Aoike Kenji (dir.) 1992. *Biwa hōshi Yamashika Yoshiyuki*. Tokyo: Ofisu KS.

Hyōdō Hiromi. 2009. Fieldwork video recording on DVD with *Biwa hōshi* (Tokyo: Iwanami Shinsho 2009)

Kawano Kusumi, Kojima Tomoko, Komoda Haruko and Nakayama Ichirō, eds. 2005. Three DVDs with *Hyūga no biwa mōsō Nagata Hōjun* (see Bibliography).

Nippon Hōsō Kyōkai. 1971. *Shin Nihon Kikō*. Tokyo: NHK.

NHK Fukuoka. 1994. *Saigo no biwa hōshi Yamashika Yoshiyuki*.

——. 1993. *Wandaarando Kyūshū: ninjō biwa-hōshi ikiru*.

Suwa Atsushi (dir.) 1983. *Satsuma Mōsōbiwa*.

RKK Kumamoto Hōsō. 1975. *Kōsei higobiwa*. RKK (Anguru Kumamoto series, no. 5).

——. 1986. *Tsuchi ni utau: biwa-shi no Yamashika Yoshiyuki* (Kumamoto Mokuyō Supesharu series.

INDEX

Numbers in *italics* refer to items contained in examples, figures, maps and tables.

Amakusa islands, 8
Ama-no-Uzume, 92
Amaterasu, 6, 92
Amayo, 27n15
Aoike Kenji, 151–153
apprenticeship, 14, 240–252
   living conditions and training experiences, 246–250
   teacher-apprentice financial relations, 250–252
   terms of contract, 241–244
   training, 244–246
Araki Hiroyuki, 51, 81, 83
Asia Grace website, 154
Asokavadana (The Legend of King Asoka), 22
azusa yumi (catalpa bow), 24–25, 24n11

Bashō Matsuo, 10n8
Benzaiten, 28, 29–31, *31*, 32, 39
Biancaitian. *See* Benzaiten
Bitō Itchō, 101
biwa
   in modern day Japan, 13–14
   music traditions, 9–13
   myth of origin, 91–93
   origins, 9
   sanctity of, 33–36, 34n22
   Tale of the Heike, association with, 14
biwa-don, 270, 270n34
biwageki, 184–185
biwa hiki, 2n1, 73
   areas of work, 6, 271–273
   competition, 233
   discrimination against, 264, 265–270, 266–267n29
   payment, forms of, 273–275
   rehabilitation of image, 279, 284–285
   settings and audiences of, 178–179
   tales, repertories of, 109–113
   See also *biwa hōshi*; *higobiwa*; *higobiwa* traditions
biwa hiki narrative performance, 179–187
   biwageki, 184–185
   concerts, 16, 77n12, 185–187
   kadozuke/kadobiki, 179–181
   zashikibiwa, 179–184
biwa hiki narrative performance, formal elements in, 187–202
   framing tales, 187–190
   instrumental elements, 191–192
   pitch and mode, 198–202
   vocal elements, 192–198
biwa hōshi, 263
   ambiguity of identity, 23–24
   ancient and medieval periods, 52–55
   decline of, 177–178
   established origin accounts, 48–51
   goryō chinkon ritual performance, 33
   Heike monogatari and, 55–56
   heikyoku and, 57, 58–59, 64
   images and depictions of, 6, 44–47, *47*
   Jijin rites and, 51–52
   katarimono and, 110–111
   lore surrounding, 33–34
   marketing value of, 19–20
   "Miraculous Sound" goddess and, 32
   in modern day Japan, 13
   rehabilitation of image, 279, 284–285
   shamanistic ability, 25
   zatō and, 10, 58, 59
   See also *biwa hiki*
biwa hōshi traditions, 20–42
   blindness, 20–28
   gender, 36–40
   identity, 27, 89–91
   musical narrative, 40–42
   sanctity, 28–36
Biwa hōshi Yamashika Yoshiyuki (film), 2, 151–153
biwa mōsō, 73–74
biwa uta (songs), 121
the blind, 236
   means of sustenance for, 237–238
blind biwa players. See *biwa hiki*; *biwa hōshi*
blind musicians, social status of, 42–44
blindness, 20–28
   as karmic punishment, 23
   shamanic status accorded to, 24–26
The Boatman (Chikanobu), *207*

bosama (blind *shamisen* players), 45n37, 271
Botan Chōja. See *Miyako Gassen Chikushi Kudari*
Buddhism, suppression of, 127, 127n81
Bukkyō-biwa (didactic tales), 118
Bunkidan (treatise on biwa traditions), 32n20
bunraku (musical theatre), 64
burakumin (low status outcasts), 172, 268
bushimono (warrior tales), 118

charimono (comic narratives), 114–115, 118, 120, 184
chari (performance technique), 115, 184
Chikamatsu Monzaemon, 45
Chikanobu Toyohara, *207*
"*Chikuzen-biwa, higozatoh-biwa*" website, 154
chikuzenbiwa tradition, 12, 13, 72, 101, 109, 197, 197n15, 249n12
chikuzen biwa (musical instrument), 12, 79, 102
concert performances, 16, 77n12, 185–187

daigo (short sung text), 188–189
Dairyū (*higobiwa* master), 95
damigoe (vocal quality), 278
danmono (lengthy narrative), 84, 116, 120, 177
See also *gedai*
dan (section of *danmono* tale), 116, 203
di guo tian (Dhrtarastra figures), 29
discrimination
  kadozuke and, 263, 265–270, 266–267n29
Dōjōji tale, 123
  transcription of Yamashika's performance of and Hyōdō's structural analysis of, 206–224, 225

eishō (non-syllabic song), 197
Embree, John, 236
engi narratives, 54, 57
eta (outcasts), 268n31
Etsuzan (*higobiwa* master), 95
exorcism rituals, 33
See also *harai* rituals

Ezaki Shotarō, 14, 173, 242, 242n7, 243, 246, 257, 259, 259n20

folk religion, 127
Fujii Masako, 38
Fujii Sadakazu, 81, 148
Fujii Setsudō, 38
Fujiwara no Akihira, 52
Fujiwara Sadatoshi, 33–34
Fukijima Junkai, 87, 178
Furejō-hikae (Higo document collection), 65
fushi (performance patterns), 121, 192, 193–196
  types of, 195–196, *196*

gagaku biwa (musical instrument), 10, 41, 49, 65
gagaku (ritual music), 41
gaku biwa. See *gagaku biwa*
Ga Machiko, 73, 81, 135, 138, 139, 145–146, 174, 260n21, 272n36
Gamō Mitsuko, 204, 204n20
Ganjin (Tōshōdaiji temple founder), 60
Gankutsu Sonja, 27
gedai (lengthy narrative), 116
  classification of, 118–119, 118n72
  See also *danmono*
Gensei Hōryū (*mōsō* organisation), 12
gidayū-bushi (narrative practice), 101
gikyō (folk sutras), 131
ginshō (syllabic vocalisation), 197
gohei (ritual wands), 133–134, 133n91
Gosukōin, 37
gottan (musical instrument), 38
goze (blind female singers), 38, 39, 59n52, 263
Groemer, Gerald, 39n32, 59n53, 116n63, 119n75, 172n68
Guardian King of the East Dhritarashtra, 29
gundan (recitation of military tales), 101
gunki monogatari (war tales), 10
Gyōbukyō no Tsubone, 37n28

ha (schools of performance), 254–255
hachinin-gei (eight-person performance), 115–116, 180
Hamaguchi Kamesaku, 245–246
harai rituals, 132–136, *134*, *135*, *136*
Harootunian, Harry, 112

Index

Hashiguchi Keisuke, 2–3, 148, 178, 282–283
  apprenticeship of, 245, 246
  gedai, classification of, 118, 119
  inter-*ha* relations, 255n18
  remuneration for *biwa hiki*, 274
hauta (songs), 113–114, 113n60
Hearn, Lafcadio, 13, 45–46
heike biwa (musical instrument), 65
heikebiwa tradition, 20–21n2, 28
Heike mabushi (authoritative text-score), 59
Heike monogatari (Tale of the Heike), 1, 10, 13, 14, 55–56, 58–59
heikemono (Gempei Wars' tales), 118
heikyoku, 57, 58–59, 64
  Kyushi narrative style and, 120–121
higobiwa (biwa narrative style), 70, 72, 74–75, 111, 279
  See also *biwa hiki*
Higobiwa dayori (newsletter), 79
Higo biwa hiki Yamashika Yoshiyuki yobanashi (Kimura Rirō), 163–164, 166–174
  constructedness and subjectivity, 170–171
  content, 171–174
  structure, 167–170
Higobiwa Hozonkai (Higobiwa Preservation Society), 7, 79, 186, 280, 282n7
Higobiwa meoto sanka (Miyagawa), 150–151
higo biwa (musical instrument), 78–79
higobiwa traditions, 93–106
  blind players, 93–94
  modern era, 99–104
  origins account, standard, 95–96
  pre-Meiji period, 95–99
  Shōwa era, 104–106
  See also Kyushu biwa traditions, repertories of
Higo no biwa-shi (Yasuda), 83, 147–148
hinin (outcasts), 266, 268n31
Hirai Yoshinobu, 32
Hirakawa Atsushi, 96, 106
Hirano Kenji, 49, 82–83
Hirata Kyokushū, 76, 145
Hirose Kōjiro, 61n56
hōshi (itinerant performers), 23–24, 23n10

Hori Kyōjun, 89–90, 89n25, *90*, 93
Hosokawa Mitsunao, 95, 99
Hyōdō Hiromi, 4, 80, 81, 105, 165
  on repertories of Kyushu biwa traditions, 114n60, 120
  shōdan and, 204–205
  Yamashika, account of, 147, 245, 286
  Yamashika's *Dōjōji* performance, structural analysis of, 206–224, *225*
  Yamashika's *Dōjōji* performances, comparison of, 226, *226–228*, 228–229
  on Yamashika's *fushi* types, 195, 195n13, 196
  zatōbiwa and, 72–73, 84–85, 112
Hyūga region, 91, 92

Ichi no Tani (tale), 189
Ikime Jinja, 26
Imai Tsutomu Kengyō, 59, 283–284n8
Ine (Yamashika's first wife), 16n13
International Herald Tribune, 153
Ishimure Michiko, 269
itako mediums, 32, 263
Iwafune Kengyō, 95, 98–99
Iwahashi Koyata, 37n27, 48, 50–51, 52

jiden (autobiography), 167
Jijinbiwa (narrative practice), 71–72
Jijin Darani-kyō sutra, 36
Jijin (deity), 129–130
Jijin mōsō kongen (Jōrakuin Hōryū document), 35
Jijin rites
  biwa hōshi identity, marker of, 51–52
Jikonjin. *See* Jijin
Jimmu (Emperor), 92
Jiten (deity), 129
Jōrakuin Hōryū (*mōsō* organisation), 12, 21n4
jōruri (narrative music genre), 58, 64
  See also *ko-jōruri*

kadozuke/*kadobiki* (performance for alms), 38, 185, 231, 263–265
  discrimination and, 263, 265–270, 266–267n29
  folk rituals and, 43–44, 108, 264
  repertories for, 179–181, 264
Kagekiyo, spirit of, 26
Kakuichi text (1371), 56, 56n45

kamado-barai (ritual), 82
  See also *Kōjin-barai*
kamado-gami. See Kōjin
kami. See Jijin; Kōjin; Suijin
kamigoto (ritual work), 126, 138-140, 174, 250-251, 258, 261, 284
Kanmon Gyoki (Gosukōin), 37
kassenmono (battle tales), 118
katari (melodic recitation pattern), 180, 191
katarimonobiwa (performed narrative biwa), 71
katarimono (performed narrative genre), 41-42, 110-111, 120
  See also vocal delivery technique
Katayama Kyokusei, 7n4, 106, 154, 280-281, 281-282, 281n3, 284
Katō masafusa nikki (Minagi village diary), 64, 94
Katō Yasuaki, 61n55, 128
Kawano Kusumi, 34, 87-88
Kelly, Kevin, 154, 154n10, 159
Kenrō Jishin/Jijin, 129
kerenmono (comic narrative), 114, 118
kikigaki (oral history), 166
kikioboe (learning by listening to others' performances), 246
Kikkawa Eishi, 76
Kikuchi Kuzure/Kikuchi Gassen, 117, 119, 123
Kimura Rirō, 139, 164-165
  biwa hiki, adoption of term, 73
  higobiwa and, 79-80
  Yamashika, relationship with, 157-158, 158n14, 160
  on Yamashika's acquisition of skills and repertory, 246n11, 261
  on Yamashika's interlocutors, 88, 143, 150, 154, 155
  See also *Higo biwa hiki Yamashika Yoshiyuki yobanashi*
Kimura Yoshio, 158
Kimura Yūshō, 76, 79n16, 106, 145, 202
  on *watamashi*, 137n93, 139
  Yamashika, relationship with, 157, 158
Kindaichi Haruhiko, 193
kingen (short sung text), 188-189
kiribushi (performance pattern), *196*
Kiyohime, *207*
Kobayashi Haru, 59n52

Kobayashi Masaki, 46
Kōgetsu, 254
Kōjin-barai (ritual), 132, 133-136, *134, 135, 136*
Kōjinbiwa (narrative practice), 71-72
Kōjin (syncretic deity), 128, 130-131
kōjō (prologue), 183
kōtō (rank within *tōdō* and clergy), 56
Kojiki (712), 25
Kojima Tomiko, 88
ko-jōruri (musical narrative), 42, 77n14
  See also *jōruri*
kokkeimono (comic narrative), 114, 118
kokyū (musical instrument), 58
Komoda Haruko, 11, 51-52, 65, 87n23, 88, 204
Konjaku monogatari-shū, 23
ko-okuri (performance pattern), 200
Kosaka Naminoichi, 95
kotoba (syllabic pitched recitation), 187, *196*, 200n18
kotoba-bushi (melodic recitation pattern), 180, *196*, 200
koto (zither), 25, 38
kuchibiwa syllables, 248-249n12
Kumabe Shūhei, 281n5
Kumamoto City, 9, *293*
Kumamoto Shimin Kaikan, 282
Kunala, 22, 23, 27
kuzushi (song form), 117n67
kuzure (battle tales), 49, 72, 116-117
kuzurebiwa (biwa narrative style), 72, 117n68
"*kuzure katari*", 117
Kwaidan (film), 46
kyokubiki (comic narrative), 115-116
kyokusetsu, 193
  See also *fushi* (performance patterns)
Kyūshū no zatōbiwa, 72
Kyushu, 6-7, *292, 293*
Kyushu biwa traditions, repertories of, 108-140
  charimono, 114-115
  gedai, danmono and *kuzure*, 116-120
  kyokubiki, 115-116
  narrative articulation, 121-123
    (See also *biwa hiki* narrative performance)
  narrative language and style, 120-121
  songs *(hauta)*, 113-114, 113n60

Index 317

tales, 109–113
textual formulaity of, 123–125
See also rites

Law, Jane Marie, 268n32
Lord, Albert, 112, 148
Lorenzo *(biwa hōshi)*, 57–58

Mahâvairocana Sūtra, 30–31n19
makura (pillow text), 188–189
Manyōshū (poetry anthology), 25
marebito, theory of, 44
marume biwa (musical instrument), 79n17
Matisoff, Susan, 45, 49–50, 54n43
Matsushita Shirō, 269
metrical articulation, 122
Mimi Nashi Hōichi (folk tale), 13, 45–46, 148
Minamoto no Shunrai, 93
Misao (Yamashika's fourth wife), 38, 150, 169
Miyagawa Kikujun. *See* Ōkawa Susumu
Miyagawa Kyōgaku the First, 103–104, 104n46, 118n72
Miyagawa Mitsuyoshi, 150
Miyako Gassen Chikushi Kudari (tale), 91, 119
Miyama Chiku Mō Yūgei Kumiai (blind performers' organisation), 106, 106n51
mōjin (the blind), 236
means of sustenance for, 237, 238
mōsō, 6, 11, 13, 41, 97
biwa, cosmological associations for, 34
biwa hōshi, distinction from, 60–63
origin account, 35–36, 48
ritual performances, 11, 27, 50, 51, 109, 128, 129, 129n83, 233
secular repertories, 109n55, 117
tōdō za, dispute with, 63–66
women, exclusion of, 36–37
mōsōbiwa (biwa narrative style)
academic usages of term, 11–12
instrumental elements, 192
mōsōbiwa (biwa narrative style), Kyushu varieties, 70–88
early studies, 75–76
higobiwa and, 70, 74–75

Kimura's writings, 79–80
populist accounts and depictions, 85–88
post-Tanabe scholarship, 80–85
Tanabe's work, 76–79
terms used to identify, 71–74
mōsō biwa (musical instrument), 48–49, 65
mōsō tradition, 21, 28, 49–50
Morita Takashi, 98, 104n46, 182n3
Mori Yoichi, 173–174, 253–254, 260
Murata Hiroshi, 35n24, 83, 130
Murayama Dōsen, 34, 38–39, 81, 146, 195, 238, 239
Myōon Benzaiten (deity), 32
Myōon Bosatsu (bodhisattva), 30, 39
Myōon Jōrakuin (temple), 31
Myōon Kō *(biwa hiki* organisation), 98, 105, 255, 271–272
Myōon Kō ceremony, 98, 105, 108, 185, 271n35
Myōon Ten (deity), 29–31, 32

nabiraki (name-taking event), 185, 256
Nagai Akiko, 51, 66n64, 83, 117
Nagamatsu Daietsu, 75–76n10, 104
Nagasaki Prefecture, 8, *292*
nagashi (musical pattern), 181, 192, *196*, 200
Nagata Hōjun, 62, 73, 87–88, 87n23, 172n27, 178, 283, 284, 285
Nakayama Tarō, 48, 49, 60–61n54, 266n28
naniwa-bushi (narrative style), 101, 101n39, 238
Nankan village, 7–8, 233–234, *293*
Narita Mamoru, 146–147
Nehan ritual, 131n88
New York Times, 153
NHK Television, 86, 150
Nihon no Gakki (Tanabe), 77n13
Nijō (as biwa player), 37, 37n28
nijūsan-ya (night of autumn equinox), 183
ningyō jōruri (musical theatre), 64
"*Ninjō biwa hōshi ikiru*" (NHK Television), 150
Nishi Honganji, *47*
Nishimoto Tsuneki, 76–77, 77n13, 201n19

Nishioka Yōko, 81, 83
Noguchi Kinryū, 102, 102n40
nori (performance pattern), 192, *196*, 200

Ōkawa Susumu, 2–3, 38, 81–82, 117
  apprenticeship of, 245, 246
  articulation by, 122, 201n19
  discrimination suffered by, 270
  gedai classification, 118
  on narrative style, 120n76, 191
  professional organisations, affiliation to, 255, 255n18
  public performances, 101–102
  zashikibiwa and, 126, 163, 182n3
ō-okuri (performance pattern), 200
o-komori ritual, 108, 185
oku jōruri tradition, 146–147
Oku no Hosomichi (Bashō), 10n8
okuri (melodic recitation pattern), 180, *196*
Ono no Komachi, 23
oral composition process, 202–206
  fixity and variability, 205–206
  (*See also* Hyōdō, comparison of Yamashika's *Dōjōji* performances)
  shōdan model, 202–205
Orikuchi Shinobu, 44, 111–112
Ozawa Shōichi, 86

Parry, Milman, 112
pipa (musical instrument), 22n6, 41
  women and, 37, 37n27
pitch and mode (performance elements), 198–202
Prince Amayo, 27n15
Prince Kunala, 22, 23, 27
Prince Saneyasu, 27, 27n15

rites, 125–140
  harai rituals, 132–136, *134, 135, 136*
  other performances, 138–140
  watamashi, 82, 91, 136–138
rōkyoku (narrative style), 101
rōshō (syllabic vocalisation), 197
"Rokudō Gozen" (Ishimure), 269
rokunin-gei (six-person performance), 116
Ruch, Barbara, 111
Ryūsen (musical piece), 33–34

Saigo no biwa hōshi Yamashika Yoshiyuki (television documentary), 150
saimon (prayers to *kami*), 131
Sakemochi Gassen (tale), 115
Sanbō Daikōjin, 130
Saneyasu, 27, 27n15
sangaku performances, 52–53
Sanger, David, 153, 286
sanjakumono (criminal underworld tales), 118
sanxian (musical instrument), 23
Sarasvati (deity), 29–30, *30*
Saru zatō (*kyōgen* play), 46
Satō Teruo, 84n20
satsumabiwa tradition, 12, 13, 72, 101, 109, 121, 249n12
  chikuzenbiwa, comparison to, 197
Satsuma mōsōbiwa (film), 87, 87n23
Satsuma mōsōbiwa tradition, 12
Seiyūki (1795 journey chronicle), 94
Sekijun, 253, 254, 256, 257, 258
seki (section of *gedai* tale), 116
sekkyō (edification tale), 191
semantic articulation, 121–122
Semimaru, 23n9, 27, 45
Semimaru (*nō* play), 45
senritsukei (melodic patterns), 193
  See also *fushi* (performance patterns)
serifu (performance pattern), *196*
"Shaka no dan" ritual, 131n88
shakumon (Buddhist deity tales), 109, 283
shamisen (musical instrument), 38, 42, 58, 64
shichinin-gei (seven-person performance), 116
Shimabara Gunki. See *Kikuchi Kuzure*
Shimada Dangetsu, 96, 100, 103
Shimaya nikki (Kumamoto historical text), 95
shimpa-mono (narratives), 119
Shin Nihon kikō (NHK television documentary series), 86
Shinsaku Sano Genzaemon (Shimada), 103
Shin saragaku-ki (Fujiwara no Akihira), 52, 53
shōdan model, 202–205
Shōren'in temple, 97
shugenja (Shugendō adherents), 127–128

Shunki-*ha* (performance school), 95
shuoshude (blind itinerant narrative singers), 23
The Singer of Tales (Lord), 148
Suijin (deity), 131
Suris, Doriano, 159, 159n16
Susanō, 92
Suwa Atsushi, 87

Taietsu-*ha* (performance school), 95
Tai no Mukoiri (tale), 115
Taira Kanemori, 52
Tajima Rintarō, 103
Takagi Seigen, 40, 86, 88, 178
Takamure Itsue, 85
Takano Shizu no Ichi, 102–103, 102n40
Takezawa Kōgyoku, 260
Takuboku (musical piece), 33–34
Tale of the Heike *(Heike monogatari)*, 1, 10, 13, 14, 55–56, 58–59
Tamagawa-*ha* tradition, 89, 91, 92
Tamagawa Kyōen. See Yamashika Yoshiyuki
Tamagawa Kyōjun, 14
Tamagawa Kyōzan, 174
  See also Mori Yoichi
Tamagawa Sekijun. See Sekijun
Tamagawa Taikyō, 104n46
Tamamuro Fumio, 127n81
Tamayohime Chikushi Kudari. See *Miyako Gassen Chikushi Kudari*
Tanabe Hisao, 49, 77n13, 104n47, 145, 185, 186
  on *higobiwa* tradition, 73, 76–79, 96n33
  mōsō biwa and, 48, 65
  Yamashika's criticism of, 143, 156
Tanaka Tōgo, 77n12, 126
tategoto (musical instrument), 58
te (biwa punctuating strokes), 191
Tetsuo (Yamashika's son), 16n13
tōdō za (guild), 10, 26–27, 26–27n14, 32, 43, 52, 100
  hierarchy of, 55, 56–57
  Higo province, 97–98
  mōsō groups' dispute with, 63–66
  women, exclusion of, 36–37
Tokita, Alison, 82
tonosama biwa (biwa narrative style), 90
Toyota Foundation, 81

tōzokumono (criminal underworld tales), 118
Tsuchi ni utau: biwa-shi no Yamashika Yoshiyuki (television program), 149
Tsukimi zatō (play), 46
tsurebushi (training technique), 249

uchideshi (live-in apprentices), 240
Uda Yasushi, 155, 246n11
urei-katari (performance pattern), 200
ureimono (tragic tales), 118
urei (performance pattern), *196,* 200

vocal delivery technique, 192, 197–198

watamashi rite, 82, 91, 136–138
water *kami,* 32
Wiswell, Ella, 274
women and biwa, 36–40

Xu gaoseng zhuang (Tang-period chronicle), 22

yamabushi (Shugendō adherents), 127–128
Yamamoto Izumi, 148–149
Yamamoto Kichizō, 84n20
Yamashika Yoshiyuki, 1, 14–16, 86, *90, 178, 182, 241*
  accolades, 15, 74
  acquisition of skills and repertory, 15, 259–262 (*See also* apprenticeship)
  areas of work, 7
  audience response, on decline of, 179
  biwa, on origin of, 91–93
  biwa hiki, factors in choice to become a, 232–233, 238, 239–240
  biwa hiki, on original purpose of, 125
  biwa hiki, on sacred origins of, 28–29
  biwa hiki earnings, 258
  blindness, onset of, 14, 235–237
  childhood and adolescence, 234–235, 238–239
  concert performances, 16, 77n12, 106, 186–187
  discrimination suffered by, 267
  on *Dōjōji* tale, 206
  on *higo biwa,* 79
  on *higobiwa* tradition, 80, 88–89, 91
  on Hori Kyōjun, 89–91

Yamashika Yoshiyuki (*continued*)
  Ikka Hiraite performance, 113–114
  katari, emphasis on, 191
  Kōjin-barai ritual, 133–136, *134*, *135*, *136*
  as last *biwa hōshi*, 19, 285–286
  on *marume biwa*, 79n17
  nabiraki (naming ceremony), 252, 254, 256–258
  oral performance style, 85, 194–196, *196*
  professional organisations, affiliation to, 15, 70–71, 105–106, 284–285
  repertory, fragmentary transmission of, 280–282
  ritual work, 34–35, 126, 132, 133–136, *134*, *135*, *136*, 139, 140
  Tamagawa-*ha*, participation in, 253–256
  Tanabe Hisao, criticism of, 143, 156
  tetrachordal profiles in *fushi* types, 200, *201*
  vocal delivery style, 197–198
  vocal pitch, stability of, 201–202
  watamashi ritual, version of, 34–35
  See also apprenticeship
Yamashika Yoshiyuki, documentation of, 144–154
  academic documentation, 145–148
  representations for the broader public, 148–154
Yamashika Yoshiyuki, experiences of interlocutors, 154–163
  de Ferranti, 159–163
  foreigners, 158–159
  Kimuras, 157–158
  scholars, 155–157
Yanagita Kunio, 32, 111–112
yashikigami ritual, 129
Yasuda Muneo, 91, 96n32, 100, 155, 253, 266
  on *higobiwa*, 70, 74, 96, 103nn42–43
  on *mōsō*, 51–52, 83
  on *watamashi*, 139–140
  Yamashika, account of, 147–148, 245, 259, 261n22
Yōshinsō (musical piece), 33–34
yogomori ritual, 108, 185
Yokomichi Mario, 193, 194n10, 202–203
yonagashi (wandering *nagashi*), 181
Yoshida Kenkō, 55–56

zadankai (group discussions), 166
zashikibiwa (pre-arranged performances in *zashiki*), 179–184, 186, 259
  remuneration for, 273, 274
zashiki (formal room), 178
zatō (low-status, blind male musicians), 10, 11, 51, 56n48, 73
  See also *biwa hōshi*
zatō arts, 58
zatōbiwa, 72
Zatō Ichi, 39n31
"Zatō Sakura" (folk tale), 46
Zeami Motokiyo, 45, 203
Zentai Heike (tale), 188, 188n6
Zhenyu (*pipa*-playing blind man), 22
zokumono (commoner tales), 118

CORNELL EAST ASIA SERIES

4 Fredrick Teiwes, *Provincial Leadership in China: The Cultural Revolution and Its Aftermath*
8 Cornelius C. Kubler, *Vocabulary and Notes to Ba Jin's Jia: An Aid for Reading the Novel*
16 Monica Bethe & Karen Brazell, *Nō as Performance: An Analysis of the Kuse Scene of Yamamba*
18 Royall Tyler, tr., *Granny Mountains: A Second Cycle of Nō Plays*
23 Knight Biggerstaff, *Nanking Letters, 1949*
28 Diane E. Perushek, ed., *The Griffis Collection of Japanese Books: An Annotated Bibliography*
37 J. Victor Koschmann, Ōiwa Keibō & Yamashita Shinji, eds., *International Perspectives on Yanagita Kunio and Japanese Folklore Studies*
38 James O'Brien, tr., *Murō Saisei: Three Works*
40 Kubo Sakae, *Land of Volcanic Ash: A Play in Two Parts*, revised edition, tr. David G. Goodman
44 Susan Orpett Long, *Family Change and the Life Course in Japan*
48 Helen Craig McCullough, *Bungo Manual: Selected Reference Materials for Students of Classical Japanese*
49 Susan Blakeley Klein, *Ankoku Butō: The Premodern and Postmodern Influences on the Dance of Utter Darkness*
50 Karen Brazell, ed., *Twelve Plays of the Noh and Kyōgen Theaters*
51 David G. Goodman, ed., *Five Plays by Kishida Kunio*
52 Shirō Hara, *Ode to Stone*, tr. James Morita
53 Peter J. Katzenstein & Yutaka Tsujinaka, *Defending the Japanese State: Structures, Norms and the Political Responses to Terrorism and Violent Social Protest in the 1970s and 1980s*
54 Su Xiaokang & Wang Luxiang, *Deathsong of the River: A Reader's Guide to the Chinese TV Series Heshang*, trs. Richard Bodman & Pin P. Wan
55 Jingyuan Zhang, *Psychoanalysis in China: Literary Transformations, 1919-1949*
56 Jane Kate Leonard & John R. Watt, eds., *To Achieve Security and Wealth: The Qing Imperial State and the Economy, 1644-1911*
57 Andrew F. Jones, *Like a Knife: Ideology and Genre in Contemporary Chinese Popular Music*
58 Peter J. Katzenstein & Nobuo Okawara, *Japan's National Security: Structures, Norms and Policy Responses in a Changing World*
59 Carsten Holz, *The Role of Central Banking in China's Economic Reforms*
60 Chifumi Shimazaki, *Warrior Ghost Plays from the Japanese Noh Theater: Parallel Translations with Running Commentary*
61 Emily Groszos Ooms, *Women and Millenarian Protest in Meiji Japan: Deguchi Nao and Ōmotokyō*
62 Carolyn Anne Morley, *Transformation, Miracles, and Mischief: The Mountain Priest Plays of Kōygen*
63 David R. McCann & Hyunjae Yee Sallee, tr., *Selected Poems of Kim Namjo*, afterword by Kim Yunsik
64 Hua Qingzhao, *From Yalta to Panmunjom: Truman's Diplomacy and the Four Powers, 1945-1953*
65 Margaret Benton Fukasawa, *Kitahara Hakushū: His Life and Poetry*
66 Kam Louie, ed., *Strange Tales from Strange Lands: Stories by Zheng Wanlong*, with introduction
67 Wang Wen-hsing, *Backed Against the Sea*, tr. Edward Gunn
69 Brian Myers, *Han Sōrya and North Korean Literature: The Failure of Socialist Realism in the DPRK*
70 Thomas P. Lyons & Victor Nee, eds., *The Economic Transformation of South China: Reform and Development in the Post-Mao Era*
71 David G. Goodman, tr., *After Apocalypse: Four Japanese Plays of Hiroshima and Nagasaki*, with introduction
72 Thomas Lyons, *Poverty and Growth in a South China County: Anxi, Fujian, 1949-1992*

74 Martyn Atkins, *Informal Empire in Crisis: British Diplomacy and the Chinese Customs Succession, 1927-1929*
76 Chifumi Shimazaki, *Restless Spirits from Japanese Noh Plays of the Fourth Group: Parallel Translations with Running Commentary*
77 Brother Anthony of Taizé & Young-Moo Kim, trs., *Back to Heaven: Selected Poems of Ch'ŏn Sang Pyŏng*
78 Kevin O'Rourke, tr., *Singing Like a Cricket, Hooting Like an Owl: Selected Poems by Yi Kyu-bo*
79 Irit Averbuch, *The Gods Come Dancing: A Study of the Japanese Ritual Dance of Yamabushi Kagura*
80 Mark Peterson, *Korean Adoption and Inheritance: Case Studies in the Creation of a Classic Confucian Society*
81 Yenna Wu, tr., *The Lioness Roars: Shrew Stories from Late Imperial China*
82 Thomas Lyons, *The Economic Geography of Fujian: A Sourcebook*, Vol. 1
83 Pak Wan-so, *The Naked Tree*, tr. Yu Young-nan
84 C.T. Hsia, *The Classic Chinese Novel: A Critical Introduction*
85 Cho Chong-Rae, *Playing With Fire*, tr. Chun Kyung-Ja
86 Hayashi Fumiko, *I Saw a Pale Horse and Selections from Diary of a Vagabond*, tr. Janice Brown
87 Motoori Norinaga, *Kojiki-den, Book 1*, tr. Ann Wehmeyer
88 Chang Soo Ko, tr., *Sending the Ship Out to the Stars: Poems of Park Je-chun*
89 Thomas Lyons, *The Economic Geography of Fujian: A Sourcebook*, Vol. 2
90 Brother Anthony of Taizé, tr., *Midang: Early Lyrics of So Chong-Ju*
92 Janice Matsumura, *More Than a Momentary Nightmare: The Yokohama Incident and Wartime Japan*
93 Kim Jong-Gil tr., *The Snow Falling on Chagall's Village: Selected Poems of Kim Ch'un-Su*
94 Wolhee Choe & Peter Fusco, trs., *Day-Shine: Poetry by Hyon-jong Chong*
95 Chifumi Shimazaki, *Troubled Souls from Japanese Noh Plays of the Fourth Group*
96 Hagiwara Sakutarō, *Principles of Poetry (Shi no Genri)*, tr. Chester Wang
97 Mae J. Smethurst, *Dramatic Representations of Filial Piety: Five Noh in Translation*
98 Ross King, ed., *Description and Explanation in Korean Linguistics*
99 William Wilson, *Hōgen Monogatari: Tale of the Disorder in Hōgen*
100 Yasushi Yamanouchi, J. Victor Koschmann and Ryūichi Narita, eds., *Total War and 'Modernization'*
101 Yi Ch'ŏng-jun, *The Prophet and Other Stories*, tr. Julie Pickering
102 S.A. Thornton, *Charisma and Community Formation in Medieval Japan: The Case of the Yugyō-ha (1300-1700)*
103 Sherman Cochran, ed., *Inventing Nanjing Road: Commercial Culture in Shanghai, 1900-1945*
104 Harold M. Tanner, *Strike Hard! Anti-Crime Campaigns and Chinese Criminal Justice, 1979-1985*
105 Brother Anthony of Taizé & Young-Moo Kim, trs., *Farmers' Dance: Poems by Shin Kyŏng-nim*
106 Susan Orpett Long, ed., *Lives in Motion: Composing Circles of Self and Community in Japan*
107 Peter J. Katzenstein, Natasha Hamilton-Hart, Kozo Kato, & Ming Yue, *Asian Regionalism*
108 Kenneth Alan Grossberg, *Japan's Renaissance: The Politics of the Muromachi Bakufu*
109 John W. Hall & Toyoda Takeshi, eds., *Japan in the Muromachi Age*
110 Kim Su-Young, Shin Kyong-Nim & Lee Si-Young: *Variations: Three Korean Poets;* trs. Brother Anthony of Taizé & Young-Moo Kim
111 Samuel Leiter, *Frozen Moments: Writings on Kabuki, 1966-2001*
112 Pilwun Shih Wang & Sarah Wang, *Early One Spring: A Learning Guide to Accompany the Film Video February*
113 Thomas Conlan, *In Little Need of Divine Intervention: Scrolls of the Mongol Invasions of Japan*
114 Jane Kate Leonard & Robert Antony, eds., *Dragons, Tigers, and Dogs: Qing Crisis Management and the Boundaries of State Power in Late Imperial China*

115 Shu-ning Sciban & Fred Edwards, eds., *Dragonflies: Fiction by Chinese Women in the Twentieth Century*
116 David G. Goodman, ed., *The Return of the Gods: Japanese Drama and Culture in the 1960s*
117 Yang Hi Choe-Wall, *Vision of a Phoenix: The Poems of Hŏ Nansŏrhŏn*
118 Mae J. Smethurst & Christina Laffin, eds., *The Noh Ominameshi: A Flower Viewed from Many Directions*
119 Joseph A. Murphy, *Metaphorical Circuit: Negotiations Between Literature and Science in Twentieth-Century Japan*
120 Richard F. Calichman, *Takeuchi Yoshimi: Displacing the West*
121 Fan Pen Li Chen, *Visions for the Masses: Chinese Shadow Plays from Shaanxi and Shanxi*
122 S. Yumiko Hulvey, *Sacred Rites in Moonlight: Ben no Naishi Nikki*
123 Tetsuo Najita & J. Victor Koschmann, *Conflict in Modern Japanese History: The Neglected Tradition*
124 Naoki Sakai, Brett de Bary & Iyotani Toshio, eds., *Deconstructing Nationality*
125 Judith N. Rabinovitch & Timothy R. Bradstock, *Dance of the Butterflies: Chinese Poetry from the Japanese Court Tradition*
126 Yang Gui-ja, *Contradictions*, trs. Stephen Epstein and Kim Mi-Young
127 Ann Sung-hi Lee, *Yi Kwang-su and Modern Korean Literature: Mujŏng*
128 Pang Kie-chung & Michael D. Shin, eds., *Landlords, Peasants, & Intellectuals in Modern Korea*
129 Joan R. Piggott, ed., *Capital and Countryside in Japan, 300-1180: Japanese Historians Interpreted in English*
130 Kyoko Selden & Jolisa Gracewood, eds., *Annotated Japanese Literary Gems: Stories by Tawada Yōko, Nakagami Kenji, and Hayashi Kyōko* (Vol. 1)
131 Michael G. Murdock, *Disarming the Allies of Imperialism: The State, Agitation, and Manipulation during China's Nationalist Revolution, 1922-1929*
132 Noel J. Pinnington, *Traces in the Way: Michi and the Writings of Komparu Zenchiku*
133 Charlotte von Verschuer, *Across the Perilous Sea: Japanese Trade with China and Korea from the Seventh to the Sixteenth Centuries*, Kristen Lee Hunter, tr.
134 John Timothy Wixted, *A Handbook to Classical Japanese*
135 Kyoko Selden & Jolisa Gracewood, with Lili Selden, eds., *Annotated Japanese Literary Gems: Stories by Natsume Sōseki, Tomioka Taeko, and Inoue Yasushi* (Vol. 2)
136 Yi Tae-Jin, *The Dynamics of Confucianism and Modernization in Korean History*
137 Jennifer Rudolph, *Negotiated Power in Late Imperial China: The Zongli Yamen and the Politics of Reform*
138 Thomas D. Loooser, *Visioning Eternity: Aesthetics, Politics, and History in the Early Modern Noh Theater*
139 Gustav Heldt, *The Pursuit of Harmony: Poetry and Power in Late Heian Japan*
140 Joan R. Piggott & Yoshida Sanae, *Teishinkōki: The Year 939 in the Journal of Regent Fujiwara no Tadahira*
141 Robert Bagley, *Max Loehr and the Study of Chinese Bronzes: Style and Classification in the History of Art*
142 Edwin A. Cranston, *The Secret Island and the Enticing Flame: Worlds of Memory, Discovery, and Loss in Japanese Poetry*
143 Hugh de Ferranti, *The Last Biwa Singer: A Blind Musician in History, Imagination and Performance*
144 Roger Des Forges, Gao Minglu, Liu Chiao-mei, Haun Saussy, with Thomas Burkman, eds., *Chinese Walls in Time and Space: A Multidisciplinary Perspective*
145 George Sidney & Hye-jin Juhn Sidney, trs., *I Heard Life Calling Me: Poems of Yi Sŏng-bok*
146 Sherman Cochran & Paul G. Pickowicz, eds., *China on the Margins*
147 Wang Lingzhen and Mary Ann O'Donnell, trs., *Years of Sadness: Autobiographical Writings of Wang Anyi*

DVD Monica Bethe & Karen Brazell: "Yamanba: The Old Woman of the Mountains" to accompany CEAS Volume 16 *Noh As Performance*

CORNELL
East Asia Series

Order online at www.einaudi.cornell.edu/eastasia/publications or contact
Cornell University Press Services, P. O. Box 6525, 750 Cascadilla Street,
Ithaca, NY 14851, USA.
Tel: 1-800-666-2211 (USA or Canada), 1-607-277-2211 (International);
Fax: 1-800-688-2877 (USA or Canada), 1-607-277-6292 (International);
E-mail orders: orderbook@cupserv.org

www.ingramcontent.com/pod-product-compliance
Lightning Source LLC
Chambersburg PA
CBHW031434230426
43668CB00007B/535